programming in
Scheme

programming in
Scheme

written by
Michael Eisenberg

edited by
Harold Abelson

foreword by
Julie Sussman

The MIT Press
Cambridge, Massachusetts
London, England

First MIT Press paperback edition, 1990

The sample outputs shown in this book were taken from the software as it was when this book went into production. Any revisions to the software could cause the output on your system to be different from that in the book.

Printed in the United States of America.

10 9 8 7 6 5 4 3 2

ISBN 0-262-55017-2

Ordering Information:

Additional copies of this trade edition are available through the MIT Press, 55 Hayward St., Cambridge, MA 02142.

The larger professional version of the software, which adds a language interface and expanded memory, is available from The Scientific Press, 651 Gateway Blvd., Suite 1100, South San Francisco, CA 94080, (415) 583-8840

Contact The Scientific Press for class adoption review copies.

About the Cover: The geometrical design on the cover was generated by the circle-squared program described in Chapter 7. The square plotted has a side length of 2154, and a bottom lefthand corner of $(-1077, -1077)$. The color-choice algorithm takes the sum of x^2 and y^2, truncates the result, divides by 7, and examines the remainder: if the remainder is less than 4, the color is set to 0 (black); if 4, 5, or 6, the color is set to 1 (cyan), 2 (magenta), or 3 (white), respectively.

Text design: Gene Smith
Cover design: Rogondino & Associates

This book is dedicated,
with admiration and affection,
to two teachers:

Sherry Fine and Fran Streeter

Contents

Foreword

When I was in high school, I was introduced to programming by some fellow students who were taking a special Saturday course offered by a college in New York. I learned a little bit of FORTRAN and wrote a few tiny programs, which I passed across the classroom to be checked. It was pretty clear that programming and I were made for each other, even though I never actually ran a program on a real computer. But hardly anyone in those days ever used or even saw a computer.

The personal computer you have on your desk is more powerful than the behemoths available in advanced research laboratories when I was in high school. So you can have even more fun than I did, and more easily.

Why is programming fun? I think the reason I like it so much is that it gives me a world I can control. The laws of nature in that world are published, and knowing them, you can make things happen to your liking. There are few limits to what you can accomplish if you just think hard enough. Not quite like the real world.[1]

You have had experience with programs in the real world whether or not you have programmed a computer. A knitting pattern, a cooking recipe, driving directions, written music, instructions for assembling a kit—these are all programs for a human to execute. You've probably written some such programs, and you have no doubt been confused and frustrated when trying to interpret a program that was unclear or had bugs in it. The author of such a program must be precise and careful if the person who uses it is to be successful in carrying it out. The same goes for programming a computer.

Learning to program is really learning to describe a procedure completely and clearly, so that someone or something can carry it out. Lots of people seem to think they won't be able to program unless they are good at math. Math and programming do have something in common: they both require clear thinking, and learning either one improves your thinking skills. But you don't have to know any math in order to program. (This book sometimes uses math in examples, but nothing beyond what you've seen in high school.)

---

1 The real world: ". . . the location of non-programmers and activities not related to programming"—Steele, et al., *The Hacker's Dictionary,* Harper and Row, 1983.

One of the thinking skills you practice a lot when you program is debugging. (Although I should know better, from the amount of experience I've had, I've somehow never gotten over the feeling of anticipation when I run a new program that this one will work the first time. Occasionally it does, but you'd think I would know enough by now not to be disappointed all the times that it doesn't.) Seymour Papert argues in *Mindstorms* that debugging is a very powerful idea that can make you smarter, because you can debug the procedures that you yourself follow. That is, instead of feeling incompetent when you can't do something, you can try to figure out what is wrong with the procedure you are following, and then fix it. One of the most important things I ever learned was the point of view that if I can't understand something, it is probably because the explanation is missing something or is confused, not because I am incapable of understanding it. So when I read or listen to an explanation, I automatically try to debug it.

Approaches to programming and to teaching programming have improved a lot since my introductory FORTRAN days. With this book you can learn to write good programs that do interesting things right off the bat. Of course, "interesting" is subjective, but the examples and exercises in this book are so varied that you're bound to find some that are up your alley. Do you like pretty patterns? Look at the pictures in Chapter 7, or try the Lissajous figures in Exercise 12.16 and the C-curve in Exercise 13.18. Do you enjoy games and puzzles? Write programs to play hangman (13.7) or peg solitaire (16.2), or to work with cryptograms (12.17). Interested in science or sports? You'll find examples from chemistry, biology, and baseball. Thinking of going into the direct mail business? Chapter 13 can help you generate personalized form letters. Wish you could live in ancient times? Well, programming won't help you with that, but you can make your computer use Roman numerals (Exercise 5.10). Even people who enjoy math will find fun things here, such as the continued fractions in Chapter 5. My own favorite part of this book is the Abbott and Costello "Who's on First?" program in Chapter 10. The introductory programming text that can teach me to write a program like that is the text I wish I had had.

Julie Sussman
Cambridge, Massachusetts

Acknowledgments

This book owes its existence to Hal Abelson. As editor, he has given generously of his time and scholarship; even more important, he has been a consistent source of encouragement and emotional support. I owe him my greatest thanks.

Thanks also to Paul Kelly of the Scientific Press, who has shown unflagging good cheer and patience in waiting for me to finish this manuscript. His energy, coupled with his commitment to the quality of the final result, have made him a joy to work with.

This manuscript has been read and commented on at various stages by a number of remarkable people. Special thanks to David Bartley, Jim Miller, Don Oxley, Mitchel Resnick, and Julie Sussman. Their input has improved the book beyond measure; those flaws that remain are entirely my own responsibility.

I also want to thank the following people for reading portions of the book and providing helpful feedback: Trina Arnett, Al Cuoco, Mike McGiffin, Tim McNerney, Barbara Miller, Guillermo Rozas, and Franklyn Turbak.

Finally, some special acknowledgments are in order:

- Mario Bourgoin, for his assistance in taking the photograph that appears on the cover of this book;

- Seth Haberman, author of the original "Who's on First" program, for allowing me to construct and present my own version in this text;

- Brian Harvey, for sharing his expertise in TeX (and for generously providing some useful TeX macros).

- Gene Smith for the typographic design of this book and typesetting the final manuscript.

CHAPTER 1

Programming in Scheme

Programming is a joy. That's why people do it. No one should spend hours in front of a computer terminal out of some dreary sense of duty, or because they have some vague notion of becoming "computer literate." That's not the point. Programming ought to be fun—and if you're not having fun, you shouldn't waste your time.

To be sure, programming can be useful as well. Any mathematician who has ever been able to construct some complicated geometric surface on the computer screen, and then stroll about on that surface; any physicist who has simulated the events at the center of a star; any musician who has experimented with programmable synthesizers; any biochemist who has gotten new insights from looking at graphical models of proteins; any artist who has created new and beautiful video images, whether static or moving; any of these people could testify to the usefulness of programming. But more than that, they have had the pleasure of watching their ideas take shape inside this strange, fascinating instrument—a feeling of surprise, of creative pride, of wonder.

This book is about having fun.

I'm telling you that here, at the outset. Ostensibly, this book is an introduction to the Scheme programming language; but really, it's about using the computer as a means of expression. There will, of course, be times when you will curse the machine in frustration; when you will struggle with some project or other; when you will have to do a certain amount of "grunge work" before getting at the really interesting ideas in your program. These things are inevitable. They come with the territory. Every means of expression—writing, painting, playing a musical instrument—similarly involves stretches of frustration and practice and toil. But we persist with the work because we have ideas that we wish to express, and a medium in which to express them. And despite all the pain and travail, we know that in some very fundamental way we are enjoying ourselves.

You should therefore read this book in a spirit of play. No matter what interests you—art, physics, linguistics, business, mathematics—you will very likely find the activity of programming to be one that expands your powers of

2

creative expression. As you read along, make up projects for yourself. Try things out. Challenge yourself. You are starting off on an intellectual adventure.

Now, on to Scheme.

Scheme

Scheme is a computer language. It is typically referred to as a dialect—an offshoot language—of Lisp. Lisp, however, is a pretty difficult thing to pin down. The earliest version of Lisp was developed in the late 1950s at the Massachusetts Institute of Technology (MIT) by John McCarthy and his associates. This makes Lisp the second-oldest major computer language still in use (the oldest is FORTRAN). By now, there are dozens of dialects of Lisp in existence, and the differences between them range from minor discrepancies in syntax to fairly important (at least in computer science terms) conflicts in underlying programming-language ideas. It is safest to say that there is no one Lisp; rather, Lisp is the collection of all existing dialects.

Even though the term "Lisp" is a catchall for many implementations, there are nevertheless some general observations we can make. Lisp dialects are distinguished by, among other things, their ability to manipulate both symbols and numbers. This property is less special than it used to be, but in many circles programming languages are still seen basically as number-crunching tools. Lisp's facility at manipulating symbols has historically made it the favorite language of the artificial intelligence (AI) community (although more recently another language, Prolog, has also become popular with AI researchers). In this book we will see many examples of symbol manipulation, and will also work on some illustrative AI-type projects.

The word "Lisp" stands for "List Programming," and perhaps the most recognizable feature common to all Lisps is the extensive use of a special data structure known as a *list*. Lists turn out to be important in Lisp not only because they are an extremely convenient and flexible way to group data elements, but for another subtle reason whose power will only become apparent later on in this book. That reason is this: Lisp programs are themselves represented as lists, and as a consequence Lisp programs can be treated as data objects by other Lisp programs. All this may sound a bit obscure at the moment, but the notion of programs accepting other programs as data has proved to be one of the most fruitful in the history of computer science.

Recently, there has been an effort to unite the various dialects of Lisp into one common language called, appropriately enough, Common Lisp. It is certainly worth your while, if you are interested in Lisp programming, to learn Common Lisp as well as Scheme; but you will find that to be a much easier task after having encountered Scheme. Moreover, it is safe to say that Scheme will itself remain a popular Lisp dialect for a long time to come; if anything, its influence is very much on the increase.

What distinguishes Scheme from other dialects of Lisp? Scheme is notable for several reasons. One of them is indicated by the size of the average Scheme manual: it is refreshingly small. Scheme is designed to be a simple, learnable Lisp. It is therefore a particularly good language for teaching computer programming.[1] There are a number of other interesting features of Scheme vis-à-vis other Lisps—features that you won't be familiar with just yet, but will come to appreciate in the course of this book. These include:

---

[1] Many universities have adopted the textbook *Structure and Interpretation of Computer Programs,* by Harold Abelson and Gerald Jay Sussman with Julie Sussman, which uses Scheme as the basis for a one-semester course in computer science. I highly recommend the Abelson-Sussman book, either as follow-up or concurrent reading to this one.

- Block structure and lexical scoping
- A "properly tail recursive" implementation
- "First-class" status for a variety of objects, including procedures, continuations, and (in many implementations) environments

Sounds hopelessly technical, no doubt. But all of these features—and the reason that they make Scheme so powerful—will be explained thoroughly in the following chapters.

The examples in this book will be drawn from the Scheme system called *PC Scheme* supplied by Texas Instruments (TI). PC Scheme runs on the various members of the IBM PC family—the PC, PC/XT, and AT—as well as on IBM's Personal System/2 and TI's Professional, Portable Professional, and Business-Pro computers. In order to use the Edwin editor, which will be included in our examples, your system should have at least 512K bytes of memory; and some examples assume that you have additional graphics hardware (such as the Color Graphics Adapter (CGA) supplied for the IBM PC computers).

> If you are using some other Scheme system, you will still find much of interest in this book, but you will have to exercise caution about the differences between your system and PC Scheme. There are a number of special features of PC Scheme, such as "window objects," which are described here but may not appear in other Scheme implementations; also, as noted above, several of our projects involve the graphics commands of PC Scheme, and commands of this sort tend to be particularly implementation-dependent. Some of TI's features and commands will have analogues in other versions of Scheme; some won't. Throughout the remaining chapters, any text which applies specifically to PC Scheme will be identified as such; but again, if you are using another Scheme, you will probably want to accompany your reading of this book with your own system manual and a certain degree of extra care.[2]

PC Scheme

This book is aimed at people who are new to Scheme and who have never worked with any dialect of Lisp. I will, however, assume that the reader has some familiarity with computers in general—that she knows, for example, what an editor is, or how to type CTRL-A at the keyboard, or what it means to save and restore files, or what a program is.

> Beyond this sort of general lore, no other programming experience is necessary as background to this book. To tell the truth, I'm not even sure how helpful other programming experience would be. If you know Basic, it would probably be worth your while to erase that knowledge from your mind for the purposes of learning Scheme—the two languages differ in such profound ways that your assumptions from the Basic world are likely to cause more confusion than anything else. Same goes for FORTRAN, Pascal, and assembly languages. Knowing Logo is probably helpful, but even a Logo expert will encounter many new ideas here. It may in fact be that the ideal background is simply experience with a good word processing program; that way, the reader would be comfortable with the computer keyboard, but would not be saddled with too many preconceptions about what a programming language has to look like.

**This Book:
An Outline**
Things Assumed

---

[2]In a similar vein, it should be mentioned that the version of PC Scheme employed in this book is version 3.0. Future versions of PC Scheme may include changes that affect a few examples in this book. The most likely of these changes are mentioned in the text; but in any case, only a very few examples should be markedly affected by the newer implementations.

Things Omitted

This book doesn't cover absolutely everything about Scheme; limitations of time and space (and the publisher's patience!) forbid it. The point of this volume is to get the reader familiar enough, and comfortable enough, with the fundamentals of Scheme so that he can go off and learn anything else on his own. In particular, some of the features of PC Scheme will be omitted here, or dealt with very briefly. This book will not discuss the SCOOPS object system supplied with PC Scheme; nor will TI's structure editor be included. The Edwin editor will be examined only sketchily, with details being supplied as needed; a mini-manual for Edwin is included as an appendix, but in any case it is suggested that you read the material about Edwin in the *User's Guide for PC Scheme*. And finally, although advanced Scheme topics like continuations and macros are included toward the end of the book, they will not be treated at length; a truly thorough discussion of such topics would require (at least!) another volume in its own right.

What's Coming Up

This book is organized as a series of "layers": each layer is a set of several chapters that advances you to a new level in Scheme. The first layer, consisting of Chapters 2 through 7, will teach you about Scheme procedures—how to define them, use them, and debug them. The next three chapters, 8 through 10, introduce lists and subprocedures. If you get only through Chapter 7 in this book, you will still be able to do a lot of interesting programming; if you get through Chapter 10, you will be able to do even more. My advice to those who want to learn only a little about Scheme is to read up through Chapter 10; hopefully you will be intrigued enough by that time to continue on, but even if you are not, you will have encountered a substantial subset of the language.

With the third and final layer—Chapters 11 through 15—this book becomes progressively more difficult. A more elaborate and powerful model of the Scheme language is introduced in Chapter 11, and the ensuing four chapters are devoted to exploring the ramifications of this model. A running theme of this section is the notion of first-class procedure objects and how they may be used in programming. This is one of the most fascinating ideas in computer science, and Scheme's handling of procedure objects sets it dramatically apart from virtually every other computer language; but the topic demands a little hard work and a lot of getting used to.

Chapter 16, the last in the book, may be regarded as an extended appendix: it touches on a number of advanced special topics, including vectors, macros, continuations, and ports. If you work through this chapter, and follow up with explorations of your own, you will probably be at a point in your life where people have to drag you away from the keyboard.

There are a number of themes that pervade this text. The first concerns techniques of programming. That may sound obvious, but many books on programming languages spend a lot of time introducing individual commands and telling you what those commands do, without giving any sense of how to actually use the language you are learning. So this book is going to introduce Scheme in the context of programming; many Scheme primitives will therefore not show up in the text, but you should have no problem using the ones we haven't looked at. It is worth your while, as you read this book, to periodically scan through your Scheme manual; that way, you will get a sense of the extent of your system, and you will progressively understand more and more of the manual's explanations.

A second theme is the notion of programming projects. At the end of each layer, there will be a chapter presenting a sample Scheme project that you might undertake. These are not intended to be completely finished projects; in fact, that's the whole point. There are many possible extensions that are left up to you, if you are interested; otherwise, you might simply read through the text and get an overview of the programming ideas illustrated. The particular projects that I chose were mainly selected because they were interesting (to me, anyhow), somewhat demanding, and relevant to the ideas of the previous chapters. But if you want to try something else, or if the selected project suggests a different one more to your liking, then so much the better. In fact, if by the end of this book you haven't thought of at least one totally original project to try out on your own, then one of us is doing something wrong (and it's probably me).

There are also exercises at the conclusion of each chapter. These range from simple drill-and-practice-type questions to more open-ended projects. Again, you should view the exercises more as suggestions than assignments; but if you choose not to try any of the exercises, then you should at least play with some ideas of your own. Reading a programming book without ever sitting at the keyboard is like reading a beginning piano book without . . . well . . . ever sitting at the keyboard.

Exercises with the symbol ☑ have answers (or, at least, possible answers) at the end of the book. Exercises with the symbol ⚹ are more in the nature of longer-term projects. This symbol ✳ indicates a particularly difficult problem.

CHAPTER **2**

Sample Projects I

Before doing anything else, let's start by writing a program. Don't worry about understanding exactly what you're doing; the purpose of this chapter is just to give you a feel for working in Scheme. Try, as you go along, to speculate about those things you find mysterious. Why did we write the program in such-and-such a way? . . . What happens if we change this word in the program? . . . Feel free to experiment and make predictions and fool around.

**Loading Up
the Scheme System**

I will assume that you know how to load a working Scheme system into your computer. The PC Scheme User's Guide gives explicit instructions on how to install and load Scheme. Once Scheme is loaded up, your screen will look something like Figure 2.1.

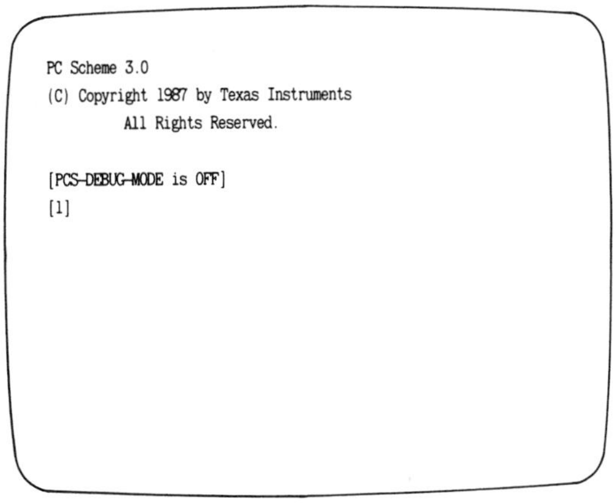

```
PC Scheme 3.0
(C) Copyright 1987 by Texas Instruments
        All Rights Reserved.

[PCS-DEBUG-MODE is OFF]
[1]
```

Figure 2.1. First view of the Scheme system

**The Scheme
Interpreter**

Every Scheme programming system contains at least two subsystems—an *interpreter* and an *editor*. These terms will become clear later, but for now suffice it to say that Figure 2.1 depicts what you see when you are first typing at the Scheme

7

interpreter. The number 1 in brackets, *[1]*, is the interpreter's prompt: anything that you type at the keyboard will appear after this prompt. (If you are using a Scheme system other than TI's, your initial interpreter screen may look different from that of Figure 2.1, but the concepts presented here are constant across all Scheme systems.)

The purpose of the interpreter is to evaluate Scheme expressions. If that sounds arcane just now, it should. The idea is that we will type in various lines of text ("expressions"); these expressions will appear, as we type them, immediately after the interpreter prompt; and when we press ↵ (ENTER key, or RETURN key on some keyboards), the interpreter will apply certain rules ("rules of evaluation") to the expression we just typed. Once the interpreter evaluates our typed-in expression, it prints out the result of that evaluation process and then provides us with a new prompt.

All this might still sound very strange. If so, don't worry; we will have plenty of opportunity to be more precise later on. But just now, let's try typing something at the interpreter. Type the number *3*, and press ↵. The interpreter should respond by printing out the number *3*, and then providing you with a new prompt; the screen now looks like Figure 2.2.

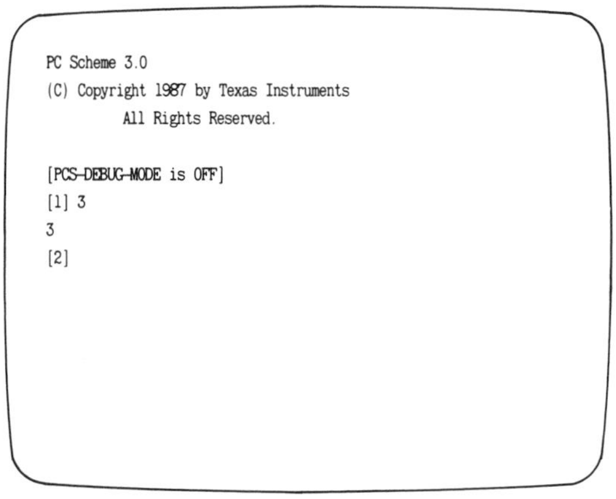

```
PC Scheme 3.0
(C) Copyright 1987 by Texas Instruments
        All Rights Reserved.

[PCS-DEBUG-MODE is OFF]
[1] 3
3
[2]
```

Figure 2.2. Typing a number, then ENTER

Now may be a good time to warn you about errors. Perhaps you made a typing mistake above—say, for instance, you typed E instead of 3 before pressing the ↵ key. In PC Scheme, the interpreter would respond with an error message, and the screen would appear as it does in Figure 2.3.

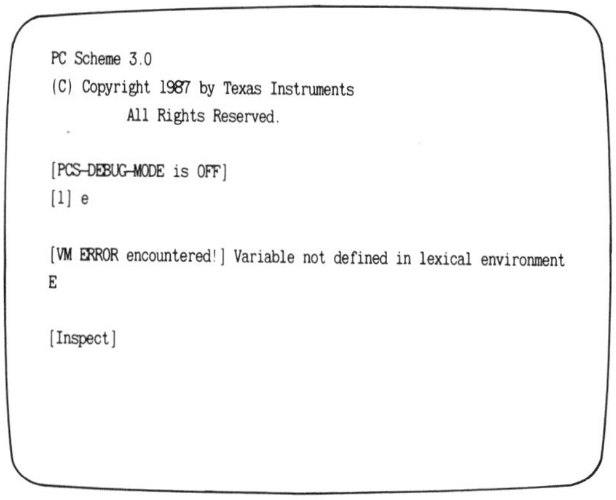

```
PC Scheme 3.0
(C) Copyright 1987 by Texas Instruments
        All Rights Reserved.

[PCS-DEBUG-MODE is OFF]
[1] e

[VM ERROR encountered!] Variable not defined in lexical environment
E

[Inspect]
```

Figure 2.3. An error message

Error messages like the one in Figure 2.3 can be very intimidating, but all that's going on is that you are looking at the prompt for yet another Scheme subsystem: the *interactive debugger*. This subsystem is useful for finding and fixing the bugs that crop up in your programs. We will look more closely at the debugger later on in this book; but for now let's not worry about it. We can go back to the Scheme interpreter by typing (CTRL)-Q at the debugger prompt (again, the particular character may vary if you are using something other than PC Scheme). Having done this, the screen will look like Figure 2.4 below.

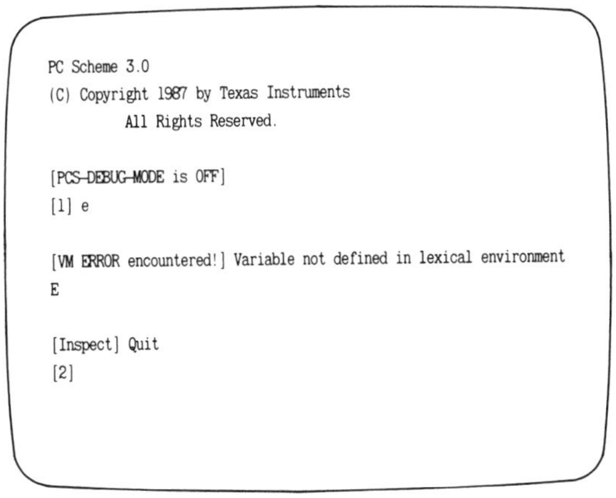

```
PC Scheme 3.0
(C) Copyright 1987 by Texas Instruments
         All Rights Reserved.

[PCS-DEBUG-MODE is OFF]
[1] e

[VM ERROR encountered!] Variable not defined in lexical environment
E

[Inspect] Quit
[2]
```

Figure 2.4. Leaving the debugger

For the present, and indeed until much later in this book, we will not discuss the debugger. If you would like to explore this subsystem, feel free; but remember that you can always (CTRL)-Q your way back to the interpreter if need be.

The number *2* in brackets, in both Figures 2.2 and 2.4, again represents the Scheme interpreter prompt. PC Scheme, as you've probably surmised, represents its interpreter prompts as a bracketed sequence of increasing numbers: *[1], [2], [3], . . .* Just to try one more expression, type

    (+ 1 3)

and press ◄┘. The interpreter should respond by printing out *4*. Perhaps you might speculate now on how to add (or subtract, or multiply, etc.) other pairs of numbers.

And before going on, I should include a brief note here on presentation: in the future, I will usually not depict interactions with Scheme by providing a view of the entire screen. More often, text like the following will be used:

    (+ 1 3)
    4

The slanted font for the number *4* indicates that this is something printed out by the Scheme interpreter, as opposed to the expression (+ 1 3), which you type in yourself. On the actual computer screen, all text is displayed in the same font. In general, I will use the slanted print-out font only to call attention to the fact that what follows is text printed out by the computer.

Writing a Scheme Program— The Scheme Editor

The typical strategy for writing a Scheme program is as follows:

1. Create the program in the Scheme editor.
2. Go back to the interpreter and test the program.
3. If there are problems with the program, try to spot them by using the debugger or through a variety of other methods. Having tentatively identified the problem, rewrite the program in the editor and then go back to step 2.

I am leaving out a lot of details here, but the basic idea is to create programs in the editor and try them out in the interpreter. With this in mind, let's create one very simple program as our first Scheme project.

The first thing we wish to do is get to the Scheme editor. In PC Scheme, the editor is called "Edwin"; we can enter the editor from the interpreter by typing

```
(edwin)
```

at the interpreter prompt. Upon entering the editor, the screen looks like Figure 2.5.

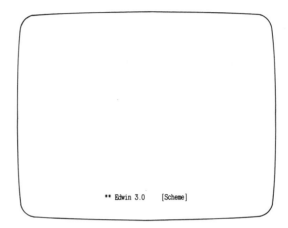

** Edwin 3.0   [Scheme]

Figure 2.5. Initial Edwin screen

Now we will create our first Scheme program inside the editor. Try typing the following:

```
(define (roulette-wheel)
  (random 37))
```

Briefly, what we are doing here is creating a new Scheme *procedure* called roulette-wheel; our first program thus consists of this one procedure. Later, we will go back to the interpreter and use our new procedure to simulate one spin of a roulette wheel; but before doing that, let's take a closer look at what we've just typed. The first thing you've probably noticed is that there are an awful lot of parentheses in our procedure. Scheme programs (indeed, programs in virtually every Lisp dialect) are characterized by a lot of parentheses. The reason for this is that in Scheme, parentheses are the characters used to group expressions into what are called *compound expressions*. Again, we'll get more formal about this later on, but keep in mind that parentheses are not, repeat *not*, optional in Scheme. Every parenthesis in a Scheme expression contributes to the meaning of that expression: you can't take any out, or put any more in, without changing the meaning of what you are writing. The parentheses in a Scheme expression must balance—that is, each right parenthesis "closes off" an expression beginning with a corresponding left parenthesis. In the text of our roulette-wheel procedure, the next-to-last right parenthesis closes off the expression beginning with the word random; the last parenthesis closes off the entire define expression.

Another point worth noting is the name of our procedure. We didn't call it rw, or fl, but rather roulette-wheel. Many programming languages, and programming texts, encourage brief and therefore cryptic names for procedures. This may have made sense in the days when computer memory was a scarce commodity, but it is a tradition worth dispensing with. It is much more important to be able to read a program and discern what it's doing than to save a few bytes of memory. In his book on Logo programming,[1] Brian Harvey writes that he will not even

---

[1] *Computer Science Logo Style* (Volume 1), MIT Press, 1985.

look at a student's program if it includes a variable named "X": the name is simply too vague. I'm not sure I'd go quite that far, but the point is well-taken: use names that tell you something about your program.

Two Procedures:
Roulette–Wheel
and Random

Now, what's going on in our roulette–wheel procedure? The idea is this: we are defining a new procedure named roulette–wheel. When we eventually use this procedure back in the Scheme interpreter, the result of a call to roulette–wheel will be a random number between 0 and 36. That is, to evaluate a call to roulette–wheel, the Scheme interpreter will have to take another step and evaluate a call to the built-in Scheme procedure random with argument 37. (I'll explain that word "argument" in just a moment.)

Random is an example of what in Scheme is called a *primitive procedure*—something that is built into the Scheme system, and that the Scheme interpreter automatically knows about. Therefore, we do not have to define our own random procedure (it isn't in any case a particularly easy thing to do). The addition procedure +, which we used earlier, is likewise a Scheme primitive. We will encounter most of PC Scheme's primitive procedures in the course of this text, and you can find the entire set in your Scheme manual.

Random is a procedure that takes one *argument*, which ought to be a positive integer. If we were to go back to the interpreter (don't do this just yet) and type:

    (random 10)

at the interpreter prompt, the interpreter would print out some integer between 0 and 9. In this example, the number 10 is the argument to the procedure random. In our roulette–wheel procedure, random will be called with an argument of 37. The purpose of random, as should be clear by now, is to return a random integer between zero and the number right before the one we used as random's argument. (Got that?) So typing

    (random 100)

at the interpreter prompt—that is, calling the random procedure with an argument of 100—would cause the interpreter to return an integer between 0 and 99.

While we're on the subject of arguments (or *parameters,* as they are sometimes called), it is worth noting that the roulette–wheel procedure which we are writing at the moment happens to take no arguments. We've already seen another procedure that takes no arguments (albeit this is a somewhat offbeat example): the procedure edwin, which we called on no arguments to get to the editor. Earlier, we used the addition procedure +, which we called with two arguments, namely the numbers 1 and 3. Whenever we define a new Scheme procedure, such as roulette–wheel, we specify the number of arguments that it takes; here, that number is zero. Very soon, we will change our definition of roulette–wheel so that it takes one argument.

**Going Back
from the Editor
to the Interpreter**

Enough talk. Hopefully by now you have actually written the above procedure and gotten used to the way the Edwin editor works. I won't go into great detail here about the editor; you should familiarize yourself with the Edwin manual in the PC Scheme User's Guide, and from time to time examine the mini-manual included as an appendix to this book. You have perhaps already discovered that the arrow keys move the cursor around the screen and that the ← (BACKSPACE) key deletes characters before the cursor position. There are many special features to the Edwin editor, but you don't need much expertise to begin using it; the features mentioned in the previous sentence are enough to get you started on your first examples.

Anyway, it's time to go back to the Scheme interpreter and use our new procedure. What we want to do is tell the Scheme interpreter to evaluate the new definition that we just typed into Edwin. That is, we want the Scheme interpreter to know about the new procedure we just created. Here's what we do: type (ESC)-O (that's the letter O, not zero). This will tell the Scheme interpreter to evaluate everything that we just wrote inside the editor, and will send us back to the interpreter subsystem. The interpreter will print out the symbol *OK*, and your screen should look like Figure 2.6.

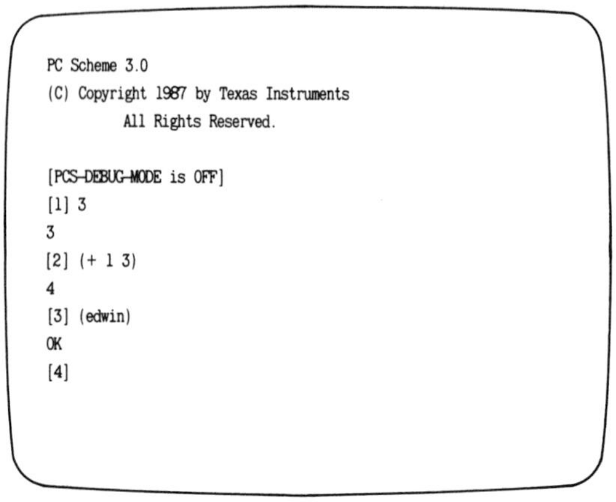

```
PC Scheme 3.0
(C) Copyright 1987 by Texas Instruments
           All Rights Reserved.

[PCS-DEBUG-MODE is OFF]
[1] 3
3
[2] (+ 1 3)
4
[3] (edwin)
OK
[4]
```

Figure 2.6. Returning from Edwin to the interpreter

This may be a good opportunity for another digression about errors. Upon returning to the Scheme interpreter, you may have seen an error message of some sort instead of the symbol *OK*. Many beginning programmers (including the author, some years past) respond to this sort of thing by physically leaping back from the screen. That won't help. What you should do is type (CTRL)-Q to leave the debugger; then return to the editor by typing

        (edwin)

and try to spot the problem in your procedure. It should look exactly like the version shown earlier, and almost certainly the problem lies in unbalanced or misplaced parentheses. Once you think the problem is fixed, return to the Scheme interpreter by typing (ESC)-O, and continue on.

Now that we're back in the interpreter, let's use our new roulette-wheel procedure. We type the following:

        (roulette-wheel)

and the interpreter should print out a number between 0 and 36. Try calling the roulette-wheel procedure a few more times.

Changing a Procedure

So far, so good. But roulette is really a gambling game, and we ought to be able to bet on the outcome of a particular spin. One simple enhancement to our existing roulette-wheel procedure would be to include an argument representing the number we wish to bet on; that is, we would like to be able to type

        (roulette-wheel 10)

at the interpreter and then find out whether we won (if the wheel came up 10) or lost. Let's go back to the editor and change our procedure to accommodate this idea. Type

```
(edwin)
```

to get back and then change the roulette–wheel procedure to look like this:

```
(define (roulette–wheel number–to–bet)
  (compare–with–bet (random 37) number–to–bet))
```

The idea is that when we eventually go back to the interpreter and call roulette–wheel with a number argument, the interpreter will call the procedure compare–with–bet using two arguments: a random number between 0 and 36, and the number we just bet on. But we're not done writing our program just yet: we have to create the compare–with–bet procedure. The following will work:

```
(define (compare–with–bet wheel–spin bet)
  (if (= wheel–spin bet)
      (display "You won! ")
      (display "You lost! "))
  wheel–spin)
```

Compare–with–bet, loosely, is a procedure that takes two numeric arguments named wheel–spin and bet; prints out a particular message depending on whether the two arguments are equal; and finally returns the value of wheel–spin. Let's look at it a bit more closely.

You will note that the body of compare–with–bet consists of two expressions: the first is a large compound expression beginning with the word if, and the second is simply the name wheel–spin. (The body of a Scheme procedure, by the way, is that portion of the definition which follows the name-and-parameters specification. The body of our new roulette–wheel procedure, for instance, consists of one expression beginning with the word compare–with–bet.) We will spend some time with if expressions two chapters hence; for now, I am going to supply a purely pragmatic explanation for what that first big expression means. Essentially, the point of the if statement is as follows: if wheel–spin and bet happen to have the same value, we print out the words "*You won!*" on the display screen; otherwise, we print out the words "*You lost!*" Take a look at the if expression, and it should be pretty trivial to intuit which portions of that expression correspond to the individual elements of the strategy I just mentioned. For instance, you might try and change our procedure so that it prints out "*Congratulations!*" instead of "*You won!*" whenever our gamble pays off.

What about the second expression, wheel–spin? Well, if the body of a procedure consists of more than one expression, then when we call that procedure on some arguments each expression will be evaluated in turn. The ultimate result of the evaluation process is simply the result of evaluating the very last expression in the procedure body. So, the result of evaluating a call to compare–with–bet is just the value of wheel–spin. (Again, don't get too hung up on understanding this just yet!) To summarize, the point of the if expression is to print something out on the screen; the point of the second expression is to return the value of wheel–spin as the result of the entire procedure call.

Try going back to the interpreter now (via ⎋-0) and using the new roulette–wheel procedure. To bet on the number 4, for instance, you would type the following at the interpreter prompt:

```
(roulette–wheel 4)
```

There is one final point worth mentioning about our program: it consists of two independent procedures. Scheme programs are typically composed of a (possibly large) set of procedures, any one of which can be called from the interpreter. For instance, you can use our new compare-with-bet procedure now just as easily as roulette-wheel. Try typing the following expressions at the interpreter, and you'll see what I mean:

```
(compare-with-bet 10 20)
(compare-with-bet 20 20)
```

Saving and Retrieving Files

To finish this first session with Scheme, let's save our program on a floppy disk. (The precise commands shown in this example may not be exactly applicable to your system; among other things, I am assuming that you have at least one floppy disk drive—i.e., an "A: drive.") You should first go back to Edwin and type (CTRL)-X (CTRL)-W. You will see a prompt asking for the name of the file you wish to write. Place a properly formatted disk in the A: drive, and type A:ROULET.SCM. Edwin will write the program onto the disk and give you a message to that effect by displaying the word "done" at the bottom of the screen.

Just so that you can see how to retrieve stored files, let's now reset the Edwin editor and clear out everything we've typed so far. Type (CTRL)-X (CTRL)-C; this sends you back to the Scheme interpreter and resets Edwin. Now go back to the editor one last time. The editor screen should look just as it did when we first used it—namely, empty of all text. We can retrieve the program that we just saved by typing (CTRL)-X (CTRL)-V; Edwin will ask for the name of the file, and (assuming that our disk is still in the A: drive) we can type A:ROULET.SCM. After a few seconds, our roulette program should be loaded back into Edwin.

Leaving Scheme

If you are done using Scheme, go back to the interpreter ((ESC)-O should still work) and type the following at the interpreter prompt:
```
(exit)
```

This will send you back to the operating system of your machine. Before completing the exit operation, however, your PC Scheme system may print out a message like the following:

Buffer Main contains changes. Write them out (Y or N)?

This means that the text currently in the editor has not been saved in any file. If you want to save that text, you can type Y in response to the message; PC Scheme will then prompt you for a file name and will save the editor contents in a new file with the name that you provide. If you want to leave Scheme without saving the editor contents, you can simply type N instead of Y.

Exercises

1. Earlier, you used the + procedure to add two numbers. Make up a few examples using the -, *, and / procedures for subtraction, multiplication, and division.

2. Both edwin and roulette-wheel are procedures that take no arguments. In this chapter, you encountered another procedure (a Scheme primitive) that takes no arguments. Can you find it?

3. In using our roulette-wheel procedure, we called it on one numeric argument as follows:

        (roulette-wheel 12)

    Try experimenting with the procedure. What happens if we call it on no arguments? On two? What happens if we just type the single word roulette-wheel (without parentheses) at the interpreter?

4. Try altering the roulette-wheel procedure in some simple ways. For example, suppose our bet represents not a number on which we wish to wager, but rather an upper limit on our wager: that is, if we type

        (roulette-wheel 10)

    we ought to win if the wheel comes up with anything below 10. How would you change our existing procedures to implement this idea? (You may find the Scheme primitive < helpful. Take a look at the description for < in the Scheme manual and compare it to the description for =.)

5. Another alteration might be to have roulette-wheel take two arguments instead of one so that you can bet on two numbers. There are any number of ways of getting this to work, but our Scheme repertoire is thus far very limited. You might leaf through the Scheme manual to see if you can come up with a solution; or, if you want to use only those constructions included in this chapter, then consider what happens if you use an if expression as one of the subexpressions of a larger if expression. That is, your strategy might be as follows: if the wheel-spin is equal to the first bet, print out *"You won!"*; otherwise, if the wheel-spin is equal to the second bet, print out *"You won!"*; otherwise, print out *"You lost!"* Using if to make this work is actually a bit clumsy, but it may be worth a try.

6. Suppose we change roulette-wheel as follows, in the hope of dispensing with the compare-with-bet procedure:

```
(define (roulette-wheel number-to-bet)
  (if (= number-to-bet (random 37))
      (display "You won! ")
      (display "You lost! "))
  (random 37)
```

    Does this work? Why or why not?

7. One special feature of the Edwin editor that is worth exploring is the use of the (TAB) key. As a rule, when you are typing a Scheme program in the editor, it is good practice to begin every line in the body of a procedure with (TAB), which tells the Edwin editor to indent the current line in "standard Scheme format." For instance, in the original roulette-wheel example, after typing the line

        (define (roulette-wheel)

    you should type ↵ (to go to the next line) and then (TAB) to start the next line at the properly indented spot (in this case, three spaces from the left margin). Note that the roulette-wheel procedure is not "wrong" even if it is typed with a weird pattern of indentation; for example, if you type the roulette-wheel procedure as follows, it will still work:

```
(define
(roulette-wheel)
(random
37))
```

As long as the parentheses and spaces between words are correct, it doesn't matter how your Scheme procedures are indented. The major reason for indenting them properly is simply that it makes them easier to read. Rather than worry about remembering rules of indentation ourselves, though, it is easier to let the editor indent our progams for us by beginning each line in the editor with a (TAB). The appendix on Edwin at the end of this book provides a little more detail on this subject.

As an exercise you should try experimenting with Edwin to see how it uses the (TAB) key to indent Scheme code. For instance, suppose that you type ↵ (to start a new line) after the word wheel-spin in the compare-with-bet procedure. What happens when you type (TAB) to begin the following line?

CHAPTER 3

Expressions
and Procedures

In this chapter we will start to explore the Scheme interpreter and the rules it uses to evaluate expressions; and we will take our first steps toward creating new procedures. Unavoidably, our initial efforts will be a bit on the simple side, but that's the way it goes. A certain amount of early effort has to be devoted to expanding our repertoire of programming techniques, so that we can eventually create more interesting and sophisticated programs.

For the time being, virtually all our examples will involve numbers as data. This is because numbers are the easiest kind of data object to understand, and by using them we can illustrate many of the key ideas in Scheme. In chapter 4 another kind of data object will be introduced, and by the end of the book there will be a large variety to play with. But for now, let's stick with numbers.

Numbers

When we type something at the Scheme interpreter and hit ↵, what we are doing is telling the Scheme interpreter to evaluate the expression we just typed. Now, we already saw in the previous chapter that when our expression is a number (i.e., when we type a number and hit ↵), the interpreter simply prints out the number. This suggests our first evaluation rule.

▶ *Rule 1: Evaluating Numbers*

Numbers evaluate to themselves.[1]

There are several allowed formats for numbers. Without getting too long-winded, let's just say that you can write integers,

    5   20   1000000

---

[1]The phrases "evaluates to," "has a value of," and "returns" are used more or less interchangeably. Thus, all of the following mean essentially the same thing:

   " (+1 3) evaluates to 4."
   "The value of (+1 3) is 4."
   "Evaluating the expression (+1 3) returns 4."

rational numbers using decimal notation,

5.   5.0   3.14159   1245.674

negative numbers preceded by a minus sign (no space),

-5   -5.0   -1245.674

and numbers in scientific notation represented as a rational or integer mantissa and integer exponent separated by E (no spaces):[2]

5E6   -5E6   -5.3E-7   156.78E75

In PC Scheme, there are upper and lower limits on scientific notation numbers. The largest exponent that you can use is 308, and the smallest is -308.[3]

Arithmetic Operations

The Scheme language contains a variety of *primitive procedures*—procedures that are built into the language. Some of these primitives perform simple numeric operations, like addition (the + procedure) and multiplication (the * procedure). We can use these numeric operations by *applying* them to *arguments* (or, as is sometimes said, *calling* them on arguments), as in the following examples:

```
(+ 5 6)
(- 75 1)
(* 88 -2.5)
(/ 43 12.2)
(expt 5 2)
```

Try typing these expressions into Scheme to see what happens. (You already saw the + procedure in the previous chapter, and may very well have discovered the others for yourself.) When we type a compound expression (that is, one surrounded by parentheses) at the Scheme interpreter, the interpreter treats this as a procedure call. The first expression after the left parenthesis is the procedure to be applied; the remaining expressions are the arguments to that procedure.[4]

The five examples above employ primitive procedures, and the Scheme interpreter evaluates them as follows: each of the operands—the arguments to the primitive procedure—is individually evaluated. Then the primitive procedure is applied to the resulting values. Note that in these five examples, evaluating the operands requires the use of our "Number Evaluation Rule," which says that numbers evaluate to themselves.

So far, so good. We can now state a rule relevant to our new examples—i.e., how the Scheme interpreter evaluates expressions that employ primitive procedures.

◆ *Rule 2: Evaluating Calls to Primitive Procedures*[5]

To evaluate a primitive procedure call, evaluate each of the operand expressions and then apply the primitive procedure to the resulting values.

---

[2]In case you are unfamiliar with this notation, the four sample numbers represented are 5 times 10^6, -5 times 10^6, -5.3 times 10^{-7}, and 156.78 times 10^{75}. In other words, a number x followed by an "E" followed by an integer n may be read as "multiply x by 10 to the nth power."

[3]Future versions of PC Scheme—i.e., versions later than 3.0—may include other types of numbers, such as a special *rational number* type and a *complex number* type. For instance, dividing the integer 3 by the integer 2 may return a rational number rather than the present version's returned value of 1.5 (which is a floating point number). It is worthwhile experimenting on your own and checking your system documentation on this point.

[4]There are certain exceptions to this statement; some Scheme expressions employ what are called *special forms* instead of procedures. We will encounter our first special form later in this chapter.

[5]In this book, the term *primitive procedure* refers to any procedure that is supplied with the Scheme system—that is, any procedure that you can find in your manual. There isn't much standardization in the Scheme community for terms like this, however, and the word "primitive" can sometimes

Our "Primitive Procedure Rule" is more powerful than it at first appears. Since we now know how to evaluate expressions like

```
(* 12 4)

(- 77 3)
```

and so on, we can use those expressions as parts (or *subexpressions*) of larger expressions. For instance, consider the following expression, in which the call to the * procedure is *nested* within the call to +:

```
(+ 5 (* 12 4))
```

This is a primitive procedure call for the procedure +, so we need to use our Primitive Procedure Rule to evaluate it. The first operand, 5, simply evaluates to itself; and the second operand expression is itself a primitive procedure call, which we can evaluate using . . . the Primitive Procedure Rule! So there is a hidden recursive quality to our new rule: namely, the notion of "evaluating operand expressions" may itself require the use of other evaluation rules, including the Primitive Procedure Rule.

Let's restate our rule, then, making this insight explicit:

▶ *Rule 2: Evaluating Calls to Primitive Procedures*

> To evaluate a primitive procedure call, evaluate each of the operand expressions and then apply the primitive procedure to the resulting values. Note that the task of "evaluating each of the operand expressions" may itself require the evaluation of procedure calls.

You should now be able to predict what happens when we evaluate the following expressions:

```
(+ (+ 2 5) (* 7 8))

(- (- 17 (- 14 2)) 1)

(* (+ 3 (* 4 5)) (- 12.6 (/ 14 2)))
```

Try typing these at the Scheme interpreter to see if your predictions are correct. And by the way: I used the word "recursive" a little earlier. Loosely, the idea there was that in order to apply the Primitive Procedure Rule to some particular expression, we might have to apply that very same rule to some subexpression. Recursion is a theme that pervades Scheme programming at every level; it is a notion both marvelous and puzzling. We will soon explore this notion in depth, in the context of writing recursive Scheme procedures.

Naming Things with Define

Several more ideas still need to be introduced before we can get any real programming under way. For one thing, we need some way of giving names to objects: in Scheme, define expressions are used for this purpose. Now, it happens that in chapter 2, define was used to create new procedures, and we'll get back to that topic shortly; here, though, we will use define in a slightly different way.

To begin, try typing the following expressions at the Scheme interpreter:

```
(define a 10)

a

(* a 2)
```

---

take on slightly different meanings. In the PC Scheme manual, not all system-supplied procedures are referred to as primitive procedures; the manual's usage is too complex to discuss here, but we will return to it briefly at the end of Chapter 11. In any case, the terminology used in this book is consistent with Abelson-Sussman [1985] and is, I believe, simpler to understand.

The Scheme interpreter should respond by printing out *A*, *10*, and *20*. The first expression tells the Scheme interpreter that henceforth a will be another name for the number 10. In evaluating the second expression, the interpreter evaluates the name a and returns the object that a names, 10. In the final expression, we are using the primitive procedure *, so the interpreter has to employ our Primitive Procedure Rule; since the first operand, a, evaluates to 10 and the second operand evaluates to 2, the resulting value is 20.

Technically speaking, the effect of the first expression is to *bind* the symbol a to the number object 10. A symbol is *bound* if it names some object, and we can therefore say—if we're into sounding impressive—that define is used to bind symbols to objects.

Something Unexpected About Define

Now that we have seen define in action, we might ask an innocent question: is define a primitive procedure? It is certainly true that define is built into the Scheme language, like +; but there is something odd about calling define a primitive procedure. The problem is this: primitive procedure calls are evaluated by the Primitive Procedure Rule. If you look carefully at that rule, you will notice its stipulation that all operands to a primitive procedure be evaluated before applying the procedure. But define doesn't quite work this way.

Consider what happens if we type the following expressions at the Scheme interpreter:

```
b

(define b 8)

b
```

The first time that we type b, the Scheme interpreter will respond with an error message. The problem is that b is not yet a name for anything (in technical terms, b is an *unbound variable*). The second expression tells the Scheme interpreter that henceforth b will be another name for 8; and when we evaluate the name b afterward, in the third expression, the Scheme interpreter will return the value 8.

Now, why is the evaluation of the define expression inconsistent with our Primitive Procedure Rule? The answer is that if define were a primitive procedure, we would have to evaluate both of its arguments—b and 8—before applying the define procedure. But we have already seen that if we evaluate b we get an error message! We can't evaluate b until the define expression has actually made it a name for something.

The upshot of all this is simply that define expressions are not evaluated via the Primitive Procedure Rule, and that therefore define is not a primitive procedure. Instead, define is an example of what is called in Scheme a *special form*. And before getting back to define, we may as well spend a few careful moments considering the whole idea of special forms.

Special Forms

Earlier, it was said that when the Scheme interpreter encounters an expression within parentheses, this expression is treated as a procedure call, and the first thing after the left parenthesis is the procedure being applied. That's true most of the time, but there are exceptions—define expressions, for instance. We just proved to ourselves that define must be a special form, not a procedure. In the previous chapter, we encountered if expressions, and as we will see later if, like define, also happens to be a Scheme special form. Expressions that begin with special forms cannot be evaluated using the Primitive Procedure Rule—it is precisely this property, in fact, that makes them distinct from procedures. The "specialness" of special forms is a kind of negative quality: they are special because we can't use the Primitive Procedure Rule to understand them.

Each special form has its own unique evaluation rule. If we wish to use one, we have to know its individual rule. Fortunately for us, there aren't many special forms in Scheme: we will encounter fewer than two dozen in this book, and you can get by very comfortably using ten or so of the most important ones.

◆ *Rule 3: Evaluating Expressions Beginning with Special Forms*

To evaluate a compound expression beginning with a special form, you cannot use the Primitive Procedure Rule. Each special form has its own unique rule for evaluation. That's why they're called special forms.

Because we have now classified `define` as a special form, we know that a unique rule will be needed to indicate how `define` expressions are evaluated. Here it is: A `define` expression may be of the form

Define Revisited—Evaluating Symbols

```
(define symbol expression)
```

An expression of this form is evaluated as follows: first evaluate the expression following the symbol, and then bind the symbol to the resulting value.

This leads us to a related rule about evaluating symbols:

◆ *Rule 4: Evaluating Symbols*

Symbols can be bound to data objects (like numbers). To evaluate a symbol, see if it is bound to a data object. If so, return that object; if not, signal an error.

Thus, the last three expressions below should return 5, 3, and 10, respectively.[6]

```
(define b 20)
(define c 4)
(/ b c)
(- b (+ 1 (* 4 c)))
(+ c (+ c (/ b 10)))
```

What kind of symbols can we use as names? Without wading too deeply into hideously trivial details, the answer is, "just about anything that doesn't include spaces, parentheses, and some other special characters, and that doesn't look like a number." All of the following are symbols which we could bind with `define` statements:

```
x
love-potion-number-9
100-yard-dash
```

We have seen how to use `define` to provide names for things like numbers. But you may recall that in the last chapter `define` was used in a different way, to create new procedures. This is the next topic to explore.

Using `Define` to Create New Procedures

Before getting formal about matters, it is best to stare at a few examples. As you encounter these procedures, try to get a sense of what they do—what the various parts of the procedure definitions mean. Use your intuition!

---

[6] At this point, you might wonder, "What about the first two expressions? What values do they return?" The answer is that `define` expressions do return values, but we virtually never care about the values that they return. `Define` expressions are useful because they give names to objects, not because they evaluate to some interesting result. In the PC Scheme manual, in fact, the returned value of a `define` expression is deliberately left unspecified.

Here's a procedure named double. It is called on one argument, a number, and returns the value of that number multiplied by two.

```
(define (double number)
  (* 2 number))
```

If we type (double 5) at the Scheme interpreter, the printed result will be *10*.

Here is a procedure named square, which when called on a number argument will return the square of that number:

```
(define (square number)
  (* number number))
```

We could equally well have written these two procedures in the following way:

```
(define (double number)
  (+ number number))
```

```
(define (square number)
  (expt number 2))
```

The point of showing these alternative versions of double and square is simply to note that even for very simple procedures, there is no one "correct" way to write them. Of course, there are many ways that won't work; and even among the ways that do work, there will often be advantages or disadvantages to some particular version. But in programming, as in life, there is no ultimate answer key; and all rules of style are made to be broken eventually.

Back to our examples. Here's a procedure that takes one argument, a number representing some length, and returns the area of a circle whose radius is that length:

```
(define (circle-area radius)
  (* 3.14159 (square radius)))
```

Notice that the procedure circle-area uses the procedure square that we created above. We can use circle-area in the definition of some other procedure; here's a procedure that takes two arguments, numbers representing radius and height, and returns the volume of a cylinder with these dimensions:

```
(define (cylinder-volume radius height)
  (* height (circle-area radius)))
```

And because the volume of a cone with a given radius and height is one third that of a cylinder with these same dimensions:

```
(define (cone-volume radius height)
  (/ (cylinder-volume radius height) 3))
```

Procedures can use other procedures which can use other procedures, and so on. Suppose we were to call cone-volume on two numeric arguments by typing at the Scheme interpreter:

```
(cone-volume 4 20)
```

The cone-volume procedure would call cylinder-volume, which would itself call circle-area, which would call square, which would call the primitive procedure * (or maybe, in our alternate version, expt). Thus, in evaluating a call to cone-volume, the Scheme interpreter would eventually call some primitive procedure; but even in this first foray into Scheme programming, you can see that it isn't hard to build ever-more-complicated procedures out of the building blocks that we ourselves create.

Now, let's get formal.

We define procedures using the following format:

```
(define (procedure-name arg1 arg2 . . .)
   body )
```

The word `define` is followed by the procedure's name and the names of its arguments (these names are all within one set of parentheses). Note that, as in our first `roulette-wheel` procedure back in Chapter 2, there may be zero arguments. After this name-and-argument specification, the remainder of the `define` expression is the *body* of the procedure; this specifies how calls to the procedure will be evaluated, in a way that will be discussed in the next section of this chapter.

If you look again at examples of the two forms of `define` that we have used in this chapter:

```
(define a 3)
```

```
(define (square number)
   (* number number))
```

you will see that the difference between them is simply that procedure definitions have the procedure name and arguments in parentheses. Thus, the first `define` expression binds the name `a` to the number 3, while the second creates a new procedure called `square`. If we type the following at the interpreter:

```
(define (a) 3)
```

then we are now defining a new procedure named `a` that when called with no arguments will return (as we shall explain in the next section) the value 3. This meaning for `a`, by the way, would replace any earlier meaning for `a`; that is, if we type the two expressions

```
(define a 100)
```

```
(define (a) 3)
```

then `a` is the name of a procedure (not a name for 100) after both expressions have been typed.

In this section I'm going to lie to you. I promise to tell the truth eventually (say, in Chapter 11), but for now, honesty compels me to admit that I'm lying. But, though the story presented here is not really true, it will serve our purposes more than adequately for a long time, and trying to puzzle through the complete story just now would be more trouble than it's worth.

What we need at this point is a rule analogous to our Primitive Procedure Rule—except where that rule dealt with primitive procedures, we will now need something dealing with the procedures that we create (so-called *compound procedures*). Here is the new rule:

▶ *Rule 5: Evaluating Calls to Compound Procedures*

> To evaluate a compound procedure call, first evaluate all the operands to the procedure. Then evaluate the body of the procedure as though the procedure arguments were actually names for the operands' values. The result of the procedure call is the value of the last expression in the body of the procedure.

Let's work through an example. Suppose we type the following at the Scheme interpreter:

```
(square 28)
```

Our new "Compound Procedure Rule" says that we first evaluate all the operand expressions. Here, the only operand expression is the number 28, which evaluates to itself. Now we wish to evaluate the body of the square procedure:

```
(* number number)
```

as though the symbol number was actually a name for 28. This is a primitive procedure call, so we use our Primitive Procedure Rule to evaluate it: both of the operand expressions are the symbol number, which we are pretending is a name for 28, so each of the operands evaluates to 28 by our "Symbol Evaluation Rule" (Rule 4 above); and finally we apply the primitive procedure * to this number and get 784 as our returned value.

Here's another example:

```
(square (double 3))
```

The Compound Procedure Rule says that we first evaluate the operand expressions. Here the operand expression is (double 3), which is a call to the double procedure and therefore has to be evaluated using the Compound Procedure Rule. (Again, the Compound Procedure Rule—like the Primitive Procedure Rule—has a recursive quality.) To evaluate (double 3), we first evaluate the operand expression 3, which evaluates to itself. Now, the body of double:

```
(* 2 number)
```

is evaluated as though number were bound to 3. The result is 6, and thus the overall operand expression (double 3) has evaluated to 6. Now we evaluate the body of square:

```
(* number number)
```

as though number were bound to 6. The result is 36, and this is finally the value of the call to square. Note that the fact that both square and double have chosen to name their argument number has absolutely no effect on the evaluation process: in each case, the binding for number is completely local to the body of the procedure in question. In fact, as long as we write a given procedure consistently, it doesn't matter what we choose to name the argument. You should convince yourself that from the standpoint of any other procedure which calls them, the following versions of double are exactly the same:

```
(define (double no)
  (* 2 no))

(define (double x)
  (* 2 x))

(define (double just-about-any-reasonable-symbol)
  (* 2 just-about-any-reasonable-symbol))
```

A Note on Practice: The Editor and the Interpreter

Usually, procedure definitions are written in the Scheme editor, as we did in Chapter 2, and then "sent back" to the Scheme interpreter (we did this via PC Scheme's ᴱˢᶜ-0 in the last chapter). The "sending back" process is equivalent to telling the Scheme interpreter to behave as though we had actually typed in all the define expressions in the interpreter itself. In other words, the purpose of the editor subsystem is to provide a place where we can write expressions that will ultimately be passed to the interpreter just as though we had typed them directly at the interpreter.

It would be perfectly all right to work entirely in the Scheme interpreter, and type all our procedure definitions directly. But it would be highly impractical, since if we wanted to make a small change in an already-defined procedure (as we did with the roulette-wheel procedure in Chapter 2), we would have to retype the entire procedure definition at the interpreter. The editor is thus a place where we can easily look at and alter old procedures, as well as create new ones.

Suppose we want to write a handy algebra procedure that will print out the solutions to any quadratic equation:

$$ax^2 + bx + c = 0$$

There are two values of x that will satisfy this equation:

$$x = (-b \pm \sqrt{b^2 - 4ac})/2a$$

Using this formula we can create the following procedure:

```
(define (quadratic-solutions a b c)
  (display (/ (+ (- 0 b) (sqrt (- (square b) (* 4 a c)))) (* 2 a)))
  (newline)
  (display (/ (- (- 0 b) (sqrt (- (square b) (* 4 a c)))) (* 2 a))))
```

This procedure, when called on three numeric arguments representing a, b, and c in the quadratic equation above, will print out the two values of x satisfying the equation. Quadratic-solutions makes use of the Scheme primitve procedures display, which we saw in the previous chapter, and sqrt, which returns the square root of its argument. The newline primitive effectively causes the next display operation to begin on a fresh line on the screen.

There are a couple of points worth mentioning about quadratic-solutions. First, this procedure (unlike, say, the double procedure) does not return a number when called; it returns the value of the second display expression, which is not a number (the PC Scheme manual mentions that expressions using the display primitive, like those using the special form define, return unspecified values). Second, quadratic-solutions doesn't always work: it fails whenever the argument to sqrt is negative. We'll fix that in the next chapter.

For our present purposes, there is another problem with quadratic-solutions. When the procedure is called, the expression

```
(sqrt (- (square b) (* 4 a c)))
```

must be evaluated twice. This seems unnecessary: having evaluated the expression once, why evaluate the exact same expression (yielding the exact same result) a second time?

We can remedy this problem using the Scheme special form let:

```
(define (quadratic-solutions a b c)
  (let ((root-part (sqrt (- (square b) (* 4 a c)))))
    (display (/ (+ (- 0 b) root-part) (* 2 a)))
    (newline)
    (display (/ (- (- 0 b) root-part) (* 2 a)))))
```

The idea here is that the let expression will evaluate the expression

```
(sqrt (- (square b) (* 4 a c)))
```

and temporarily bind root-part to the resulting value. The display expressions are then evaluated with the binding for root-part in effect. Thus, the call to sqrt is only evaluated once. Even though the difference in actual computation time between our two versions of quadratic-solutions is hardly noticeable, there will be many occasions in the future when using let saves a great deal of time. Perhaps more importantly, the code for quadratic-solutions is more readable than before; in fact, we can make what is perhaps an even cleaner version:

```
(define (quadratic-solutions a b c)
  (let ((root-part-over-2a (/ (sqrt (- (square b)(* 4 a c))) (* 2 a)))
        (minus-b-over-2a (/ (- 0 b) (* 2 a))))
    (display (+ minus-b-over-2a root-part-over-2a))
    (newline)
    (display (- minus-b-over-2a root-part-over-2a))))
```

Here, we make two temporary bindings (for the names root-part-over-2a and minus-b-over-2a) and evaluate the two display expressions with those bindings in effect.

The formal rule for evaluating let expressions is as follows. Let expressions are of the form:

```
(let ( (name-1  exp-1 )
       (name-2  exp-2 )
       . . . )
   body)
```

Evaluate each of the various expressions *exp-1*, *exp-2*, and so on. Once they are all evaluated, temporarily bind the names *name-1*, *name-2*, etc., to the respective resulting values: i.e., bind *name-1* to the result of evaluating *exp-1*, bind *name-2* to the result of evaluating *exp-2*, and so on. Then evaluate the expressions in *body* with the new temporary bindings in effect; the value of the let expression is the value of the last expression in *body*.

If you examine this rule carefully, you'll see why the following attempted version of quadratic-solutions would not work:

```
(define (quadratic-solutions a b c)
  (let ((denominator (* 2 a))
        (root-part-over-2a
          (/ (sqrt (- (square b)(* 4 a c))) denominator))
        (minus-b-over-2a (/ (- 0 b) denominator)))
    (display (+ minus-b-over-2a root-part-over-2a))
    (newline)
    (display (- minus-b-over-2a root-part-over-2a))))
```

This is not a bad idea, but there's a problem. The expression whose value will be bound to root-part-over-2a contains the name denominator, and denominator is not yet bound to anything. (We also run into the same difficulty with minus-b-over-2a.) Recall, from the description of let above, that all the expressions *exp-1*, *exp-2*, and so on have to be evaluated before any bindings can be done. So although we can use the name denominator in the body of the let expression, we cannot use it in the various "binding-portion" expressions that precede the body.

A Little Vocabulary Expansion

We have covered a fair amount of ground in this chapter, although there is still much further to go. But before moving on to the next chapter, we may as well pick up a little extra vocabulary. Here is a brief sampling of useful Scheme primitives:

▶ 1+

Adds 1 to its argument. Thus (1+ 3) evaluates to 4.

▶ −1+

Subtracts 1 from its argument. So (-1+ 3.6) evaluates to 2.6.

◆ `floor, ceiling`

Returns the integer immediately below (for `floor`) or above (for `ceiling`) the argument. Thus

(floor 2.3)　　(ceiling 2.6)　　(floor -5.5)

evaluate to 2, 3, and −6, respectively.

◆ `cos, sin, tan`

Each of these takes a numeric argument interpreted as a number of radians (recall that 2π radians is equivalent to 360 degrees). They return the cosine (or sine, or tangent) of the argument. So the following expressions:

(cos 3.14159)　　(sin 3.14159)　　(tan (/ 3.14159 4))

evaluate to (approximately) −1, 0, and 1, respectively.

There are many other numeric procedures that you should have no trouble understanding. Some of them are mentioned in the exercises at the end of the chapter.

Here, in summary form, are the evaluation rules that we have encountered thus far:

A Summary of Scheme Evaluation Rules

◆ *Rule 1: Evaluating Numbers*

Numbers evaluate to themselves.

◆ *Rule 2: Evaluating Calls to Primitive Procedures*

To evaluate a primitive procedure call, evaluate each of the operand expressions and then apply the primitive procedure to the resulting values. Note that the task of "evaluating each of the operand expressions" may itself require the evaluation of procedure calls.

◆ *Rule 3: Evaluating Expressions Beginning with Special Forms*

To evaluate a compound expression beginning with a special form, you cannot use the Primitive Procedure Rule. Each special form has its own unique rule for evaluation. That's why they're called special forms. (So far, we have seen two special forms—namely, `define` and `let`—along with their associated unique rules. In the next chapter we will meet some more special forms.)

◆ *Rule 4: Evaluating Symbols*

Symbols can be bound to data objects (like numbers). To evaluate a symbol, see if it is bound to a data object. If so, return that object; if not, signal an error.

◆ *Rule 5: Evaluating Calls to Compound Procedures*

To evaluate a compound procedure call, first evaluate all the operands to the procedure. Then evaluate the body of the procedure as though the procedure arguments were actually names for the operands' values. The result of the procedure call is the value of the last expression in the body of the procedure.

Exercises

1. Try to predict the values of the following expressions; then type them at the Scheme interpreter to see if your predictions were correct.

   ```
   (+ 22.5 3)
   (expt 3 4)
   (- (+ 75 12) 4)
   (* (* 2 2.5) (/ 36.3 3))
   (expt 2 (/ 1 2))
   (* (+ 14 -6) 3E5)
   (+ (* 4E9 2.2E15) (+ 2E23 8E23))
   (+ (* 2 (/ 20 4)) (/ 600 (* (+ 1 3)(expt 5 2))))
   ```

   You probably can't predict the result of evaluating this expression:

   ```
   (expt 5 100)
   ```

   but it is worth your while typing it in; it is a good demonstration of how PC Scheme handles very large integers.

2. Suppose we type the following expressions, one by one, at the Scheme interpreter. See if you can predict the values that the interpreter will return:

   ```
   (define a 2)
   (define b 7)
   (+ a b)
   (* (- b a) (+ 1 b))
   (expt (- b a) a)
   (define b 8)
   (+ a b)
   ```

3. Here are several simple procedures. Can you determine (in a qualitative sense) what they are intended to do? What would be better choices of names for these procedures?

   ```
   (define (mystery-1 number)
     (expt number (/ 1 3)))
   (define (mystery-2 number)
     (* 3.14159 (* 2 number)))
   (define (mystery-3 number-1 number-2)
     (/ (+ number-1 number-2) 2))
   ```

4. Write a procedure called `rectangle-area` that takes two number arguments, `base` and `height`, and returns the area of the rectangle with these two numbers as its base and height, respectively. We should be able to use the procedure as follows:

   ```
   (rectangle-area 12 4)
   48
   ```

5. Write a procedure called `triangle-area` that takes two arguments, `base` and `height`, and returns the area of the appropriate triangle:

   ```
   (triangle-area 12 4)
   24
   ```

6. Write another triangle-area procedure—maybe this one ought to be called triangle-area-2—that takes three arguments: two side lengths and the angle (in radians) between them. Here are a couple of sample calls (one for a right triangle and one for an equilateral triangle):

```
(triangle-area-2 1 4 (/ 3.14159 2))
2

(triangle-area-2 4 4 (/ 3.14159 3))
6.928
```

7. The distance between two points (x_1, y_1) and (x_2, y_2) is expressed by the formula:

$$\sqrt{(x_2 - x_1)^2 + (y_2 - y_1)^2}$$

Write a procedure, distance-between-points, that takes four numbers as arguments x1, y1, x2, and y2, and returns the distance between the appropriate points.

8. The volume of a sphere of radius r is

$$\text{volume} = 4\pi r^3/3$$

Write a procedure sphere-volume that takes one argument, radius, and returns the volume of the sphere with that radius. Then write a new procedure, shell-volume, that takes two arguments, inner-radius and outer-radius, and finds the volume of a hollow spherical shell with the appropriate inner and outer radii. (What we want is the volume between the two spheres.)

9. Inspired by Dave Johnson's success in using computer-maintained statistics to help manage the New York Mets, your local baseball manager asks you to write several Scheme procedures on his behalf. He has provided a Scheme procedure called baseball-statistics, but his program is incomplete: three more procedures, batting-avg, slugging-pct, and on-base-pct, are needed.

```
(define (baseball-statistics
            at-bats singles doubles triples home-runs walks sac-flies)
  (newline)
  (display "Batting average: ")
  (display (batting-avg at-bats singles doubles triples home-runs))
  (newline)
  (display "Slugging percentage: ")
  (display (slugging-pct at-bats singles doubles triples home-runs))
  (newline)
  (display "On-base percentage: ")
  (display
    (on-base-pct
       at-bats singles doubles triples home-runs walks sac-flies)))
```

Your job is to write the three needed procedures. The formula for batting average is total hits divided by times at bat; the formula for slugging percentage is total bases divided by times at bat (thus, for example, doubles count as two bases); and the formula for on-base percentage is hits plus walks divided by times at bat plus walks plus sacrifice flies (in calculating on-base percentages sacrifice flies count as times at bat, whereas in calculating batting averages sacrifice flies do not count as a time at bat).

10. The period of a pendulum of length l (in meters) is given by the formula:

$$\text{period} = 2\pi\sqrt{l/g}$$

where g is the acceleration due to gravity: $g = 9.8$ meters/sec^2

Write a procedure `pendulum-period` that takes one argument `length` and returns the period of the appropriate pendulum.

✳ 11. Use a nested `let` expression (that's as much of a hint as I'm going to give) to implement the strategy of the failed `quadratic-solutions` which was shown earlier and is repeated below:

```
(define (quadratic-solutions a b c)
  (let ((denominator (* 2 a))
        (root-part-over-2a
           (/ (sqrt (- (square b)(* 4 a c))) denominator))
        (minus-b-over-2a (/ (- 0 b) denominator)))
    (display (+ minus-b-over-2a root-part-over-2a))
    (newline)
    (display (- minus-b-over-2a root-part-over-2a))))
```

The idea is that we wish to bind `denominator` and then bind `root-part-over-2a` and `minus-b-over-2a` using the existing binding for `denominator`.

12. Suppose the following expressions are typed at the Scheme interpreter in the order shown. Try to predict what values the interpreter will return; then actually perform the experiment to see if your predictions were correct. (Some of these expressions will signal errors; others will return values which you probably won't be able to anticipate just yet.)

```
(define a 3)
(define (b) 4)
a
b
(a)
(b)
(+ a (b))
(+ a b)
(+ (a) (b))
```

13. Some numeric primitives were not described in this chapter, but they should be straightforward to understand. Look for the following procedures in your Scheme manual and try to use them in a Scheme expression:

```
max
min
abs
round
truncate
remainder
modulo
log
acos
asin
atan
```

CHAPTER **4**

Making
Choices

When we struggle with some problem, we often find ourselves considering among
a set of alternative actions. In a game of chess, for instance, we might think: "If
I move my rook to K6, my opponent will probably counter by moving her bishop
to K2. . . . On the other hand, if I leave my rook where it is and push that pawn,
she will probably move her king. . . ." It's hardly a surprise that in writing
computer programs to solve some problem, we similarly have to select among
alternatives. A typical computer program will be filled with what programmers
call *conditional choices* (or *branch points*, or *conditional branches*, or a variety
of other terms). Even the most familiar activity of computer programs, doing
something *n* times, can be expressed informally as a choice: "if the action has
been performed *n* times, we are finished; otherwise do it again." In this chapter,
we will learn how to make Scheme programs that make choices.

Let's start by looking once more at the quadratic-solutions procedure from the
previous chapter:

```
(define (quadratic-solutions a b c)
  (let ((root-part-over-2a (/ (sqrt (- (square b)(* 4 a c))) (* 2 a)))
        (minus-b-over-2a (/ (- 0 b) (* 2 a))))
    (display (+ minus-b-over-2a root-part-over-2a))
    (newline)
    (display (- minus-b-over-2a root-part-over-2a))))
```

If we try to call this procedure on arguments 1, 2, and 5, as follows:

```
(quadratic-solutions 1 2 5)
```

we will get an error message from the Scheme interpreter because the argument to
sqrt turns out to be -16. Depending on our purposes, we might wish to alter the
procedure in several ways: for instance, if the argument to sqrt is negative, we
might simply want the procedure to print out "*No solutions.*" Or we might want the
procedure to print out the solutions as complex numbers, in some reasonable

format. Here is one way of accommodating the first of these strategies; we write a new procedure, new–quadratic–solutions, as follows:

```
(define (new-quadratic-solutions a b c)
  (if (negative? (- (square b)(* 4 a c)))
      (display "No solutions")
      (quadratic-solutions a b c)))
```

Now, instead of calling quadratic-solutions, we would call new–quadratic-solutions. If the expression under the square root sign is negative, new–quadratic-solutions prints out *"No solutions"*; otherwise it simply goes ahead and calls our original quadratic–solutions procedure. This is not the most elegant way to handle the problem, but it's a simple illustration of the if special form. We first encountered if in Chapter 2, but now it's time to examine this special form a little more closely.

The If Special Form

The structure of an if expression is as follows:

(if *predicate-exp consequent-exp alternative-exp*)

That is, the special form if is followed by three expressions, called the predicate, consequent, and alternative. Here is the Scheme interpreter's rule for if: to evaluate an if expression, first evaluate the predicate. If the result is #t, evaluate the consequent expression and return its value as the value of the entire if expression; but if the predicate evaluates to #f, then evaluate the alternative expression and return its value. (Should the predicate evaluate to anything besides #t or #f, by the way, then the value of the consequent expression is returned.)

So far, we don't quite know what "evaluating to #t" or "evaluating to #f" means; these phrases will be explained very soon. Loosely, the idea is that if the predicate is true, then the value of the consequent expression is returned; otherwise, the value of the alternative is returned.

Here are some examples.

```
(if (= 1 1) 2 3)
(if (negative? 4) (* 3 6) (/ 10 2))
(if 1 2 3)
(if (= (+ 12 4)(double 8)) (square 5)(square 7))
```

These expressions return 2, 5, 2, and 25, respectively. In the third example, the first subexpression after the if evaluates to 1 (which is neither #t nor #f); so the value of the second subexpression, 2, is returned. Also, in the fourth example, we assume that double and square have been defined as in the previous chapter.

Now, why is if a special form, and not a procedure? Consider the following two expressions:

```
(+ (* 2 19) (/ 1 0))
(if (= 3 3) (* 2 19) (/ 1 0))
```

If we type the first expression at the Scheme interpreter, we will get an error message, since both arguments to + have to be evaluated and we can't divide a number by 0. But the second expression will return 38; the third expression after the if will never be evaluated, since the predicate expression is true. In other words, the "arguments" of the if special form—unlike those of primitive and compound procedures—do not all have to be evaluated.[1] In fact, in evaluating an

---

[1] A note on terminology: typically, the term "argument" is only used in the context of describing procedures, not special forms. Thus, in the expression if (= 1 2) 4 10) the subexpression (= 1 2) is simply referred to as "the first expression following the if" and not as "the first argument to if."

if expression, only two of the three expressions following the if will be evaluated: namely, the predicate and either the consequent or the alternative.

Most of the Scheme primitives that we have encountered thus far expect numeric arguments and return numeric results. The + procedure is an obvious example: + returns the sum of its arguments. (In fact, most of the compound procedures that we have created likewise take numeric arguments and return numeric values— double and square, for instance.) But there are some other primitives which accept numeric arguments and return, instead of numbers, the special Scheme objects #t and #f. One such procedure is =, which we first encountered in chapter 2, and which we employed in a couple of the if examples above. The expressions:

    (= 2 2)
    (= 2 3)

evaluate to #t and #f, respectively.[2]

Procedures like = that return #t or #f as their results are called *predicates*. The new–quadratic–solutions procedure employed another predicate, the Scheme primitive negative?, which returns #t if its argument is negative and #f otherwise. Two other numeric predicates are:

    <

Takes two numeric arguments and returns #t if the first is less than the second.

    >

Takes two numeric arguments and returns #t if the first is greater than the second. Thus,

    (> 4 3)
    (< 4 3)

evaluate to #t and #f, respectively. There are other numeric predicates, several of which are mentioned in the exercises.

Now, just what are these things, #t and #f? In Scheme, they are called *boolean objects*, or *booleans* (they are in fact the only boolean objects). Like numbers, booleans evaluate to themselves. So here's a new rule to add on to the list from the previous chapter:

▶ *Rule 6: Evaluating Booleans*

Booleans (namely, #t and #f) evaluate to themselves.

One of the problems at the end of Chapter 2 suggested a modification to our roulette-wheel program so that we could bet on two numbers instead of one. There are a variety of ways to do this, but an especially easy method uses the Scheme special form or inside the compare–with–bet procedure:

```
(define (roulette–wheel bet–1 bet–2)
  (compare–with–bet (random 37) bet–1 bet–2))

(define (compare–with–bet wheel–spin bet–1 bet–2)
  (if (or (= wheel–spin bet–1)(= wheel–spin bet–2))
      (display "You won! ")
      (display "You lost! "))
  wheel–spin)
```

---

[2]If you actually evaluate the second expression at the PC Scheme interpreter, what you will see on your screen is (). It happens that in Scheme, #f and the "empty list" () are the same object. This will be discussed later, in Chapter 8; for now, you can simply think of () as the (admittedly strange) representation used by PC Scheme interpreter for printing out #f.

The new `compare-with-bet` procedure simply checks whether the value of `wheel-spin` is equal either to `bet-1` or `bet-2` and prints either the message *You won!* or *You lost!* depending on the result.

Perhaps you tackled this problem earlier, using a "nested `if`" expression as the heart of your strategy. If so, you can probably appreciate the usefulness of the `or` special form. `Or` and its cousin special form `and` provide simple ways of combining predicate expressions. Their names give a fair indication of what they do: basically, an `or` expression returns `#t` if any of the predicate expressions following the symbol `or` evaluate to `#t`, and `#f` otherwise. An `and` expression returns `#t` if all of the predicate expressions following the symbol `and` return `#t`, and `#f` otherwise. Here are the formal rules governing the evaluation of `and` and `or` expressions:

To evaluate an expression beginning with `and`, start evaluating the expressions following the `and`, one by one. As soon as one of these expressions evaluates to `#f`, we are done; the result of the entire evaluation process is `#f`, and we don't have to evaluate any of the remaining expressions. On the other hand, if none of the expressions following the `and` evaluates to `#f`, then the result of the entire process is the value of the last expression.

To evaluate a compound expression beginning with `or`, start evaluating the expressions following the word `or`. Should any of these evaluate to something other than `#f`, return that value and ignore the remaining expressions. Otherwise, return `#f`.

The following examples return `#t`, `#t`, `3`, and `#f`, respectively.

```
(or (= 1 1) (> 5 4))
(and (= 1 1) (> 5 4))
(and 1 2 3)
(or (< 3 1) (and (= 3 1) (= 1 1)))
```

A brief word about that first example above. When we use the word "or" in day-to-day conversation, we often mean "one or the other but not both," as in the statement, "Give me liberty or give me death!" This is what logicians call the *exclusive or*. However, the Scheme interpretation of "or" is closer to the so-called *inclusive* version; a Scheme `or` expression has value `#t` if at least one (and maybe more) of the predicate subexpressions has value `#t`. Had George III been a Scheme programmer, he might have responded to Patrick Henry by freeing him and then killing him.

The primitive procedure `not` is another useful tool for manipulating predicates. `Not` takes a single argument (typically a boolean argument—i.e., either `#t` or `#f`) and returns `#t` if the argument is `#f` and `#f` otherwise. So you can think of `not` as an "opposite-returner": give it `#f`, it returns `#t`, and vice versa.

Here is a sample procedure, using `not`, which takes as argument a year and returns the number of days in that year; it uses the rule that century years are not leap years unless they are divisible by 400:

```
(define (number-of-days year)
  (if (or (= (remainder year 400) 0)
          (and (= (remainder year 4) 0)
               (not (= (remainder year 100) 0))))
      366
      365))
```

Defining New Predicates

The `number-of-days` procedure above would be a bit more readable if we had a `divisible?` predicate that took two numeric arguments and returned `#t` if the first was evenly divisible by the second:

```
(define (number-of-days year)
  (if (or (divisible? year 400)
          (and (divisible? year 4)
               (not (divisible? year 100))))
      366
      365))
```

Scheme doesn't have a divisible? primitive, but we can write one ourselves:

```
(define (divisible? number-1 by-number-2)
  (= (remainder number-1 by-number-2) 0))
```

Our new procedure divisible? is a sort of "custom predicate." Try using the various evaluation rules that we have encountered thus far to convince yourself that divisible? will correctly return #t or #f depending on its arguments.

Another way of writing the same program, using a new predicate leap-year?, might be:

```
(define (number-of-days year)
  (if (leap-year? year) 366 365))

(define (leap-year? year)
  (or (divisible? year 400)
      (and (divisible? year 4)
           (not (divisible? year 100)))))
```

There is really no difference in principle between writing new predicates, as we've just done, and writing numeric procedures like double or square. It just happens that some of the procedures we write can return numbers (like double) while others (like leap-year?) can return boolean values. As a matter of Scheme "culture," it may be worth noting that most primitive Scheme predicates end in a question mark; and by convention, when Scheme programmers define new predicates they like to end those predicates' names with question marks as well, for readability.

Making Choices with Cond

If you leaf through this book and look at some of the programs we will be working on later, you will notice that a significant percentage of Scheme procedures contain just one large expression—a cond expression—in their body. The special form cond is Scheme's most general and powerful tool for making choices. In fact, once you have read this section, you don't ever have to use if again, since any if expression can easily be rewritten in cond form. (Usually, when Scheme programmers employ if expressions, they are doing so because in simple situations the if expression is a little easier to read than its equivalent cond version.)

The name cond is short for "conditional," and the overall point of a cond expression is to choose some action based on a variety of conditions. Unfortunately, the evaluation rule for cond is a bit complicated; but with practice, it'll eventually become second nature.

The form of a cond expression is as follows:

```
(cond clause-1
      clause-2
      .
      .
      .
      final-clause )
```

Each clause in the format above consists of two portions: a predicate expression and a set of one or more consequent expressions. Thus, another way of writing the form of a cond expression is:

```
(cond (predicate expression . . . )
      (predicate expression . . . )
            .
            .
            .
      (else expression . . .))
```

Here's the rule that the Scheme interpreter uses to evaluate cond expressions:

Start by evaluating the first clause's predicate expression. If this returns #t (or to be exact, anything other than #f), then evaluate the consequent expressions in the first clause and return the result of the last consequent expression; that is, the value of the entire cond expression is that of the last expression within the first clause. If the first clause's predicate evaluates to #f, however, then go on to the next clause and evaluate its predicate expression. If that predicate is true, then evaluate the second clause's consequent expressions, and so on. The last cond clause typically begins with the word else; you might think of this as a predicate expression that is always true. Thus, if all the earlier predicates return #f, the consequent expressions of the else clause get evaluated, and the value of the last consequent in the else clause is returned.

A brief recap of the above description: evaluate the predicate portions of the clauses, one by one, until you find one that evaluates to #t (or rather, anything besides #f). When this happens, evaluate the consequent expressions of that clause, one by one, and return the value of the last consequent expression in the clause.

Let's do a simple example, very slowly.

```
(cond ((= 0 1) 3)
      ((or (< 5 4) (= 2 9)) 4)
      (else 5))
```

This expression evaluates to 5. We initially evaluate the predicate expression (= 0 1), which returns #f; so we go on and evaluate the next predicate expression, (or (< 5 4) (= 2 9)), which likewise returns #f; so we again go on, and since the else clause is next, we finally evaluate the consequent expression in this clause and return the result—namely, 5.

Here's a more useful example—a procedure named color that takes as argument a number representing a wavelength of light (in angstroms) and prints out the color of that wavelength:

```
(define (color wavelength)
  (cond ((> wavelength 7000) (display "infrared"))
        ((> wavelength 6470) (display "red"))
        ((> wavelength 5850) (display "orange"))
        ((> wavelength 5750) (display "yellow"))
        ((> wavelength 4912) (display "green"))
        ((> wavelength 4240) (display "blue"))
        ((> wavelength 4000) (display "violet"))
        (else (display "ultraviolet"))))
```

Note that writing the above procedure using if would be awfully clumsy:

```
(if (> wavelength 7000)
    (display "infrared")
    (if (> wavelength 6470)
        (display "red")
        (if ... etc)))
```

It's obvious, then, that cond is a more flexible construct than if. In general, instead of writing

> (if *predicate consequent alternative*)

we could always write

> (cond (*predicate consequent*)
>   (else *alternative*))

These two expressions have exactly the same meaning. And sometimes, we can rewrite other expressions as well. For instance, you can verify for yourself that the following two versions of the leap-year? predicate—one of which we created earlier—are equivalent:

```
(define (leap-year? year)
  (or (divisible? year 400)
      (and (divisible? year 4)
           (not (divisible? year 100)))))
```

```
(define (leap-year? year)
  (cond ((divisible? year 400) #t)
        ((divisible? year 100) #f)
        ((divisible? year 4) #t)
        (else #f)))
```

Exercises

1. Suppose the following expressions were typed at the Scheme interpreter in the order presented. Try to predict the values that the interpreter would return; then do the experiment to see if your predictions were correct.

   ```
   (if (= 0 1) 3 4)
   (if (+ 0 1) 3 4)
   (define b 6)
   (if (< b 7) b (1+ b))
   (if (< 2 b) (if (> 6 b) 3 5) (if (> 9 b) 7 8))
   ```

2. Write a predicate speeding? which takes one argument, mph, and returns #t if that argument is greater than 55.

3. One problem in the previous chapter involved writing a triangle–area procedure which takes two numbers, base and height, as arguments and returns the area of the appropriate triangle. But it is probably a mistake to call triangle-area with negative values for either base or height. Rewrite triangle-area so that it prints out some sort of admonishing message if either base or height is negative, and returns the correct area otherwise.

4. Write a predicate close? which takes two numbers as arguments and returns #t if they are within, say, .001 of each other. You might extend this to write a new version of close? which takes three arguments—number-1, number-2, and limit—and returns #t if the two numbers are within a distance of limit from each other.

5. Here are some possible elaborations you could make to our roulette-wheel program:

   (a) Change the roulette–wheel procedure so that it will not accept illegal bets (less than 0 or greater than 36).

(b) Change the program so that roulette-wheel will take two bets representing a high and low limit: if the wheel comes up with any number in between the two limits, then the bettor wins. For instance, if we call (roulette-wheel 3 6), then we will win if the wheel comes up with either 4 or 5.

(c) Change the program so that the color of the particular spin—red or black—is printed out. (Look at a genuine wheel to see which numbers are red and which are black.)

6. Try to predict the results of typing in the following expressions, one by one, at the Scheme interpreter; then actually try the experiment to see if your predictions were correct.

```
(define a 12)

(define b 6)

(cond ((< a b) a)
      ((= a b) 0)
      ((< b a) b)
      (else -1))

(cond ((= a (* 2 b)) (display "First clause result: ") 0)
      (else (display "Second clause result: ") 1))

(cond (a 0)
      (else 1))

(define (a-less-than-b?)
  (< a b))

(a-less-than-b?)

(define b 15)

(a-less-than-b?)
```

7. Write a program to tell how many days you have been alive. You will probably need some procedure that takes six arguments—the current month, day, and year, and the month, day, and year of your birth—and returns the number of days from the earlier to the later date. It is very likely that you will find the leap-year? predicate helpful.

8. Here is one of our working versions of the leap-year? predicate:

```
(define (leap-year? year)
  (or (divisible? year 400)
      (and (divisible? year 4)
           (not (divisible? year 100)))))
```

Suppose we tried reversing the expressions following the and:

```
(define (leap-year? year)
  (or (divisible? year 400)
      (and (not (divisible? year 100))
           (divisible? year 4))))
```

Would this procedure still work?

Here is another of our versions of leap-year?, using cond:

```
(define (leap-year? year)
  (cond ((divisible? year 400) #t)
        ((divisible? year 100) #f)
        ((divisible? year 4) #t)
        (else #f)))
```

Suppose the first two clauses of the cond expression were reversed:

```
(define (leap-year? year)
  (cond ((divisible? year 100) #f)
        ((divisible? year 400) #t)
        ((divisible? year 4) #t)
        (else #f)))
```

Would this procedure still work?

9. Write a procedure describe-temperature, which takes as argument degrees-fahrenheit and prints out (using display) some description of the weather based on the current temperature. The procedure should work as follows:

```
(describe-temperature 105)
sweltering
(describe-temperature 70)
pleasant
(describe-temperature -60)
I'm surprised you're alive to read this
```

10. Here are some predicates that were not mentioned in this chapter. Examine their descriptions in the Scheme manual, and try to use them in a Scheme expression:

```
>=
<=
<>
zero?
even?
integer?
float?
```

CHAPTER 5

Recursion

I want you to try an experiment. Put your face very close to a mirror and stare yourself in the eye. If you look very hard you will see a smaller image of yourself in your eyeball; and the eyeball of that image contains (though it's really too small to see) yet a smaller image of yourself, and so on, indefinitely. You've no doubt observed that similar tricks can be played with two mirrors facing each other.

Now, why did I ask you to do that? Actually, we will have cause to return to this experiment a little later; but mostly, the purpose was to put you in the proper frame of mind for the upcoming discussion.

In this chapter, we are going to look at recursive Scheme procedures. A procedure is *recursive* if it contains a call to itself. We can start by looking at a popular example, the `factorial` procedure:

```
(define (factorial number)
  (if (= number 0)
      1
      (* number (factorial (-1+ number)))))
```

The purpose of this procedure, when called on a positive integer argument, is to return the factorial of that argument. The *factorial* of a number n, written $n!$, is defined as the product:

$$n! = n \times (n - 1) \times (n - 2) \cdots 1.$$

Thus, the factorial of 1 is 1; the factorial of 2 is 2; of 3 is 6; and so on. The factorial of 0 is defined by convention to be 1.

We could use our new procedure by typing, say, (factorial 5) at the Scheme interpreter: the value returned would be 120, which is 5!. Our `factorial` procedure is indeed recursive, since it contains a call to itself (within the alternative portion of the `if` expression).

Let's explore this a little further. Consider the following observations:

1a. The factorial of 0 is 1.

1b. The factorial of a positive integer n is $n \times (n - 1) \times \cdots 1$.

2a. The factorial of 0 is 1.

2b. The factorial of a positive integer n is n multiplied by the factorial of $n - 1$.

Most people learn about factorials through the first pair of statements, 1a and 1b. This is the definition that they are given (in fact, this is essentially the definition that I presented a little earlier). Now, knowing this definition, there is no difficulty agreeing to the truth of statements 2a and 2b. Clearly the factorial of 6 is equal to 6 multiplied by the factorial of 5. But what might be difficult is seeing that statements 2a and 2b are not only true: they constitute by themselves a complete definition of the factorial function. That is, we could deduce statements 1a and 1b from statements 2a and 2b. We will see how this could be done a little later, but for now simply note that our Scheme procedure embodies this second definition. An informal statement of the factorial procedure's strategy is as follows: If the argument is 0, return 1; otherwise, evaluate the result of calling the factorial procedure with the next lowest argument, and multiply the result by the present argument.

I am going to have to beg your indulgence at this point. In the next several sections, we are going to examine the factorial procedure from several different angles. The reason for doing this is not because factorials are such interesting things (you will probably be very tired of them after a while); rather, I would like to follow the example set by Brian Harvey in his marvelous book on Logo and present several different models for understanding recursion. Each of these models provides its own unique insights; but, more importantly, in becoming familiar with recursion it helps to have a grab-bag of images from which to draw. You will no doubt find that you have favorites—one way of thinking will seem much easier than another. There's nothing wrong with that: if one explanation starts sounding too obscure, then try reading another. Eventually, though, it would be worth your while to spend at least a little time mulling over each of the individual models.

Model 1: Actors

Imagine that the factorial procedure is a kind of script. Any time a call to factorial is evaluated, a new actor is hired to "act out" a freshly-made copy of the script. Thus, when we type (factorial 4) at the Scheme interpreter, we are in effect hiring a new actor and providing him with the "factorial script":

```
(define (factorial number)
  (if (= number 0)
      1
      (* number (factorial (-1+ number)))))
```

This actor—let's call him Humphrey—now sets to work. Since we called factorial with an argument of 4, Humphrey knows that he must enact the factorial script, pretending that number is another name for 4. The only expression that he needs to evaluate is the if expression: since number is not equal to 0, he will have to evaluate the alternative expression, (* number (factorial (-1+ number))). Now, the first thing Humphrey must do is evaluate the two arguments to *. It doesn't matter in which order he does this: let's say that he starts out by evaluating the second argument, (factorial (-1+ number)). Again, the argument to factorial must be evaluated, and since number is another name for 4, this argument evaluates to 3. Thus, Humphrey wishes to call factorial with an argument of 3: when he gets the result of this call, he will use it to proceed with his evaluation of the call to *.

Humphrey thus sets out to call factorial. To do this, a new performer must be hired for the occasion. Let's call her Meryl. Meryl is given a fresh copy of the factorial script and is told that the argument for this call is 3. She therefore will enact her copy of the script, pretending as she does so that number is another name for 3. Eventually, she will have to call factorial yet again, with an argument of 2: when she gets this result, she will be able to complete her own call to * and thus obtain a final value as the result of all her work.

In calling the factorial procedure yet again, a new actor—Dustin—is hired. Dustin will eventually have to call factorial with an argument of 1: and Sigourney gets hired for this job. She will eventually call factorial with an argument of 0, and this job is taken by Marlon.

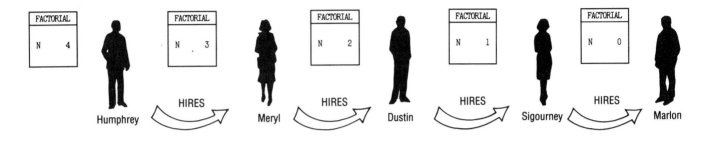

Figure 5.1. The Great Chain of Actors

Marlon is the first actor whose job has not required him to make another call to factorial: since he is reading the script under the pretense that number is another name for 0, he immediately returns 1 as the result of his call. Now Sigourney is able to complete her call to *: since Marlon has finished his reading by returning a value of 1, she goes on to evaluate the other argument to *, which is simply number. Sigourney is reading her script while pretending that number is another name for 1, so the result of her call to * is 1. This result gets passed back to Dustin, who is now able to complete his call to * and pass the result of 2 back to Meryl. Meryl completes her job and passes the result of 6 back to Humphrey. Finally, Humphrey can evaluate the other argument to *, which again is simply number; and since he is assuming that number is another name for 4, he completes the call to * and returns 24. This is the final result of the call to factorial that we originally typed in.

There are a few important elements in this scenario. One is that each actor gets his or her own copy of the factorial script. Thus, the factorial procedure that we defined is a sort of "master script"; each time factorial is actually called, a fresh copy gets made and handed to the newly-hired actor. In technical terms, the actors and their scripts represent individual *invocations* of the factorial procedure. There may be many copies of one script being worked on at one time: in our example, when Marlon received his copy, there were four other actors waiting to finish their own reading of the script. Another way of phrasing this is to say that there may be many active invocations of a given procedure at any one time.

In our scenario, it does not matter in which order the arguments to * are evaluated. This is an important point: you will notice, if you look back at the two rules for evaluating procedure calls (Rules 2 and 5), that the order in which operands are evaluated is not specified. When the Scheme interpreter evaluates a procedure call, it may choose to evaluate the operands from left to right, or right to left, or (if we were working with a sufficiently powerful computer) all at once, in parallel. In the actor model, it would not have made any difference had Humphrey first evaluated the argument number and then the second argument (factorial (-1+number)) in evaluating the call to *. You should convince yourself of this statement by tracing through the various actors' activities, assuming as you go that procedure arguments are always evaluated from left to right.

There are one or two elements of the actor scenario as presented that may also be a bit misleading. First, to be absolutely consistent, we should hire new actors for primitives and special forms as well. Thus, in this more elaborate version of the actor model, Humphrey would hire an actor to evaluate the if expression; that actor would hire a new actor to evaluate the * expression; that second actor would hire both an actor for the -1+ expression, and, later, Meryl to evaluate the call to factorial. Meryl would now hire her own if actor, and so on. You can see that this more elaborate actor model can get rather messy; in any case, it ends up giving the same results—i.e., Humphrey eventually returning 24—as the simpler scenario. On infrequent occasions, it may be necessary to take a more fine-grained view in order to see what the Scheme interpreter is doing.

Perhaps a bigger difficulty with the actor model is that it doesn't really indicate what happens to actors (invocations) once they are done with their work. Usually, when a real-life actor is finished with one script, he goes off and looks for other work. In the actor model, however, actors only exist for the duration of one script-reading: a procedure invocation no longer exists once it has returned a final value for the procedure call. Thus, an actor is associated only with one particular script for his entire existence. (Come to think of it, there are a few real-life actors of that description, also!)

Model 2: Mathematical Induction

Mathematical induction is a well-known technique for proving mathematical statements. The basic idea is that a particular statement is proved for one simplest case (the *base case*); then it is proved that if the statement holds for any case at all, it must hold for the next most complicated case (this part of the proof is known as the *inductive step*). Here's a classic example:

Statement:

For any number $n \geq 0$:

$$0 + 1 + 2 + \cdots n = n \times (n + 1)/2$$

Base Case:

For $n = 0$, we have $0 = 0 \times 1/2$.

Inductive Step:

Suppose the statement is true for some number n. Then it must also be true for $n + 1$, since:

$$
\begin{aligned}
0 + 1 + \cdots n + (n + 1) &= (0 + 1 + \cdots n) + (n + 1) \\
&= [n \times (n + 1)/2] + (n + 1) \\
&= (n^2 + 3n + 2)/2 \\
&= (n + 1) \times (n + 2)/2
\end{aligned}
$$

Together, the base case and inductive step prove our statement for all n. Since the statement is true for 0, which we know from the base case, then it must (by the inductive step) be true for 1. But since it is true for 1, it must also (again by the inductive step) be true for 2, and so on.

Now, what does all this have to do with recursion? Take another look at the factorial procedure:

```
(define (factorial number)
  (if (= number 0)
      1
      (* number (factorial (-1+ number)))))
```

It should be clear from looking at this procedure that if we evaluate (factorial 0), we will get a correct result of 1. Thus, we are now in possession of a procedure named factorial which—we are agreed—returns the correct result if called on 0. Suppose, now, that we evaluate (factorial 1). This will result in a call to the primitive *: the first argument number is bound to 1 for this call, while the other argument to * is the result of evaluating a new call to factorial with argument 0. But we know that factorial must return the correct answer when called with an argument of 0. Thus, the result of our call to * will be the product of 1 and 1, which is the correct result for (factorial 1).

We are now in possession of a procedure named factorial that returns the correct result if called on either 0 or 1. If we evaluate (factorial 2), this will result in a call to * with arguments number—which is bound to 2 for this call—and the result of evaluating a new call to factorial with an argument of 1. But again, we have proved that our factorial procedure returns the correct result when given an argument of 1. Thus, the value of the expression (factorial 2) is 2.

You can see that in this way, we can continue to show that our factorial procedure works correctly for any positive integer. Essentially, we can boil this explanation down to the standard format for inductive proofs:

Base Case:

>The factorial procedure works correctly when called with an argument of 0.

Inductive Step:

>If factorial returns the correct result for some positive integer *n*, then it also returns the correct result for *n* + 1, since in this case the procedure will return the product of *n* + 1 and the (correct) result of calling factorial with argument *n*; and we know that the factorial of *n* + 1 is indeed equal to the product of *n* + 1 and the factorial of *n*.

Exactly the same sort of reasoning can be used to show that the two statements (2a and 2b) we made earlier serve to define the factorial function. Deriving statement 1b by induction from these two statements is straightforward.

Using inductive reasoning is a good way to convince yourself that some particular recursive procedure actually works the way it's supposed to. More than that, inductive reasoning is especially helpful for writing your own recursive procedures; we'll return to this point in a little while.

Model 3: Scheme Rules

The previous two chapters were largely concerned with presenting the rules that the Scheme interpreter uses to evaluate expressions. It would hardly be fair for me to make you go through all those explanations without showing that they are adequate for understanding the factorial procedure. In point of fact, the actor model we looked at earlier is only a slightly-concealed version of the Scheme rules; but just in case you find the metaphor of actors a little undignified, let's go through the call to (factorial 4) once more, this time using the language of Chapters 3 and 4.

When we type (factorial 4) at the Scheme interpreter, the interpreter uses the Compound Procedure Rule (Rule 5 in Chapter 3). The first step of this rule is to evaluate the operand expressions: here, there is only one, 4, and since it is a number it evaluates to itself. Now, according to the Compound Procedure Rule, the Scheme interpreter must evaluate the body of the factorial procedure, treating number as a name for 4.

The body of factorial is an if expression, and the predicate portion of this expression evaluates to #f, so the interpreter must now evaluate the alternative expression, (* number (factorial (-1+ number))). This is a call to a primitive procedure, so the interpreter uses the Primitive Procedure Rule (Rule 2). The first step of this rule is to evaluate the operands; we can start with the second operand, (factorial (-1+ number)). This is a call to a compound procedure, so by the Compound Procedure Rule the argument expression (-1+ number) must be evaluated; and since number is being treated as a name for 4, this expression (using the Primitive Procedure Rule for the call to -1+) evaluates to 3.

Let's recap the path so far: evaluating (factorial 4) causes the interpreter to evaluate the if expression with number as a name for 4; since the predicate is #f, the alternative expression (* number (factorial (-1+ number))) must be evaluated; and in evaluating the second argument to *, the interpreter calls factorial with argument 3.

Now, since the interpreter is calling factorial again, the if expression must be evaluated on the assumption that number is a name for 3. Before going any further, note that once the call to (factorial 3) is complete, the result will be used to complete the evaluation of the * expression for the (factorial 4) call. What we are doing in evaluating (factorial 3), then, is finding a result to pass back to the still-incomplete evaluation of (factorial 4). When the result of (factorial 3) is found—it will turn out to be 6—it will be multiplied with the value of number for *that previous invocation* of factorial. Thus, the result of the call to (factorial 3) will ultimately be multiplied by 4. The reason I am going to such lengths about this is merely to note that the value of number is local to each invocation of factorial: whenever the factorial procedure is called, its argument is evaluated and that argument becomes—for that particular invocation—the value of number. The value of number for any previous invocation is totally unaffected.

Anyway, let's proceed with our discussion. The call to (factorial 3) will result in yet another call to (factorial 2), as one step in evaluating a * expression; the call to (factorial 2) will result in a call to (factorial 1), which will result in a call to (factorial 0), which finally returns 1. Now, the previous invocation of factorial (with argument 1) which was waiting to evaluate its * expression will be able to continue. Since for this invocation, number is bound to 1, the result of this invocation of factorial is the product of 1 and 1—namely, 1. This result gets passed back to the still-incomplete previous invocation, and so on. You should now be able to finish this trace of the evaluation process yourself.

Writing Recursive Procedures

Scheme programmers do not typically trace through recursive procedure calls as we just did; life is too short for that. And in writing recursive procedures, it would be impossible (or at least impracticable) to start with a complete step-by-step account of how calls to this procedure should run. How, then, does one actually sit down and devise a recursive procedure?

Unfortunately, there is no hard-and-fast answer to that question. There is no surefire way of starting with a problem—say, the problem of finding factorials—and deriving a recursive solution to it. Sometimes no such solution exists. But there are a few patterns of thought—gimmicks, really—that can help in the activity of writing recursive procedures.

Here is one trick that often works. It is really based on the notion of induction that was introduced a little earlier. The idea is to take a particular problem and decide:

(a) How to solve the very simplest, most trivial version of the problem, and

(b) How you would solve the problem assuming that you had a procedure which solved the next-simplest case.

In terms of induction, what we are doing is devising a "base-case" solution, and an "inductive-step" solution, and putting the two together.

Let's take a simple example to start. Suppose we want to write an expt procedure to raise a given number base to some power. (As we know, Scheme already has a primitive expt procedure, but there's no harm in writing our own.) Let's also assume that power will always be a nonnegative integer. What we would like, then, is a procedure that we could call as follows:

```
(expt 6 2)

(expt -2 3)
```

These two expressions should evaluate to 36 and -8, respectively.

Now, what should we call the "simplest case" of raising some number to some power? A good candidate would be the case in which we raise a number to the zero-th power, since for all n, $n^0 = 1$. So we might start out our expt procedure as follows:

```
(define (expt base power)
  (cond ((= power 0) 1)
        ??????))
```

The next step is a little tougher. Suppose we want our procedure to solve some more complicated case—say, 6^5. Let's assume that we have an expt procedure which will solve the next-simplest case, and use that expt procedure to solve our present case. In other words, let's take the next-simplest expt problem, and see if we can find our current answer in terms of the answer to that simpler problem. A worthwhile candidate for "next-simplest case" is when the number power is one less than our present case: for instance, if our problem is to find 6^5, we can call the next-simplest problem 6^4. The reason this looks like a good choice is because for any number n, $n^m = n \times (n^{(m-1)})$. Thus, if we had an expt procedure which gave the correct result for (expt 6 4), we could multiply that result by 6 and get the correct result for (expt 6 5).

Here, then, is our suggested expt procedure:

```
(define (expt base power)
  (cond ((= power 0) 1)
        (else (* base (expt base (-1+ power))))))
```

Believe it or not, we're done. Expt works. It would probably be a good idea to check this assertion via, say, the actor model; but the point of our construction was to show that we could set about writing a recursive procedure without working through the recursive calls, step by step. This type of programming style is an example of what is sometimes called "wishful thinking": we pretend that the simpler problem is solved, and use that (pretended) solution for our current problem.

Now, you may feel that the construction of expt above pulled a lot of rabbits out of hats: How did we know that the zero-th power was the best "base case"? How did we know that subtracting one from a nonzero power would be the best "simpler case"? The answer is, we didn't. We guessed—or rather, we made an educated guess. Finding an appropriate "base case" and "simpler case" is part experience, part knowledge, and part luck. But there are some more-or-less "typical" choices to consider. For instance, in writing recursive numeric procedures, the base case will often be the one where some relevant number n is equal to 0, or perhaps 1. Or perhaps the simplest case is when some n is greater or less than a particular limit. The "next-simplest" case may be the one in which n is increased or decreased by 1.

A few examples may help to make these observations a little more concrete. Look closely at each of the following procedures, and see if you can identify how the particular problem has been handled: how the base case has been chosen, and how all other cases use the next-simplest solution.

Here's a procedure that prints out the word "hello" n times. (This procedure uses PC Scheme's `writeln` primitive, which is like `display` in that it prints a value on the screen. Unlike `display`, however, `writeln` starts a new line after the given value.)

```
(define (print-hello n)
  (cond ((= n 0) (writeln "done"))
        (else (writeln "hello") (print-hello (-1+ n)))))
```

Here's a procedure that finds the number of digits in a given positive integer:

```
(define (number-of-digits number)
  (cond ((< number 10) 1)
        (else (let ((last-digit (remainder number 10)))
               (1+ (number-of-digits (/ (- number last-digit) 10)))))))
```

Here's a procedure that repeatedly takes the square root of a given positive number until the result is within .001 of 1:

```
(define (sqrt-till-1 number)
  (cond ((<= (abs (- number 1)) 0.001) (writeln number)(writeln "done"))
        (else (writeln number) (sqrt-till-1 (sqrt number)))))
```

Recursion and the Big Questions of Life

Recursion is a subject that goes far beyond its applications in Scheme programming. The notion of "processes described in terms of themselves" is not only useful and thought-provoking but, to many people, beautiful. People tend to get taken up with it. A particularly wonderful tribute to recursion is Douglas Hofstadter's book *Gödel, Escher, Bach: An Eternal Golden Braid*; Hofstadter explores recursive ideas in language, mathematics, music, and art.

Once you have spent some time working with recursion in Scheme, you will probably find yourself "thinking recursively" about a lot of other things as well. You may find yourself reinterpreting or redefining various phenomena in everyday life:

A staircase of level 0 is flat ground.

A staircase of level n is a single step up followed by a staircase of level $(n - 1)$.

A wedding cake of level 0 is a little pair of (bride-and-groom) statuettes.

A wedding cake of level n is a pastry of radius $2n$ inches topped by a wedding cake of level $(n - 1)$.

A target of level 0 is a point (or, a circle of radius 0).

A target of level n is target of level $(n - 1)$ surrounded by an annulus of inner radius $(n - 1)$ inches and outer radius n inches.

A checkerboard of level 0 is a single black square.

A checkerboard of level n is a checkerboard of level $(n - 1)$ with: a row of $n + 1$ squares of alternating color above it; and a column of n squares of alternating color to the right of it. The leftmost square of the new row and the bottom square of the new column should be white if n is odd, black if n is even.

A mirror-image of level 0 is your face.

A mirror-image of level n is your face with a mirror-image of level $(n - 1)$ inside the eyeball.

These examples are only slightly facetious; every one of them might be the basis for a Scheme program. For instance, we might write a Scheme procedure to draw a checkerboard by using the strategy mentioned above. One of the reasons that Scheme is a powerful language is precisely because it is an elegant medium in which to model the recursive patterns visible in the world.

An Extended Example: Continued Fractions

Consider this equation:

$$x = 1 + \frac{1}{x}$$

If you do a little algebraic manipulation of this equation, you will find that it has one positive solution: $(1 + \sqrt{5})/2$. But we can try manipulating this equation in a different way. Since

$$x = 1 + \frac{1}{x}$$

we can substitute in for that second x and get the following equation:

$$x = 1 + \frac{1}{1 + \frac{1}{x}}$$

Repeating this process indefinitely, we get a *continued fraction*:

$$x = 1 + \frac{1}{1 + \frac{1}{1 + \cdots}}$$

We can write a Scheme procedure to approximate this continued fraction, using the following strategy:

The level 0 approximation for x is 1.

The level $n > 0$ approximation for x is

$$1 + \frac{1}{\text{level } (n-1) \text{ approximation for } x}$$

Here is a realization of this strategy in Scheme:

```
(define (golden-ratio level)
  (cond ((= level 0) 1)
        (else (1+ (/ 1 (golden-ratio (-1+ level)))))))
```

The procedure is named golden-ratio because that is what this number has historically been called. The golden ratio has an illustrious literature devoted to it: it is a number which appears in a variety of biological contexts. For instance, the ratio of the average person's height to the height of their navel is reputed to be the golden ratio (I've never measured). The ratio also plays a role in the history of art and architecture; it is visible in certain proportions of the Parthenon, among many, many other structures.[1]

Try calling the golden-ratio procedure with various values for level, and compare the results to a straightforward computation of $(1 + \sqrt{5})/2$; how quickly does our approximation converge to the "true" value?

---

[1] A good source of information about the golden ratio is Matila Ghyka's book *The Geometry of Art and Life*, from which the facts in the paragraph above were taken.

Continued fractions provide an interesting and elegant way of computing square roots. Suppose we wish to find $\sqrt{n}$: that is, we wish to find the x such that $x^2 = n$. We could also write this as follows:

$$x = 1 + \frac{n-1}{1+x}$$

If you solve for x in this equation, you will see that this is precisely the condition that $x^2 = n$.

Taking our cue from the golden-ratio example, we could repeatedly substitute in for x to get the following equation:

$$x = 1 + \cfrac{n-1}{1 + \left(1 + \cfrac{n-1}{1 + \cdots}\right)}$$

A recursive strategy for finding the square root of n, then, would be this:

The level 0 approximation for x is 1.

The level $k > 0$ approximation for x is

$$1 + \frac{n-1}{1 + \text{level } (k-1) \text{ approximation}}$$

We could express this strategy in the following Scheme procedure:

```
(define (sqrt number level)
  (cond ((= level 0) 1)
        (else (1+ (/ (-1+ number) (1+ (sqrt number (-1+ level))))))))
```

You might want to experiment with this Scheme procedure. You will find, for instance, that a level 10 approximation for $\sqrt{2}$ is fairly accurate, but much less accurate for larger square roots. As with our expt example, we are again defining our own version of a Scheme primitive. There is no harm in doing this—if you define your own procedure with the name of a Scheme primitive, that name is now bound to your procedure. For instance, if you define sqrt as above, the name sqrt now refers to the procedure you just defined, not to the Scheme primitive procedure. Of course, you will no longer be able to use the original Scheme procedure (at least until you start up your system again); if this prospect makes you uncomfortable, then you might simply name the new procedure my-sqrt, or new-sqrt, instead of sqrt.[2]

Rethinking a Recursive Procedure

Suppose we wish to use our new sqrt procedure to find the square root of 300. How do we know the appropriate level argument to use? If we type (sqrt 300 20) we will, as it happens, get a rather inaccurate answer; on the other hand, if we type (sqrt 300 500), we will get an accurate answer—but a smaller value of level might have provided about the same level of accuracy with less computation time. One strategy that we could use would be to evaluate a series of expressions with increasing level values, as follows:

```
(sqrt 300 20)
(sqrt 300 50)
(sqrt 300 80)
```

---

[2] In PC Scheme, some primitives cannot be redefined so easily. For instance, redefining the primitive + takes some extra effort; the subject is a little complicated, so we will leave it unexplored until the appendix of Chapter 11. Suffice it to say for now that you can write your own definitions of sqrt and expt, if you want to, without event.

We could keep typing in these expressions until we find that the answers don't vary too much; then we would conclude that our answer is reasonably accurate. But that might take a lot of work; and besides, we might want to write other Scheme procedures that use the sqrt procedure. How would some other Scheme procedure know what level to use in calling sqrt?

There are any number of approaches to this problem, but one strategy is to rewrite the sqrt procedure so that it does its own testing for accuracy. Rather than have a level argument, our new sqrt procedure will be called with a approximation argument, representing the current approximation for the square root value. The strategy for the new sqrt procedure is as follows:

- Check the current approximation. If it is close enough to the square root of the given number, we are done; return the approximation as our result.

- If the approximation is not good enough, call the sqrt procedure again, this time with a new approximation:

$$1 + \frac{n - 1}{1 + \text{old approximation}}$$

Here is a Scheme program that realizes this strategy:

```
(define (sqrt number approximation)
  (cond ((close-enough? approximation number) approximation)
        (else (sqrt number (1+ (/ (-1+ number) (1+ approximation)))))))
(define (close-enough? approximation number)
  (> 0.001 (abs (- (square approximation) number))))
```

We have defined two procedures here: the second is a predicate close-enough?, which returns #t if the square of approximation is within 0.001 of number. When we first call our new sqrt procedure, our initial approximation should always be 1: this initial choice is consistent with the "level 0" approximation of our earlier sqrt procedure. Thus, to find the square root of 300, we would type (sqrt 300 1) at the Scheme interpreter. The returned value is about 17.3205, and we know—because of the way in which sqrt was written—that this must be within 0.001 of the true value.

Tail Recursion

It happens that our new sqrt procedure, unlike the earlier one, exhibits a special kind of recursion called *tail recursion*. A tail recursive procedure is one in which the value of the recursive call provides the complete result of the original call. In other words, once the recursive call is evaluated, there is no additional work to do to find the result of the original call.

This probably sounds very obscure. Let's consider an example using our old friend, the factorial procedure. Here are two ways of defining factorial:

```
(define (factorial-A number)
  (cond ((= number 0) 1)
        (else (* number (factorial-A (-1+ number))))))
(define (factorial-B number)
  (fact-helper number 1))
(define (fact-helper count result)
  (cond ((= count 0) result)
        (else (fact-helper (-1+ count) (* count result)))))
```

The factorial-A procedure, which is essentially the same one we used above (it uses cond instead of if), has a recursive call in the else clause: but once the value of this recursive call is found, it must be multiplied by number to get the result of the original call. For instance, if we call (factorial-A 4), the result of the call to (factorial-A 3) will have to be multiplied by 4 to get our final result.

Now look at the second procedure, factorial-B. It simply calls another procedure named fact-helper. If we type (factorial-B 4) at the Scheme interpreter, the factorial-B procedure will call fact-helper with arguments 4 and 1. Now, if you follow through the recursive calls to fact-helper, you will see that they look as follows:

```
(fact-helper 4 1)
(fact-helper 3 4)
(fact-helper 2 12)
(fact-helper 1 24)
(fact-helper 0 24)
```

When fact-helper is finally called with a first (count) argument of 0, it simply returns the value 24. But note that this is the final answer for the original fact-helper call: the previous invocations of fact-helper do not need to do any additional computation using the returned value of 24. It is this property that makes fact-helper a tail recursive procedure: the recursive call to fact-helper produces the complete answer for the original call.

Why do we even bother classifying procedures as tail recursive? We can illustrate the reason by looking back at the actor model. Suppose we hire a new actor—for consistency's sake, let's call him Humphrey again—to evaluate (fact-helper 4 1). Eventually, Humphrey will hire Meryl to evaluate a new call to fact-helper with arguments 3 and 4. But now, there is no need for Humphrey to exist any more: the answer to Meryl's problem is the exact same as the answer to Humphrey's. Unlike our original situation, in which Humphrey had to multiply Meryl's eventual result by 4, we have a situation in which Humphrey needn't wait around to do anything with Meryl's result. (That is to say, the result of evaluating (fact-helper 4 1) is the same as the result of evaluating (fact-helper 3 4)—you can prove this yourself by typing both expressions at the Scheme interpreter.) Likewise, when Meryl eventually passes her problem on to Dustin, she too needn't exist anymore, since Dustin's result will be the same as hers. What is going on here is that we don't have to maintain invocations that have no additional work to do: when an invocation is finished with its work, it can disappear.

In terms of actual Scheme systems, maintaining a waiting procedure invocation requires a certain amount of memory within the computer: thus, when an invocation "disappears," as it does in the evaluation of tail recursive calls, some memory space is reclaimed. Tail recursive procedures thus require only enough space for one active invocation at a time: each invocation disappears upon calling the next. Tail recursive procedures are therefore more space-efficient than other kinds of recursive procedures: in technical terms, they "run in constant space."[3]

If tail recursive procedures are so great, why don't we write *only* tail recursive procedures? Why did we bother with that first version of factorial altogether? Or the first version of sqrt? The answer is that tail recursive procedures, although space efficient, are often more difficult to create and to read than their non-tail-recursive counterparts. For instance, the old version of sqrt is somewhat easier to read than the newer version. This is not an uncommon trade-off in programming:

---

[3]In some Lisp dialects—Logo is one example—tail recursive procedures will not run in constant space in every implementation. However, every Scheme system *must*, by the very definition of the language, have this property; Scheme is thus called a *properly tail recursive* language. (You may recall that this term was mentioned in Chapter 1.) A properly tail recursive language is simply one in which tail recursive procedures always run in constant space in every implementation. If your implementation doesn't have this property, then it may say "Scheme" on the diskette, but it ain't Scheme.

often, in order to make a particular program run a little faster or use less memory, we must change the program in ways that make it harder to decipher.

Tail recursive procedures are often used to provide *infinite loops* in Scheme. (In fact, the very name "tail recursive" was, I believe, coined to suggest the ultimate "looping" image—that of a snake swallowing its own tail.) Here is an example:

```
(define (print-hello-forever)
  (writeln "hello")
  (print-hello-forever))
```

Because this procedure is tail recursive, it needs only constant space in which to run, and thus if you type (print-hello-forever), the procedure should, as the name suggests, run forever. (Try following through a call to print-hello-forever using your favorite model of recursion.) If you wish to stop such a procedure, you have to use some sort of special "abort" mechanism (for instance, on the IBM PC, one types (CTRL)-BREAK to halt a running process).

Sometimes an infinite loop is precisely what we want. But usually we find that we have created an infinite loop by mistake. For instance, suppose we had written this (incorrect) version of fact-helper:

```
(define (fact-helper count result)
  (cond ((= count 0.1) result)
        (else (fact-helper (-1+ count) (* count result)))))
```

If we call (factorial-B 4), the factorial-B procedure will eventually call fact-helper with arguments 4 and 1; and since the value of the count argument will always remain an integer on every recursive call to fact-helper, this procedure will run indefinitely. (To be exact, it might run until the value of count becomes too large for the computer to keep track of—but for our purposes, that's a long enough time to call "indefinitely.") Should you find yourself in a situation like this—i.e., you have called a procedure that seems to be running without end—you can use your machine's "abort" key to stop the procedure.

A similar problem often occurs with non-tail-recursive procedures. For instance, suppose we mistakenly wrote the following:

```
(define (factorial number)
  (cond ((= number 0.1) 1)
        (else (* number (factorial (-1+ number))))))
```

Suppose you were now to call (factorial 4). In this case the procedure would not run forever: it is not tail recursive, and thus the computer must generate space for each successive invocation of factorial. However, the procedure would obviously not return the correct value either. What you would eventually see is an error message from the Scheme interpreter—most likely something to the effect that the computer had run out of available memory. In such a situation, one might hypothesize that there is something wrong with the "base case" of our procedure: somehow this simplest case is never reached. One would then return to the Scheme editor and examine the procedure for bugs, paying particular attention to the base case. But since the next chapter deals with the topic of debugging, let us not get ahead of ourselves any further.

Exercises

1. Write a procedure that takes as input a positive integer n and returns the sum $0 + 1 + \cdots n$.

2. This procedure, called `roll-till-you-win`, takes as argument a particular `bet` and simulates the rolling of a die until the bet wins:

```
(define (roll-till-you-win bet)
  (let ((die-roll (1+ (random 6))))
    (writeln die-roll)
    (cond ((= die-roll bet)(display "You won!"))
          (else (roll-till-you-win bet)))))
```

Modify `roll-till-you-win` so that the procedure makes a random bet at each roll. The new procedure should take no arguments and simply keep rolling the die until the random bet happens to be the same as the new roll. Here's a sample printout of the result:

Bet: 5   Result: 4
Bet: 1   Result: 3
Bet: 4   Result: 4
You won!

How many rolls, on average, do you think it will take before a win? Can you modify the procedure so that it returns the total number of rolls required?

3. Use whatever model you prefer to predict the behavior of the two following procedures:

```
(define (recursive-proc-1 number)
  (cond ((= number 0) (writeln number))
        (else (writeln number) (recursive-proc-1 (-1+ number)))))
```

```
(define (recursive-proc-2 number)
  (cond ((= number 0) (writeln number))
        (else (recursive-proc-2 (-1+ number)) (writeln number))))
```

Now try evaluating the following two expressions:

```
(recursive-proc-1 10)
```

```
(recursive-proc-2 10)
```

Did the procedures behave as you predicted?

4. One of the now-classic recursive procedures is described by Schroeppel, Gosper, Henneman, and Banks in *Hakmem*, a thoroughly amazing paper produced in 1972 by members of the MIT Artificial Intelligence Lab. The procedure works as follows: it takes a positive integer argument `number`. If `number` is even, we recursively call this procedure with the integer divided by 2; if odd, we triple the integer, add one, and call the procedure with this new value. Your job is to write this procedure (it might be called `odd-up-and-even-down`); and you should write the procedure so that it prints out the value of `number` at each call. Once your procedure is working, you will see the sequence of numbers generated by any particular starting value.

The interesting thing about this procedure can be illustrated by trying it with a few small starting numbers—say, 7. The values generated by the procedure are:

7, 22, 11, 34, 17, 52, 26, 13, 40, 20, 10, 5, 16, 8, 4, 2, 1, 4, 2, . . .

As you can see, the sequence ends up "stuck" in the loop 4, 2, 1, 4, 2, 1, . . . But one question that no one has been able to answer is whether *every* starting positive integer causes the procedure to eventually end up in this loop. According to Schroeppel et al., all integers up to 60 million do end up in the "4, 2, 1-loop" (though for some it takes a very long time); but there is no proof that every integer must do so.

5. Consider the following recursive procedure:

```
(define (familiar-number level)
  (cond ((= level 0) 1)
        (else (sqrt (1+ (familiar-number (-1+ level)))))))
```

Try calling this procedure with increasing values of level. Does the result look familiar? Can you explain why the familiar-number procedure returns this number?

6. Consider the tail recursive version of sqrt shown earlier. It is of some interest to see how many recursive calls this procedure requires to come up with a good approximation to the square root of its number argument. Try the following experiment: first, modify close-enough? so that it returns #t if the square of its first argument is within 0.01 percent (rather than 0.001) of its second argument. Then change sqrt so that it keeps a running count of the number of recursive calls made, and returns the value of this count (instead of returning the square root approximation). Now see how many recursive calls are required to compute the square roots of the following numbers: 10, 100, 1000, 10000, 100000. Do you see any pattern?

7. Go through some of the recursive procedures shown in this chapter and decide which ones are tail recursive and which aren't. What about, for instance, recursive-proc-1 and recursive-proc-2 in Exercise 3 above?

8. Write a program to print out the prime factorization of a positive integer. For instance, the prime factorization of 60 is 2 × 2 × 3 × 5. Thus, the program might be used as follows:

```
(print-factors 60)
2
2
3
5
```

Now write a procedure called count-number-of-factors to return the number of prime factors of a given number; and use it to write a predicate procedure prime? that returns #t if its input is a prime number. You should then be able to write a procedure that will take a positive integer argument limit and return the number of primes less than or equal to limit.

9. Write a program for printing decimal numbers in binary (base 2) representation. There should be some procedure that takes as input a decimal number and prints out the binary representation of that number. Here is how the program might be used:

```
(print-out-binary 6)
110

(print-out-binary 37)
100101
```

Now you can write a procedure which takes two arguments: a decimal number and a base (between 2 and 10, inclusive) in which to print out the number. Here are a couple of examples:

```
(print-out-in-base 22 8)
26

(print-out-in-base 22 7)
31
```

⊛ 10. From Steven Levy's book *Hackers*:

> Peter Samson hacked the night away on a program that would instantly convert Arabic numbers to Roman numerals, and Jack Dennis, after admiring the skill with which Samson had accomplished this feat, said, "My God, why would anyone want to do such a thing?"

Write a program to convert positive integers into Roman numerals. The program should probably include some sort of print-out-roman procedure analogous to the print-out-binary procedure of the previous problem.

☑ 11. The PC Scheme primitive runtime takes no arguments and returns the time of day in units of 0.01 seconds. Thus, evaluating (runtime) should return some value between 0 (just after midnight) to 8639999 (just before midnight). Using this primitive, write a procedure called wait which takes a positive integer argument and waits for the appropriate number of 0.01-second units. For instance, evaluating (wait 500) should cause the interpreter to wait 5 seconds before printing out the next prompt.

⊛⊛ 12. Imagine a little bug walking on the number line. Every second, the bug flips a coin; if the result is heads, he walks to the next higher integer on the line, and if the result is tails, he walks to the next lower integer. Thus, if the bug starts at 0, his path may take him as follows:

$$0, 1, 2, 1, 0, 1, 0, -1, -2, -1, \ldots$$

This sequence of numbers corresponds to the bug flipping a head on the first two flips, followed by two tails, then a head, then three tails, and so on.

The bug on the number line is an example of a *random walk*. Random walks form an incredibly rich study in mathematics; there are applications in physics (e.g., the Brownian motion of particles), chemistry (e.g., configurations of polymers), microbiology (e.g., the motion of bacteria), and other areas.

Try writing a procedure to simulate the walk of the bug on the number line. Your procedure should print out a sequence of numbers like the sample shown above. You can also investigate a number of other issues:

(a) Suppose the bug always ends his walk when he has arrived at some net distance from the origin. For instance, if the distance is 20, then the bug will stop if he gets to either 20 or −20. How many steps, on average, does it take for the bug to finish his walk? How does the average number of steps depend on the net distance at which the bug stops?

(b) Suppose the bug's coin is not perfect, and comes up heads, say, 60 percent of the time. How does this affect the sequence of steps that the bug takes?

(c) Suppose the bug has a kind of "momentum" in his walk; that is, if he took a step forward at the last move, he is a little more likely to move forward this time as well. (You might think of this as the bug's using two coins: one that is more likely to come up heads—the bug uses this coin if the previous flip was heads—and one that is more likely to come up tails.) How does this affect the sequence of steps that the bug takes?

(d) Suppose the bug is walking on the *x, y*-plane and can take a step either horizontally or vertically. (This is a *two-dimensional random walk*.) What observations can you make about this situation?

CHAPTER 6

Debugging

By now you have probably done a fair amount of exploratory Scheme programming. You have no doubt also encountered a fair number of bugs in your programs. Maybe it took several tries before you got the parentheses to balance in your first original procedure; or perhaps your initial attempts at recursion resulted in unintended infinite loops; or you wrote a procedure that worked correctly most of the time but—maddeningly—behaved unexpectedly for certain infrequently-used argument values.

Debugging is a complicated activity, and this chapter will hardly scratch its proverbial surface. For one thing, as with programming, there are no hard-and-fast rules for debugging. Sometimes the best strategy for finding a mistake in a program is to go eat lunch and come back to the work after a few hours' rest. Sometimes talking to another programmer about the problem can be helpful. The activity of debugging transcends questions of Scheme programming, or computer programming; it has as much to do with your own preferred style of work.

Moreover, the Scheme programs that we have been working with are still very small—perhaps three or four procedures at most. Debugging these small programs can be difficult enough, of course, but when projects get large and complicated different kinds of debugging techniques come into play. We will see some of these techniques in later chapters; here, our focus will be on smaller programs, although the material in this chapter will be useful later on as well.

And, as a final note, it should be mentioned that we are not yet in a position to make good use of all the debugging facilities provided by most Scheme systems. PC Scheme, for instance, has an elaborate subsystem called the *Inspector* that is useful for analyzing programs; but until we achieve a deeper understanding of the Scheme language, most of the Inspector's features will remain unintelligible. Toward the end of this book, in Chapter 14, we will return to the issue of debugging, and there we will examine the Inspector at length.

Debugging and Mental Health

Perhaps the most important dimension along which to analyze bugs is the emotional one. People tend to react to programming mistakes in extreme ways. Sometimes they throw up their hands and decide to give up on a project altogether;

or they start to rewrite their entire program from scratch; or they blindly change every conceivable expression, one by one, in a furious attempt to fix the problem; or they add extra lines to their program to undo the symptom of the bug without analyzing its source. These reactions—all of which are likely to do more harm than good—usually stem from an attitude of severe self-criticism. For many people, a programming bug is evidence (in some vague sense) of "poor" thinking.

There are any number of alternative, and certainly more beneficial, ways to view bugs. You might think of them as a puzzle: finding the flaw in a program can be a mystery in the spirit of Agatha Christie and Ngaio Marsh. Or you might make a project out of analyzing the more interesting bugs that you encounter to see if they suggest another programming strategy or even another project altogether: the history of creative work is filled with mistakes that turned into great ideas.[1] Or, as Seymour Papert has suggested in his book *Mindstorms*, you can use programming bugs as a window into your own mind. The errors that you make—and how you uncover them—can give you new insights into your own learning process; and you may even be able to consciously improve your own learning abilities by a careful analysis of past bugs. In this respect, keeping a "bug notebook" would be a terrific project (though I have never actually met anyone with the discipline to do it).

In any event, it's important to maintain a certain equanimity about bugs. Though programmers will always strive to avoid, find, and fix them, mistakes remain an inevitable (and fascinating) part of the programming process.

Syntactic versus Semantic Bugs

The most straightforward kinds of programming errors are purely syntactic: that is to say, errors that one could conceivably spot without even knowing what the program is supposed to do. Mismatched parentheses are a case in point. The following procedure definition must be wrong, regardless of what bar and blah are intended to mean:

```
(define (bar x) (blah x)))
```

Another kind of syntactic mistake involves calling a procedure with too few or too many arguments. For instance, the recursive procedure wrong-args below cannot work:

```
(define (wrong-args x y)
  (cond ((= x 0) 0)
        (else (wrong-args (-1+ x) x y))))
```

Syntactic errors are usually not too hard to find. In fact, your Scheme system will find many of them automatically. For instance, if you create the bar procedure above in the PC Scheme editor, then when you type the mistaken final parenthesis, the editor will make a warning "beep" sound. In other cases of mismatched parentheses, the problem should become apparent when you return to the Scheme interpreter: you will get some sort of error message telling you that there was difficulty in reading the editor's contents. (For instance, if there are not enough matching right parentheses to balance the existing left parentheses, PC Scheme will print out *WARNING—EOF encountered during READ* when you enter the interpreter.[2]) And if you try creating the wrong-args procedure in the PC Scheme editor, then when you return to the interpreter you will see a message like: *Wrong number of arguments in call WRONG-ARGS*.[3]

---

[1]My favorite story along these lines concerns W. H. Perkin, a nineteenth-century chemist who discovered the dye mauve by accidentally spilling the contents of a reaction vessel onto his lab coat.

[2]The letters EOF, by the way, stand for "end of file." Without drowning in detail, the point is simply that in trying to read the contents of the editor, the Scheme interpreter encountered the end of the text before finding a right-parenthesis match for every left parenthesis.

[3]In many cases, procedure calls with the wrong number of arguments will not be detected "automatically" by your Scheme system. In the example above, the mistaken call to wrong-args was part of the

Unfortunately, most programming errors are harder to uncover; rather than being purely syntactic, they involve the *semantics*, or meaning, of the program in question. Consider our recursive expt procedure from the previous chapter:

```
(define (expt base power)
  (cond ((= power 0) 1)
        (else (* base (expt base (-1+ power))))))
```

Knowing whether this procedure is "correct" depends on our perception of what it is supposed to do. To exaggerate the matter just a bit, expt is a reasonable procedure for doing exponentiation, and a dreadful procedure for doing multiplication; if we use expt thinking that it will multiply its arguments, then we will quickly conclude that expt is a very buggy procedure indeed. A slightly subtler point is illustrated by typing the following at the Scheme interpreter:

```
(expt 2 -5)
```

Here, the machine will churn away in silence for a while, and eventually we will see an error message indicating that the Scheme system has run out of space. The problem, upon inspection, is that we called expt with a negative value for power, and thus the base case in which power equals 0 is never reached. So again, whether a procedure is correct depends on how we intend to use it. If expt is always going to be called with positive integer values for power, then it's fine as is; but if we want to use negative or noninteger values for power, then there are bugs in the procedure.

When we use a program and do not see any error messages as a result, our first reaction tends to be positive; but the absence of error messages is a somewhat ambiguous phenomenon. All it really means is that the program contains no bugs that prevent it from returning some value. In the previous example—calling expt with a negative value for power—we knew something was amiss when we saw the error message. But a problem of some other sort—accidentally using sqrt, for example, instead of square—might be buried somewhere in an apparently working program. Only by carefully examining the values returned by our program could we determine that something was in fact wrong. These examples are deliberately on the obvious side, but the point is still meaningful: bugs that do not cause a program to "bomb" are if anything more treacherous than those that do.

A Brief Zoology of Bugs

It would be impossible to list all the mistakes one can make in programs. There are many exotic varieties of bugs and, for better or worse, new ones are invented all the time. What follows, then, is just a sampler of some of the more common sorts of errors that you may have run into in your work thus far. This section is intended to jog your mind a bit and additionally provide a little vocabulary for identifying bugs in the future.

Errors in
Recursive Procedures
Missing Base Case

Occasionally in writing a recursive procedure, programmers neglect to include a base case for the procedure. Often, this happens when the procedure in fact requires more than one base case. Here's an example. Suppose we want to write a procedure called even-or-odd-factorial that works as follows: if the argument (which is always a nonnegative integer) is odd, find the product of all odd numbers from 1 up to and including the argument. If the argument is even, find the product of all even numbers from 2 up to and including the argument. Thus, for example, if the argument is 6, we want the product $2 \times 4 \times 6 = 48$. Here is a procedure that comes close but doesn't work:

wrong-args procedure itself, so that particular call could not possibly be correct. On the other hand, if the same mistaken call to wrong-args were to occur in some other procedure, the Scheme system would not know this is an error; you may, after all, decide to redefine wrong-args before calling the other procedure. In this case—assuming, of course, that you do not redefine wrong-args—you will get an error message when you actually use the other procedure.

```
(define (even-or-odd-factorial number)
  (cond ((= 0 number) 1)
        (else (* number (even-or-odd-factorial (- number 2))))))
```

The problem here is that if we call this procedure with an odd argument, the base case will never be reached. We need to add another base case as follows:

```
(define (even-or-odd-factorial number)
  (cond ((= 0 number) 1)
        ((= 1 number) 1)
        (else (* number (even-or-odd-factorial (- number 2))))))
```

A Recursive Call That Does Not Lead to the Base Case

Another problem that sometimes crops up is the presence of a recursive call that does not lead to the intended base case. For instance, we might make a simple omission in writing the factorial procedure:

```
(define (factorial number)
  (cond ((= number 0) 1)
        (else (* number (factorial number)))))
```

Because the recursive call uses the same value for number as the original call, the base case is never reached. A procedure suffering from this sort of flaw will typically cause the Scheme system to run out of space by generating a never-ending chain of procedure invocations; or, if the problem involves a tail recursive call, using the procedure may result in an infinite loop. (What happens if we try the factorial procedure above by typing, say, (factorial 2) at the Scheme interpreter?)

Fencepost Errors

This one is a killer. The name "fencepost error" comes from the following puzzle: There are ten fenceposts placed in the ground in a straight line, each one ten feet away from the next. What is the distance from the first to the last post? The answer is ninety feet, since although there are ten fenceposts there are only nine gaps between the posts.

A fencepost error arises when a procedure that is intended to do something, say, n times instead does something $n + 1$ times—or perhaps $n - 1$ times. The problem involves keeping track of when the procedure is actually done. Here's an example: the following program is intended to print out the word "hello" n times. See if you can find (and fix) the bug:

```
(define (print-hello n)
  (print-hello-helper 0 n))

(define (print-hello-helper count limit)
  (cond ((> count limit) (writeln "done"))
        (else (writeln "hello")
              (print-hello-helper (1+ count) limit))))
```

Type Errors

Type errors arise when an object of one particular type is used as though it were an object of another type. For instance, suppose we write the following procedure:

```
(define (add3 number)
  (+ 3 (number)))
```

Here, we wanted the value of number to be, straightforwardly enough, a number; but the expression (number) only makes sense if number is the name of a procedure—a procedure that in this case takes zero arguments. Thus, we are mistakenly using a number object as though it were a procedure. The same sort of error would be caused by typing in these expressions at the Scheme interpreter:

```
(4)
(+ 3 (= 0 0))
```

The first expression illustrates the same error that we had in our add3 procedure: a number is being used as though it were a procedure. The second expression tries to add 3 to the result of evaluating (=0 0); but this result is #t, which is a boolean value instead of a number and hence cannot be added to another number.

Often, a program seems to work correctly for a long time—until one fateful day when someone innocently tries to use the program to handle some slightly unusual situation. For instance, I remember hearing a story (possibly apocryphal) of an alphabetic sorting program that worked correctly until it was given as input a list that happened to be sorted already—at which point the program crashed. Problems of this sort fall under the heading of "special case situations," and they are ubiquitous. In fact, even discussing special cases in the context of debugging is a little specious, since many programs are nothing but huge collections of "special case handlers"—portions designed to deal with one special case or another. Nevertheless, since so many errors arise from neglecting offbeat cases, it seems worthwhile to mention the issue here.

Special Cases

What constitutes a special case depends, of course, on what situations the program is usually intended to handle. In our earlier expt example—in which the procedure failed to work with a negative power argument—we might have said that a negative value for power is a special case of exponentiation. More typically, there is some unique case that the program fails to handle. Here, for instance, is a program that averages n roulette spins:

```
(define (average-n-roulette-spins n)
  (roulette-helper 0 n 0))
(define (roulette-helper count limit sum-so-far)
  (cond ((= count limit) (/ sum-so-far count))
        (else (roulette-helper
                (1+ count) limit (+ (random 37) sum-so-far)))))
```

This works unless we try to average 0 spins—in which case we will get an error resulting from trying to divide the value of sum-so-far by 0. If we thought that averaging 0 spins was a reasonable thing to ask for, we might want to change average-n-roulette-spins as follows:

```
(define (average-n-roulette-spins n)
  (cond ((= n 0) (writeln "Averaging zero spins returns 0 by default") 0)
        (else (roulette-helper 0 n 0))))
```

Here's another example: suppose we want to write a procedure to print out the prime factorization of a positive integer. For instance, for the number 60, we want the procedure to print out 2, 2, 3, and 5, since the prime factorization of 60 is $2 \times 2 \times 3 \times 5$. The following procedure will work in most cases:

```
(define (prime-factors number)
  (prime-factors-helper number 2))
(define (prime-factors-helper number factor)
  (cond ((= number factor) (writeln factor))
        ((= (remainder number factor) 0)
         (writeln factor)
         (prime-factors-helper (/ number factor) factor))
        (else (prime-factors-helper number (1+ factor)))))
```

The prime-factors procedure fails on an input of 1—assuming, that is, that we regard finding the prime factors of 1 as a reasonable special case. It is left to the reader to explain why the procedure fails for an input of 1, and to devise a possible emendation of the program.

When a program crashes for some reason, the Scheme interpreter prints out an error message. It is always worth examining the error message closely: often it provides useful information about what went wrong. For instance, when we defined the wrong-args procedure earlier, the Scheme error message told us that there was some problem involving a call to wrong-args with the wrong number of arguments. This should at least give us a hint as to where the bug in our program might be.

There are other sorts of error messages. The documentation for your Scheme system will provide a complete list, but most of these will probably look obscure just now. There are a few common messages, however, which correspond to some of the errors mentioned above. For example, suppose we make a type error by trying to evaluate the following expression at the Scheme intepreter:

```
(+ 2 (= 0 0))
```

PC Scheme's error message in this case is:

```
Non-numeric operand to arithmetic operation
(+ #T 2)
```

The error message indicates the sort of type error that we made: using something that is not a number (in this instance, a boolean object) as an argument to +. As another example of a type error, suppose we create the following procedure in the editor:

```
(define (factorial number)
  (if (= number 0)
      1
      (* (number) (factorial (-1+ number))))))
```

When we type (factorial 3) at the Scheme interpreter, we get the following error message:

```
Attempt to call a non-procedural object with 0 argument(s) as follows:
(3)
```

Again, the message indicates the sort of type error that we made: using something other than a procedure (here a number) as a procedure of zero arguments.

Another standard sort of error is illustrated by the following example. Suppose we write this procedure in the editor:

```
(define (factorial number)
  (if (= no 0) 1 (* number (factorial (-1+ number)))))
```

When we use this procedure in the interpreter by typing (factorial 3), we will see the following error message:

```
Variable not defined in lexical environment
NO
```

Ignoring for the moment that phrase "lexical environment," the gist of the message is that we are using a name, no, which is not bound to any particular value. Examining the factorial procedure reveals that we accidentally used the name no instead of number in the predicate portion of the if expression.

Now, suppose we are writing a program in which we anticipate the possibility of certain sorts of errors. We can create our own error messages using Scheme's error special form. Here's an example, using our earlier program to average n roulette spins:

```
(define (average-n-roulette-spins n)
  (cond ((= n 0)(error "Trying to average zero spins" n))
        (else (roulette-helper 0 n 0))))
```

The idea here is that we have decided that averaging zero spins is not a sensible thing to do and that calling average-n-roulette-spins with an argument of 0 should be treated as an error.

The error special form is followed by two expressions: a message (in double quotes), and a second "irritant" expression. If the error expression is evaluated, then the message is printed out, the irritant expression's value is printed out, and (in PC Scheme) the Inspector subsystem is entered. Thus, if we type (average-n-roulette-spins 0) at the interpreter, we should see the following response:

```
Trying to average zero spins
0
```

This is more informative than our original error message: recall that if we typed (average-n-roulette-spins 0) with our original version, we got a divide-by-zero error in the roulette-helper procedure. Even though both our original and current versions crash on the same input, our customized error condition tells us precisely what the problem is.

Tracing

Often when something is going wrong with a program, our Scheme system does not provide us with a lot of helpful information about the problem. Consider, for instance, the situation described earlier in which we tried a negative value for power in the expt procedure below:

```
(define (expt base power)
  (cond ((= power 0) 1)
        (else (* base (expt base (-1+ power))))))
```

All that we saw for a long time was a blank screen; and eventually we saw a message that the Scheme system had run out of available space. Not too meaningful.

Our first idea might be to find out what the problem is by having the expt procedure print out the values of its arguments base and power every time it is called. Thus, we might change the expt procedure to read as follows:

```
(define (expt base power)
  (newline)
  (display "Base: ")
  (display base)
  (newline)
  (display "Power: ")
  (display power)
  (newline)
  (cond ((= power 0) 1)
        (else (* base (expt base (-1+ power))))))
```

This is not a bad idea. If we now evaluate (expt 2 -3) in the interpreter, we will almost certainly discover what the problem is—namely, that the negative power argument is decremented on each successive call and never achieves a value of 0. But we had to do a lot of editing of expt for this purpose; and once the problem is understood, we will presumably want to take out all those display lines from expt, since they are no longer needed.

Scheme provides a primitive called trace that makes this sort of debugging a good deal easier. If we type (trace expt) at the interpreter, then from that point on every time expt is called the values of its arguments will be printed on the screen.[4] (In this case, we say that we are "tracing the procedure expt.") For instance, typing (expt 2 -3) would result in the following messages:

```
>>>Entering #<PROCEDURE EXPT>
Argument 1: 2
Argument 2: -3
>>>Entering #<PROCEDURE EXPT>
Argument 1: 2
Argument 2: -4
>>>Entering #<PROCEDURE EXPT>
Argument 1: 2
Argument 2: -5
...
```

These messages, of course, will continue printing out for a long while; you can stop the process by using (on the IBM PC) the [CTRL]-BREAK key. The point, though, is that using the trace primitive enables us to look at the argument values of a given procedure every time that procedure is called—and we don't have to do any elaborate editing for that purpose.

Once we have identified the problem with expt we can "untrace" the procedure by typing (untrace expt) at the interpreter. The untrace primitive, like trace, is followed by the name of a procedure; untrace will in effect return a traced procedure to "normal."

There are actually several tracing primitives in Scheme. Besides trace, there is a procedure called trace-exit which prints out the returned value of a procedure invocation every time that invocation is completed. Thus, whereas trace prints out messages every time a procedure invocation *begins* its work, trace-exit prints out messages when the invocation is *done* with its work. Suppose, as an example, we type (trace-exit expt) and then (expt 2 2) at the Scheme interpreter. We will see the following messages printed out:

```
<<<Leaving #<PROCEDURE EXPT> with value 1
<<<Leaving #<PROCEDURE EXPT> with value 2
<<<Leaving #<PROCEDURE EXPT> with value 4
```

Here, a message is printed out every time an invocation of expt is finished: the returned value of the particular invocation is printed out as well. (If you are puzzled by the order in which the values are printed out—1, 2, and 4—you should think about how the call to (expt 2 2) is evaluated, perhaps using the actor model.) The procedure can be untraced by typing (untrace-exit expt) at the interpreter.

If you wish to print out both the argument values and the returned values of a particular procedure's invocations, you can use both trace and trace-exit on that procedure; or you can use the Scheme primitive trace-both, which has the effect of both trace and trace-exit combined. Experimenting with trace-both and its "inverse" untrace-both is left as an exercise.

Preventive Debugging

The only thing more fun than debugging is not debugging: i.e., having your program run correctly the first time. This happens a good deal less often than one

---

[4]In the current version (3.0) of PC Scheme, in order to trace recursive procedures like expt, you have to evaluate the following expression:

```
(set! pcs-debug-mode #t)
```

before defining expt. The special form set! will be explained later in this book, but for now simply treat this expression as a sort of "incantation." If a recursive procedure is defined before this expression is evaluated, only the first (top-level) invocation of that procedure will be traced. See also Exercise 3.

might like, but a little effort beforehand can save many hours of debugging later. One of the best techniques of "preventive debugging"—providing meaningful names for variables and procedures—was alluded to in the second chapter of this book. There are other techniques that are perhaps more applicable to large programs, but that are nonetheless worth mentioning here.

Although we have thus far created programs consisting of only a few procedures at most, it won't be long before our programs grow to larger sizes: ten, twenty, one hundred procedures and more. Later in this book we will discuss some strategies for managing larger programs, but for now one simple rule of thumb is to group procedures according to their purpose. For instance, if we were writing a baseball-statistics program with some thirty procedures in it, we might place all the procedures relating to batting statistics at the top of the program and all the pitching-statistics procedures at the bottom. Otherwise, we might find ourselves searching back and forth through the Scheme editor every time we wanted to look at several related procedures.

A similar policy is to include comments in programs. Comments are portions of programs that are written solely to explain the program to someone reading it; they do not affect the running of the program. In Scheme, comments are set off by the semicolon character (;). Everything following the semicolon on a particular line is treated as a comment by the Scheme system. Thus, for example, we might have written a version of average-n-roulette-spins as follows:

```
(define (average-n-roulette-spins n)
  (cond ((= n 0) 0) ;averaging 0 numbers returns 0 by default
        (else
          (roulette-helper 0 n 0))))
```

How much commenting you should do is to some extent a matter of taste. It's easy to go too far and write copious comments about everything in a given program; in that case, the program is as hard to read as it would have been without any comments at all. But more often than not, programs are under- rather than over-commented.

All of these tips on preventive debugging really deal with the common notion of "good programming style." Obviously, it is a good idea to make programs readable and understandable by organizing procedures according to topic, using meaningful variable names, and including comments. But at the risk of belaboring an earlier idea, it's worth mentioning again that the reason we are programming at all is because the activity is fun; and part of the point of "good programming style" is simply that it is more fun to watch a program work than to try to understand why it doesn't.

Exercises

1. Investigate the behavior of the trace-both primitive and compare it with trace and trace-exit.

2. The following procedure, count-down, is tail recursive:
   ```
   (define (count-down n)
     (cond ((= n 0) (writeln n))
           (else (writeln n)(count-down (-1+ n)))))
   ```

From our earlier discussion of tail recursion, we can conclude that there should be only one active invocation of count-down at any one time: if we call (count-down 5), then the first invocation (for which n is bound to 5) disappears once the recursive call to count-down is made.

Now, suppose we type (trace–both count–down) at the interpreter. This means that we will see a message printed out every time an invocation to count–down is begun and ended. Try doing this, and examine the result of typing, say, (count–down 5). Can you explain the sequence of trace messages that you see?

3. Try loading up your PC Scheme system, creating a recursive procedure, and tracing it. Then evaluate the following expression:

```
(set! pcs–debug–mode #t)
```

Now reevaluate the define expression that you used to create your recursive procedure, and trace it again. What sorts of differences do you see? Do these differences apply to all traced procedures?

If you wish to change the PC Scheme system back to its original state, you can evaluate the following expression:

```
(set! pcs–debug–mode #f)
```

Sample
Projects II

Before we proceed any further in our study of Scheme, now would be a good time to put together some of the techniques that we have acquired and tackle a small project. This chapter provides one example; if you are interested in the topic described, you may find yourself elaborating on the program developed here. Even if you prefer some project of your own, it would be worth your while at least to skim through the procedures in this chapter, since they serve as a review of many of the programming ideas we've encountered thus far.

Circle²

Our example will be a graphics project, based on the "circle²" program described by A. K. Dewdney in the September 1986 *Scientific American*. (The original version is credited to John E. Connett of the University of Minnesota.) The name "circle²" derives from features of the program that will become apparent—the designs that we will make have both "circle-like" and "square-like" aspects. As you will see, the program is fairly easy to implement, but the images created are stunning; and there is tremendous range for exploration.

I will assume, in this and future graphics examples, that you are working with PC Scheme on an IBM PC (or PC/XT or AT) computer with a Color Graphics Adapter and color monitor. If you are working with some other Scheme system, or with PC Scheme on a Texas Instruments machine, you may have to make some alterations; you should consult the PC Scheme User's Guide and your own system documentation in this case.

**A Primer on
PC Scheme Graphics**

In PC Scheme, the IBM monitor screen is treated as a rectangular portion of the standard x, y-plane: the visible points range from $(-160, -100)$—the lower left corner—to $(159, 99)$—the upper right corner. The center of the monitor screen thus corresponds to the origin $(0, 0)$ of the plane. (See Figure 7.1.)

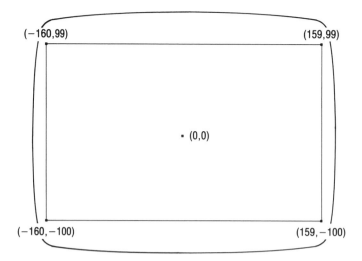

Figure 7.1. PC monitor screen treated as *x, y*-plane

Each location with integer coordinates—like, say, $(25, 44)$—corresponds to one unique pixel (picture element) on the monitor screen. This is just another way of saying that the screen has a 320 (horizontal) by 200 (vertical) resolution, with each pixel corresponding to one plottable point with integer *x*- and *y*-values.

Any particular point can be set to white or black by the draw-point and clear-point primitives. For instance, typing (draw-point 10 0) will cause the point corresponding to $(10, 0)$ to light up on the screen. (For reasons that will be given later, I will ask you for the moment not to try this on your computer: we have to get some more preliminaries out of the way first.) Similarly, typing (clear-point 10 0) will cause the lit spot to disappear.

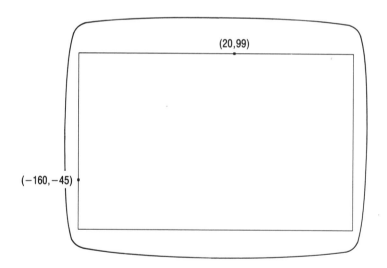

Figure 7.2. Points (20,99) and (−160,−45) have been illuminated

Only integer values can be used as arguments to the draw-point and clear-point primitives. For instance, typing (draw-point 10.1 0.2) will result in an error message from the Scheme interpreter. In general, if you want to plot some point with noninteger *x*- and *y*-values, you should first round those values to the nearest integer using the Scheme round primitive: thus (draw-point (round 10.1) (round 0.2)) will cause the same location to light up as typing (draw-point 10 0). The rationale is that draw-point and clear-point are being applied to pixel coordinates, which must be integer values; and if you want to plot noninteger values, you have to choose the nearest appropriate pixel.

We can view the entity actually doing the drawing as a sort of "invisible pen." The color of this pen can be changed by using the set–pen–color! primitive. Typically, the color of the pen is white; but if we type (set–pen–color! 1) the pen will be light blue (IBM documentation calls this color "cyan"). The set–pen–color! primitive takes as argument one of the integers 0, 1, 2, or 3, corresponding to the colors black, cyan, magenta, or white, respectively. When we draw a point, the color that point is set to is the current pen color. Thus, suppose we type the following at the Scheme interpreter:

```
(set-pen-color! 1)
(draw-point 0 10)
(set-pen-color! 2)
(draw-point 0 20)
(set-pen-color! 3)
(draw-point 0 30)
(set-pen-color! 0)
(draw-point 0 40)
```

The four points $(0, 10)$, $(0, 20)$, $(0, 30)$, and $(0, 40)$ will be set to colors cyan, magenta, white, and black, respectively. Thus, when I said earlier that draw–point will set a pixel location to white, I wasn't telling the whole truth: actually, draw–point will set the location to the current pen color. And you can also see that another way of clearing a point—besides using the clear–point primitive—is to set the pen color to 0 (black) and then use draw–point.

There are still a couple more graphics primitives to mention before we get down to work. The position–pen primitive can be used to place the invisible pen at any particular pixel location on the screen. (Like clear–point and draw–point, position–pen takes two integer arguments.) The draw–line–to primitive will cause the pen to draw a line from its present position to the designated pixel location. Here's an example:

```
(position-pen 0 0)
(draw-line-to 0 50)
(draw-line-to 50 50)
(draw-line-to 50 0)
(draw-line-to 0 0)
```

The first command, (position–pen 0 0), places the pen at the origin without drawing any lines. The next command, (draw–line–to 0 50), causes the pen to move from its starting position of $(0, 0)$ to the point $(0, 50)$, drawing a (vertical) line in the process. The net result of the five commands is to draw a square as in Figure 7.3.

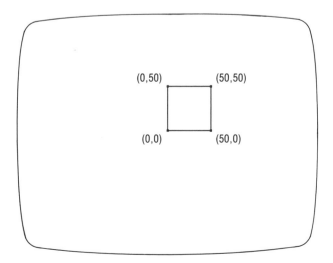

Figure 7.3. A square with a side-length of 50 pixels

As it turns out, we will need only the draw–point, clear–point, and set–pen–color! primitives for our present project; but the others are so useful that I included them in the introduction above. There are some other somewhat more obscure graphics primitives that we will encounter in the next section and later in this book.

Some Preliminary Procedures

I'm really sorry about this, but before we proceed with our project, I am going to give you the following "canned" procedures. These procedures are used to provide different "modes" for PC Scheme on the IBM PC. The first procedure sets up a "graphics mode" in which you can type commands at the bottom of the screen and view the graphical results in the upper portion of the screen. (That is to say, in graphics mode all interaction with the Scheme interpreter takes place in a region toward the bottom of the screen.) The second procedure, text–mode, returns your screen to its usual appearance when using the Scheme interpreter. The final procedure enables you to go directly from graphics mode to the Edwin editor; if you were to type (edwin) at the Scheme interpreter while in graphics mode, you would get a rather strange result (try it if you don't believe me!).

What you should do, then, is type the following procedure definitions into your editor buffer. In the remainder of this book, it will be assumed that all programs using graphics will contain these three procedures, and that any time a graphics example is employed—that is, any time a picture-making procedure is called from the Scheme interpreter—the screen will be in graphics mode at the time.

```
(define (graphics-mode)
  (window-set-position! 'console 18 0)
  (window-set-size! 'console 6 80)
  (set-video-mode! 4)
  (set-line-length! 40)
  (clear-graphics)
  *the-non-printing-object*)

(define (text-mode)
  (window-set-position! 'console 0 0)
  (window-set-size! 'console 24 80)
  (window-clear 'console)
  (set-video-mode! 3)
  *the-non-printing-object*)

(define (g-edwin)
  (text-mode)
  (edwin))
```

At the moment, I am only going to give a rather hand-waving description of what these procedures do. A more thorough explanation will be provided in Chapter 16, in the section on windows; but for the curious, here is the general idea. Both graphics–mode and text–mode begin with two commands to set the position and size of the Scheme interpreter area (called 'console) on the monitor screen. In graphics–mode the Scheme interpreter area starts at row 18 and column 0, and occupies 6 rows down and 80 columns across; you can figure out for yourself the position and size of the interpreter area in text–mode. The third expression in the body of graphics–mode is a call to the special graphics primitive named set–video–mode! which sets the monitor on IBM PC-family machines to its four-color graphics mode.[1]

The set–line–length! command in graphics–mode causes the interpreter area to use a line length of 40 characters instead of the usual 80. The (clear–graphics)

---

[1]The meaning of set–video–mode! depends on the machine you are using. If you are running PC Scheme on a Texas Instruments computer, or are not using IBM's Color Graphics Adaptor, you should consult your Scheme User's Guide for a description of the set–video–mode! command.

primitive clears the screen; this is a useful graphics primitive, and we will employ it later in this chapter. The final returned value is a special Scheme object whose name is *the-non-printing-object*. The only remarkable thing about this object is that the Scheme interpreter prints it as nothing! That is, if you type *the-non-printing-object* at the Scheme interpreter, you will see no returned value at all; you can think of this object as something which prints out as "invisible."

As for the text-mode procedure: it ends with a call to window-clear which clears the interpreter area on the screen, and a call to set-video-mode! which sets the monitor on IBM PC-family machines to its usual "text" mode.

Before going on, it would be a good idea to test the three procedures you have just created. Try defining the following additional procedure in the editor:

```
(define (draw-square side)
  (position-pen 0 0)
  (draw-line-to 0 side)
  (draw-line-to side side)
  (draw-line-to side 0)
  (draw-line-to 0 0))
```

Now go back to the Scheme interpreter, and type (graphics-mode). The "interpreter area" should now consist of only the lower fourth or so of the screen. If you now type (draw-square 50), your screen should look like Figure 7.4.

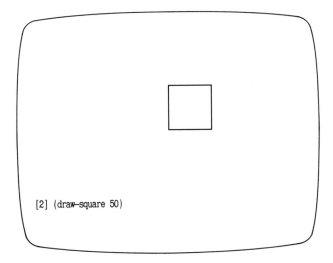

[2] (draw-square 50)

Figure 7.4. A sample graphics mode screen

Now, if you type (g-edwin) you will clear the screen (any graphic design on the screen is thus lost), and go back to the Edwin editor; if you type (text-mode) while in graphics mode, you will go back to the full-screen version of the Scheme interpreter.

One final point before we go on to our project. If you go back to graphics mode and type (draw-square -80), you will see a square drawn with diagonal corners (0,0) and (-80, -80) as expected; but you will also see that the text area of the interpreter interferes with the graphics on the screen. Unlike some machines that have separate "planes" on the screen for graphics and text (thus allowing text to overlay graphics without interference), on the IBM PC the text and graphics both occupy the same plane on the screen. I don't want to go into gory detail on this matter (you can check various IBM PC books on the subject) except to say that you may sometimes have to be careful not to let the text on your screen overlap your graphics designs; if you are intending to do any graphics work that requires the entire screen, you may have to use some fairly straightforward programming tricks for that purpose (see Exercise 3).

**Circle²:
A Top-Level
Description**

And now, at last, we can get to our project itself.

We start out by reserving a 100-pixel by 100-pixel square region on the screen: say, the region whose bottom left corner pixel is $((0, 0)$ and whose upper right corner pixel is $(99, 99)$. What we are going to do is look at each pixel location in this region; and, based on a choice which will be explained below, we will either set the pixel to white or leave it blank.

Now, what is the nature of this choice? The idea is this: imagine a square of any side length you like, sitting anywhere on the x, y-plane. For instance, suppose we choose the square of side length 91 whose bottom left corner is the point $(-10, -20)$. What we now wish to do is set up a correspondence between the 10,000 pixels of our screen region and 10,000 points of our imagined square. Here's how we'll do it: for each pixel in the screen region, we will compute its horizontal and vertical distance in pixels from the lower left corner of the region. We'll call these values the pixel's x- distance and y-distance respectively. Thus, because our screen region has its lower left corner at the origin $(0, 0)$, the x-distance and y-distance of the pixel $(25, 44)$ are simply 25 and 44, respectively.

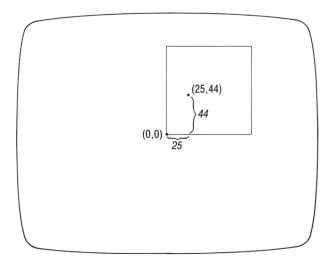

Figure 7.5. The x-distance and y-distance of the point (25,44)

To find the matching point in our imagined square, we'll locate the point in the square which has the same relative distance from the square's bottom left corner as our pixel does from the screen region's bottom left corner. In other words, we'll take our pixel—say $(25, 44)$—and find its x- and y-distances (here, 25 and 44, respectively). These x- and y- distances mean that the pixel is (in this case) 25 percent of the way along the x-direction of the screen region and 44 percent along the y-direction. We now find the point of our imagined square which is 25 percent of the way from the lower left corner in the x-direction and 44 percent in the y- direction. For our particular example, since the bottom left corner is at $(-10, -20)$ and the side length is 91, the point we are looking for is

$$((-10 + 0.25 \times 91), (-20 + 0.44 \times 91)) = (12.75, 20.04)$$

The process of finding a matching point for a given pixel can be summarized by the following formulas:

percent-pixel-x-distance = pixel-x-distance/side-length-of-screen-region

percent-pixel-y-distance = pixel-y-distance/side-length-of-screen-region

matching-point-x = square-bottom-left-x
                    + (percent-pixel-x-distance $\times$ square-side-length)

matching-point-y = square-bottom-left-y
                    + (percent-pixel-y-distance $\times$ square-side-length)

Now, once we find the matching point (x, y) for a particular pixel, we:

1. Compute the sum $x^2 + y^2$.
2. Truncate (find the nearest integer below) the sum.
3. If this integer is even, we set the screen pixel; if odd, we clear the screen pixel.

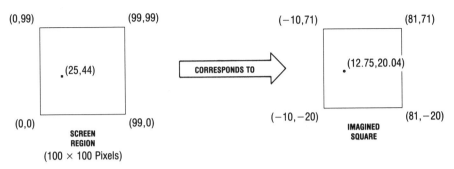

Figure 7.6. Finding a matching point in our square for a given pixel

We will follow this same recipe for each pixel in our screen region: find the pixel's matching point, sum the squares of the x- and y-values of that matching point, truncate, and—depending on whether the resulting number is even or odd—set or clear the pixel.

Let's see if we can now implement these ideas in a program.

Some Useful Procedures

There are dozens of alternative ways one could go about writing the program described above. The version that I am going to present is not by any means the "right" way; in fact, it is patently improvable, and you may very well find ways to improve it as you go along. What follows is simply one possibility among many.

We can start by writing procedures that express the notion of "pixel-x-distance" and "pixel-y-distance":

```
(define (pixel-x-distance pixel-x)
  (- pixel-x 0))
(define (pixel-y-distance pixel-y)
  (- pixel-y 0))
```

These two procedures implicitly assume that the bottom left corner of our screen region is the screen origin $(0, 0)$. I'm not sure I like that assumption. What I'm going to do, then, is create two new names screen-region-left-x and screen-region-bottom-y, and then rewrite the two procedures:

```
(define screen-region-left-x 0)
(define screen-region-bottom-y 0)
(define (pixel-x-distance pixel-x)
  (- pixel-x screen-region-left-x))
(define (pixel-y-distance pixel-y)
  (- pixel-y screen-region-bottom-y))
```

The first two define expressions create new names screen-region-left-x and screen-region-bottom-y whose values both happen to be 0. We can then use these names in the bodies of the two procedures pixel-x-distance and pixel-y-distance.

Now we can create two procedures to find a particular pixel's matching x- and y-coordinates in our imagined square:

```
(define (matching-x pixel-x square-left-x square-side-length)
  (+ square-left-x (* square-side-length
                      (/ (pixel-x-distance pixel-x) 100))))

(define (matching-y pixel-y square-bottom-y square-side-length)
  (+ square-bottom-y (* square-side-length
                        (/ (pixel-y-distance pixel-y) 100))))
```

There are several noteworthy aspects to these two procedures. First, their arguments both include the side length of our imagined square and its bottom left corner x- or y-coordinate. Second, there is a clear correspondence between these procedures and the earlier description of how to find a pixel's matching points (you should check that description if you find the procedures puzzling). Finally, note that these procedures assume that the screen region has a side-length of 100: this is implicit in the expressions (/ (pixel-x-distance pixel-x) 100) and (/ (pixel-y-distance pixel-y) 100). If we wanted to, we could drop that assumption and define a new name screen-region-side-length in the same way that we used the names screen-region-left-x and screen-region-bottom-y above. Implementing this idea will be left as an exercise.

Finally, here is a predicate procedure to see whether a particular pixel should be set or not:

```
(define (set-this-pixel? pix-x pix-y sq-left-x sq-bottom-y sq-side-length)
  (even?
   (truncate
    (+ (expt (matching-x pix-x sq-left-x sq-side-length) 2)
       (expt (matching-y pix-y sq-bottom-y sq-side-length) 2)))))
```

The Pixel-by-Pixel Loop

So far, we have created a bunch of procedures that enable us to find out whether a given pixel should be illuminated. Now we need some procedures that will perform this test for every pixel in our screen region.

Let's start by writing a procedure that will simply perform the test for 100 consecutive pixels in one particular row of the screen region. The following procedure, single-row-loop, is called with five arguments: the row on which we will work, the starting column on this row, the bottom left x- and y-coordinates of our imagined square, and the side-length of our imagined square. When first called, the value for the starting column should be the value of screen-region-left-x, which for our example is 0.

```
(define (single-row-loop row-y column-x sq-left-x sq-bottom-y sq-side-length)
  (cond ((= (- column-x screen-region-left-x) 100) row-y)
        (else (if (set-this-pixel?
                      column-x row-y sq-left-x sq-bottom-y sq-side-length)
                  (draw-point column-x row-y)
                  (clear-point column-x row-y))
              (single-row-loop row-y (1+ column-x)
                               sq-left-x sq-bottom-y sq-side-length))))
```

If we type the following expression at the Scheme interpreter:

```
(single-row-loop 10 screen-region-left-x -10 -20 91)
```

then 100 consecutive pixels on row 10 of the screen—the pixels ranging from (0, 10) to (99, 10)—will be tested and set or cleared accordingly.

Let's look at the procedure single-row-loop carefully. The first clause of the cond expression is the "base case" of our recursive procedure: if the current x-value exceeds the leftmost x-value of our screen region by 100, we are done.

(The returned value of row-y is not especially important here.) Otherwise we test the current pixel and set or clear it depending on the result; and then we recursively call single-row-loop with the next higher *x*-value.

The next step is to create a procedure that will test the entire region—all 100 rows starting with the bottom row of the screen region. The following procedure, region-loop, does this. You should be able to follow the strategy through for yourself and see its similarity to that of single-row-loop above.

```
(define (region-loop row-y sq-left-x sq-bottom-y sq-side-length)
  (cond ((= (- row-y screen-region-bottom-y) 100) (display "done"))
        (else
          (single-row-loop
            row-y screen-region-left-x
            sq-left-x sq-bottom-y sq-side-length)
          (region-loop (1+ row-y) sq-left-x sq-bottom-y sq-side-length)))))
```

We are now almost done. We simply need a top-level calling procedure, circle-squared:

```
(define (circle-squared sq-left-x sq-bottom-y sq-side-length)
  (clear-graphics)
  (region-loop
    screen-region-bottom-y sq-left-x sq-bottom-y sq-side-length))
```

Circle-squared clears the screen—using the clear-graphics primitive mentioned earlier—and then calls region-loop. The call to region-loop will result in 100 rows being tested, one by one, starting with row 0 and working upward to row 99.

The program works now, and if you have been typing in the procedures as given you might enjoy trying it out. Here are some argument values for circle-squared that might be worth a go:[2]

```
(circle-squared -1000 -2000 8773)

(circle-squared -83 -83 166)

(circle-squared 10 10 12)
```

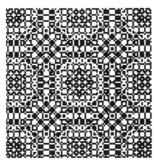

Figure 7.7. Some calls to circle-squared

Sometimes the designs include whorl-like patterns, or octagonal blocks, or floret-like portions, depending on the arguments to circle-squared. Personally, I have had a spectacular lack of success in predicting the program's behavior.

[2]You will find that circle-squared designs take a while to draw—on the order of twenty minutes or so. So be patient. You might also try making smaller designs (say, 50-pixels-by-50-pixels); see Exercise 2 at the end of this chapter.

**Notes on the
Circle² Program**

A sense of textbook-writer's duty compels me to include a few paragraphs here about the mathematical content of the circle² program. (Heaven forbid the program should only be *fun!*) First, you may have noticed that the values I chose above for the sq–side–length argument to circle–squared did not include 100. The reason for this can be illustrated by trying the following call:

```
(circle–squared 0 0 100)
```

The result is uninteresting, because in this case every pixel in our 100-by-100 screen region is being mapped to a point (x, y) where both x and y are integers; if both are odd or even, the sum of their squares is even, and if only one is odd, the sum of their squares is odd. Thus, you can easily convince yourself that the pixels plotted in our screen region will simply alternate in checkerboard fashion.[3]

Another theme worth exploring is the notion of magnifying a given circle–squared design around a particular point. For instance, consider the designs created by the following calls:

```
(circle–squared -10 -10 20)
(circle–squared -5 -5 10)
(circle–squared -1 -1 2)
```

What we are doing is viewing the circle–squared design for smaller and smaller regions centered on the origin—essentially, zooming in on the origin. As our square gets smaller and smaller, we eventually get to the situation in which the truncated sum $x^2 + y^2$ is 0 for the entire region; thus, our circle–squared design will simply be a block of white.

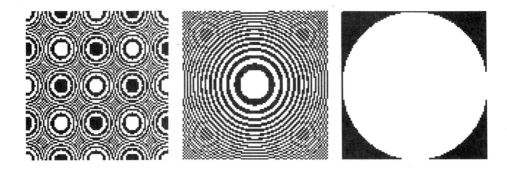

Figure 7.8. Circle–squared designs zooming in on the origin

Suppose we want to zoom in on some point other than the origin. No matter which point we choose, there is some "magnification"—some sufficiently tiny square—for which our circle–squared design will be a block of one color, black or white. But depending on the point that we are zooming in on, we may need a different level of magnification. In particular, as the point that we choose gets more distant from the origin, we need a higher magnification level to get the circle–squared design to come out as a single block. For instance, compare the designs for squares of side-length 2 centered around the points $(0, 0)$ and, say, $(7648, 4346)$.

And then there is the other direction: zooming out. I had rather expected that by choosing a huge value for sq–side–length, some of the apparent regularity of the circle–squared designs for "medium-sized" squares would disappear. I haven't

---

[3]If you try this call to circle–squared you may find that the plotted result is almost but not exactly a checkerboard pattern—at least, this is what happens with my own system. The discrepancy between the plotted result and a "pure" checkerboard pattern is due to slight rounding-off errors in PC Scheme's floating-point arithmetic operations.

seen that happen, even for values of sq-side-length in the millions: the designs still evince boxy, square-like properties. And why do we see square-like patterns in the designs, anyway? As Dewdney writes, "There are mysteries here."

The circle-squared program really takes off when you add color to the designs. In using PC Scheme with the IBM PC, we can generate four-color designs; you may be able to get more colors on your own system.

Adding Color

Here is one way to change our program so that it generates four-color patterns. The idea is that instead of testing whether or not to illuminate a given pixel, we are going to use the result of our earlier formula to get a number between 0 and 3, and this number will indicate the pen-color in which to draw the pixel. We need to change one earlier procedure—the single-row-loop procedure—and add a new procedure, choose-pen-color.

```
(define (single-row-loop row-y column-x sq-left-x sq-bottom-y sq-side-length)
  (cond ((= (- column-x screen-region-left-x) 100) row-y)
        (else (set-pen-color!
                (choose-pen-color
                  column-x row-y sq-left-x sq-bottom-y sq-side-length))
              (draw-point column-x row-y)
              (single-row-loop
                row-y (1+ column-x) sq-left-x sq-bottom-y sq-side-length)))))
(define (choose-pen-color pix-x pix-y sq-left-x sq-bottom-y sq-side-length)
  (remainder
    (truncate
      (+ (expt (matching-x pix-x sq-left-x sq-side-length) 2)
         (expt (matching-y pix-y sq-bottom-y sq-side-length) 2)))
    4))
```

The new procedure choose-pen-color is much like our earlier set-this-pixel?, except it returns a number between 0 and 3—namely, the remainder of our formula's result when divided by 4. The new version of single-row-loop uses this value as the argument to set-pen-color! and then draws the pixel in the chosen color.

You might want to experiment with different color-choosing procedures. Perhaps limiting the designs to three colors produces good results; or you might try increasing the likelihood of a pen-color of 0 (black) to get sparser designs.

Exercises

1. The pictures that we have drawn appear toward the right of the monitor screen. Modify the program so that the 100-by-100 pixel region is centered on the y-axis (i.e., the column for which $x = 0$).

2. Create a new global variable screen-region-side-length, which indicates the side length of the square screen region whose pixels are being tested. By going to the editor and changing this variable's value, you should be able to change the size of the squares drawn by the program: for instance, changing the value to 40 should cause the program to draw 40-by-40 squares on the screen. How many procedures in the existing program have to be modified to accommodate this idea?

3. Suppose you incorporate the changes of Exercise 2 above and attempt to draw a very large picture—that is, your screen region takes up the bulk of the monitor screen. You will find that the text printed out within the "interpreter area" toward the bottom of the screen interferes with the picture that you have drawn.

   There are a number of ways to deal with this. One is to ensure that after the picture is drawn, no text will appear on the screen until you are ready to type at the interpreter again. What you can do is create a procedure called final-loop which is simply an infinite loop:

   ```
   (define (final-loop)
     (final-loop))
   ```

   If we place a call to final-loop at the end of the body of circle-squared, we will not see the interpreter prompt until we explicitly stop the procedure (using (CTRL)-BREAK) after the picture is drawn. Try incorporating this idea in the program. Why is it important that final-loop be tail recursive?

   Can you think of other ways around the "text interference" problem? Might the wait procedure of Exercise 11 in Chapter 5 be helpful?

4. Try making the screen region a rectangle instead of a square. You might consider having two global variables: screen-region-x-length and screen-region-y-length instead of the single variable screen-region-side-length of Exercise 2.

5. Try other formulas instead of $x^2 + y^2$ as the basis of your test. What happens if you try, say, $x^2 - y^2$? Or $x^3 + y^3$? Or $x^2 + y^2 + |x| + |y|$?

6. Change the choose-pen-color procedure so that it is more likely to choose black (as suggested earlier). Suppose, for example, that you truncate $x^2 + y^2$ and take the remainder when divided by 7 instead of 4; and if the result is 3 or less the pen color will be set to 0 (if the result is 4, 5, or 6 we set the pen color to 1, 2, or 3, respectively). How does this change the pictures drawn?

CHAPTER 8

Pairs, Lists, and Symbols

The Scheme language can be thought of as a collection of different object types—a sort of menagerie of various "species." So far we have paid attention to two of these species: numbers and booleans. We have written procedures (like `double` and `factorial`) that take number arguments and return number values; or predicate procedures (like `leap-year?`) that take number arguments and return boolean values. Most of the primitive procedures we have encountered have been likewise restricted. For instance, `+` takes number arguments and returns a number value; `not` takes a boolean argument and returns a boolean value; `negative?` takes a number argument and returns a boolean value; and so on.

It's time to expand our repertoire. In this chapter we will encounter two new types of objects: *pairs* and *symbols*. Before getting into details, though, here's a two-paragraph overview of what these object types are all about:

Pairs are objects that are composed of accessible parts; they are therefore useful for representing "compound" data. We often think of objects in the world as being the sum of two or more sub-objects; to take a simple example, telephone numbers might be thought of as a three-digit "area code part" and a seven-digit "local number part." Pairs are Scheme's most general mechanism for representing things of this sort—i.e., data objects composed of other objects.

Symbols are names. We have encountered symbols in the context of using `define`, whose purpose is to bind symbols to values. In fact, we have employed symbols since we began programming in Scheme, since Scheme expressions are typically lists of symbols (you don't know what a *list* is just yet, either, but we'll get to that). As mentioned in the first chapter, programming with symbols is a standard activity in the field of artificial intelligence; and we will see our first example of a symbol-manipulating program later in this chapter. For now, the key point to keep in mind is that besides being used as names for *other* Scheme objects, symbols are themselves Scheme objects.

Pairs Informally, a pair is a two-part object in which two other objects are stuck together. Pairs are often represented in what is called *box-and-pointer* notation; a pair in this system is depicted as two squares side by side, each with an arrow pointing to one sub-object. For instance, Figure 8.1 shows the pair consisting of the number objects 3 and 4.

Figure 8.1. The pair of 3 and 4

Pairs are created by the cons primitive in Scheme. We could create the pair depicted in Figure 8.1 by evaluating the expression (cons 3 4), as in the following example:

```
(define sample-pair (cons 3 4))
```

This binds the name sample-pair to the pair of 3 and 4. Now if we evaluate the name sample-pair, the Scheme interpreter would respond as follows:

```
sample-pair
(3 . 4)
```

That is, the Scheme interpreter indicates the pair object consisting of 3 and 4 by printing out (3 . 4).[1] To access the individual parts of the pair, we use the Scheme primitives car and cdr. Each of these primitives takes a pair as its argument; car returns the first object in the pair, and cdr the second. Thus, we could continue our session with the Scheme interpreter as follows:

```
(car sample-pair)
3
(cdr sample-pair)
4
```

Let's step back a moment and summarize what we've seen so far:

• Cons is a Scheme primitive that takes two arguments (of any type) and creates a pair composed of those two arguments.

• Car is a Scheme primitive that takes a pair as argument and returns the first object in that pair.

• Cdr is a Scheme primitive that takes a pair as argument and returns the second object in that pair.

The three statements above comprise a purely pragmatic—and surprisingly, reasonably formal—definition of pairs. We could say that pairs are things created by cons, and whose parts are accessed by car and cdr. What exactly happens inside the machine when we use the cons primitive is not really relevant to this definition; all we are concerned with is the guarantee that when we cons two objects x and y, we get something whose car is x and whose cdr is y.[2] Period.

---

[1] This is spoken "three-dot-four" to distinguish it from the decimal number 3.4; note that the spaces on either side of the period are crucial.

[2] The name cons is short for "construct," since this procedure is a pair constructor. The names car and cdr stand for "Contents of Address Register" and "Contents of Decrement Register"; these names refer to registers on the IBM 704 computer, on which the first Lisp system was implemented. This information is of course totally useless, but if I didn't include it here you might waste time looking it up elsewhere. A couple of other notes: the name cdr is pronounced "could-er," rhyming with "gooder." Also, since these procedures are so common, their names are often used colloquially: "we're consing two objects together," "it's getting the car of that pair," and so on.

Actually there is a little more to the story than this, but before going any further it might be worthwhile looking at a few examples. This will hopefully provide some motivation for slogging through the confusion that follows.

Suppose we want to create Scheme objects to represent points in the x,y-plane. Until now, we have had no straightforward method of doing this, since we could only work with individual numbers; thus, in the previous chapter, we had no way of referring to the x- and y-coordinates of our "imagined square" as parts of one single point—one entity.

A reasonable approach is to represent points as pairs; the car of the pair will be the x-coordinate, and the cdr of the pair the y-coordinate. To implement this idea, we might create the following procedures:

```
(define (make-point x-cor y-cor)
  (cons x-cor y-cor))
(define (x-coordinate point)
  (car point))
(define (y-coordinate point)
  (cdr point))
```

This seems like a very simple notion, but because we are now able to refer to points as objects, a large number of point-manipulating procedures become feasible. For instance, one operation that people often perform on points is to reflect them about the x- or y-axis. [The reflection of a point (x, y) about the x-axis is $(x, -y)$; the reflection about the y-axis is $(-x, y)$.] Thus, we could write the following procedures:

```
(define (reflect-about-x-axis point)
  (make-point (x-coordinate point)
              (* -1 (y-coordinate point))))
(define (reflect-about-y-axis point)
  (make-point (* -1 (x-coordinate point))
              (y-coordinate point)))
```

And of course, we could continue this process of creating point-manipulating procedures:

```
(define (reflect-about-origin point)
  (reflect-about-y-axis (reflect-about-x-axis point)))
```

Here's another example. Suppose we wish to create Scheme objects representing dates in time, and consisting of three parts: year, month, and day. Now the question is this: how do we use pairs, which consist of only two parts, to represent three-part objects?

The answer is simple. The two portions of a pair—the car and cdr—can be objects of any type at all. So far, we have created pairs whose car and cdr both happen to be numbers; but there is no reason at all why the sub-objects of a pair cannot themselves be pairs. Thus, we could represent a date as a pair whose car is a number representing the year, and whose cdr is a pair of two numbers, month and day. Here, in box-and-pointer notation, is an object representing the date July 4, 1776:

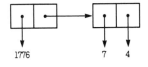

Figure 8.2. A Scheme object representing July 4, 1776

Here are some Scheme procedures implementing this representation of dates:

```
(define (make-date year month day)
  (cons year (cons month day)))

(define (year date)
  (car date))

(define (month date)
  (car (cdr date)))

(define (day date)
  (cdr (cdr date)))
```

There are, of course, many alternative ways that we could represent dates as objects. For instance, we could create a pair whose car is a pair indicating year and month, and whose cdr is the number indicating day. In this representation, the date July 4, 1776 would be represented as in Figure 8.3; creating procedures to implement this new representation is left as an exercise.

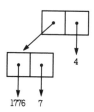

Figure 8.3. July 4, 1776 in the new representation

Lists   In creating compound data objects, we have a lot of leeway over how to arrange the various pairs to represent sub-objects. We have just seen, for example, that a variety of ways exist to represent dates in time: two possibilities were outlined above, and you could no doubt come up with many others. Historically, though, one particular type of structure known as a *list* has been associated with Lisp programming. In fact, as mentioned in the opening chapter, the very name "Lisp" stands for "List Programming"; so the concept has been an important part of the Lisp language since day one. Lists embody, as we will soon see, a particularly flexible and powerful way of combining objects together.

So what is a list, anyway? Essentially, it is a series of pairs linked together, ending in the special object nil. Figure 8.4 shows an example: this list consists of the three numbers 1, 2, and 3.

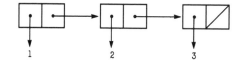

Figure 8.4. Box-and-pointer diagram of list (1 2 3)

Take a look at the box-and-pointer diagram of Figure 8.4. The list has three cons pairs lined up end-to-end, like a line of circus elephants. Each of the first two pairs has a number as its car, while its cdr is the next pair in the list. The final pair has the object nil as its cdr. In the diagram, the final cdr pointer is omitted, and a slash is drawn through the second "sub-box" of the third pair; this is the conventional Lisp way of indicating a cdr pointer to the object nil. If you prefer, you can think of this as shorthand for a familiar cdr arrow pointing to the nil object.

Figure 8.4 illustrates the standard format of a list: a list is any series of pairs such that if you chase down successive cdr arrows from pair to pair, you eventually arrive at nil. (The object nil, by the way, is sometimes referred to as *the empty list*—i.e., the list of zero pairs.[3])

How would we create the sample structure of Figure 8.4 in Scheme? One way is illustrated below:

```
(define sample-list (cons 1 (cons 2 (cons 3 nil))))
```

This would work: if you examine Figure 8.4, you will see that the suggested series of cons operations produces precisely the box-and-pointer structure that we want. Nevertheless, creating lists this way is a bit clumsy. A somewhat cleaner approach would be to use the Scheme primitive list:

```
(define sample-list (list 1 2 3))
```

The list primitive takes any number of arguments, of any type whatever, and creates a list of those objects. Thus, the expression

$$(\text{list } exp_1 \; exp_2 \; \ldots \; exp_n)$$

is equivalent to

$$(\text{cons } exp_1 \; (\text{cons } exp_2 \; \ldots \; (\text{cons } exp_n \; \text{nil}) \; \ldots \;))$$

That is to say, the list primitive simply conses its final argument to the empty list and then continues consing up its arguments, one by one, going from right to left.

Earlier, lists were described as a series of pairs such that the process of chasing down cdr pointers would eventually result in nil (i.e., the empty list). The discussion of the list primitive above suggests another, entirely equivalent description: a list is either the empty list or a pair whose cdr is a list. The self-referential quality of this second definition sounds confusing at first, but if you reflect on the matter a while you will see that there is no contradiction in it. Take, for example, the list of 1, 2, and 3 diagrammed in Figure 8.4: this is a pair whose car is 1 and whose cdr is the list of 2 and 3. Thus, by our new definition, this object is indeed a list, since it is a pair whose cdr is a list.

In a similar vein, you can prove to yourself that consing any object to a list will return a new list. Consider:

$$(\text{cons } \textit{any-object-whatever} \; \textit{some-list})$$

This expression will return a new list. The car of this list will be the object that was the first argument to the cons procedure, and the cdr of this list will be the original list that was the second argument to the cons procedure.

Having seen how to create lists, let's explore how the Scheme interpreter prints them out. Suppose, for instance, that we actually define sample-list as suggested earlier:

```
(define sample-list (list 1 2 3))
```

If we now evaluate the name sample-list, the Scheme interpreter will respond as follows:

---

[3]The notation that I am using in these paragraphs—i.e., nil to indicate the empty list—is slightly inaccurate; I am temporarily bending the rules of Lisp terminology for pedagogical purposes. Later in the chapter we will see a better notation for the empty list; and an extensive discussion of this idiosyncratic object is provided in Exercise 6. For now, I will mention two facts that you may find helpful. First, if you evaluate the name nil at the PC Scheme interpreter, what you will see printed out is (). This, you may recall, is exactly the same as the printed representation for the boolean object #f. In point of fact, the empty list and the object #f are the same object. Whether we want to think of this single object as an empty list or something representing the notion of "falseness" depends on the context of the program that we are writing. Second, although I am (for now) referring to nil as the empty list, it is in fact just a name—a symbol—that is *bound* to the empty list. There is a distinction between the symbol object nil and the empty list object to which it is bound. However, it is not uncommon for programmers to use phrases like, "the cdr of that pair is nil," on the assumption that everyone knows what they mean.

sample-list
(1 2 3)

That is, the list of 1, 2, and 3 is printed out as *(1 2 3)* by the Scheme interpreter. In general, a list of objects is represented in Scheme as the series of those objects surrounded by parentheses. (The objects are often referred to as the *elements* of the list.) Here is a sample session at the Scheme interpreter:

(list 6)
(6)

(list 1 4 2 3)
(1 4 2 3)

(list (list 1) 2 (list 3 4))
((1) 2 (3 4))

The third example above illustrates something that you might have anticipated already—namely, that lists can contain other lists as elements. The third list consists of three elements, two of which happen themselves to be lists; we could represent this structure in box-and-pointer notation as in Figure 8.5.

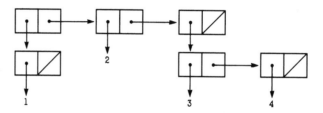

Figure 8.5. Box-and-pointer diagram of ((1) 2 (3 4))

The first example, the list (6), is also worth a second look. We have seen that the pair of two objects *x* and *y* is printed out in what is called "dotted pair notation," as (*x* . *y*). For example, the pair of 2 and 5 prints out as (2 . 5). But we have also seen that the single-element list 6 is simply the pair consisting of 6 and nil. Why, then, does this list print out as (6) and not as *(6 . ())*?[4] The answer is that the Scheme interpreter automatically prints out lists in the standard list format; although the dotted pair notation *could* have been used without any ambiguity, the list notation is somewhat easier to read. Since lists are such a common data structure in Scheme, all systems adopt the simpler notation when printing them out.

Lists:
A Summary

We have covered a fair amount of ground thus far. Let's pause a bit to codify some of this information:

- Lists are data structures consisting of a series of pairs; if we take the cdr of each pair in succession, we eventually arrive at the special object nil. The only exception to this definition is nil itself, which contains no pairs and which is sometimes called "the empty list."

- A list can also be defined as something that is either nil or a pair whose cdr is a list.

- If we cons any object to some list sample-list, we get a new list whose car is the object and whose cdr is the original list sample-list.

---

[4]Note that in this hypothetical dotted-pair notation I am employing the printed representation of nil—namely, *()*.

- The Scheme primitive `list` takes any number of objects as arguments and creates a list whose elements are those objects.

- A list is printed out by the Scheme interpreter as a series of elements within parentheses.

- Lists may contain other lists—indeed, objects of any type—as elements.

There are some handy gimmicks for remembering how certain Scheme primitives, like `cons` and `list`, work. These are not surefire—there are subtle exceptions to each of them—but they do the job often enough.

You can think of the primitive `cdr` as something that takes a list as input and returns that portion of the list following the first element. Pictorially, this is equivalent to moving the starting left parenthesis of the list one element over to the right.

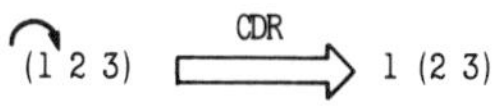

$$\widehat{(1}\ 2\ 3)\quad\overset{\text{CDR}}{\Longrightarrow}\quad 1\ (2\ 3)$$

Figure 8.6. A picture of cdr in action

Some examples:

```
(cdr (list 1 2 3))
(2 3)
(cdr (list (list 1) (list 2 3) 4))
((2 3) 4)
(cdr (list 3))
()
```

Note that in this last example, the empty list prints out as *()*; happily, this is consistent with our "graphical" interpretation of `cdr`.

The primitive `cons` can take an object and a list as its two arguments. In this case, `cons` returns the list whose `car` is the object and whose `cdr` is the original list. Pictorially, we might represent this as taking the left parenthesis of the list and "hooking it over" the first argument to `cons`.

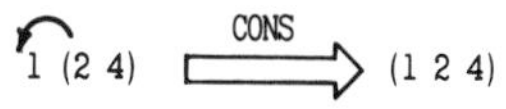

$$\widehat{1}\ (2\ 4)\quad\overset{\text{CONS}}{\Longrightarrow}\quad (1\ 2\ 4)$$

Figure 8.7. A picture of cons in action

Some examples:

```
(cons 1 (list 2 4))
(1 2 4)
(cons (list 1 2) (list 2 3))
((1 2) 2 3)
```

The `list` primitive, pictorially, can be seen as "surrounding its arguments with parentheses."

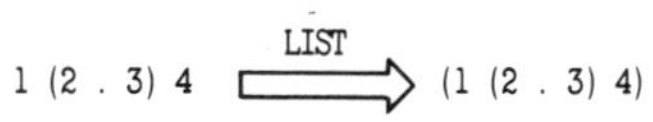

$$1\ (2\ .\ 3)\ 4\quad\overset{\text{LIST}}{\Longrightarrow}\quad (1\ (2\ .\ 3)\ 4)$$

Figure 8.8. A picture of list in action

An example:

```
(list 1 (cons 2 3) 4)
(1 (2 . 3) 4)
```

There is another Scheme primitive worth including here—the append procedure. Append takes two lists as arguments and creates the list whose elements consist of the elements of the first followed by the elements of the second:

```
(append (list 2 3) (list 5 6))
(2 3 5 6)
(append (list 1 2 3) nil)
(1 2 3)
(append (list 1) (list (list 2)))
(1 (2))
```

Pictorially, what append is doing is "dissolving" the central parentheses from its two arguments to create one long list.

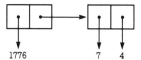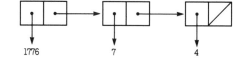

Figure 8.9. A picture of append in action

Recursive List Procedures

We have now acquired a little familiarity with list structure. But why, after all, are lists so important? In some ways, lists seem like a rather inefficient way to group objects together. Consider, for example, our earlier Scheme objects representing dates: we created a pair whose car indicated the year and whose cdr was a pair indicating month and day (as in Figure 8.10). But suppose instead we decided to make a list of three numbers—year, month, and day—to represent dates (as in Figure 8.11). In this case, we need three cons pairs to represent a date, whereas in our earlier version we needed only two. Since in fact pairs do take up some memory space inside the computer, the list representation of dates is certainly less space-efficient than the original representation. So why are lists so popular?

Figure 8.10. July 4, 1776   **Figure 8.11.** July 4, 1776 as a list

The answer is that in many cases, lists are a particularly easy structure for procedures to handle. The reason they are so easy to handle can be found staring out at us from the original definition that we used—if you keep chasing down cdr arrows, you eventually get to the special object nil. What this means is that many Scheme procedures can work with a list element by element: do something to the first element, then take the cdr of the list, then do something to the first element of *that* list, then take the cdr again, and so on until the object nil is finally reached.

Suppose, for example, we want to write a procedure that will take a list of numbers as input and return as its result the sum of all the numbers in the list. That is, we would like a procedure that could work as follows:

```
(sum (list 1 2 3 4))
10
(define sample-list (list 5 6 7))
sample-list
(sum sample-list)
18
(sum (cdr sample-list))
13
```

Here's how we could express the desired strategy: if the argument list is empty—that is, if the list is nil—then our sum procedure should return 0. Otherwise, our sum procedure should add the number which is the car of the list to the result of calling sum on the cdr of the list.

```
(define (sum list-of-numbers)
  (cond ((null? list-of-numbers) 0)
        (else (+ (car list-of-numbers)
                 (sum (cdr list-of-numbers))))))
```

This is a recursive procedure in the same mold as the ones we saw in Chapter 5: the "base case" is the case in which the argument list is empty, and the "next-simplest case" is the one in which the argument to sum is the cdr of the current list argument. Let's follow through a sample call to sum:

```
(sum (list 5 6 7))
```

The argument to the first invocation of sum is (5 6 7). Thus, we will evaluate the body of sum with the name list-of-numbers temporarily bound to (5 6 7). The first clause of the cond expression uses a Scheme primitive that we haven't encountered yet: the predicate null?. This predicate returns #t if its argument is nil and returns #f otherwise. Since in this case, the value of list-of-numbers is not the object nil, the next clause of the cond is tried; and since this is the else clause, we go on to evaluate the call to +. The first argument to + is the car of list-of-numbers, which is 5; so far, so good. The second argument to + is the result of calling the sum procedure on the cdr of our list argument—that is, we want to call the sum procedure on the list (6 7). The result of this call will be summed to 5 to produce the final result of our original invocation of sum. You can follow through for yourself the continuation of this process; eventually, there will be an invocation of sum with an argument of nil, and the result of this invocation will be 0. This result will be used by the previous invocation of sum, and so on; the value returned by the call to sum with argument (6 7) will be 13. Thus, the value returned by our original invocation will be the sum of 5 and 13, or 18, as desired.

Here are a few more examples. Take a look at them and see if you can identify the standard recursive patterns that we have employed in the past.

This is a procedure that returns the length of a list of objects:

```
(define (length list-of-objects)
  (cond ((null? list-of-objects) 0)
        (else (1+ (length (cdr list-of-objects))))))
```

Here's a procedure that returns the maximum of a list of numbers.

```
(define (maximum list-of-numbers)
  (cond ((null? (cdr list-of-numbers)) (car list-of-numbers))
        (else (let ((max-of-rest (maximum (cdr list-of-numbers)))
                    (first-element (car list-of-numbers)))
                (if (> first-element max-of-rest)
                    first-element
                    max-of-rest)))))
```

Here's another way to write maximum:

```
(define (maximum list-of-numbers)
  (cond ((null? (cdr list-of-numbers)) (car list-of-numbers))
        ((> (car list-of-numbers) (car (cdr list-of-numbers)))
         (maximum (cons (car list-of-numbers)
                        (cdr (cdr list-of-numbers)))))
        (else (maximum (cdr list-of-numbers)))))
```

Here's a procedure that counts the number of zeroes in a list of numbers:

```
(define (number-of-zeroes list-of-numbers)
  (cond ((null? list-of-numbers) 0)
        ((= 0 (car list-of-numbers))
         (1+ (number-of-zeroes (cdr list-of-numbers))))
        (else (number-of-zeroes (cdr list-of-numbers)))))
```

Procedures that Return Lists

The recursive procedures shown above take lists as arguments and return numbers as values. But we can also write procedures that return lists. Here are some examples.

This procedure takes a number n as argument and returns a list of n zeroes:

```
(define (make-list-of-zeroes n)
  (cond ((= n 0) nil)
        (else (cons 0 (make-list-of-zeroes (-1+ n))))))
```

If we type (make-list-of-zeroes 3) at the Scheme interpreter, we should see the result *(0 0 0)*. You should *definitely* work through a sample call to make-list-of-zeroes using your favorite model of recursion, to make sure that you understand how it works.

Our next example makes a list of n consecutive integers, counting down from n to 1:

```
(define (make-countdown-list n)
  (cond ((= n 0) nil)
        (else (cons n (make-countdown-list (-1+ n))))))
```

If we type (make-countdown-list 3) at the interpreter, we should see the result *(3 2 1)*.

Here is a procedure named increment-list that takes a list of numbers as argument and returns a new list of numbers, each of which is one greater than the corresponding number in the original argument. Thus, if we type (increment-list (list 2 4 6)) at the interpreter, we should see the response *(3 5 7)*.

```
(define (increment-list list-of-numbers)
  (cond ((null? list-of-numbers) nil)
        (else
         (cons (1+ (car list-of-numbers))
               (increment-list (cdr list-of-numbers))))))
```

Finally, you should be able to convince yourself that the following definition of append would behave just like the existing Scheme primitive:

```
(define (append list-1 list-2)
  (cond ((null? list-1) list-2)
        (else
         (cons (car list-1)
               (append (cdr list-1) list-2)))))
```

A Meta-Comment

As you may have noticed, this is a long chapter, and there is still a fair amount to go. If you are reading straight through, I would advise you to take a break now and digest the material covered thus far. Try creating some list-manipulating procedures (if you need suggestions, check out the exercises). Try using the trace primitive to see how your procedures work and to debug them when they don't. When you feel relatively comfortable with the topics covered so far, go on to the next section.

The special form quote is probably the most difficult that we have encountered thus far. Essentially, quote means "don't evaluate what follows." Thus, if we type the following at the Scheme interpreter:

    (quote (1 2 3))

the response will be *(1 2 3)*—that is, the unevaluated list of elements 1, 2, and 3. The idea is that quote tells the Scheme interpreter to treat the expression that follows as something which should not be evaluated. Ordinarily, the expression (1 2 3) would be treated by the Scheme interpreter as a procedure call: it looks as though we want to call the procedure 1 on the arguments 2 and 3. This would result in an error—a "type error" of the sort described in Chapter 6. But since in this case the expression (1 2 3) follows the quote special form, the Scheme interpreter treats it as what it looks like—namely, a list of three elements.

In a sense, the role of quote is similar to that of quotation marks in everyday conversation. A standard example is to contrast the instructions, "Say your name," and "Say 'your name'." In the first case, the phrase "your name" is meant to be evaluated, and the proper answer is (in my own case) "Mike." In the second case, the phrase "your name" is meant to be left unevaluated, and the proper answer is "your name." The concept of quotation, and the difficulties that arise from it, are part of a long tradition of philosophical investigation: a language that allows quotation is thereby able to include statements referring to other statements, and this opens up a variety of difficult logical questions.[5] The concept of quotation has an equally honorable place in the history of humor: many hoary old jokes are based on misunderstandings of the placement of quotation marks. One example was used by the comedy team of Dan Rowan and Dick Martin to close their show every week:

> *Rowan:* Say "goodnight," Dick.
>
> *Martin:* Goodnight, Dick!

To get back to Scheme: the quote special form has several idiosyncrasies. First, it is rarely written out as such. Usually, the expression

    (quote (1 2 3 4))

is abbreviated using the apostrophe character:

    '(1 2 3 4)

The apostrophe ' is a kind of shorthand for the quote special form. Note that the apostrophe doesn't just stand for the symbol quote itself; rather, when an expression is preceded by the apostrophe this is equivalent to that expression being part of a larger compound expression beginning with quote. That is, *'exp* is equivalent to (quote *exp*), not quote *exp*.

Just to play with these notions a bit, consider the difference between the following expressions:

    (car '(1 2 3))
    (car ''(1 2 3))

The result of the first expression is 1. In this case, we are taking the car of the list returned by the quote special form. The result of the second expression is quote. In this instance, the list being quoted by the first apostrophe is the list (quote (1 2 3)),

---

[5]For instance, suppose John is Mary's brother. Then if the statement "John has brown eyes" is true, the statement "Mary's brother has brown eyes" will also be true. But even though the statement "'John' is four letters long" is true, the statement "'Mary's brother' is four letters long" is not. The introduction of quotation in the language means that "John" and "Mary's brother" may not be substituted for each other in all statements, even though the two expressions refer to the same object.

and it is the car of this list that we get as our returned value. I strongly urge that you type in some examples at the Scheme interpreter and investigate this phenomenon for yourself.

Now that we have become acquainted with quote, we can also dispense with our previous notation for writing the empty list—namely, nil. In Scheme, the preferred notation for writing the empty list is (). If we want to write a Scheme expression that evaluates to the empty list (), we simply use the quoted empty list, '(). Here are two examples:

```
(cons 5 '())
(5)
(null? '())
#t
```

Note that the notation '() is consistent with our notation for quoted lists in general: that is, when the Scheme interpreter evaluates '(), it returns an (unevaluated) empty list. Just as the Scheme expression '(1) evaluates to the list (1), the expression '() evaluates to the empty list (). Henceforth in this text, I will use the notation () to indicate the empty list, and I will use '() in programs whenever a Scheme expression that evaluates to () is needed.

And one more fact about the quote special form: when the expression following quote is a number, the value of the quote expression is simply that number. In other words, the quote has no effect in this instance. Thus (+ '1 '4) evaluates to 5.

Symbols

The quote special form enables us to use symbols—essentially, "unevaluated names"—as data objects. Consider the following session at the Scheme interpreter:

```
(define a 10)
A
a
10
'a
A
```

When we typed the symbol a at the Scheme intepreter, the response—consistent with the rule for evaluating symbols—was the value to which a is bound, or 10. However, by typing 'a we told the Scheme interpreter to leave the name a unevaluated; therefore, the returned value was simply the symbol a itself.

When the quote special form precedes a list including symbols, the returned value is just the unevaluated list. This is illustrated in the following examples:

```
(car '(a b c))
A
(car (list a))
10
(car (list 'a))
A
(car '(list a))
LIST
```

In the first example, the list whose car we want is the unevaluated list of symbols a, b, and c—so the result is the symbol a. In the second example, the argument to car is the list whose one element is the value of a—that is, the list (10). You should be able to work through the last two examples on your own.

Just as two numbers can be compared for equality with the predicate =, two symbols can be compared for equality with the predicate eq?. The expression (eq? 'a 'a), for instance, returns #t, while (eq? 'a 'b) will return #f. Here, as an example, is a predicate called contains-olives? that uses eq?. Contains-olives? takes a list of symbols as argument and returns #t if the symbol olives is anywhere in the list:

```
(define (contains-olives? list-of-symbols)
  (cond ((null? list-of-symbols) #f)
        ((eq? (car list-of-symbols) 'olives) #t)
        (else (contains-olives? (cdr list-of-symbols)))))
```

We could use this predicate as follows:

```
(contains-olives? '(lettuce tomatoes onions))
()
(contains-olives? '(pepper olives lettuce))
#t
```

The contains-olives? predicate is recursive, of course, and is completely analogous in structure to many other recursive procedures that we have already seen. If you find it problematic, try comparing it to some of the earlier recursive examples; the number-of-zeroes procedure, which counts the number of zeroes in a list, is a good one to look at. Here it is again, for your convenience:

```
(define (number-of-zeroes list-of-numbers)
  (cond ((null? list-of-numbers) 0)
        ((= 0 (car list-of-numbers))
         (1+ (number-of-zeroes (cdr list-of-numbers))))
        (else (number-of-zeroes (cdr list-of-numbers)))))
```

One more point about symbols: you may have noticed that the Scheme interpreter prints out all symbols in capital letters. Thus, if we evaluate the symbol 'a, the interpreter will respond A. This property is known as *case insensitivity*, which simply means that, as far as symbols are concerned, the Scheme interpreter ignores any distinction between capital and lowercase letters. The symbols olives, OLIVES, oLiVeS, and so on are therefore all treated as the same symbol by the interpreter; comparing any two of them with eq? will yield a value of #t. When symbols are printed out, the interpreter does so by using—as a default—the all-capitalized version of the symbol. (In this text, the interpreter's responses are generally written in lowercase for readability.)

An Extended Example: Molecular Weights

A common activity for chemists is finding molecular weights. Given some molecular formula—like that for glucose: $C_6H_{12}O_6$—the problem is to find the mass in grams of a mole of the substance. (A *mole* is 6.022×10^{23} molecules; it is a standard measure for obtaining molecular weights.)

Here's how the problem is usually handled: we go to the periodic table of elements and look at the atomic weight for each individual element in our formula. For the example of glucose, we would find that the atomic weight of carbon (C) is 12.011; this means that a mole of carbon has a mass of 12.011 grams. Looking up hydrogen (H) and oxygen (O) as well, we find that the atomic weights of these elements are 1.0079 and 15.9994, respectively. Now, since one mole of glucose contains 6 moles of carbon, 12 moles of hydrogen, and 6 moles of oxygen, we know that the molecular weight of glucose is:

$$(6 \times 12.011) + (12 \times 1.0079) + (6 \times 15.9994) = 180.1572$$

Let's create a Scheme program that will compute molecular weights automatically. We want a procedure named molecular-weight that can be called on lists of symbols and numbers representing chemical formulas:

```
(molecular-weight '(C 6 H 12 O 6))
180.1572

(molecular-weight '(C O 2))
44.0098

(molecular-weight '(Na Cl))
58.4428
```

The examples above show molecular-weight returning results for glucose, carbon dioxide, and sodium chloride (table salt). As you can see, molecular formulas here are represented by lists; the numbers that usually appear as subscripts simply appear after the appropriate chemical symbol.

Here is the basic strategy that we will employ: if the argument list is empty, then our procedure should return the number 0. (This is the "base case" of the problem.) Now, if the list is not empty, then we will consider two possibilities: either the list begins with an element followed by a subscript number, as in the list (C 6 H 12 O 6), or else the list begins with an element without a subscript, as in the list (C O 2). In the former case we want to multiply the atomic weight of the beginning element by the appropriate number, and add the result to the weight calculated for the rest of the list; in the second case, we simply add the atomic weight of the beginning element to the weight calculated for the rest of the list.

Here is a procedure to realize this strategy:

```
(define (molecular-weight formula-list)
  (cond ((null? formula-list) 0)
        ((null? (cdr formula-list)) (atomic-weight (car formula-list)))
        ((number? (car (cdr formula-list)))
         (+ (* (car (cdr formula-list)) (atomic-weight (car formula-list)))
            (molecular-weight (cdr (cdr formula-list)))))
        (else (+ (atomic-weight (car formula-list))
                 (molecular-weight (cdr formula-list))))))
```

A couple of points before we go on. First, we are of course not yet done with our program: molecular-weight employs a procedure named atomic-weight which we haven't yet written. This is a very typical way of going about writing Scheme programs; we work out a "top-level" procedure like molecular-weight and later write the other, subsidiary procedures that it uses. Second, our procedure uses a new primitive: the predicate number?, which returns #t if its argument is a number object.

In English, this is what the molecular-weight procedure is doing: the first cond clause tests to see whether the formula is empty. If so, the procedure returns the number 0. The second clause sees whether the formula consists of just a single element symbol; in this case the molecular weight is the atomic weight of the element. The third clause ascertains whether the list begins with a symbol followed by a number. In this event, the number is multiplied by the atomic weight of the element, and the result is added to the molecular weight of the formula list following the number. Finally, if the formula begins with an element symbol followed by another symbol, we add the atomic weight of the beginning element to the molecular weight of the rest of the formula.

Writing the atomic-weight procedure is tedious, but simple in principle. All we want is a procedure that will take an element's symbol as input and return the atomic weight of the element. Here is one possible version, covering eight common elements:

```
(define (atomic-weight element)
  (cond ((eq? element 'h) 1.0079)  ;hydrogen
        ((eq? element 'c) 12.011)  ;carbon
        ((eq? element 'n) 14.0067) ;nitrogen
        ((eq? element 'o) 15.9994) ;oxygen
        ((eq? element 'na) 22.9898) ;sodium
        ((eq? element 'p) 30.9738) ;phosphorus
        ((eq? element 's) 32.06)  ;sulfur
        ((eq? element 'cl) 35.453) ;chlorine
        (else (error "This element not handled: " element))))
```

Naturally, a complete version of this procedure would handle all one-hundred-or-so elements.

Our program now works—at least for the examples shown—but we can make some minor improvements before going on to make a major improvement. First, in the molecular-weight procedure, there are a couple of expressions of the form:

```
(car (cdr formula-list))
(cdr (cdr formula-list))
```

Taking the car of the cdr of a list is a common activity; this returns the second element in the list. Because we so often want to do repeated car and cdr operations on lists, Scheme includes some primitives representing sequences of these operations. For the examples above, we would write:

```
(cadr formula-list)
(cddr formula-list)
```

The general form of these "abbreviated" primitives is

```
c....r
```

where the blanks indicate as many as four successive a's or d's. These are read from right to left as indicating successive car and cdr operations. Thus, the following expressions:

```
(car (cdr (cdr lis)))
(cdr (cdr (car (car lis))))
(car (car lis))
```

could be written, respectively, as:

```
(caddr lis)
(cddaar lis)
(caar lis)
```

A second minor improvement involves the atomic-weight procedure. Although the cond special form is perfectly adequate, there is a related special form called case, which is a little cleaner in this instance. A description of case and a suggestion for rewriting atomic-weight are included in the exercises at the end of this chapter.

Now for the large improvement. Chemical formulas often include portions in parentheses which represent groups of elements. For instance, the formula for isopropyl alcohol is $(CH_3)_2CHOH$; this represents the structure shown in Figure 8.12. It would be nice if our molecular-weight procedure could handle formulas of this sort:

```
(molecular-weight '((C H 3) 2 C H O H))
60.0956
```

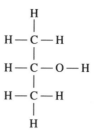

Figure 8.12. Isopropyl alcohol

There are a number of ways that we could change `molecular-weight` to accommodate this idea. One reasonable version is illustrated below:

```
(define (molecular-weight formula)
  (cond ((null? formula) 0)
        ((symbol? formula) (atomic-weight formula))
        ((null? (cdr formula))(molecular-weight (car formula)))
        ((number? (cadr formula))
         (+ (* (cadr formula)(molecular-weight (car formula)))
            (molecular-weight (cddr formula))))
        (else (+ (molecular-weight (car formula))
                 (molecular-weight (cdr formula))))))
```

Notice that `molecular-weight` can now accept either a list or a lone symbol as argument; hence, the name of the argument is now `formula` instead of `formula-list`. The first clause again checks to see whether the formula is the empty list, in which case we return 0. The second clause is new, and employs the primitive predicate `symbol?`, which returns #t if its argument is a symbol. If the formula is simply an atomic symbol, then `molecular-weight` returns the atomic weight of the appropriate element.

The remaining clauses illustrate the interesting new strategy in our procedure. Note that they are very similar to the final three clauses of our original version, except where our original version used `atomic-weight` in these clauses we now use a recursive call to `molecular-weight`. The point is this: it is easy to show that our new `molecular-weight` procedure handles all the same cases as the original one—that is, the new procedure handles all "one-level" formula lists. (You should work through an example—say, the list (C O 2).) Now consider what happens when the argument list to `molecular-weight` begins with a list, as in:

```
(molecular-weight '((C H 3) 2 C H O H))
```

In this case, the predicate for the fourth clause returns #t, since the `cadr` of this argument list is indeed a number. Therefore, `molecular-weight` will return the sum of two numbers: one is the product of 2 and the result of calling `molecular-weight` on the argument (C H 3), and the other is the result of calling `molecular-weight` on the argument (C H O H). Both the arguments for these recursive calls are therefore "one-level" lists. But we have just seen that `molecular-weight` does indeed work correctly for such lists. Therefore, our procedure also works correctly on a "two-level" list. Indeed, continuing by induction, we could show that our new procedure works for lists involving *any* level of grouping. For instance, here's a conceivable formula: $((CH_3)_3C)_2CHOH$. We could use this as an argument for `molecular-weight`:

```
(molecular-weight '(((C H 3) 3 C) 2 C H O H))
144.2564
```

The key idea here is that our new `molecular-weight` can call itself recursively on both the `car` and the `cdr` of its argument. Because the two recursive calls may be seen as a sort of "branching"—one call handles the car of the list, and another the cdr—this type of strategy is sometimes known as *tree recursion*. Exercise 18 at the end of this chapter suggests another example of a tree recursive procedure.

George Orwell's book *Animal Farm* includes the famous declaration, "Some animals are more equal than others." In Scheme, there are also different sorts of "equality" between objects. Which type of equality we use depends on our needs at the moment.

We have already seen that two numbers can be compared for equality with the predicate =. Similarly, two symbols can be compared with eq?.

The eq? predicate is actually a bit more general. It can be used to compare two pairs to see if they are the same object. Now, this is trickier than it sounds. Each time we perform a cons operation, we create a new pair. Thus, although two pairs may *look* alike when printed out, they may not be eq? to one another. Here's an example:

```
(define first-list (list 1))
first-list
(define second-list (list 1))
second-list
(define third-list (cons 2 first-list))
third-list
first-list
(1)
second-list
(1)
third-list
(2 1)
(eq? first-list second-list)
()
(eq? first-list (cdr third-list))
#t
```

Although the two lists first-list and second-list have the same elements, and look the same when printed out, they are not the results of the same cons operation. However, when we created third-list, we did so by consing the number 2 onto the already-existing pair to which first-list is bound. Therefore, the cdr of this new list is eq? to first-list. The situation is illustrated in Figure 8.13.

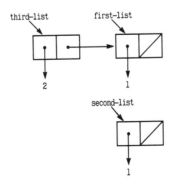

Figure 8.13. First-list, second-list, and third-list

There are two other equality predicates worth knowing about: eqv? and equal?. Both of these are a little more "lenient" than the eq? predicate.

The eqv? predicate can be used to compare any two objects. It acts as a sort of combination of eq? and =. The eqv? predicate returns #t if its arguments are equal numbers, identical (in the sense of eq?) pairs, or identical symbols. (There are a few other cases in which eqv? returns #t, but these cases involve object types that we haven't examined yet.) Thus, if you need a predicate that can compare both numbers and symbols, eqv? is the way to go. Here are some examples:

```
(eqv? 'a 'a)
#t

(eqv? (cons 1 2) (cons 1 2))
()

(eqv? 3 3)
#t

(eqv? 3 'a)
()
```

The equal? predicate takes two objects of any type and returns #t if they look the same when printed out. That is, two lists that print out in the same way will be equal? to one another, even if they contain nonidentical pairs. In addition, as with eqv?, identical symbols and equal numbers are equal?. Here are some examples:

```
(equal? (list 1) (list 1))
#t

(equal? (list 1) (list 2))
()

(equal? 'a 'a)
#t
```

Exercises

1. Create a Scheme representation of telephone numbers, including area code and local number. Your representation should include procedures make-telephone-number, area-code, and local-number. Using this representation, and knowing that Los Angeles has area code 213 and that toll-free numbers have area code 800, write predicates los-angeles-number? and toll-free-number?.

2. Implement the alternative representation of dates suggested earlier—i.e., a pair whose car is another pair indicating year and month, and whose cdr indicates the day. Using this representation, write a procedure start-of-next-month that, given a date as argument, will return the date that is the first day of the following month. For instance, if the argument to start-of-next-month represents the date July 4, 1776, the date returned should represent August 1, 1776.

3. Using the representation of points given earlier, create Scheme objects to represent line segments. (A line segment is determined by its two endpoints.) You should include procedures make-line-segment, endpoint-1, and endpoint-2. Using your representation, write a predicate vertical-segment? that takes a line segment as argument and returns #t if the segment is vertical. Also write a procedure unit-vector that takes an angle angle (in radians) as argument and returns a line segment of length 1 beginning at the origin $(0, 0)$ and at the appropriate angle from the x-axis. For example, calling unit-vector with an argument of π should return the line segment from $(0, 0)$ to $(-1, 0)$.

4. For each of the following expressions, show the box-and-pointer representation of the structure created. Also show how the Scheme interpreter would print the given structure.

```
(list 4)
(cons 4 '())
(list 4 5)
(list (list 3 5) 6)
(list (cons 1 2) (cons 3 4) (cons 5 6))
(cons 5 (cons 7 8))
(list 1 (list 2 3) (list (list 4)))
```

5. For each of the following lists (as printed out by the Scheme interpreter), write an expression that could create that list. For example, the list printed out as *(1)* could be created by (list 1).

(4 5)
(4 (5))
((1 . 2) 3)
((1) ((2)) 3 (4 5 6))

6. The special object () is worth some investigation. First, experiment with your Scheme system to determine the value of the following two expressions:

```
(car '())
(cdr '())
```

For many Scheme systems, these expressions signal an error.

In Chapter 4, it was mentioned that evaluating the object #f causes the Scheme interpreter to respond *()*. You will get the same response if you evaluate the object '(). As it happens, in PC Scheme (and in all Scheme systems that I know of), the object #f is identical to (). Thus, the empty list is, strictly speaking, a boolean object. Check this with your own system by evaluating (eq? '() #f).

There are still other observations to make about this special object. For instance, in this chapter we made use of the fact that in PC Scheme, the symbol nil is bound to the empty list; the name nil derives from older Lisp dialects. Yet another designation, in some systems, is #!null. Typically, we use the term "the empty list" or nil or () when this object is used as a list with no elements; when the object is to be returned by some predicate it is referred to as #f. In most systems the name false is bound to this object also. (And, by the way, the name true is similarly bound to the boolean object #t.) Keeping track of all the names for the empty list is marginally easier than keeping track of the names in a Russian novel.

As to why the objects () and #f are identical, the answer is that some common procedures that have been written in Lisp through the years run somewhat more efficiently given this identification. Many people feel that identifying the two objects is a historical artifact and not really desirable.

Oh, yes—this is supposed to be an exercise, isn't it? Well, as noted above, () is a boolean object, but we sometimes like to think of it as "the empty list." It might be nice to have a predicate list? that returns #t if its argument is () or some nonempty list. Using the primitive predicate pair?, which returns #t if its argument is a pair object, you should be able to write the list? predicate.

7. Write a procedure product that takes a list of numbers as argument and returns the product of the numbers. For instance, evaluating (product '(2 5 6)) should return 60.

8. Write a procedure average that takes a list of numbers as argument and returns the average of the numbers. For instance, evaluating (average '(2 5 11)) should return 6.

9. Write a procedure golf-score that takes as arguments two 18-element lists of numbers: the first represents the scores of a particular player and the second represents the par values of the holes on the course. The procedure should return the number above or below par of the player's score. You might also want your procedure to display the number of birdies (holes for which the player scored 1 below par), eagles (holes for which the player scored two below par), bogeys (the player was 1 above par), double bogeys (the player was 2 above par), and other special scores.

10. There is a common party game in which one person acts as "answerer" and everyone else acts as "questioners." The answerer must answer "yes" or "no" to every question based on some rule or other. For instance, the rule might be: "If the question includes the word 'you' then answer 'yes'; otherwise, answer 'no'." The object of the questioners is to try and guess the rule.

Write a procedure answer-me that allows the computer to act as answerer. The procedure should take as argument a list of symbols representing a question (it's probably simpler not to include punctuation), and returns either the symbol yes or no depending on some rule of your own choice. As an example, here's a sample session with answer-me using the rule mentioned above: namely, if the argument list contains the symbol you then the procedure returns yes.

```
(answer-me '(do you answer yes to everything))
yes
(answer-me '(you really do))
yes
(answer-me '(really))
no
```

11. Write a procedure filter-out-symbol that takes as argument a list and a symbol and returns a list whose elements are the same as the argument list except with all instances of the symbol deleted. For example, evaluating

```
(filter-out-symbol '(no no a thousand times no) 'no)
```

should return the list (a thousand times).

12. The *association list* is a common data structure in Scheme (actually, it is common in all Lisp programming). Each element of an association list is a two-element list (or sometimes, a two-element cons pair like our "point objects" at the beginning of the chapter). Each two-element list in the association list can be thought of as an "index-value pair": that is, the first of the two elements is a keyword or an identifier of some sort, and the second of the two elements is a "value-marker." Here's an example: the association list menu has two-element lists representing particular dishes and their prices in a Chinese restaurant.

```
(define menu
   '((egg-drop-soup 1.75)
     (won-ton-soup 2.00)
     (beef-with-snow-peas 7.00)
     (chicken-with-almonds 6.75)
     (shrimp-lo-mein 6.50)
     (mixed-vegetables 5.00)))
```

Write a predicate procedure on-the-menu? that returns #t if the given argument (a symbol) is one of the foods on the menu. Write a second procedure `price-of` that returns the price of a given menu item. Finally, write a procedure `price-of-meal` that takes as argument a list of symbols representing a meal and returns the price of the entire meal. Thus, if we evaluate:

```
(price-of-meal '(egg-drop-soup beef-with-snow-peas shrimp-lo-mein))
```

the result should be 15.25.

13. Write a `connect-the-dots` procedure that takes a list of points as argument and draws on the graphics screen the figure consisting of line segments from one point to the next point. For instance, calling

```
(connect-the-dots (list (make-point 0 0)(make-point 0 50)(make-point 50 50)
                        (make-point 50 0)(make-point 0 0)))
```

will draw a square.

14. Write a procedure `reverse-list` that takes a list as argument and returns a list whose elements are the same as those in the argument but in reverse order. Here's an example:

```
(reverse-list '(1 2 3))
(3 2 1)
```

15. Write a procedure `permutations` which takes a list of distinct elements as argument and returns a list of all lists representing possible orderings of those elements. Here's an example:

```
(permutations '(1 2 3))
((1 2 3) (1 3 2) (2 1 3) (2 3 1) (3 1 2) (3 2 1))
```

You will probably need to define other procedures besides `permutations`.

16. Write a procedure `shuffle` that will take a list as argument and return a list containing the same elements in some "random" order. For instance (`shuffle '(h e l l o)`) might return (`l o l h e`). You might use this procedure as part of a program to generate anagram puzzles.

17. The `case` special form is a "choice-making" feature of Scheme similar to `cond`. Although `case` is less general than `cond`, it sometimes proves cleaner to use.

The format of `case` expressions is as follows:

```
(case expression
      clause
      clause . . . )
```

Each *clause* is of the form (*selector consequents*) where *selector* is a number, boolean, symbol, or non-nested list (i.e., a list without any lists as elements). The *consequents* may be any series of expressions.

Here, in a nutshell, is how `case` expressions are evaluated. First, the *expression* at the top is evaluated. The result of this evaluation is compared with each *selector* in turn. If the result is `eqv?` to the *selector* (when the *selector* is a boolean, number, or symbol) or if the result is `eqv?` to some element in the *selector* (when the *selector* is a list), then we don't go on to the next clause; rather, we evaluate the *consequents* in this clause and return the value of the last one. Otherwise—if no match is found—we go on and compare the *expression* result to the *selector* of the next clause. The last clause in the `case` statement typically has the symbol `else` as its *selector* value; this is analogous to the `else` clause in `cond` expressions, and is treated as a *selector* that always matches.

Once again, even more briefly: evaluate *expression*; compare the result to the *selector* of each clause, one by one; as soon as a match is found, evaluate the consequents of the matching clause and return the value of the last consequent in the clause.

As an example:

```
(case (1+ 3)
  ( 5 'a)
  ((2 6) 'b)
  ((3 4) 'c)
  (else 'd))
```

This expression returns the symbol c. The top expression evaluates to 4; this matches an element in the selector of the third clause; and the value of the consequent in that clause is returned.

Rewrite the atomic-weight procedure that we saw earlier in the chapter, using case instead of cond.

18. Write a procedure atoms-in-molecule that takes as argument a molecular formula of the kind we used earlier and returns the number of atoms in the given formula. Here are some examples of the procedure in action:

```
(atoms-in-molecule '(C 0 2))
3

(atoms-in-molecule '((C H 3) 2 C H 0 H))
12
```

Note that your procedure should work on "multilevel" formulae as in the second example above.

19. Investigate the behavior of the primitives member, memq, and memv. Check the definitions of these procedures in the Scheme manual. How do they differ?

20. Why is quote a special form?

21. The DNA molecule constitutes a kind of "code" for proteins. Each DNA molecule (really, each half of the molecule) is a long sequence of the bases adenine (A), thymine (T), guanine (G), and cytosine (C). Thus, a DNA molecule might be expressed as a list:

```
(C A G A G T G G A A T A . . . )
```

This molecule consists of a cytosine base, followed by an adenine base, followed by a guanine base, and so on.

Each sequence of three bases codes for a particular amino acid. For instance, the sequence (C A G) codes for leucine, while (A G T) codes for threonine. Thus, the protein coded by the DNA molecule above has amino acid leucine followed by threonine, and so on.

Develop a program for translating DNA molecules, expressed as lists of bases, into protein molecules expressed as lists of amino acids. You can find a complete description of how DNA codes for proteins in any standard undergraduate biology text.

22. Write a program for generating simple sentences. Your program might create random sentences of the form:

"article—subject-noun—verb—article—object-noun"

by selecting choices from lists of possible nouns, verbs, and articles. Thus, a session with your program might look as follows:

```
(make-random-sentence)
(the cow kicked the computer)

(make-random-sentence)
(a horse saw the cow)

(make-random-sentence)
(the computer kicked a person)
```

You could elaborate on this program. How might adjectives or adverbs be included? Can you restrict the choices of nouns and verbs so that the sentences make more sense, or focus on some topic?

23. A matrix is a two-dimensional array of numbers, as in the following example:

$$\begin{pmatrix} 1 & 3 & 4 \\ 2 & 3 & 6 \\ 4 & 5 & 7 \end{pmatrix}$$

Matrices might be represented in Scheme as a list of sublists, where each sublist represents a row. For instance, the following Scheme list could represent the matrix shown above:

```
((1 3 4) (2 3 6) (4 5 7))
```

Investigate the subject of matrices[6] and write a program using the suggested representation (or some other, if you prefer) to perform matrix operations.

24. Many programming languages—Scheme included—include an object type known as *strings*. Strings are text objects, and we use them in many cases when we want to work with textual material, as for word-processing applications. In Scheme, strings are surrounded by double quotes. We have in fact already seen these objects as arguments to the display primitive:

```
(display "This is a string")
```

Here, the argument to display is the string object "This is a string".

Because symbols, like strings, have a "textual" quality, students of Scheme (especially those with previous experience in other languages) often confuse symbols and strings. However, they are *not* the same type of object. If something is a string it is not a symbol, and vice versa.

It should be stated, though, that the "real" differences between strings and symbols—i.e., whether these two types of objects embody some deep philosophical division—is a matter of some debate. To some extent, the distinction between strings and symbols is a matter of common usage. Strings, as noted above, are typically used for purposes like displaying messages and doing word processing (e.g., a form-letter-writing program would probably use strings as data objects). Symbols, on the other hand, are distinguished in that the process of comparing them for equality (via the eq? primitive) happens to be very fast and efficient.

We will not spend a lot of time on string objects in this book. However, this would not be a bad time for you to begin investigating the subject on your own. As a start, you might experiment with the string? primitive, which takes one argument and returns #t if that argument is a string object and #f otherwise:

```
(string? "a")
#t

(string? 'a)
()
```

You might also play with the string=? primitive, which takes two string arguments and returns #t if the two strings contain the same characters:

```
(string=? "ab" "ab")
#t

(string=? "ab" "ac")
()
```

---

[6]Serge Lang's book *Introduction to Linear Algebra* (Springer-Verlag, 1986) provides a good introduction.

Using these two primitive predicates, you can rewrite the molecular weight program in this chapter so that it works with lists of numbers and strings, rather than lists of numbers and symbols:

```
(molecular-weight '("Na" "Cl"))
58.4428

(molecular-weight '(("C" "H" 3) 2 "C" "H" "O" "H"))
60.0956
```

This example is provided to help you get your feet wet, but you should snoop around for string primitives in your Scheme system's manual and make up some projects for yourself. The subject of strings will also be briefly revived in Chapter 13, Exercise 21, and in Chapter 16, Exercise 22.

25. One of the interesting features of Scheme (and Lisp in general) is that compound expressions are simply lists. We will return to this topic in Chapter 16, but for now you might enjoy pondering the following examples. See if you can predict what values these expressions will return; then type them in at the interpreter to see if your predictions were correct.

```
(car (list 1 2 3))

(car '(list 1 2 3))

(list (car (+ 2 3)))

(list (car '(+ 2 3)))

(list '(car (+ 2 3)))

(list '(car '(+ 2 3)))
```

The key point in all of this is that under certain circumstances the expression (+ 2 3) may be viewed as something for the interpreter to evaluate; while under other circumstances it may be viewed as a list of three elements— namely, the symbol + and the two numbers 2 and 3.

Subprocedures

Imagine that you're working along on a Scheme program, and at some point you decide to enter the editor so that you can examine your program. In the editor, you are faced with, let's say, forty or fifty procedures. How do you know which procedures are currently working and which are obsolete? Or which procedures are definitely debugged, and which are still tentative? Or which procedures are subsidiary to others (i.e., which are viewed as "helper" procedures for others)?

Scheme programs are collections—sometimes, large collections—of procedures. And you've probably noticed that as your programs become larger and larger, it becomes increasingly important to maintain some kind of organization in your Scheme code. Several techniques for this purpose were mentioned earlier, in our discussion of debugging. In this chapter we will examine yet another organizational stratagem: the use of subprocedures. Subprocedures certainly don't solve all our problems—in particular, they apply mainly to the last of the three questions in the paragraph above. Nevertheless, subprocedures represent a tremendously useful addition to our arsenal of programming skills.

"Top-Level" and "Helper" Procedures

Think back to the blissful, simple days of Chapter 2. One of the first programs that we looked at was composed of two procedures, roulette-wheel and compare-with-bet:

```
(define (roulette-wheel number-to-bet)
  (compare-with-bet (random 37) number-to-bet))

(define (compare-with-bet wheel-spin bet)
  (if (= wheel-spin bet)
      (display "You won! ")
      (display "You lost! "))
  wheel-spin)
```

The point of this program, as you may recall, was that we could call roulette-wheel from the interpreter; the number argument to roulette-wheel represents the bet for one particular spin.

The reason I am resurrecting this program now is to point out a fairly obvious structural relationship between the two procedures. If we view procedures as occupying a sort of hierarchy based on "who calls whom," then roulette–wheel is a "top-level" procedure; it calls compare–with–bet, but not vice versa. Similarly, we can view compare–with–bet as a subsidiary, "helper" procedure specifically written to work for roulette–wheel. And moreover, as users of the program, we intend to work only at the top level; that is, we intend to call roulette–wheel, not compare–with–bet. Thus, roulette–wheel is the only procedure that prospective users need to be told about.

All this is true enough, you might say, but how often does such a clearcut structural relationship exist between procedures? The answer, as it turns out, is "pretty often." Consider the tail recursive factorial procedure presented as factorial-B in Chapter 5, and shown here with the name factorial:

```
(define (factorial number)
  (fact-helper number 1))

(define (fact-helper count result)
  (cond ((= count 0) result)
        (else (fact-helper (-1+ count) (* count result)))))
```

Once more, one procedure is subsidiary to the other; their relationship is openly indicated by their names. And again, as users of this program, we never intend to call fact-helper; the only procedure we care about is the top-level factorial procedure.

It wouldn't be hard to find more examples of this sort of hierarchical structure among the programs we saw in earlier chapters. The roulette–wheel and factorial examples, however, should serve to convey the general idea.

Subprocedures: A First Look

Before going on to any of the formal rules regarding subprocedures, let's get an overall impression of how they look. Here, then, are the two programs above, rewritten to use subprocedures:

```
(define (roulette-wheel number-to-bet)
  (define (compare-with-bet wheel-spin bet)
    (if (= wheel-spin bet)
        (display "You won! ")
        (display "You lost! "))
    wheel-spin)
  (compare-with-bet (random 37) number-to-bet))

(define (factorial number)
  (define (fact-helper count result)
    (cond ((= count 0) result)
          (else (fact-helper (-1+ count) (* count result)))))
  (fact-helper number 1))
```

The common pattern to these two procedures is straightforward. In each case, the body of the new procedure begins with a define expression—an *internal definition*—and then the remainder of the procedure body uses the internally-defined procedure as in our earlier versions. In essence, we have placed the definition of the "helper" procedure inside the "top-level" one.

Writing Multi-Level Procedures

If you want to write a procedure with internal definitions, those definitions must be the first expressions in the procedure body. The following examples, therefore, are wrong:

```
(define (factorial number)
  (fact-helper number 1)
  (define (fact-helper count result)
    (cond ((= count 0) result)
          (else (fact-helper (-1+ count) (* count result))))))

(define (factorial number)
  (display "The factorial is: ")
  (define (fact-helper count result)
    (cond ((= count 0) result)
          (else (fact-helper (-1+ count)(* count result)))))
  (fact-helper number 1))
```

In the first example, we have simply reversed the order of the call to fact-helper and the internal definition. In the second example, the display expression precedes the internal definition. Neither of these will work. (Try it if you don't believe me; in fact, try it even if you *do* believe me!)

Subprocedures may contain their own subprocedures, and so on. Thus, you can (in principle, anyway) write "deeply nested" procedures with many levels of subprocedures. Let's try an example: as it happens, the number of ways of choosing *k* items from a larger group of *n* items is

$$\frac{n!}{k! \times (n-k)!}$$

To take one instance, the number of different 5-card poker hands is

$$\frac{52!}{5! \times 47!}$$

So, here is a procedure that takes arguments n and k and returns the number of ways of choosing k items from a set of n:

```
(define (n-choose-k n k)
  (define (factorial number)
    (define (fact-helper count result)
      (cond ((= count 0) result)
            (else (fact-helper (-1+ count) (* count result)))))
    (fact-helper number 1))
  (/ (factorial n)(* (factorial k)(factorial (- n k)))))
```

In practice, Scheme programmers rarely nest subprocedures to a depth of more than two or three. For one thing, we start to run up against bothersome limitations like the width of the monitor screen: it becomes difficult to write procedures when every expression begins very far to the right of the screen and thus must be broken over two or more lines. Also, deeply nested procedures can be hard to read: one has to keep track of which "level" of code one is presently reading. For two- or three-level procedures, this isn't so bad, but for five- or six-level procedures it could start to be confusing.

There is another reason that the specific n-choose-k example above is a little unlikely; we'll get to that a little later in this chapter.

Blocks

Intuitively, the point of subprocedures is fairly clear: they are subsidiary procedures that are defined at the beginning of the body of a top-level procedure. There are, however, more observations to make about this subject.

Subprocedures can be called inside the procedure where their definition appears (and inside any more deeply nested procedure), but not outside. For instance, consider our factorial procedure:

```
(define (factorial number)
  (define (fact-helper count result)
    (cond ((= count 0) result)
          (else (fact-helper (-1+ count) (* count result)))))
  (fact-helper number 1))
```

You will notice that fact-helper is called within the body of factorial (in the final expression), and in the body of fact-helper itself. However, we could not call fact-helper from the interpreter, nor could we call it from some newly-defined procedure. Another way of phrasing this is to say that the procedure fact-helper is local to the body of factorial.

What we are touching on here is the subject of *scoping*. Scheme is what is called a *lexically scoped* language. We'll see a more formal definition of that term a little later, but right now we can use a graphical illustration of the idea. Imagine that each procedure definition sets up a "block"—a sort of barrier—that extends from the beginning of the define expression to the end. Within this block, other procedures may be defined; these definitions set up their own blocks internal to the larger one. Figure 9.1 shows an example: here, block 1 has two sub-blocks, 2 and 4; and block 2 has one sub-block, block 3.

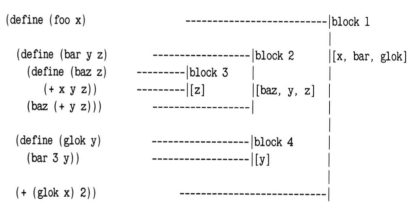

Figure 9.1. A Scheme program with "block" outlines drawn.
The names in brackets are those variable names whose bindings occur within the given block.

The point of all these barriers is simply to get at the following rule: any name first bound within a block may be used inside that block's boundaries, but not outside it. Thus, names bound within block 1 may be used in blocks 1, 2, 3, and 4; names bound within block 2 may be used in blocks 2 and 3; names bound within block 3 may be used only in block 3; and names bound within block 4 may be used only within block 4.

Now, when a procedure definition occurs within some block, the name of that procedure is bound within the block. Thus, the names bar and glok are bound within block 1; the name baz is bound within block 2. From the preceding paragraph, we conclude that the bar procedure, to take one example, can be called anywhere in blocks 1, 2, 3, and 4 (but not outside block 1).

The name of the outer procedure, foo, is said to be *globally* bound: we can use the foo procedure from the interpreter or from inside any other procedure. You can think of the area surrounding the entire definition as one big "global block." The global block is subject to the same rules as all other blocks; names bound within it, like foo, may be used anywhere inside it. The only special property of the global block is that it is the biggest one around: it is not a sub-block of any other.

The rules that dictate where procedure names can be used also dictate where argument names can be used. Procedure arguments are bound in the block associated with the procedure definition. Thus, the name x is bound in block 1; y and z are bound in block 2; z is bound in block 3; and y is bound in block 4. You have no doubt noticed that there is something a little funny here in that y and z are bound separately in two blocks; we'll get to that. In the meantime, we can note that the name x can be used inside blocks 1, 2, 3, and 4, consistent with the rules we have seen so far.

There is really no problem with the name y in this example. Since blocks 2 and 4 are mutually exclusive, the only possible binding for y in block 2 is the one associated with block 2; that is, inside block 2 we could not refer to names bound in block 4.

What about z? The rule here is that, should more than one apparent binding exist for a name, the value to which that name is bound is taken from the most local binding. Thus, inside block 3, we use the binding for z associated with the baz procedure; inside block 2, we use the binding associated with the bar procedure.[1]

Lexical Scoping

Now, where does the name "lexical scoping" come from? The *scope* of a name is that area of the program text in which the name's binding is in effect. Thus, we say that the scope of bar in Figure 9.1 is the interior of block 1. The term *lexical* means that we can always find the scope of a name simply by looking at the text of the program itself. That is, to find the scope of the name x in Figure 9.1, we note the block boundary of the definition in which x occurs.

The lexical scoping discipline has some subtle implications. Consider the following example:

```
(define (proc-1 x)
  (define (proc-2 y)
    (+ x y))
  (define (proc-3 x)
    (proc-2 (* 2 x)))
  (proc-3 (1+ x)))
```

Now suppose we call proc-1 with an argument of 4. This will result in a call to proc-3 with an argument of 5, which results in a call to proc-2 with an argument of 10. So far, so good. But now we observe that the body of proc-2 uses the name x. Which value of x should we use: the one associated with the argument for proc-1—that is, the binding of the surrounding block—or the one associated with the argument for proc-3—that is, the binding of the procedure which called proc-2?

The answer is that we use the binding associated with the surrounding block: for this call to proc-2, the name x is bound to 4. This is entirely consistent with the scoping rules outlined above, but it nonetheless requires a little additional thought. In terms of our actor model from Chapter 5, we might say that if there are names in a procedure "script" that are not argument names (like x in proc-2), then the actor hired to perform the script will have to find the binding of those names by looking at the larger script inside which his own script was written. Thus, the

[1] A brief terminology note: you may recall that in Chapter 1, I touted Scheme as having the desirable feature of *block structure*. This indicates that Scheme programs are arranged in nested blocks of the kind we have just explored. The term is historically associated with the programming language Algol 60, which uses similar name-binding rules and which also structures its programs in nested blocks. Other languages employing block structure (besides Scheme) include those in the "Algol family"—notably, Pascal.

actor hired to perform the script will have to find the binding of those names by looking at the larger script inside which his own script was written. Thus, the actor hired to perform proc-2 must find the binding for x by looking at the value for x in the script for proc-1, and *not* the script for proc-3 (even though he was hired by the proc-3 actor).

Actually, we can illustrate the same principle without using subprocedures in our example. Consider:

```
(define a 10)
(define (proc-4 b)
  (+ a b))
(define (proc-5 a)
  (proc-4 a))
```

You should be able to convince yourself that evaluating (proc-5 2) from the Scheme interpreter will return 12: the value of a in the body of proc-4 is derived from the surrounding (global) block, not from the value of a in the procedure (proc-5) that hired proc-4.

The Pragmatics of Subprocedures

There are trade-offs associated with most decisions in life, and the decision to use subprocedures is no exception. When we rewrote factorial to use fact-helper as a subprocedure rather than as a separate procedure, we lost the ability to call fact-helper directly from the interpreter, since the name fact-helper in our newer version is bound only inside the factorial block. This is no great loss, of course: we were unlikely to call fact-helper directly in the first place. It might even be seen as an advantage to have one less "global name" to think about.

On the other hand, in our n-choose-k example, you might recall that the factorial procedure was written as a subprocedure to n-choose-k, rather than as a separate procedure. In most circumstances, this wouldn't be a very good decision: we might very well want to use the factorial procedure ourselves, calling it from the interpreter. And we might want to write other procedures that can use factorial as well. So making factorial the "private property" of n-choose-k will probably cause more trouble than it's worth.

There are other trade-offs besides. Subprocedures are used mainly to improve the organization and readability of programs. If some other programmer comes upon the code for the factorial procedure and sees the fact-helper subprocedure, she will immediately see how the program is structured: fact-helper is a subsidiary procedure for factorial. But as noted before, if some procedure has ten levels of nested subprocedures, it might be difficult for that other programmer to read the code and keep track of the level being examined. So although subprocedures can enhance program readability up to a point, they can also detract from it if over-used. Like many other aspects of programming, the notion of "proper use of subprocedures" is not a timeless, universal one, but is rather a matter of common practice and cultural acceptance.

Exercises

1. Rewrite the circle^2 program of Chapter 7 so that it uses subprocedures wherever you think sensible.

2. Consider the following unbelievably arcane procedure:

```
(define (foo x y)
  (define (bar x)
    (+ x x))
  (define (baz y)
    (+ y x))
  (define (blat x z)
    (- z x))
  (+ (bar y) (baz 3) (blat y x)))
```

What is the result of calling (foo 1 2)?

3. One advantage of using subprocedures that was not mentioned in this chapter is that by making a "helper" procedure a subprocedure, one can often eliminate redundant arguments in the subprocedure. An example should make this clear. Consider the rewritten roulette–wheel procedure shown earlier:

```
(define (roulette-wheel number-to-bet)
  (define (compare-with-bet wheel-spin bet)
    (if (= wheel-spin bet)
        (display "You won! ")
        (display "You lost! "))
    wheel-spin)
  (compare-with-bet (random 37) number-to-bet))
```

Here, we simply took our original "helper" procedure compare–with–bet, and made it a subprocedure of roulette–wheel. But now, the argument bet is no longer necessary in compare–with–bet, since the value of bet will always be just the same as the value of number–to–bet in the surrounding roulette–wheel procedure. So we can rewrite our code as follows:

```
(define (roulette-wheel number-to-bet)
  (define (compare-with-bet wheel-spin)
    (if (= wheel-spin number-to-bet)
        (display "You won! ")
        (display "You lost! "))
    wheel-spin)
  (compare-with-bet (random 37)))
```

Note that compare–with–bet uses the name number–to–bet in its body; the value of number–to–bet will be taken from its value in the call to roulette–wheel.

Your task is to rewrite the following program:

```
(define (factorial no)
  (fact-helper 0 1 no))

(define (fact-helper count result limit)
  (cond ((= count limit) result)
        (else (fact-helper (1+ count)
                           (* (1+ count) result)
                           limit))))
```

Make fact–helper a subprocedure of factorial and then rewrite fact–helper so that it takes fewer arguments than before.

CHAPTER 10

Sample Projects III

In the very early days of computers (the 1950s or thereabouts), the conventional wisdom was that these new machines were good at "number crunching," but not much more. According to one writer, Paul Ceruzzi, "the computer pioneers understood the concept of the computer as a general-purpose machine, but only in the narrow sense of its ability to solve a wide range of mathematical problems."[1] Time has revealed this point of view to be a little embarrassing in retrospect. However one chooses to describe computers—as "symbol manipulators" or "information processors" or whatever[2]—they are certainly much more than high-speed arithmetic machines. And now that we have made the acquaintance of objects like symbols and pairs, our programming activities can branch out into a variety of nonmathematical topics.

In this chapter, our sample project will be a simple conversational program in the mold of many early artificial intelligence (AI) efforts. Although not profound, it should provide good experience in working with lists as data structures; and it might suggest more elaborate projects for you to try on your own. Later in the book, in Chapter 15, we will attempt a more ambitious symbol-manipulation example—one that illustrates the notions of "pattern matching" and "rule-based inference" characterizing more recent work in expert systems.

Who's on First?

One of the more famous AI demos of early years was Joseph Weizenbaum's ELIZA program, which was able to hold "conversations" with its user in the manner of a psychiatrist interviewing a patient.[3] Although the program appeared to be participating in meaningful dialogue—responding as a psychiatrist might—it was in point of fact looking only at very superficial aspects of the user's input. For instance, if the user were to type in the sentence "I am feeling depressed today" the

---

[1] From P. Ceruzzi, "An Unforeseen Revolution: Computers and Expectations, 1935–1985" in *Imagining Tomorrow*, J. Corn, ed., MIT Press, 1986.

[2] The best description that I have heard for computers is that they are "telescopes for the complex."

[3] A brief account of the program is provided in Weizenbaum's book *Computer Power and Human Reason*, W. H. Freeman, 1976.

program might answer, "*You say you are feeling depressed today.*" All that ELIZA did in this instance is change a first-person sentence to second person and repeat it; but the effect is deceptively impressive.

Ours will be a similar conversational program, though more restricted in scope. We will create a program that participates in the classic Abbott and Costello routine "Who's on First?": the computer will play the role of Bud Abbott, and the user will play Lou Costello.[4] For those young people in the audience who have never seen the routine, it begins something like this:

> *Costello*: Hey, Bud, now that we're at the ballgame, tell me the names of the guys on our team.
>
> *Abbott*: Who's on first, What's on second, I Don't Know on third.
>
> *Costello*: Who's on first?
>
> *Abbott*: Right.
>
> *Costello*: Who?
>
> *Abbott*: Yes.
>
> *Costello*: What's the name of the first baseman?
>
> *Abbott*: What's the name of the second baseman.
>
> *Costello*: I don't know!
>
> *Abbott*: He's on third . . .

Our Scheme program will work pretty much the same way (though we will not employ any punctuation, and all sentences will be written as lists of symbols). Let's pick up the bit from where we left off above:

```
(whos on third)
(no whos on first)

(whats his name)
(hes on second)

(who is)
(hes on first)

(hey abbott)
(now calm down)
```

Note that our program will follow the general outline of the routine—it does not use a complete script. Thus, the user does not have to memorize Costello's lines, but only has to know, roughly, the sort of things that Costello might say. And of course, each time we work with the program, the performance may go somewhat differently.

Starting Out: Some Useful List Procedures

Before getting to the heart of our program, we can start by creating some handy list-manipulating procedures. The eventual role of these procedures will not be apparent just now, but they will prove useful later on.

Our first procedure is named select-any-from-list; its purpose is to select a random element from a list. That is, we would like select-any-from-list to work as in the following examples:

```
(select-any-from-list '(a b c d))
b
```

---

[4]Special thanks to Seth Haberman, author of the original "Who's on First?" program, for kindly allowing me to use his idea.

```
(select-any-from-list '(a b c d))
```
d
```
(select-any-from-list '((1) 2 (3 4) 5 (6)))
```
(1)

Here is one version of select-any-from-list:

```
(define (select-any-from-list lis)
  (let ((length-of-list (length lis)))
    (list-ref lis (random length-of-list))))
```

Our procedure uses two potentially unfamiliar Scheme primitives: length and list-ref. Length takes a list as argument and returns the number of elements in the list (we wrote our own version, in fact, in Chapter 8). List-ref takes two arguments, a list and a nonnegative integer *n*, and returns the *n*th element of the list counting from 0 upward (that is, the "0th" element is the car of the list). The strategy of select-any-from-list is thus to find the length of the given list; use this number *n* as the argument to random; and use the resulting number (anything from 0 to *n* − 1) as the second argument to list-ref in order to select a random element from the given list.

Let's go on. We need a predicate procedure that takes two arguments—a sentence fragment and a sentence—and returns #t if the fragment occurs in the sentence. Here are some sample calls to our procedure (which we will call fragment-of?):

```
(fragment-of? '(their names) '(just tell me their names))
```
#t
```
(fragment-of? '(first base) '(whos the first baseman))
```
()

The following procedure should do the job:

```
(define (fragment-of? fragment sentence)
  (cond ((null? sentence) #f)  ;fragment is not empty but sentence is
        ((eq? (car fragment)(car sentence))
         (or (starting-part? fragment sentence)
             (fragment-of? fragment (cdr sentence))))
        (else (fragment-of? fragment (cdr sentence)))))
(define (starting-part? fragment sentence)
  (cond ((null? fragment) #t)
        ((null? sentence) #f)
        ((eq? (car fragment) (car sentence))
         (starting-part? (cdr fragment)(cdr sentence)))
        (else #f)))
```

Expressed in prose, the strategy of fragment-of? is as follows: if the sentence is the empty list (), then obviously the fragment (which is never the empty list) cannot be contained in the sentence. Now, suppose the fragment and sentence begin with the same symbol. Then our procedure should return #t if the sentence in fact begins with the fragment, or if the fragment is contained later in the sentence. Finally, if the fragment and sentence do not start off the same way, then we check to see whether the fragment is contained later on in the sentence.

Doing a similar analysis of the starting-part? procedure is left to the reader.

As it turns out, we are going to use fragment-of? as a "helper" to a top-level procedure that takes as argument a sentence and a list of fragments, and checks to see whether any of the fragments are contained in the sentence. Here is the top-level procedure, any-good-fragments?:

```
(define (any-good-fragments? list-of-fragments sentence)
  (cond ((null? list-of-fragments) #f)
        ((fragment-of? (car list-of-fragments) sentence)
         #t)
        (else (any-good-fragments? (cdr list-of-fragments)
                                   sentence))))
```

Here are a couple of examples of any-good-fragments? at work:

```
(any-good-fragments? '((what) (whats)) '(whats his name))
#t
(any-good-fragments? '((who is) (who) (whos)) '(i dont know))
()
```

Since both fragment-of? and starting-part? will be used only as helpers to any-good-fragments?, it might be a good idea to rewrite what we've done, changing the former two predicates into subprocedures of the top-level predicate.

Overall Strategy: The Top-Level Loop

Our program will be structured as a tail recursive loop:

1. Read in Costello's line.
2. Examine it and reply to it appropriately.
3. Go back to step 1.

Thus, a very rough outline of our program would look as follows:

```
(define (whos-on-first-loop)
  (let ((costello (read)))
    ‹ make some sort of reply ›
    (whos-on-first-loop)))
```

The read primitive, when applied to no arguments, causes the Scheme interpreter to wait until the user has typed in a Scheme expression (usually a symbol or list), and returns that object. (You should try it now to familiarize yourself with how it works.) Thus, every time whos-on-first-loop is called with no arguments, it will read in the user's next line, bind the name costello to the read-in expression, and then execute the (as yet unspecified) body of the let statement with that binding in effect.

Now, how should our program decide on an appropriate reply? The idea is that "Abbott" will first look for strong cues—cues that tell him to respond in a specific way. For instance, if Costello (you) types in (i dont know), Abbott will always respond with either (third base) or (hes on third).

Suppose that there are no strong cues in Costello's input. In that case, Abbott will look for weaker cues; the response to these weaker cues depends on the particular surrounding context of the dialogue. For instance, if Costello says (whats his name), then Abbott will respond with some affirmative—like (right)—if we are talking about second base, and with something like (hes on second) if we are talking about anything else.

If Costello's input contains neither strong nor weak cues, Abbott will simply hedge with a response like (now calm down) or (but you asked).

Finally, Abbott will also check whether Costello is trying to end the performance with a standard "closer."

Here, then, is the top-level loop of our program:

```
(define (whos-on-first-loop old-context)
  (let ((costello (read)))
    (let ((new-context (get-context costello old-context)))
      (let ((strong (try-strong-cues costello))
            (weak (try-weak-cues costello new-context)))
        (cond ((not (null? strong))
               (writeln strong)
               (whos-on-first-loop (get-context strong new-context)))
              ((not (null? weak))
               (writeln weak)
               (whos-on-first-loop (get-context weak new-context)))
              ((wants-to-end? costello) (wrap-it-up))
              (else (writeln (hedge))
                    (whos-on-first-loop new-context)))))))
```

In the procedure above, we are using (as yet unwritten) procedures named try-strong-cues and try-weak-cues. These procedures should return a possible response if Costello's input contains an appropriate cue, and the empty list () otherwise. The predicate wants-to-end? returns #t if Costello's line is a closer, and #f otherwise; the wrap-it-up procedure will finish the performance in response to a closing cue from Costello. Finally, the hedge procedure will simply select from a list of possible hedges.

You will also note that our new whos-on-first-loop procedure takes a "context" argument. This is, roughly, the most recent context of the conversation (e.g., "first base" or "second base"). Keeping track of the current context is necessary because the possible responses provided by try-weak-cues will depend on context. The get-context procedure, which is used several times within the body of whos-on-first-loop, takes as its arguments a sentence and a previous context, and returns a new context (if any); that is, get-context is employed to see if its first argument, the new sentence in the conversation, has changed the context.

All this discussion no doubt seems abstruse. The best way to deal with the confusion for now is to forget about it. Go on and examine how the program is built, step by step; then, from time to time, come back to this section and reexamine the top-level procedure and the exposition of the previous two paragraphs.

Hedging and Strong Cues

Let's write the easiest procedure—the hedge procedure—first. We will need a list of possible hedges:

```
(define *hedges*
  '((its like im telling you)
    (now calm down)
    (take it easy)
    (its simple lou)
    (im trying to tell you)
    (but you asked)))
```

Then the hedge procedure will be:

```
(define (hedge)
  (select-any-from-list *hedges*))
```

Calling hedge on no arguments returns one of the sentences inside the list *hedges*, chosen at random.

Now let's write the portion of the program that deals with strong cues. We will create another large list like *hedges*, but this one will be more complicated. Each element in the list (which we'll call *strong-cues*) will itself contain two lists: a "cue-part" that includes a bunch of synonymous strong cues to look for, and a "response-part" that includes a bunch of synonymous replies to select from. For instance, here is one element in *strong-cues*:

```
(((suppose) (lets say))
 ((okay) (why not) (it could happen)))
```

This element indicates that if Costello's sentence includes the words "suppose" or "let's say," then Abbott will always respond with either "okay," "why not," or "it could happen." Thus, if we type in the sentence

```
(suppose i throw the ball to first)
```

Abbott might respond (okay).

Here is the list *strong-cues*:

```
(define *strong-cues*
  '(
    (((the names) (their names))
     ((whos on first whats on second i dont know on third)))
    (((suppose) (lets say))
     ((okay) (why not) (it could happen)))
    (((i dont know))
     ((third base) (hes on third)))
  ))
```

Now we are ready to write the try-strong-cues procedure. As you may recall, this procedure takes as argument Costello's sentence and returns a possible response if the sentence contains a strong cue, or () if it doesn't.

```
(define (try-strong-cues costello)
  (define (strong-helper cue-list)
    (cond ((null? cue-list) '())
          ((any-good-fragments?
             (cue-part (first-element cue-list))
             costello)
           (select-any-from-list
             (response-part (first-element cue-list))))
          (else (strong-helper (rest-elements cue-list)))))
  (strong-helper *strong-cues*))
```

The try-strong-cues procedure defines a big subprocedure, strong-helper, and then calls it with argument *strong-cues*. Let's run through the strategy of strong-helper to see how it works. The point of strong-helper is to look at each cue-response element in *strong-cues* and see whether any of the cues are contained in Costello's sentence; if so, strong-helper returns one of the appropriate responses. The first clause of the cond expression in strong-helper is the "base case" check: if the giant list of cue-response elements is empty, then we return (). Otherwise, we look at the "cue" portion of the first element and check all its fragments against Costello's sentence; if we find a match, we return one of the possible responses in the first element. If no match is found, though, we recursively call strong-helper with the remainder of the giant list.

The `strong-helper` procedure makes use of several *selector* procedures, like `first-element` and `cue-part`. These are procedures that retrieve a specific portion of a larger data structure. For instance, the `first-element` procedure takes a giant cue-list as argument and returns the first cue-response element in that list. Here are the procedures that we need:

```
(define (first-element cue-list) (car cue-list))

(define (rest-elements cue-list) (cdr cue-list))

(define (cue-part strong-cue-list-element)
  (car strong-cue-list-element))

(define (response-part strong-cue-list-element)
  (cadr strong-cue-list-element))
```

Making Context-Specific Responses

We're not quite done yet: we still have to implement the weak cue portion of our program. In this case, we will need a still more complicated data structure that allows for different responses to Costello's cues depending on the current context of conversation. The list *weak-cues* below represents one possible approach. Each element in the list *weak-cues* is composed of a list of cues followed by "context-response" lists. Each of these "context-response" lists contains a list of contexts followed by a list of possible context-dependent responses. Before describing the data structure any further, I will present it:

```
(define *weak-cues*
  '(
    (((who) (whos) (who is))
     ((first-base)
        ((thats right) (exactly) (yes) (right)
         (perfect) (now youve got it)))
     ((third-base second-base)
        ((no whos on first) (whos on first) (first base))))

    (((whats the name))
     ((first-base third-base)
        ((no whats the name of the guy on second)
         (whats the name of the second baseman)))
     ((second-base)
        ((now youre talking) (you got it))))

    (((what) (whats) (what is))
     ((first-base third-base)
        ((hes on second) (i told you whats on second)))
     ((second-base)
        ((right) (sure) (you got it lou))))
    ))
```

To take an example: the last element in *weak-cues* shows the possible responses to sentences containing one of the phrases "what," "what's," or "what is." If we are currently talking about first or third base, Abbott will respond with either "He's on second," or "I told you, What's on second." If we are talking about second base, however, Abbott will respond with some affirmative like "Right."

The `try-weak-cues` procedure will use the *weak-cues* data structure to find a possible response:

```
(define (try-weak-cues costello context)
  (define (weak-helper weak-list)
    (cond ((null? weak-list) '())
          ((any-good-fragments?
             (cue-part (first-element weak-list))
             costello)
           (let ((possible-response
                   (try-to-respond
                     context
                     (context-response-part
                       (first-element weak-list)))))
             (if (null? possible-response)
                 (weak-helper (rest-elements weak-list))
                 possible-response)))
          (else (weak-helper (rest-elements weak-list)))))
  (define (try-to-respond current-context context-response-list)
    (cond ((null? context-response-list) '())
          ((memv current-context
                 (context-part
                   (first-element context-response-list)))
           (select-any-from-list
             (weak-response-part
               (first-element context-response-list))))
          (else (try-to-respond
                  current-context
                  (rest-elements context-response-list)))))
  (weak-helper *weak-cues*))
```

Try-weak-cues defines two subprocedures and then calls one of them—weak-helper—with the argument *weak-cues*. Let's go through the weak-helper subprocedure's strategy, in words: if there are no more elements in the giant list, we are done. Otherwise, we look at the first element and see if there are any weak cues in Costello's input. If so, we call try-to-respond which will return a possible response if the current context is one of the available choices (like first-base, second-base, etc.) or () otherwise. If try-to-respond can't find an available response, we recursively call weak-helper with the remaining elements in the giant list, just in case there are other weak cues present in Costello's input. Finally, if there were no cues from the first element present in Costello's input, then we recursively call weak-helper.

The only unfamiliar feature of the try-to-respond subprocedure is that it uses the memv primitive, which takes two arguments: any Scheme object and a list. The result of calling memv is #f if the object is not eqv? to any elements in the list; if, however, the object is eqv? to some element in the list, then the portion of the list beginning with the matching object is returned. Informally, then, memv may be used to test whether some object is contained in a list. Memv was also mentioned, by the way, in Exercise 19 of Chapter 8; so if you didn't look at that problem before, you might want to do so now.

We still need to implement a few remaining selectors used by try-weak-cues:

```
(define (context-part contexts-and-responses)
  (car contexts-and-responses))
```

```
(define (weak-response-part contexts-and-responses)
  (cadr contexts-and-responses))
```

```
(define (context-response-part weak-list-element)
  (cdr weak-list-element))
```

And this next portion of our program, which I will leave to you to examine on your own, determnes the context of a given sentence:

```
(define *context-words*
  '(
     (((first)) first-base)
     (((second)) second-base)
     (((third)) third-base)))
(define (get-context sentence old-context)
  (define (context-helper context-list)
    (cond ((null? context-list) old-context)
          ((any-good-fragments?
             (context-words (first-element context-list))
             sentence)
           (apparent-context (first-element context-list)))
          (else (context-helper (rest-elements context-list)))))
  (context-helper *context-words*))
(define (context-words context-element)(car context-element))
(define (apparent-context context-element) (cadr context-element))
```

Finishing and Starting the Routine

We need a couple of procedures to close the routine. The closer that Abbott and Costello used went something like this:

> *Costello*: Well, I don't give a darn!
> *Abbott*: Oh, he's our shortstop.

We'll employ a similar closer:

```
(define (wants-to-end? costello)
  (equal? costello '(well i dont give a darn)))
(define (wrap-it-up)
  (writeln '(oh hes our shortstop))
  (writeln '(thank you youve been a beautiful audience)))
```

That should almost do it; we need one top-level procedure to start everything off:

```
(define (whos-on-first)
  (whos-on-first-loop '()))
```

Working with the Program

It would be criminal to do all this work writing our program and then not enjoy the final product. So here is a sample performance of the "Who's on First" routine:

```
(hey abbott now that were at the ballgame tell me the names
of the guys on our team)
```
(whos on first whats on second i dont know on third)
```
(tell me their names)
```
(whos on first whats on second i dont know on third)
```
(hold it whos on first)
```
(right)
```
(who)
```
(exactly)
```
(suppose i throw the ball to first)
```
(okay)

(who gets the ball)
(yes)

(who gets it)
(yes)

(whats the name of the guy on first)
(no whats the name of the guy on second)

(i dont know)
(third base)

Exercises

1. Add more responses to the various "Abbott response lists" scattered throughout the program; also, try adding more cue-response elements to the list *strong-cues* and more cue-context-response elements to the list *weak-cues*.

2. One potential improvement to our program would be to make Abbott's response lists change over the course of the routine. For instance, after several exchanges have taken place, the response

    (i keep telling you and telling you)

    might be included in the list of hedges. (If this response were used early in the routine, it would look inappropriate.)

    To implement the idea of "changeable responses," include a costello-count argument to the whos-on-first-loop procedure; the value of this argument should be the number of Costello's responses that have been made thus far. You can use the value of this counter to determine the variation in Abbott's response. A simple plan, for instance, is to include two lists of hedges: the first is used until Costello has made five or more responses, after which the second hedge-list is used.

3. The original "Who's on First?" routine contained a number of additional elaborations. For instance, the catcher on the team was named Today and the pitcher was named Tomorrow. Thus, the following exchange might occur:

    Costello: Okay, tell me the pitcher's name.

    Abbott: Tomorrow.

    Costello: Why won't you tell me now?

    Abbott: I'm telling you.

    Costello: Tell me his name!

    Abbott: Tomorrow.

    Add this "sub-routine" to the overall routine.

4. Suppose we wanted to make a computer play the role of Costello instead of Abbott. Do you think this would be a harder project? What about other comedy teams? Would it be possible to create a similar program for a Mike Nichols–Elaine May routine? Or a George Burns–Gracie Allen routine? What is it about the structure of certain comedy performances that makes them good or bad candidates for programming projects?

5. There are many (maybe distressingly many) types of conversations that seem to consist of large numbers of cliches with a few situation-specific elements thrown in. For instance, one could argue that all postgame football interviews sound pretty much the same:

Announcer: That was a great game you played, Joe.

Joe: Well, we knew we had to get some points on the board, and that's just what we did . . .

Announcer: Throwing four touchdown passes must please you quite a bit.

Joe: Well, that's the kind of thing that can give the whole team a boost . . .

See if you can take some "class" of conversations such as this one and write a program that will participate in those conversations. A program to represent Joe the athlete, for instance, might take as input a list of a few specific facts about the game just played, and use that list to provide a generic postgame interview.

CHAPTER 11

Environments

It's truth time. We have come a reasonable distance by employing a not-altogether-honest model of Scheme evaluation; but now, in order to go much further, we will have to take a closer look at our language.

Paradoxically, we will prepare for our forward leap by spending the bulk of this chapter reexamining things that we have already done: in particular, we will look very carefully at the heretofore deceptively simple notions of *procedure* and *definition*. Because there will be no "new" material in this chapter—in the sense that we will not be able to write any programs that we couldn't have written before—the following explanations may seem a little pedantic. Why go over things that we already know how to do? The point of our new approach will become apparent in the succeeding chapters, where we will encounter some extremely powerful programming techniques.

I should also warn you that this chapter, and the chapters that follow, are more difficult than those that you have already read. This is not meant to scare you off, or induce you to stop reading; but you should not be surprised if you find that you have to concentrate harder in reading the remainder of this book.

Suppose we type the following at the Scheme interpreter: **Bindings**

```
(define a 3)
```

As we have seen, after evaluating this expression we can treat a as another name for the number 3:

```
a
3
(+ a (* 2 a))
9
```

In technical phraseology, we have *bound* the name a to the number object 3; alternatively, we could say that we have created a *binding* between the name a and the number object 3. A binding is an association between a name (a Scheme symbol) and any other Scheme object. And the whole point of define expressions

124

is that they create bindings—when we evaluate a define expression we are associating a particular Scheme symbol with some other Scheme object. Consider the following sample expressions:

```
(define b (* 8 2))
(define c (= b 16))
(define d 'e)
(define (increment no) (1+ no))
```

The first expression above binds the name b to the number object 16. The second expression binds the name c to the boolean object #t (of course, it is important that the name b already be bound in order to evaluate this define expression). The third expression binds the name d to the symbol e; I have included this example just to make it clear that a symbol may be bound to any type of Scheme object, including some other symbol.

What about the last expression? Well, we know from experience that this is the type of define expression that we use to create new procedures. For the moment, we will simply say that the last expression binds the name increment to a procedure; but we will postpone the question of how to represent the exact thing to which the name increment is now bound. But even though this question will be put off for now, I urge you to reflect a bit on the notion that increment is a name for something in the same sense that b, c, and d are. Up until now, we have avoided looking upon procedures as "objects" like boolean or number objects; but just as b in our example above is bound to a number, so increment is bound to a procedure.

The Initial Environment

Whenever we start up our Scheme system, we are automatically provided with a bunch of "prearranged" bindings. For instance, the name + is already bound to something—a primitive procedure. Similarly, the names * and cons and exit and many, many others are also already bound. Most of these bindings concern primitive procedures; that is, in most cases the bound names correspond to our familiar collection of Scheme primitives.

As before, with our increment example, we might ask just what the name + is bound to: how is this primitive procedure to be represented? And, again, we will put this question off until a little later. For now, let's just say that names like + and cons are bound to primitive procedures (however those may be represented), just as the name b above was bound to the number 16, and increment was bound to a compound procedure.

In any case, we know that when we are typing at the Scheme interpreter there is some collection of bindings currently in effect. This collection of bindings is known as the *initial environment*. When we type an expression at the Scheme interpreter, we sometimes say that we are *evaluating this expression within the initial environment*. Immediately after our Scheme system is loaded up, the initial environment consists of all the prearranged bindings like those for +, *, and so on; and we can evaluate expressions like (* 3 (+ 2 4)) within the initial environment. By evaluating define expressions at the Scheme interpreter, we can add new bindings to the initial environment.

Let's imagine a sample session at the Scheme interpreter, just to make some of these ideas a little more concrete. Suppose we load up our Scheme system. Then if we evaluate the name a, the Scheme interpreter will respond with an error message, indicating that the name a is not bound. If we evaluate the expression (+ 2 4), the interpreter will of course respond by printing out 6. We can conclude, then, that the symbol + is currently bound in the initial environment, whereas the name a is not.

To continue our session, let's try an experiment and simply evaluate the name +. In PC Scheme, the interpreter will respond by printing out #*‹Procedure +›*. This too indicates that the symbol + is bound to something; if it were not, we would get an "unbound variable" error like the one we saw with the name a before.

We can represent the initial environment graphically as a box containing a bunch of bindings, as in Figure 11.1. The contents of the box in Figure 11.1 reveal that a variety of names are bound: the symbol +, for instance, is bound to a primitive procedure, as is the symbol cons. Figure 11.1 is not, of course, a thorough depiction of the initial environment—there are many other symbols (like *) that are bound but are not, for reasons of space, included in the diagram.

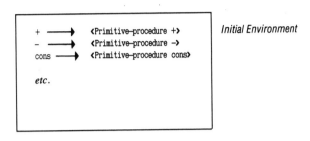

Figure 11.1. The initial environment

Now, suppose we evaluate the expression (define a 1) at the Scheme interpreter. In this case, a binding is created between the symbol a and the number object 1. The contents of the initial environment have thus been augmented, and a diagram of our new environment would look like Figure 11.2.

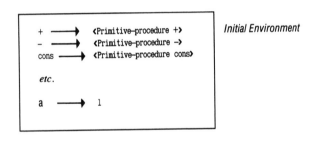

Figure 11.2. The initial environment after a is defined

Now, of course, if we evaluate the name a within the initial environment as we did before—that is, if we type a at the Scheme interpreter—then the result will be the number object 1.

As it happens, the initial environment is a particular (and in some ways special) example of a Scheme environment. The environment concept in Scheme is tremendously important, and we will turn to a discussion of that concept now.

A General Definition of Environments

The initial environment, as we have seen, is a collection of bindings. That's all that any Scheme environment is—a collection of bindings. Any name that is bound in a given environment may be evaluated in that environment. For example, in Figure 11.2 we can evaluate the name a since it is bound to 1; similarly, we can evaluate the name + since it is bound to a primitive procedure (though we've left the entire notion of "procedure" a little bit up in the air for now). So one way to think of an environment is as a "package" of usable names.

Before saying any more about the uses of environments, let's examine their structure more carefully. Thus far, the only specific example that we have looked at is the initial environment. As we continue our investigation of Scheme, however, we will encounter other environments. Figure 11.3 shows a hypothetical example.

126

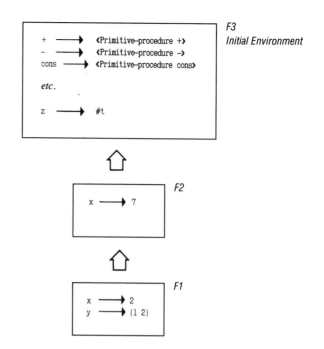

Figure 11.3. A hypothetical Scheme environment

Figure 11.3 shows three boxes (called *frames*) linked together by arrows to form a chain: frame F1 is linked to F2, which is linked to F3. All Scheme environments are structured just this way—namely, as a collection of one or more frames linked together in chainwise fashion. The initial environment, in Figure 11.2, is an even simpler example. It happens to consist of only one frame.

You may have noticed something else about Figure 11.3: the top frame is the initial environment. This is a general property—the uppermost frame of every Scheme environment is the initial environment.

Let's recap some of the ideas we have encountered thus far:

- A binding is an association between a Scheme symbol and some Scheme object (such as a number, boolean, symbol, pair, procedure, etc.).

- An environment is a collection of bindings.

- A Scheme environment is structured as a collection of frames linked together as a chain.

- The uppermost frame of every Scheme environment (i.e., the last frame in the chain) is the initial environment.

- The initial environment is the current collection of bindings that we are working with when we type expressions at the Scheme interpreter.

Environment structure is in some ways a rather subtle concept. For one thing, it must be admitted that Figure 11.3 actually depicts *three* separate environments: the one whose bottom frame is labeled F1, the one whose bottom frame is labeled F2, and the one whose bottom frame is labeled F3. The last of these is, of course, the initial environment; and the first is the environment that we have loosely identified with Figure 11.3 in our discussion thus far. The environment consisting of F2 and F3 is a perfectly good environment in its own right: it consists of a chain of two frames, where the topmost frame is the initial environment.

Another point worth noting is the difference between environments and frames. An environment is *not* a frame. An environment is rather a chain of frames. But even so, each frame is uniquely *associated* with one particular environment: namely, the environment with the given frame at the bottom. For instance, the frame F1 is not an environment, but it uniquely specifies the environment consisting of F1, F2, and F3.

Frames contain zero or more bindings. And a name is bound in an environment precisely if a binding exists in any frame of that environment. For example, in the three-frame environment of Figure 11.3, the names x, y, and z are bound, along with all the names in the initial environment. In the case of the name x we are able to find two bindings—one in F1 and one in F2. In a situation like this, where bindings for a name can be found in more than one frame, the current binding in the environment is taken from the lowest possible frame. Thus, in the three-frame environment of Figure 11.3, x is bound to 2; in the two-frame environment consisting of F2 and F3, the name x is bound to 7. You can verify for yourself that in the three-frame environment, y is bound to the list (1 2) and z is bound to #t. And you can also verify that our earlier discussion of the initial environment is consistent with the ideas we have just presented—that is, that names are bound in the initial environment precisely when they can be found in the lone frame that constitutes the initial environment.

Evaluating Expressions in Environments

So far, we have seen a fairly elaborate description of what environments *are*; but we still don't really have a good sense of what they're *for*. The brief answer is this: environments are places in which to evaluate expressions. For instance, we have mentioned that when we type in expressions at the Scheme interpreter, they are evaluated within the initial environment. Similarly, we could say of any given environment and expression that we are evaluating the expression within the environment.

In Chapters 3 and 4, we encountered a bunch of evaluation rules for Scheme. What was really going on was that we were speaking (roughly) of evaluation proceeding within the initial environment. We will be more precise about these matters very shortly, but the key point is this: *all evaluation takes place within some environment.* Expressions typed at the Scheme interpreter are evaluated in the initial environment. But in order to understand the Scheme language, we need to know how *any* expression can be evaluated in *any* environment.

Defining Things in Environments

Let's start out by reexamining what it means to evaluate a define expression. When we evaluate a define expression in an environment, we create a binding in that environment (or perhaps alter an existing binding). The new (or changed) binding appears in the lowest frame of the environment.

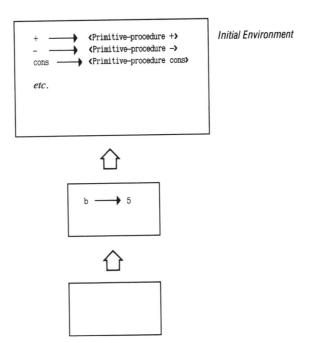

Figure 11.4. A hypothetical Scheme environment

128

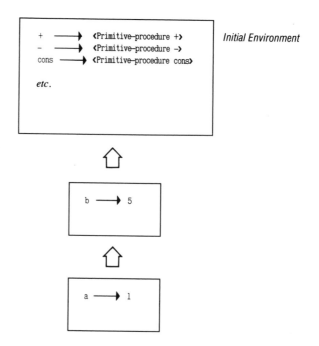

Figure 11.5. The environment after binding the symbol a

To take one example, consider the three-frame environment shown in Figure 11.4. If we evaluate the expression (define a 1) in this environment, the symbol a is now bound to the number 1, and this binding appears in the lowest frame of the environment, as in Figure 11.5. Note that the symbol a is not bound in the two-frame environment of Figure 11.5, nor in the single-frame (initial) environment, since the binding for a appears in the bottom frame only.

Now suppose we evaluate two more expressions in this environment: (define b #t) and (define a (cons 1 2)). Then the first define expression adds a new binding for b to the bottom frame, while the second expression changes the previous binding for a. The new situation is depicted in Figure 11.6.

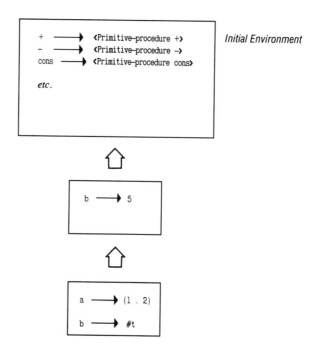

Figure 11.6. The environment after defining a and b

Now both a and b have new values in our environment, but for different reasons. In the case of a, our define expression changed the previous binding for this symbol in the lowest frame. In the case of b, there is a new binding in the lowest frame; thus, b is still bound to 5 in the two-frame environment of Figure 11.6. The symbol a, of course, remains unbound in that two-frame environment.

We have seen what it means to use define to create new bindings within environments. But an important topic still needs to be addressed: defining new procedures.

Let's return our discussion to the initial environment. Suppose we evaluate the expression

```
(define (square no)
  (* no no))
```

by typing it at the Scheme interpreter. As mentioned earlier, a define operation like this does indeed create a new binding—in this case, a binding for the symbol square. But how shall we represent the thing that square is bound to?

To answer this, I'm going to introduce a new notation to represent compound procedures. (The rationale behind this notation will become apparent only in the next section, so for the present you will just have to bear with me.) A compound procedure will be represented as a two-part *procedure object* consisting of:

(a) The text of the procedure.

(b) The environment in which the procedure was defined.

Graphically, we would represent our new square procedure as in Figure 11.7. The name square is now bound to a two-part procedure object, which we have drawn as two adjacent circles: one with an arrow pointing to the text of the procedure, and one with an arrow pointing back to the environment in which square was defined (in this case, the initial environment). The choice of circles (instead of, say, squares or diamonds or whatever) is completely arbitrary; the essential point is that the compound procedure to which the name square is now bound may be said to "know about" two things—its text and its environment.

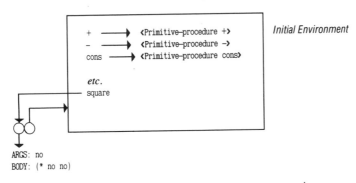

Figure 11.7. The initial environment with the square procedure

Let's continue with our square example. Figure 11.7 depicts the initial environment after the square procedure has been defined. Suppose we now type the expression (square 2) at the Scheme interpreter. How does this expression get evaluated?

Back in Chapter 3, we would have used the "Compound Procedure Rule" to answer this question. But now we will employ a new method. Our new rules for evaluating an expression like (square 2) are as follows:

Evaluating Procedure Calls

▶ *Step 1:*

First, evaluate each subexpression in the procedure call. In this case, the subexpression 2 evaluates to itself, and the name square evaluates to the thing to which it is bound—namely, the procedure object depicted in Figure 11.7.

● *Step 2:*

Create a new frame in which the argument names of the procedure are bound to the results of evaluating the operand subexpressions. Here, the result of evaluating the lone operand subexpression is the number 2, and the argument name of the square procedure is no; so we create a new frame in which the name no is bound to 2, as in Figure 11.8.

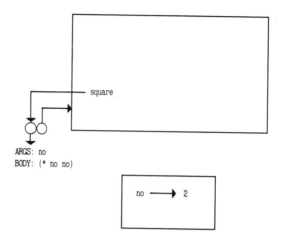

Figure 11.8. The new frame with no bound to 2

● *Step 3:*

Link this new frame to the environment pointed to by the procedure. In this case, the square procedure points to the initial environment, so we link our new frame to that environment, as in Figure 11.9. The point of this step is to create a brand new environment with our just-created frame at the bottom.

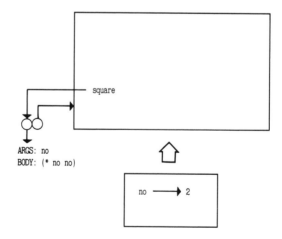

Figure 11.9. After linking the new frame to the procedure's environment

● *Step 4:*

Within the environment created by step 3, we now evaluate the body of the procedure being applied. In this case, we wish to evaluate the expression (* no no) in the environment shown in Figure 11.9. Let's go ahead and perform this step. Again, we have to evaluate each subexpression: the name no evaluates to 2, and the name * evaluates to the primitive multiplication procedure. Primitive procedures may simply be applied directly, so the result of evaluating this expression is just 4. And that completes the evaluation of the expression (square 2).

I want to call your attention to several points about the example we just completed. First, note how the two portions of the procedure object are used: the environment portion tells us where to attach the new frame, and the text portion tells us what expressions to evaluate in the newly-created environment. Second, there is again a recursive quality to these steps: in step 4, we are told to evaluate the body of a procedure in a new environment. But the body of a procedure may itself contain other procedure calls, and if that should occur then we have to employ these steps all over again. (We'll see an example of this scenario shortly.) A similar observation can be made about the very first step, since "evaluating subexpressions" may require evaluating more procedure calls, as in the expression (square (cube 3)); in this case, the second subexpression is the procedure call (cube 3).

Finally, notice that primitive procedure calls are not evaluated according to these steps: they take place directly (i.e., without creating any new frames, etc.). We will formalize this notion later on in the chapter.

Before going on, let's summarize the steps involved in evaluating a compound procedure call within some environment.

1. Evaluate each of the subexpressions in the given environment.

2. Create a new frame in which the argument names of the procedure being applied are bound to the results of evaluating the operand subexpressions.

3. Attach this new frame to the environment pointed to by the procedure being applied.

4. Within the new environment created by step 3, evaluate the body of the procedure being applied, and return the result of this evaluation.

In the example above, we evaluated the expression (square 2) in the initial environment. Let's go on and try some other examples.

Evaluating Compound Procedure Calls: Three Examples

Our first example will be fairly straightforward. Suppose we first define a new double procedure:

```
(define (double no)(* 2 no))
```

and now we type the following expression at the Scheme interpreter:

```
(square (double 1))
```

Let's follow the rules above to see how this expression would be evaluated in the initial environment. First, we have to evaluate each of the subexpressions. In this case the name square evaluates to our familiar procedure object; and now we have to evaluate the subexpression (double 1). This is itself a procedure call, and we must recursively apply our evaluation rules.

To evaluate (double 1) in the initial environment, we first evaluate each subexpression. The number 1 evaluates to itself; and the name double evaluates to a procedure object that can be depicted as in Figure 11.10.

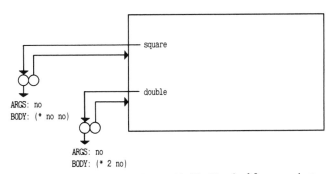

Figure 11.10. The double procedure

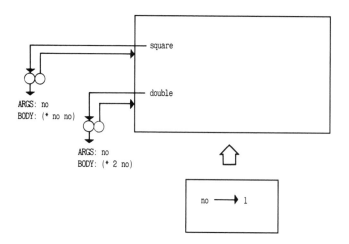

Figure 11.11. In the course of evaluating (double 1)

The next step in evaluating (double 1) is to create a new frame in which the argument name of the double procedure, no, is bound to the result of evaluating the operand subexpression—namely, 1. We then attach this frame to the environment pointed to by the double procedure, and the situation looks as in Figure 11.11.

Now we evaluate the body of the double procedure in the environment we just created. I leave it to you to show that the result of this process is 2. This, then, is the final result of evaluating (double 1), and with this result we are able to continue evaluating our original expression, (square (double 1)).

Having completed this first phase—i.e., having evaluated each of the subexpressions of (square (double 1))—we now create a frame in which the argument of the square procedure, no, is bound to the result of evaluating (double 1), or 2. The new frame is then attached to the initial environment, since this is the environment pointed to by the square procedure. From here on, of course, the scenario looks exactly as it did for our original example, so you can follow through the remainder of this evaluation process yourself and show that the result will be 4.

One point to note is that both square and double employed an argument named no; but if you review the evaluation process you will see that this caused no problems. Our new evaluation model therefore makes explicit a principle that was mentioned earlier, in Chapter 3: namely, that argument names are only bound within the body of the procedure that uses them.

Let's try a second example. Suppose we define the procedure cube as follows:

```
(define (cube number)
  (* number (square number)))
```

This is not the most elegant way to define cube, but it will be illustrative for our purposes.

Now suppose we evaluate the expression (cube 2). Again, the first step is to evaluate subexpressions. The number 2 is self-evaluating, and the name cube evaluates to a procedure object. We create a new frame with the name number bound to 2 and attach it to the initial environment. The environment thus created is shown in Figure 11.12.

Now we have to evaluate the body of cube—that is, the expression (* number (square number))—in the environment of Figure 11.12. The first step is to evaluate subexpressions. The name number evaluates to 2; the expression (square number) must now be evaluated. (Still with me?) Let's evaluate the subexpressions of (square number), then: number evaluates to 2 and square to a procedure object. We create a new frame in which no is bound to 2 and attach it to the initial environment (since that is the environment pointed to by the square procedure object).

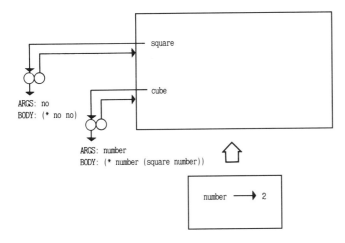

Figure 11.12. The environment in which to evaluate the body of cube

Figure 11.13 is an environment diagram acting as a "snapshot" of this point of the evaluation process. The bottom frame on the left specifies the environment in which we are evaluating the body of the cube procedure. The one on the right specifies the environment in which we will now have to evaluate the body of the square procedure in order to continue evaluating the body of the cube procedure.

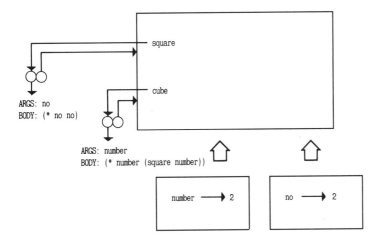

Figure 11.13. Midway in evaluating (cube 2)

Let's go on. The body of the square procedure is evaluated in the environment specified by the bottom right frame, and the result is 4. Now we are able to complete the evaluation of the expression (* number (square number)) in the environment specified by the bottom left frame, and the result of the entire process is 8.

Most likely, you found this example tedious. Everyone does, but the purpose of exercises like these is to show that our evaluation rules do in fact work. And unfortunately, it's necessary to slog through a few such trials to become comfortable with the ideas involved. Nevertheless, part of the message here is that we human beings don't have to follow through every evaluation process step by step in order to understand what a program does; once we are comfortable with the evaluation model of our language, we can easily treat procedures as "black boxes." I recall seeing an instructor at MIT go through an example like the one we just did, upon which one student commented, "Hey, you could get a machine to do that!" Well, . . . that's the whole point. We *have* a machine that does this—a computer equipped with a Scheme interpreter.

Before going on to the final example, I want to mention one more point about our previous one. One question that is often raised is, "What happens to old frames once an expression is completely evaluated?" For instance, what happens to the frames created in evaluating (cube 2) once the result, 8, is returned by the interpreter? The answer is that these frames are no longer needed. Since creating frames does in fact require memory space within our computer, that memory must be reclaimed—otherwise, we might cause our Scheme system to run out of space simply by typing many expressions like (cube 2) at the interpreter. The exact nature of this memory reclamation is beyond the scope of this book; suffice it to say that it is accomplished in large part by a subsystem of our Scheme system known as the *garbage collector*. The garbage collector works intermittently and invisibly—though it is the major cause of the brief pauses that you may have occasionally noticed in running your programs. In PC Scheme, the occurrence of garbage collection is signalled by a message reading *Garbage collecting* at the bottom of the screen.

Our final example is more elaborate than the two earlier ones—it illustrates both recursion and subprocedures within our new evaluation model. Suppose we create the following procedure:

```
(define (factorial number)
  (define (fact-helper count result)
    (cond ((= count number) result)
          (else (fact-helper (1+ count) (* (1+ count) result)))))
  (fact-helper 0 1))
```

This new procedure is depicted in Figure 11.14.

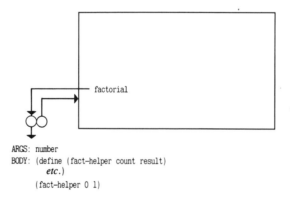

ARGS: number
BODY: (define (fact-helper count result)
           etc.)
      (fact-helper 0 1)

Figure 11.14. The factorial procedure

Suppose we now evaluate (factorial 2) in the initial environment. The first step, as usual, is to evaluate subexpressions. Here, the operand subexpression, 2, is self-evaluating; and the symbol factorial evaluates to the procedure object shown in Figure 11.14. We proceed, then, to create a new frame in which the name number—the argument to factorial—is bound to 2; and we attach this frame to the initial environment (since that is where the factorial procedure object points). Figure 11.15 depicts the environment that we have just made.

Now we have to evaluate the body of the factorial procedure in the environment of Figure 11.15. The first expression is a define expression. Thus, in accordance with our earlier discussion of define, we will create a binding in the bottom frame of Figure 11.15 between the name fact-helper and a procedure object; the updated environment diagram is shown in Figure 11.16.

The second expression in the body of factorial is a call to fact-helper. The operand subexpressions here are the numbers 0 and 1, and the first subexpression, the symbol fact-helper, evaluates to the new procedure object of Figure 11.16. So we now have to create a frame in which the names count and result are bound to 0 and 1 respectively; and since the fact-helper procedure object points to the bottom

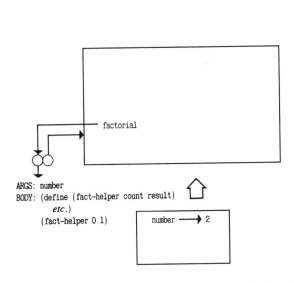

Figure 11.15. In the course of evaluating (factorial 2)

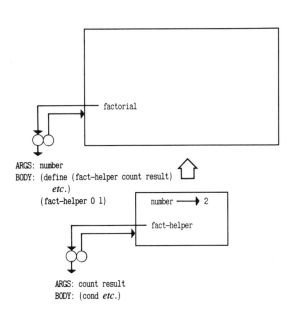

Figure 11.16. After evaluating the internal define expression

frame of Figure 11.16, our new frame will be attached to this bottom frame, as in Figure 11.17.

Now we have to evaluate the body of the fact-helper procedure in the environment we just created. (I will describe the first several steps carefully, but then speed up the presentation a bit.) The first clause of the cond statement has a predicate whose operand expressions count and number are bound to 0 and 2, and whose initial subexpression = is bound to a primitive equality-testing procedure; so this expression returns #f. We therefore evaluate the else clause, which involves a recursive call to fact-helper. The new arguments for this recursive call (you can check this on your own) evaluate to 1 and 1; so we create a new frame in which the names count and result are bound to 1 and 1 and again attach this frame to the environment pointed to by the fact-helper procedure. An environment diagram showing the work we have done so far is shown in Figure 11.18.

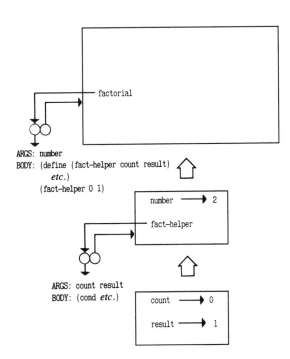

Figure 11.17. Evaluating (fact-helper 0 1)

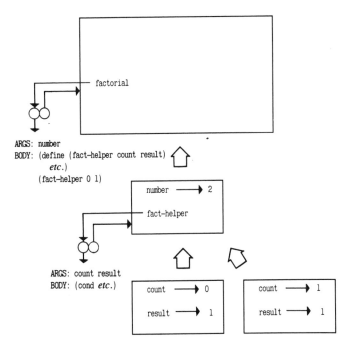

Figure 11.18. Calling fact-helper with arguments 1 and 1

Once more, we have to evaluate the body of the fact-helper procedure in a new environment—the one at the right of Figure 11.18; and (you can verify this) we will find that another recursive call to fact-helper is required. This time we will create a new frame in which count and result are bound to 2 and 2 respectively, so that the appropriate environment diagram appears as in Figure 11.19.

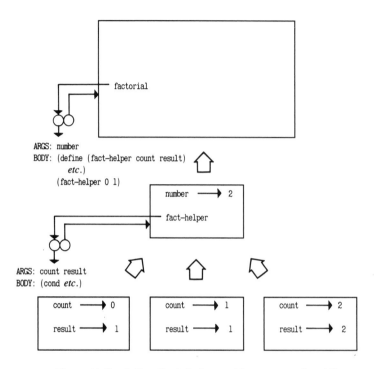

Figure 11.19. Calling fact-helper with arguments 2 and 2

Finally, in evaluating the body of fact-helper in the environment at the right of Figure 11.19, we find that the predicate in the first clause of the cond statement returns #t. So the result of this call (and, as you can check, the result of the very original call to factorial) is 2.

Loose Ends   It is actually worth your while running through the last two examples before reading this section, since I am going to refer to them in clearing up some loose ends in our evaluation model. So go back and review the factorial and cube examples and then come back here.

The fact-helper procedure in the previous example was recursive (tail recursive, to be more specific), and the environment diagram of Figure 11.19 is notable in that it shows several frames "hanging off" the frame associated with fact-helper. This is not an unusual diagram structure when working through recursive examples: if you try, as an exercise, evaluating (factorial-B 2) for the procedure:

```
(define (factorial-B number)
  (if (= number 0) 1 (* number (factorial-B (-1+ number)))))
```

you will arrive at an environment diagram in which several frames are similarly "hanging off" the initial environment frame. This feature—finding many "son" frames hanging from a single "parent" frame when working through recursive calls—is a direct consequence of our evaluation rules, since at each recursive call, a new frame is created and appended to the environment in which the recursive procedure was originally created. (See also Exercise 9.)

Another observation worth making is that environment diagrams do not convey complete information about the evaluation process. For instance, if we were to come upon the environment diagram of Figure 11.19 without knowing the context in which it was drawn, we would have a hard time deducing the original expression—(factorial 2)—that gave rise to it. In a similar vein consider Figure 11.13, which we drew in the course of evaluating a call to the cube procedure and which is reproduced as Figure 11.20.

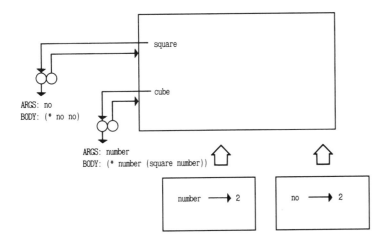

Figure 11.20. Midway in evaluating (cube 2)

Looking at this diagram, students sometimes ask, "But how does the value of the call to square get returned in evaluating the body of the cube procedure?" The answer is that the value *does* indeed get returned; but environment diagrams do not indicate anything about how this is done, nor are they intended to. Environment diagrams only represent collections of environments; the context in which those environments are to be employed—the way in which expressions evaluated in one environment "pass" their results back to another environment—is something that we have to be aware of independently.

Finally, it is worth relating environment diagrams to the topic of lexical scoping introduced in Chapter 9. This is a fairly subtle point, but the crucial observation is that procedure objects "remember" the environment in which they were created. Whenever a procedure is called, the body of the procedure will be evaluated in an environment composed of local argument bindings "added to" the environment in which the procedure was originally defined. Thus, any bindings that exist in the environment where the procedure was defined will be in effect when the body of the procedure is evaluated: and this is precisely equivalent to our earlier definition of lexical scoping. By way of example, look at Figure 11.19 once more and notice how our fact-helper procedure made use of the binding for the symbol number: whenever the body of fact-helper was evaluated, the operative environment included the environment in which fact-helper was originally defined, and hence in which number was bound. In the terminology of Chapter 9, we would say that the binding for number is in the "block" surrounding the definition of fact-helper and thus must be in effect whenever the body of fact-helper is evaluated.

A Few More Loose Ends and a Meta-Comment

You have now encountered a picture of Scheme evaluation much closer to the truth than our earlier one. We will begin to reap the benefits of our new understanding in the next chapter; but before getting to that, there are a few remaining comments to be made.

First, back to the subject of primitive procedures. Primitive procedures, as we have seen, are different from the procedures that we define in that they are applied directly. Thus, no new frames get created during their application, there are no "bodies" to be evaluated in new environments, and so on. The kind of notation that we use to represent primitive procedures, then, is distinct from the representation for compound procedures. Or, to put it yet another way, we need a "procedure object" representation appropriate for primitive procedures.

My own notation for primitive procedures is to include the most common name for the primitive in angle brackets, as in the following examples:

〈Primitive-procedure `cons`〉

〈Primitive-procedure `*`〉

〈Primitive-procedure `sqrt`〉

This is the notation that I have employed in this chapter, and will continue to employ throughout the remainder of the book. (It is not a standard notation, but at the present moment in Scheme culture no standards exist for this purpose—so it's every writer for him- or herself.) An important caveat, however: writing the primitive square-root procedure as 〈Primitive-procedure `sqrt`〉 does not mean that the Scheme symbol `sqrt` has to be bound to this primitive. Every Scheme system includes this binding in its initial environment, but it is certainly possible to rebind the symbol `sqrt` to some other Scheme object; and conversely, there may be many names for the square-root primitive. To take one example, consider the following session at the Scheme interpreter:

```
(define sqrt 4)
sqrt
(+ 3 sqrt)
7
(sqrt 9)
Attempt to call a non-procedural object with 1 argument(s) as follows: (4 9)
```

Here, the symbol `sqrt` has been rebound by a `define` operation to be the number 4.[1] This is not, of course, the sort of thing that a Scheme programmer typically does—generally, we like to leave the names of primitive procedures alone—but it illustrates the fact that a symbol like `sqrt` may in principle be bound to any Scheme object. Exercise 8 examines some other instances of the same idea.

Special forms, by the way, remain special in this respect: they are not bound in the same way that primitive procedures are. For instance, you may have remarked that I avoided including bindings for `define`, `cond`, `if`, `quote`, `let`, and so on in depictions of the initial environment. That is because these symbols really *aren't* bound—they are treated specially by the Scheme interpreter. Suppose, for example, we evaluate the symbol `if` at the Scheme interpreter. We will find that it is in fact an unbound variable. We might go on and try to "rebind" the name `if` as we did with the symbol `sqrt` a little earlier:

```
(define if 2)
```

Not every Scheme system will respond to this example in the same way, but you can be sure that it won't work the way our `sqrt` example did.[2]

The key point, really, is this: unlike numbers, booleans, primitive procedures, compound procedures, pairs, symbols, and so on, special forms are *not* Scheme objects. You cannot create new special forms with our standard `define` operation, and you cannot rebind special form names, since they are not "bound" in the first place. Special forms, as we have seen all along, have to be understood on an ad hoc basis, each according to its own rule.

---

[1] If you try rebinding certain "special" primitive names like `*` in PC Scheme, you will run into obscure and unexpected phenomena. For a partial explanation, see the appendix at the end of this chapter.

[2] For a brief description of PC Scheme's response to this example, see the appendix at the end of this chapter.

We can summarize the message of this chapter by noting the differences between our new model of Scheme evaluation and the old one that we developed in Chapters 3 and 4:

- We now have a more accurate definition of what it means to evaluate an expression. In particular, we know that every expression must be evaluated in an environment, and that when we type expressions at the Scheme interpreter they are evaluated in the initial environment.

- We have a new model of how compound procedure calls are evaluated in environments: each subexpression is evaluated; a new frame is created in which the argument names of the procedure are bound to the values of the operand subexpressions; this new frame is attached to the environment of the procedure (i.e., the environment in which the procedure was created); and the procedure's body is evaluated inside the newly-created environment.

- Primitive procedures are applied directly. Thus, for a primitive procedure call, each subexpression will be evaluated; and then the primitive procedure will be applied to the values of the operand expressions.

- A symbol is evaluated in an environment by locating the "nearest" binding for that symbol (that is, the binding in the lowest possible frame).

- Expressions beginning with the names of special forms must still be evaluated "specially." Each special form is associated with its own particular rule for evaluation. We have seen that the rule for evaluating a define expression within some environment involves creating a new binding in the lowest frame of that environment.

- We have a new notation for representing "procedure objects"—that is, the things to which procedure names are bound. The procedure object representation for a compound procedure is a pair of adjacent circles, one pointing to the text of the procedure and the other pointing to the environment in which the procedure was created. The procedure object representation of a primitive procedure is the "standard" name of the primitive within angle brackets.

Finally, a meta-comment. The environment concept and the new evaluation rules associated with it are deeply ingrained in the remainder of this book. You may therefore find it profitable, as you read through the next several chapters, to refer back to this one from time to time. As your familiarity with the environment concept deepens, you might even consider taking another look at the earlier chapters: try, for instance, to re-understand some of the recursive procedures of Chapters 5 and 8 in the light of our new model of Scheme. And before anything else—before looking either forward or backward in the book—see if you can work through some of the exercises that follow.

Exercises

1. Three environment diagrams—labeled (A), (B), and (C)—are shown below:

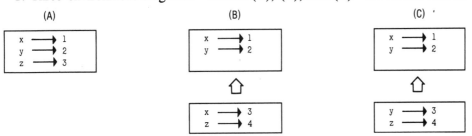

Figure 11.21. Three environment diagrams

Within each of these three environments, evaluate each of the following expressions:

```
x

(+ x y)

(list y z)
```

2. Draw environment diagrams that depict the results of evaluating each of the following expressions, one by one, in each of the environments of Exercise 1. (That is, show environment *A* after each of these expressions is evaluated in turn; then do the same for *B*; then for *C*.)

```
(define x 3)

(define z y)

(define x 5)
```

After all three expressions have been evaluated, what is the result of evaluating (list x y z) in each of the three environments?

3. Suppose we define the following procedures:

```
(define (greeting? symbol)
  (memv symbol '(hello hi greetings)))

(define (leave-taking? symbol)
  (memv symbol '(goodbye bye so-long)))

(define (conversation-boundary? symbol)
  (or (greeting? symbol) (leave-taking? symbol)))
```

Use environment diagrams to follow through the evaluation of these expressions:

```
(greeting? 'hello)

(conversation-boundary? 'rosebud)

(not (leave-taking? (car '(hi there))))
```

4. Consider the following procedure for determining the area of a circle:

```
(define (circle-area radius)
  (* 3.14 (square radius)))
```

The square procedure, of course, has been defined in the usual way:

```
(define (square no) (* no no))
```

Using environment diagrams, follow through the evaluation of these three expressions:

```
(circle-area 2)

(- (circle-area 3) (circle-area 1))

(circle-area (square 2))
```

5. Here is a recursive procedure that can be used to test whether a list of numbers is in ascending order:

```
(define (in-ascending-order? lis)
  (cond ((null? lis) #t)
        ((null? (cdr lis)) #t)
        ((<= (car lis) (cadr lis)) (in-ascending-order? (cdr lis)))
        (else #f)))
```

Use environment diagrams to depict the evaluation of the following expression:

```
(in-ascending-order? (list 2 5 4))
```

6. Suppose we choose to represent points in the x, y-plane as pairs: the car of the pair corresponds to the x-coordinate, the cdr to the y-coordinate. Here are several relevant procedures:

```
(define (make-point x-value y-value)
  (cons x-value y-value))

(define (x-coord point)(car point))

(define (y-coord point)(cdr point))
```

Now we can write a procedure named midpoint that takes two points as its argument values, and returns a point that is midway between the two:

```
(define (midpoint point1 point2)
  (define (average no1 no2)
      (/ (+ no1 no2) 2))
  (make-point (average (x-coord point1) (x-coord point2))
              (average (y-coord point1) (y-coord point2))))
```

Using environment diagrams, work through the evaluation of this expression:

```
(midpoint (make-point 0 0) (make-point 2 4))
```

7. In this chapter, we have represented the initial environment as consisting of a single frame. For many Scheme systems, including PC Scheme, this representation is not entirely truthful. PC Scheme's initial environment actually consists of two frames, as in Figure 11.22 below; thus, after defining our usual square procedure, the appropriate environment diagram would appear as in Figure 11.23.

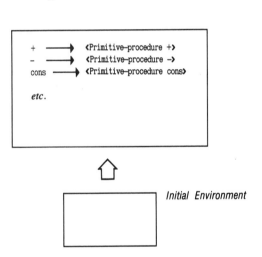

Figure 11.22. The initial environment in PC Scheme

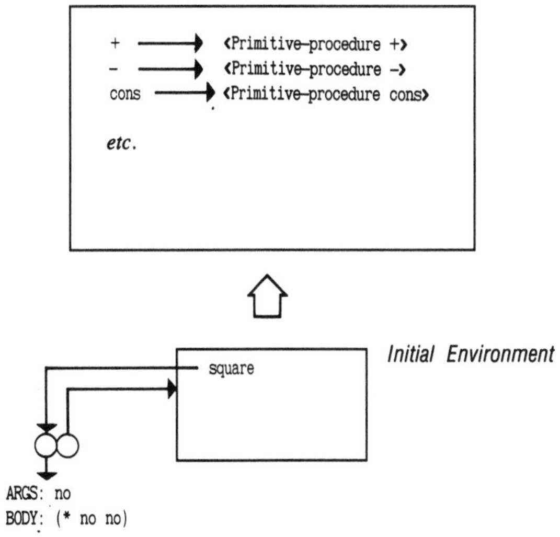

Figure 11.23. After defining square in PC Scheme's initial environment

We will address this topic later, in Chapter 14; but for now, it is worth your while to confirm that the examples we've worked through are only marginally affected by this new initial environment representation. As a start, you might evaluate the expression:

```
(square 2)
```

in the two-frame initial environment shown in Figure 11.23. Also, try reworking a few other examples; Exercises 3 and 4 above are good candidates. You will find that from the standpoint of someone evaluating expressions in the two-frame initial environment, the results of all our examples are the same as if we assume a one-frame initial environment. For instance, calling square with an argument of 2 will return a value of 4 regardless of whether the initial environment is composed of two frames or one. In fact, the most important change introduced by the two-frame initial environment structure—at least for our present purposes—is that it adds an extra frame to all our diagrams.

8. One of the notions that we touched on in this chapter was that of rebinding primitive procedure names. Consider the following example:

```
(define (add-two-to *) (+ 2 *))
```

Here, add-two-to is a procedure that takes a number argument named * and returns the value of that argument incremented by two. Use environment diagrams to evaluate the expression:

```
(add-two-to 1)
```

You will find that in the course of evaluating this expression, an environment is created in which the name * is bound to 1. Of course, the code for add-two-to is objectionable on stylistic grounds . . . but the procedure does work. (Try it!)

9. Earlier in this chapter, it was mentioned that once a frame is no longer needed, it will have its memory space automatically reclaimed by our Scheme system. This reclamation process is particularly important when analyzing tail recursive procedures. Tail recursive procedures, you may remember, are procedures containing a recursive call and in which there is no additional work to be done (i.e., no additional expressions to evaluate) once the recursive call has been evaluated.

Consider the following sample procedure:

```
(define (infinite-loop)
  (infinite-loop))
```

If we call infinite-loop on no arguments, it should run forever; as mentioned in Chapter 5, tail recursive procedures are used for precisely this purpose—to generate "endless processes"—because they run in constant space. But let's see what happens when we analyze the call to infinite-loop using environment diagrams.

When we call infinite-loop on zero arguments, we create a frame in which there are no bindings (i.e., a frame in which the zero argument names of the procedure are bound to the zero operand subexpression values); and we attach this frame to the initial environment, as in Figure 11.24.

Now we have to evaluate the body of infinite-loop in this newly-created two-frame environment. But the body of infinite-loop is just another call to

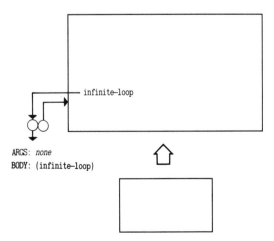

Figure 11.24. In the course of evaluating (infinite-loop)

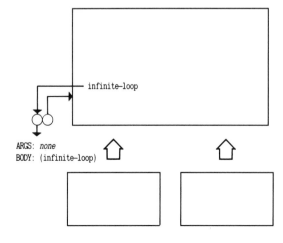

Figure 11.25. Still evaluating (infinite-loop)

infinite-loop; so we create yet another frame with zero bindings, and attach that to the initial environment, as in Figure 11.25.

Now, of course, we could keep going on this way forever. But there is an important point here: the frame on the left of Figure 11.25 is *no longer needed*. There are no additional expressions left to evaluate in this environment, so it may be reclaimed. Thus, we could have dispensed with the leftmost frame in Figure 11.25, and drawn our environment diagram as in Figure 11.26.

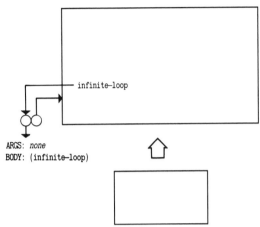

Figure 11.26. A "better" version of Figure 11.25

The reclamation of needless frames is what enables tail recursive procedures to run in constant space; if these frames were *not* reclaimed, you can see that the number of frames in our environment-diagram analysis of infinite-loop would eventually grow to astronomical proportions.

To sum up, then, a frame's memory space may be reclaimed (or, if you want to think in terms of drawing environment diagrams, a frame may be erased from the page) once there are no more expressions to evaluate in that frame. This is true of any frame that we draw—not just those that we draw in the course of evaluating tail recursive procedures—but the need for reclaiming needless frames jumps out at us when we are analyzing tail recursive procedures.

Here are two exercises along these lines: first, consider the following procedures:

```
(define (double x) (* 2 x))
```

```
(define (times-4 y) (double (double y)))
```

Using environment diagrams, work through the evaluation of (times-4 5), taking care to erase frames once they are no longer needed. You should find that at the moment when the eventual result of the evaluation is found, there is only one frame in your diagram (besides the initial environment frame), in which the name x is bound.

Finally, consider the procedure that we employed for one of our examples earlier in this chapter:

```
(define (factorial number)
  (define (fact-helper count result)
    (cond ((= count number) result)
          (else (fact-helper (1+ count) (* (1+ count) result)))))
  (fact-helper 0 1))
```

Noting that the fact-helper subprocedure is tail recursive, once more work through the evaluation of (factorial 2), this time taking care to erase needless frames.

As an aside, it is worth mentioning that the type of environment diagram that we saw as typical of recursive procedures, in which many frames "hang from" a single parent frame, is in fact a more accurate depiction of recursive procedures that are not tail recursive. For instance, the other factorial procedure that we analyzed:

```
(define (factorial-B number)
  (if (= number 0) 1 (* number (factorial-B (-1+ number)))))
```

gives rise to environment diagrams that do *not* contain needless, "reclaimable" frames after each recursive call. Try evaluating (factorial-B 2), reclaiming frames wherever possible, and compare the environment diagrams you generate to those for the factorial procedure above.

10. Suppose we evaluate the following expressions:

```
(define x 4)
```

```
(define y 5)
```

```
(define (proc-1 x)
  (define (proc-2 y)
    (+ x y))
  (proc-2 (1+ x)))
```

Predict the result of evaluating (proc-1 1) using the notions of block structure and lexical scoping discussed in Chapter 9. Then work through the same evaluation with an environment diagram. (The two analyses should of course give you the same result.) At the moment when the body of proc-2 is being evaluated, how many frames in your environment diagram contain bindings for x? How many contain bindings for y?

Appendix

Rebinding the Names
of Primitives in PC Scheme

The following is a note on PC Scheme; if you have some other Scheme system, or are not interested in some of the more obscure aspects of PC Scheme, you can ignore this appendix.

Earlier in this chapter, we looked at an example of rebinding the name of a Scheme primitive procedure; specifically, we rebound the name sqrt to 4. Suppose we attempt this experiment in PC Scheme—but this time, instead of sqrt, let's rebind the name * as follows:

```
(define * 4)
```

In PC Scheme, the interpreter will respond to the define expression with a warning:

*Warning: modifying an 'integrable' variable: **

There are now several strange phenomena to account for. When the name * occurs as the first subexpression in a procedure call, it is still treated as a procedure:

```
(* 3 5)
```

But when it occurs as something other than the first subexpression, it is treated as a number:

```
(+ 3 *)
7
```

Weird, right? In fact, by typing the following expression, you can use both of the values of *:

```
(* * *)
16
```

What's going on? Well, PC Scheme happens to treat certain names, including *, specially. The idea is that * is what is known in PC Scheme as an "integrable" primitive name: when the interpreter reads an expression beginning with the symbol *, it is able to speed up the evaluation process by assuming that this expression involves a call to the multiplication primitive. I will not go into the details of this process except to say that it is a very reasonable optimization, and that since names like * are almost never rebound by programmers these unusual issues (e.g., of names that seem to have two meanings) seldom come to our attention.[3]

In order to "turn off" this special feature of PC Scheme, you can type this expression at the interpreter:

```
(set! pcs-integrate-primitives #f)
```

Once this is done, you can continue with the following sample session:

```
(define * 4)
*  ;now you won't see a warning message
(+ * 3)
7
(* 4 3)
Attempt to call a non-procedural object with 2 argument(s) as follows: (4 4 3)
```

Be advised, however, that if you try this example you will not be able to undo the change to *, except of course by exiting PC Scheme altogether and starting up the system afresh. (There are ways around this problem, but the whole issue is not worth going into here.) Thus, that strange set! expression above makes PC Scheme behave more like the "pure" Scheme described in the text.

As for the subsequent example in the text:

```
(define if 2)
```

In this case, the PC Scheme interpreter will not respond with a warning of any kind. The name if will now be treated as a special form if it occurs as the first symbol in a compound expression, and as a number if it occurs anywhere else:

```
(if #t 1 2)
1
(+ 3 if)
5
(if #t if 3)
2
```

---

[3]In fact, the PC Scheme Reference Manual uses the term "primitive" to refer to precisely these integrable procedures. Thus, *, +, and car among others are "primitives" in PC Scheme's notation, whereas other system-supplied procedures like sqrt are not. As I mentioned in Chapter 3, the meaning of the term "primitive" has not really been standardized in this respect. Once more, I use the term to refer to *all* system-supplied procedures, whether integrable in a given implementation of Scheme or not.

You may have noticed that PC Scheme's treatment of if in this case is rather like its treatment of * above, in that the name if seems to have two different meanings (a special form or a number) depending on where it occurs in an expression. However, the two situations are not identical. In particular, evaluating the set! expression above has no effect on PC Scheme's response to the if example. Again, the crucial point is that the names of special forms are not "bound." Although we are able to bind the name if to some Scheme object (such as a number), the name if will *always* be treated as a special form at the beginning of a compound expression.

CHAPTER 12

Procedures

The mantra for this chapter is "Procedures are objects." You should discipline your mind by repeating that sentence over and over—in the bathtub, at mealtimes, to total strangers on the subway. I guarantee results.

It is, in all honesty, difficult for people to get used to the notion of a procedure as an object. Procedures are typically seen as "doers," whereas the term "object" implies a more passive sort of entity. And the natural division between procedures and objects seems to spill over to the term "data" as well. Objects are identified with the notion of data—something that is operated upon—as opposed to procedures, which do the operating.

I believe that this procedure-versus-object dichotomy is due to very deeply rooted (perhaps biologically programmed) predilections. The distinction is analogous to that between verbs and nouns in natural language; and young children seem to pick up the difference between verbs and nouns very early in the course of learning to speak. Perhaps we human beings automatically partition our conceptual worlds into "active" (verb/procedure) concepts and "passive" (noun/object) concepts.

In any case, Scheme procedures can't be pigeonholed quite so easily. It is true that they can be used to operate upon obvious sorts of data objects, like numbers; but they also have some "data-like" properties of their own. Exploring the properties of Scheme procedures can radically change one's ideas about the very nature of "object-hood."

First-Class Objects

In discussing computer languages, programmers often make use of the notion of *first-class objects*.[1] A first-class object is one that has the following properties:

- It may be named by a variable (i.e., a symbol may be bound to this object).
- It may be passed as an argument to a procedure.
- It may be returned as the value of a procedure call.
- It may be an element of larger data structures (such as lists).

---

[1] Cf. Joseph Stoy, *Denotational Semantics*, MIT Press, 1977.

As a start, let's affirm that these properties apply to numbers in Scheme. Numbers may indeed be named by variables:

```
(define a 15)
(define x 12.4)
(+ x a)
27.4
```

Numbers may be passed as arguments to procedures:

```
(ceiling 3.8)
(expt 5 6)
```

The value returned by a procedure call may be a number (see the two expressions just above); and finally, numbers may be elements inside larger data structures, such as lists:

```
(define list-of-numbers (list 3.4 2.25 7))
```

All of these examples are straightforward, and represent activities that have become familiar to us—passing numbers as arguments to procedures, creating lists of numbers, and so on. We should not be surprised, then, to hear that numbers are first-class objects.

In Scheme, virtually *every* type of object has first-class status. Booleans are first-class objects; so are pairs; so are symbols. And so are procedures (both primitive and compound). The remainder of this chapter will be an exploration of the idea of first-class procedure objects.

Naming Procedures with Variables

Procedures are objects. And one thing that we can do with objects is name them with variables (or, in other words, bind symbols to them). This is, in fact, the only one of the "first-class properties" listed above that we have exploited so far in our experience with procedures; we have been binding symbols to procedures right and left since the second chapter of the book. For instance, when we evaluate the expression:

```
(define (double number) (* 2 number))
```

we are binding a name to a procedure object; specifically, we are associating the name double with the procedure object shown toward the left of Figure 12.1.

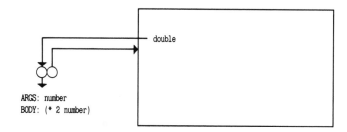

Figure 12.1. The name double is bound to a procedure object

Although this seems straightforward enough, there is a subtle point that deserves mention. Take a look at the following expression:

```
(define times-two double)
```

Here, we are binding the name times-two to the result of evaluating the symbol double. But the result of evaluating the symbol double is a procedure—the one depicted in Figure 12.1. So the expression above will bind the symbol `times-two` to the very same procedure object to which the symbol `double` is bound:

```
(times-two 3)
6
```

The interesting feature of this example is that the name `double` is bound to a procedure, and that we can make use of this binding in ways other than applying the `double` procedure to arguments. Just because the name `double` is bound to a procedure, it does *not* have to appear at the beginning of every expression in which it appears. That is to say, we *expect* to use `double` in expressions like the following:

```
(double 5)
10
```

But we are unused to seeing the name `double` appear in some other position within an expression:

```
(eq? times-two double)
#t
```

Again, the crucial point is that if a symbol is bound to a procedure, the result of evaluating that symbol is the procedure, *regardless* of whether we intend to apply the procedure to arguments or not. In the last expression above, the procedure named `double` was not applied to arguments, but the example is perfectly reasonable nonetheless. (See also Exercise 1.)

To summarize, then: procedures have the first property of first-class objects. They can be named by variables.

Procedures as Arguments to Other Procedures

Procedures are objects. And one thing that we can do with objects is pass them as arguments to procedures. So it ought to be true that procedures can be passed as arguments to other procedures.

Let's look at a very simple example of this idea. Consider the following procedure:

```
(define (apply-to-3 function)
  (function 3))
```

The procedure `apply-to-3` takes as argument a procedure and returns the value of applying that procedure to the number 3. We could use our new procedure as follows:

```
(apply-to-3 1+)
4
(apply-to-3 sin)
0.141120013
(apply-to-3 square)
9
```

In the first two examples above, the argument to `apply-to-3` is a primitive procedure; in the third, the argument is a compound procedure (I am assuming that we have already defined `square` in the usual way—otherwise we would get an "unbound variable" error message in attempting to evaluate this expression).

Let's work through one of these calls to `apply-to-3` using the evaluation model from the previous chapter. Consider the third expression, `(apply-to-3 square)`. The first step in evaluating this expression is to evaluate each subexpression. The name apply-to-3 evaluates to a compound procedure; similarly the name square evaluates to a compound procedure. Both these objects are shown in Figure 12.2 below.

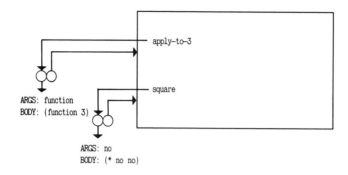

Figure 12.2. The apply-to-3 and square procedures

Now, we create a new frame in which function, the argument name of apply-to-3, is bound to the result of evaluating the expression square. The new frame is shown in Figure 12.3.

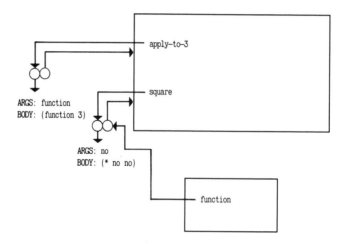

Figure 12.3. Creating a frame in which the name function is bound

All we are doing here is following the evaluation rules as slavishly as possible. The name square happens to evaluate to a procedure object, so this is the object to which the name function will be bound in our new frame. There is no logical problem, of course, in having two names bound to one procedure object—any more than there would be a problem in having two names bound to a number object.

To continue with our evaluation process: we now attach the new frame of the previous step to the environment associated with apply-to-3—that is, the initial environment. Having done this, we evaluate the body of apply-to-3 in the newly-created environment shown in Figure 12.4.

The body of apply-to-3 is simply the expression (function 3); and we can evaluate this expression according to our usual rules. The second subexpression, 3, evaluates to itself; and the name function evaluates to a procedure object. So we create a new frame in which the argument name no is bound to the number 3 and we attach this frame to the environment pointed to by the procedure object being applied. The resulting situation is depicted in Figure 12.5.

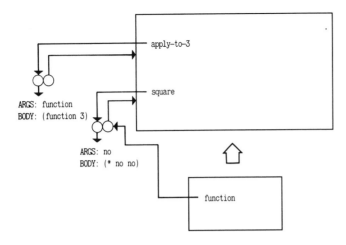

Figure 12.4. The environment in which to evaluate the body of `apply-to-3`

The environment on the left of Figure 12.5 is the one that we created earlier—the same one as in Figure 12.4. It is in this environment that we are evaluating the body of `apply-to-3`. The environment on the right of Figure 12.5 is the one that we had to create in the course of evaluating the body of `apply-to-3`. We now evaluate the body of the `function` (and `square`) procedure object inside this new environment—and the body is just the expression `(* no no)`. The result of evaluating this expression in the environment on the right of Figure 12.5 is 9 (you can verify this for yourself), so this is the result of our entire evaluation process.

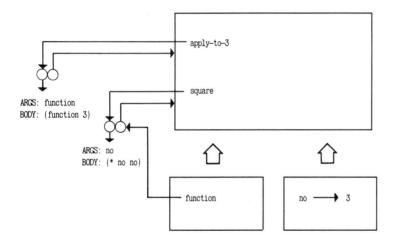

Figure 12.5. Evaluating the call to `function` in the body of `apply-to-3`

The discussion above should convince you that the notion of procedures as arguments is consistent with our Scheme evaluation rules. But let's step back a moment. Is this notion *really* as offbeat as all that? Consider the following two procedures:

```
(define (double number)
  (* 2 number))
(define (apply-to-3 function)
  (function 3))
```

The `double` procedure employs its argument, `number`, as an argument to the primitive multiplication procedure; while `apply-to-3` employs its argument as a procedure to apply to a number. But look at that symbol `*` inside the `double` procedure. It is a symbol that happens to be bound to a procedure; the binding for this symbol can be found in the initial environment. The apply-to-3 procedure is every bit as reasonable—it employs a symbol, function, which like * will be bound to a procedure. It just happens that the binding for the symbol function will be found not in the initial environment but rather in the frame created by calling the apply-to-3 procedure.

To put the matter another way: why should we expect argument names to be used only at the ends of expressions—as in (* 2 number)—and not at the beginnings of expressions—as in (function 3)? The answer, of course, is that we *shouldn't* expect this restriction; using argument names as the names of procedures is perfectly okay.

Examples of Procedures as Arguments

Just for practice, let's look at a few more simple examples of the procedure-as-argument idea. Here is a procedure that takes as argument a numeric function, a number, and a limit value. If the result of applying the function to the number exceeds the limit, then the limit is returned; otherwise the value of applying the function to the number is returned.

```
(define (apply-but-with-limit function number limit)
  (let ((value (function number)))
    (if (> value limit) limit value)))
```

Some examples of apply-but-with-limit in use:

```
(apply-but-with-limit square 20 1000)
400

(apply-but-with-limit tan (/ 3.14 2) 1000)
1000
```

Here is a procedure called find-maximum-value that takes as argument a numeric function and two integers, low and high. The two integers represent the bottom and top ends of a range of possible argument values. We will apply the function to all integers starting with low and working our way up to high; and our procedure will return the highest value that we find along the way.

```
(define (find-maximum-value function low high)
  (cond ((= low high) (function high))
        (else (let ((max-of-rest
                      (find-maximum-value function (1+ low) high))
                    (first-val (function low)))
                (if (>= first-val max-of-rest) first-val max-of-rest)))))
```

Here is an example of find-maximum-value in action:

```
(define (test-function number)
  (- 35 (square (- number 20))))

(find-maximum-value test-function 0 40)
35
```

The following is a general-purpose list-sorting procedure called sort-by-rule. This procedure will be given as argument a list and a comparison predicate; the predicate can be used to compare any two elements of the list. Our procedure will return a sorted list—sorted, that is, according to the comparison rule—as its result. For instance, if the comparison predicate is <, then a list of numbers can be sorted from low to high; if the predicate is the Scheme primitive string<?, then a list of strings can be sorted in alphabetical order.

```
(define (sort-by-rule comparison lis)
  (define (insert-by-rule element lis)
    (cond ((null? lis) (list element))
          ((comparison element (car lis)) (cons element lis))
          (else (cons (car lis) (insert-by-rule element (cdr lis))))))
  (cond ((null? (cdr lis)) lis)
        (else (insert-by-rule (car lis)
                              (sort-by-rule comparison (cdr lis))))))
```

The sort-by-rule procedure employs a recursive strategy; it sorts all but the first element of the list, and then inserts the first element into the now-sorted remainder, using the comparison rule to indicate where the first element should be inserted. For instance, suppose we wish to sort the list (5 3 6 4) from low to high. Our strategy would be to first sort the cdr of the list, obtaining (3 4 6) as our result; then we would insert the element 5 in the sorted list between 4 and 6, obtaining (3 4 5 6).[2]

Here are a few sample applications of sort-by-rule:

```
(sort-by-rule > '(4 7 5 2 9))
```
(9 7 5 4 2)

```
(sort-by-rule string<? '("apple" "orange" "banana"))
```
("apple" "banana" "orange")

```
(define (odds-then-evens? number1 number2)
  (cond ((and (even? number1)(even? number2)) (< number1 number2))
        ((and (not (even? number1)) (not (even? number2)))
         (< number1 number2))
        ((even? number1) #f)
        (else #t)))
```

```
(sort-by-rule odds-then-evens? '(2 3 4 5 6 7 8))
```
(3 5 7 2 4 6 8)

Mapping

In all Lisp dialects—Scheme included—the classic use of procedural arguments is to create *mapping* procedures. Typically, a mapping procedure takes two arguments: a procedure, and a list. The idea is that the procedure argument will be applied to each element of the list, one by one (programmers sometimes say that the procedure is being *mapped* over the list).

Here is the most widely used procedure of this type; it is called, naturally enough, map.

```
(define (map proc lis)
  (cond ((null? lis) '())
        (else (cons (proc (car lis)) (map proc (cdr lis))))))
```

Map takes a procedure and a list as arguments, and it applies the procedure in turn to each element of the list, returning a list of the results. Here are some examples:

```
(map 1+ '(2 3 6 7))
```
(3 4 7 8)

```
(map square '(3 4 6))
```
(9 16 36)

---

[2]It should be mentioned that this is not the most efficient sorting strategy in current use (not by a long shot!), but it's easy to understand for our purposes. That is to say, sort-by-rule is meant only to illustrate the basic notion that a "sorting algorithm" may be parametrized by comparison procedures like < and string<?. Our procedure is not, however, an exemplar of how to sort lists; better techniques may be found in any undergraduate text on algorithms.

```
(define (weekend-day? symbol)
  (or (eq? symbol 'friday)
      (eq? symbol 'saturday)
      (eq? symbol 'sunday)))
(map weekend-day? '(tuesday friday sunday monday))
(() #t #t ())
```

Another mapping procedure is called for-each. This procedure also takes a list and procedure as arguments, and simply applies the procedure to each element of the list.

```
(define (for-each procedure lis)
  (cond ((null? lis) #t)
        (else (procedure (car lis))
              (for-each procedure (cdr lis)))))
```

Here are two examples. Instead of depicting the results, I will leave it to you to predict what will happen and experiment with your own PC Scheme system:

```
(for-each writeln '("This" "should appear" "on three lines"))
(define (draw-point-from-pair pair)
  (draw-point (car pair)(cdr pair)))
(for-each draw-point-from-pair '((0 . 50) (25 . 0) (-25 . 0)))
```

The procedure argument to for-each will typically be something like writeln—that is, a procedure that is used not because it returns some interesting value when applied to arguments, but rather because it produces some effect (e.g., it prints out a string). By way of contrast, consider the following application of for-each:

```
(for-each 1+ '(2 3 5 6))
#t
```

There isn't much point using for-each here, since our returned value does not include any of the results of applying the 1+ procedure to the elements of the list. All that our expression evaluates to is #t—and we could have predicted that result from examining the code of for-each.

Both map and for-each are Scheme primitives, so we really needn't have written them afresh[3]; but the notion of mapping can loosely extend to other constructs. For instance, this procedure maps a two-argument function over adjacent pairs of elements (followed by a sample application):

```
(define (map-over-pairs function lis)
  (cond ((or (null? lis) (null? (cdr lis))) '())
        (else (cons (function (car lis) (cadr lis))
                    (map-over-pairs function (cddr lis))))))
(map-over-pairs * '(3 7 4 5 2 2))
(21 20 4)
```

The Lambda Special Form

We have now explored two of the reasons for dubbing procedures first-class objects: procedures can be named by variables, and they can be passed as arguments to other procedures. In both these respects, procedures are no different than numbers. But before going on to examine the other first-class properties of procedures, let's pause to discuss another issue.

---

[3] Actually, the versions of map and for-each that we wrote are a bit "stronger" than the Scheme versions. For example, our for-each always returns #t as its result, whereas Scheme's for-each returns an unspecified result. But, for all intents and purposes, our versions work the same as the Scheme primitives.

So far, we have seen only one way to create new procedures—namely, by writing `define` expressions. For instance, our standard example of `double` was created by typing the following expression at the Scheme interpreter:

```
(define (double number)
  (* 2 number))
```

By evaluating this expression, we bound the name `double` in the initial environment to the procedure object shown in Figure 12.1.

There is, however, another way of creating procedures—by using the special form `lambda`. Unlike the `define` method, our new `lambda` method does not bind a name to the newly-created procedure object: it simply creates the procedure object and leaves it unnamed.

The general form of a `lambda` expression is:

```
(lambda (argument-names) body)
```

When a `lambda` expression is evaluated in some environment, it returns a procedure object whose argument names and body are specified by the expression, and whose associated environment is the one in which we are doing the evaluation.

The best way to understand this idea is through experimentation. Try typing the following expressions at the Scheme interpreter:

```
((lambda (number) (* 2 number)) 5)

((lambda (symbol) (eq? 'joe symbol)) 'fred)

(map (lambda (number) (* 6 number)) '( 2 3 4 5))
```

Consider the top expression of the three above. Here, the first subexpression will evaluate to a procedure object that has the same arguments, body, and associated environment as the one in Figure 12.1. This new procedure object is not identical to the one to which the name `double` is bound—that is, these two procedure objects are not `eq?`—but both objects behave the same when applied to arguments. Figure 12.6 depicts the two procedures: note that the one we created by using `lambda` is not associated with any name.

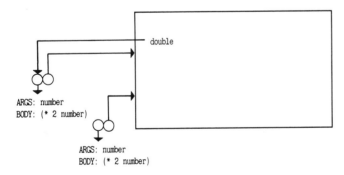

ARGS: number
BODY: (* 2 number)

ARGS: number
BODY: (* 2 number)

Figure 12.6. Two procedure objects

Now, in evaluating the expression

```
((lambda (number) (* 2 number)) 5)
```

the Scheme interpreter evaluates each subexpression. The first subexpression, as we have just seen, evaluates to a procedure object, while the second subexpression, 5, evaluates to itself. If we apply our newly-created procedure object to 5 using our familiar evaluation rules (create a new frame, bind the name `number` to 5, etc.), we will find that the value of this entire expression is 10.

The second example:

```
((lambda (symbol) (eq? 'joe symbol)) 'fred)
```

works similarly. The first subexpression evaluates to a procedure object—the one shown in Figure 12.7. The second subexpression, 'fred, evaluates to the symbol fred. You can follow through the rest of the evaluation process yourself and show that the entire expression evaluates to #f.

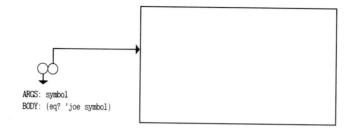

ARGS: symbol
BODY: (eq? 'joe symbol)

Figure 12.7. The procedure object in the second example

The third example:

```
(map (lambda (number) (* 6 number)) '(2 3 4 5))
```

shows that the result of evaluating a lambda expression is a perfectly good procedure object and hence can be passed as an argument to the map procedure that we encountered earlier. The two arguments to map in this case are the procedure object depicted in Figure 12.8, and the list (2 3 4 5).

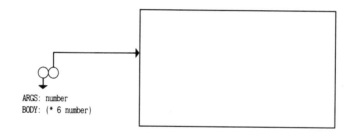

ARGS: number
BODY: (* 6 number)

Figure 12.8. The procedure object in the third example

Again, you can follow through the evaluation process and show that the value of the entire expression is the list (12 18 24 30).

The name lambda, sounding as it does Greek and mathematical, scares some people. In fact, the name does have mathematical roots: lambda expressions in Lisp were originally meant to model similar expressions in the "lambda calculus," a notation developed by the logician Alonzo Church for studying function application. But if it makes you feel more comfortable, you can think of the expression:

```
(lambda (args) body)
```

as shorthand for "the procedure that takes arguments *args* and has body *body*." Perhaps it would have been better had the pioneers of Lisp used a more mnemonic (and less intimidating) name than "lambda" for this special form; but by now, the name has become commonplace in the Lisp programming community, and what's done is done.

A more important question than why we use the name is why we use lambda expressions at all. What's the point? After all, instead of the map expression above, we could have first created a new procedure:

```
(define (times-6 number)(* 6 number))
(map times-6 '(2 3 4 5))
```

Well, yes, we could do it this way. But now we have a new procedure called times-6 that we probably don't care about and don't ever want to use again. Sometimes we actually *like* the fact that lambda expressions create unnamed procedures: we don't have to clutter up our programs with a lot of needless define expressions. Lambda expressions are handy when we have a simple procedure to use just this one time, and we don't want to bind a new name for this one-time-only procedure.

A situation of this sort, in fact, occurred a little earlier when we were illustrating the find-maximum-value procedure. You may recall that we created a procedure called test-function to try out as an argument value:

```
(define (test-function number)
  (- 35 (square (- number 20))))

(find-maximum-value test-function 0 40)
35
```

Rather than create test-function just for this purpose, we could have written:

```
(find-maximum-value (lambda (no) (- 35 (square (- no 20))))
                    0 40)
```

It should also be mentioned that unnamed procedure objects created with lambda do take up memory space within the computer. Since these procedure objects are inaccessible to us after they have been applied, they are subject to reclamation by the garbage collection mechanism mentioned in the previous chapter. For instance, after evaluating the expression in our earlier example:

```
((lambda (number) (* 2 number)) 5)
```

we are left with an unnamed procedure object (the one shown in Figure 12.6 above). But we will never be able to use this procedure again—it doesn't have a name, and if we evaluate another similar-looking lambda expression, we will get a brand-new procedure object. Thus, the object shown in Figure 12.6 is now taking up needless memory space which will eventually have to be reclaimed.

Just to drive the point home: there's a particularly simple illustration of the ideas of the previous paragraph. Suppose we type the following expression at the Scheme interpreter:

```
(lambda (number) (* 2 number))
```

The result of evaluating this expression will be an unnamed procedure object. But because it's unnamed, there is no way that we can refer to this procedure object anymore; it too will be reclaimed by the Scheme garbage collector.

Another Look at Define Expressions

Throughout this book, we have been using two kinds of define expressions: one for binding names to objects of various sorts—as in (define a 1)—and one for creating new procedures—as in (define (square no) (* no no)). In point of fact, the second kind of define expression is unnecessary. Consider the following two expressions:

```
(define square (lambda (no) (* no no)))

(define (square no) (* no no))
```

The second expression employs our standard define method for creating new procedures. But let's examine the evaluation process for the first expression. We have to evaluate the subexpression (lambda (no) (* no no)) and bind the name square to the resulting procedure object. The situation then appears as in Figure 12.9 below. But this is precisely the same situation we would have achieved by evaluating the second expression!

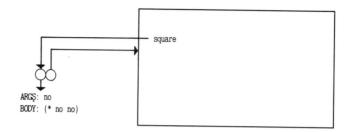

Figure 12.9. Binding the name `square` to a procedure object

In general, then, we could always use the first kind of `define` for naming procedures as well as anything else. To create a new procedure named `blah`, we would use an expression of the form:

(define blah (lambda (*args*) *body*))

This binds the symbol `blah` to the result of evaluating a `lambda` expression. The second kind of `define`—the one that we have been using up to now to make new procedures—is just a convenience. Most people find the second type of `define` expression easier to read. But if you prefer, you can avoid this syntax and use the first kind of `define` expression exclusively.[4]

Another Look at `Let` Expressions

In chapter 3, we first encountered the `let` special form. `Let`, as you recall, is handy for setting up "temporary bindings" so that we can evaluate expressions with those bindings in effect.

Now that we have encountered the `lambda` special form, it is time to reveal a secret: `let` is just shorthand for applying procedures created with `lambda` expressions. Specifically,

```
(let ((var-1 exp-1)
      (var-2 exp-2)
          .
          .
       .)
   body)
```

is just a cleaner way of writing:

((lambda (*var-1 var-2* ...) *body*) *exp-1 exp-2* ...)

So the following two expressions are equivalent:

(let ((a 3)) (* 8 a))

((lambda (a) (* 8 a)) 3)

_____

[4]This equivalence between (define (blah x) ...) and (define blah (lambda (x) ...)) is true of Scheme according to the latest definition of the language. (Cf. J. Rees and W. Clinger, eds., "Revised[3] Report on the Algorithmic Language Scheme," *ACM Sigplan Notices*, December 1986.) But some implementations, including the current version (3.0) of PC Scheme, work slightly differently. In PC Scheme, there is yet another special form called `named-lambda`; and, as it happens, the expression (define (blah x) ...) is equivalent to (define blah (named-lambda (blah x) ...)). For our purposes, the distinction between `lambda` and `named-lambda` is unimportant—so even if you are using PC Scheme, you can treat the discussion above as the truth (if not quite the whole truth). But as always, feel free to consult your language manual and play around.

And the following two procedures return the same results when applied to arguments:

```
(define (procedure-with-let x)
  (let ((x-squared (* x x)))
    (+ x x-squared)))
(define (procedure-with-lambda x)
  ((lambda (x-squared) (+ x x-squared)) (* x x)))
```

In other words, let is just an aid to readability—rather like our second syntax for define. (If you compare the two procedures above, you'll probably agree that the one using let is easier to understand.) Exercise 11 at the end of this chapter provides more practice with this special form.

Procedures are objects. And one of the things that we can do with objects is return them as the results of applying procedures to arguments.

Procedures as Returned Values

This is, for some people, the most difficult aspect of first-class procedures to get a handle on. But suppose we imagine the following dialogue between two friends, Alice and Bob:

Alice: Give me a number between 1 and 10.

Bob: Six.

Alice: x^6.

Bob: Okay . . . How about three?

Alice: x^3.

What Alice is doing here is acting as a procedure that takes as argument a number and returns a new procedure as its result. If the argument is 3, the resulting procedure is a "cube" procedure; if the argument is 2, the result is a "square" procedure.

Here's how Alice's procedure would be written in Scheme:

```
(define (expt-maker number)
  (lambda (x) (expt x number)))
```

The expt-maker procedure takes one argument, number; when we call expt-maker on a numeric argument, we get as our returned value a procedure that itself takes one argument x and returns (when applied) the value of x raised to the number power. Here are several examples of expt-maker in use:

```
((expt-maker 5) 2)
32
((expt-maker 4) 3)
81
(define cube (expt-maker 3))
(cube 5)
125
```

Let's follow through the evaluation of the top expression, ((expt-maker 5) 2), according to our Scheme evaluation rules. The first step is to evaluate subexpressions. The second subexpression, 2, evaluates to itself. The first subexpression, (expt-maker 5), must now itself be evaluated.

Okay: let's evaluate (expt-maker 5). The second subexpression is 5, which evaluates to itself. The first subexpression is expt-maker, which evaluates to the procedure object shown in Figure 12.10.

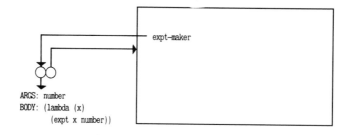

Figure 12.10. The expt–maker procedure object

We now have to create a frame in which the name `number` is bound to 5, and attach this frame to the initial environment (since that is the environment to which our `expt-maker` procedure is pointing). Now, in this newly-created environment, we evaluate the body of `expt-maker`. The body is a `lambda` expression, and the result of evaluating this expression is a procedure object—the one shown in Figure 12.11.

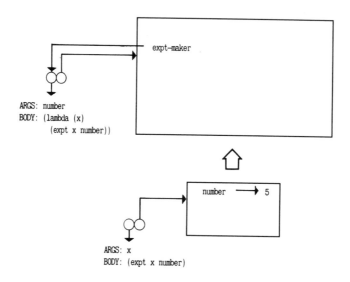

Figure 12.11. The procedure object returned by the call to expt–maker

Note that the procedure object in Figure 12.11 is not associated with the initial environment, but with a two-frame environment. The body of `expt-maker`—that is, the `lambda` expression—was evaluated in this two-frame environment; and whenever a `lambda` expression is evaluated, the resulting procedure object is associated with the environment in which the evaluation takes place. Another way of phrasing this is to say that procedure objects are associated with the environment in which they are created.

Anyhow, we have now completed evaluating the expression (`expt-maker 5`), and our result is the procedure object of Figure 12.11. So we now have a procedure object to apply to 2. Again we follow our evaluation rules: we create a new frame in which the name `x` is bound to 2 and attach that frame to the two-frame environment of Figure 12.11, since that is where our procedure object points. The resulting environment is shown in Figure 12.12.

Within *this* environment, we now evaluate the body of our procedure object—namely, (`expt x number`). You can complete the evaluation and show that the result is 32.

You should also, as an exercise, try evaluating the expression:

```
(define cube (expt-maker 3))
```

The environment diagram that you end up with should look like Figure 12.13. The interesting feature of this diagram is that we have a name in the *initial*

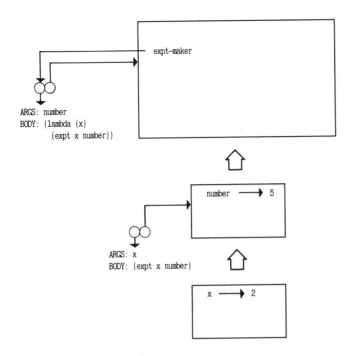

Figure 12.12. Calling the procedure object of Figure 12.11

environment that is bound to a procedure object associated with some *other* environment. There is no problem in doing this, but it's the first time we've seen such a situation. We will run across this kind of environment diagram again, when we discuss object-oriented programming.

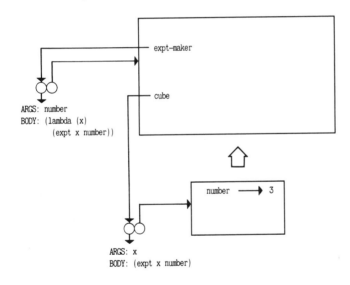

Figure 12.13. The cube procedure

Once you have arrived at the environment diagram of Figure 12.13, you should follow through the evaluation of the expression (cube 5), and show that the result is indeed 125.

Let's look at a few more examples of procedures that return other procedures. Here's one: make-list-accessor takes as argument a number n and returns a procedure that will get the nth element of a list.

Examples of Procedures as Returned Values

```
(define (make-list-accessor n)
  (lambda (lis) (list-ref lis n)))
```

Make–list–accessor uses the Scheme primitive list-ref, which we encountered in Chapter 10; just to refresh your memory, list-ref takes two arguments—a list and a nonnegative integer—and returns the appropriate element from the list. (The "zeroth" element, by convention, is the car of the list.)

Here are some examples of make–list–accessor in use:

```
((make-list-accessor 3) '(a b c d))
d

(define first (make-list-accessor 0))
(define second (make-list-accessor 1))
(define third (make-list-accessor 2))

(second (first '((5 6 7) (8 9 10))))
6

(third '(1 2 3))
3
```

Here's another example: the function–applied–twice procedure takes as argument a function and returns the procedure that applies that function two times in succession:

```
(define (function-applied-twice function)
  (lambda (object) (function (function object))))
```

The function–applied–twice procedure combines two principles relating to first-class procedures: it takes a procedure as argument and returns a procedure as its result. Here are some examples of its use:

```
(define 4th-power (function-applied-twice square))

(4th-power 2)
16

(define increment-by-two (function-applied-twice 1+))

(increment-by-two 3)
5

(define log-log (function-applied-twice log))

(log-log 58)
1.4013
```

You should definitely work through one of the examples above—say, the increment-by-two example—using environment diagrams.

We can generalize the function–applied–twice idea: suppose we wish to create a procedure that repeatedly applies a given function n times? Here is a Scheme procedure called function–applied–n–times that realizes this idea. Function–applied–n–times takes as argument a function and a number n, and returns a procedure which will apply the given function n times to its argument. (This one is scary, so hold onto your hat.)

```
(define (function-applied-n-times f n)
  (cond ((= n 1) f)
        (else (lambda (object)
                (f ((function-applied-n-times f (-1+ n)) object))))))
```

You will note that function–applied–n–times uses a recursive strategy: if we only want to apply f one time, then our procedure returns the function itself. Otherwise, function–applied–n–times returns a new procedure that takes an argument; applies f to that argument repeatedly, one less than n times; and then applies f to the result.

Here are some examples of `function-applied-n-times` in use. In a way, you have to see it work before you really trust it.

```
((function-applied-n-times 1+ 5) 3)
8
(define 8th-power (function-applied-n-times square 3))
(8th-power 2)
256
(define (delete-random-element lis)   ;returns the list minus one element
  (define (delete-nth n lis)
    (cond ((= n 0) (cdr lis))
          (else (cons (car lis)
                      (delete-nth (-1+ n) (cdr lis))))))
  (delete-nth (random (length lis)) lis))
(define (delete-n-random-elements number-to-delete)
  (function-applied-n-times delete-random-element number-to-delete))
((delete-n-random-elements 3) '(1 2 3 4 5))
(1 4)
```

As a last example, let's use the `sort-by-rule` procedure that we wrote earlier in this chapter. We will create a new procedure named `make-sorter` that takes as argument a comparison predicate and returns a sorting procedure that uses that predicate.

```
(define (make-sorter comparison)
  (lambda (lis) (sort-by-rule comparison lis)))
```

Now we have an all-purpose construction kit for creating sorting procedures:

```
(define sort-high-to-low (make-sorter >))
(define sort-low-to-high (make-sorter <))
(define sort-in-alphabetical-order (make-sorter string<?))
(sort-high-to-low '(3 5 8 2 4))
(8 5 4 3 2)
(sort-in-alphabetical-order '("i" "wanna" "hold" "your" "hand"))
("hand" "hold" "i" "wanna" "your")
```

An Extended Example: Plotting Functions

Let's put some of the ideas of the previous sections together and create a useful program. Our project will be to construct a function-plotter: a procedure that takes as argument any numeric function and plots it on the display screen.

Here's a first cut at our desired program. It isn't quite right yet, but it's close enough to illustrate what we have in mind. Note that this program uses the PC Scheme graphics primitive `draw-point`; if you find this primitive unfamiliar, you may find it helpful to go back and review the discussion of graphics in Chapter 7.

```
(define (plot-function f)
  (define (plot-loop x)
    (cond ((> x 150) (loop-forever))
          (else (draw-point x (f x))
                (plot-loop (1+ x)))))
  (plot-loop -150))
(define (loop-forever)(loop-forever))
```

The idea is that `plot-function` will take some function as its argument and then use the subprocedure `plot-loop` to draw the points corresponding to the function's value on integer arguments from -150 to 150. That is, plot-loop should plot the value of the function applied to -150, then -149, then -148, and so on all the way up to 150. After the plotting process is finished, the program goes into an infinite loop; this is done to prevent the PC Scheme interpreter from printing out a new line (and new line number), which might interfere with the just-created graph. You can stop the program in the usual way, with the (CTRL)-BREAK key.

Our plan isn't a bad one, and in fact the program will work on functions like the following:

```
(define (test-function-1 number) 1)

(define (test-function-2 number) (truncate (/ number 10)))
```

That is to say, (plot-function test-function-1) should work correctly.[5] But there are still several problems. The most serious bug is that we cannot plot functions that produce noninteger values; the draw-point primitive requires two integers as arguments. Thus, if we tried to plot the following function:

```
(define (test-function-3 no) (/ no 2))
```

our program would crash.

One way to deal with this problem is to make sure that no function that we try to plot ever produces noninteger values. To that end, we define the procedure make-plottable:

```
(define (make-plottable f)
  (lambda (no) (round (f no))))
```

Make-plottable takes as argument a function f and returns the function that "approximates" f, but only returns integer values. Thus, if f applied to, say, 1 would return 4.8, then our new function would instead return 5.

Now we could rewrite plot-function as follows:

```
(define (plot-function f)
  (define (plot-loop function x)
    (cond ((> x 150) (loop-forever))
          (else (draw-point x (function x))
                (plot-loop function (1+ x)))))
  (plot-loop (make-plottable f) -150))
```

This is an improvement: our new program will graph any function that we pass to it as an argument. But if some point that we are trying to plot has a y-value greater than 99, then that point will not appear in our graph. For example, try plotting the following:

```
(define (test-function-4 no) (+ 100 (* 2 no)))
```

The graph of this function "runs off" the top of the screen, and we don't get a very informative picture. The difficulty is that draw-point can't set any points outside the range of the screen. So once more, we set about improving our program: we will scale our function f so that it never has to plot a value with a y-coordinate greater than 99 (or less than -99). Here's our strategy: we find the largest y-coordinate (either maximum or minimum) that f would ordinarily plot between -150 and 150; then we create a new function which has the same shape as f but which has its maximum just at the top of the screen. For instance, our test-function-4 above has a maximum y-coordinate of 400 (corresponding to an x-coordinate of 150). We want this highest value to be plotted at the top of the

---

[5]If you are trying this program out on your PC, remember to use the graphics-mode, text-mode, and g-edwin procedures introduced in Chapter 7.

screen, so we'll create a new function that is just test-function-4 divided by 400/99; the highest *y*-value of this new scaled-down function will be 99.

Here's our final version of the program:

```
(define (plot-function f)
  (define (plot-loop function x)
    (cond ((> x 150) (loop-forever))
          (else (draw-point x (function x))
                (plot-loop function (1+ x)))))
  (let ((function-to-really-plot
          (make-plottable f (find-biggest-y-value-of f))))
    (plot-loop function-to-really-plot -150)))

(define (make-plottable f scale)
  (lambda (no) (round (* 99 (/ (f no) scale)))))

(define (find-biggest-y-value-of f)
  (max (abs (find-maximum-value f -150 150))
       (abs (find-minimum-value f -150 150))))
```

The find-biggest-y-value-of procedure takes as argument a function f and finds the largest absolute value of y that f will attain in the range from $x = -150$ to $x = 150$. Find-biggest-y-value-of uses the find-maximum-value procedure that we wrote earlier in this chapter, and a similar find-minimum-value procedure that is left as an exercise for the reader. We have also changed the make-plottable procedure: our current version takes as argument a function f and a maximum value scale, and returns a new function whose *y*-values will be scaled down by a factor of scale divided by 99. As before, the function returned by make-plottable rounds its returned value to the nearest integer.

The program ought to work now, and you might try graphing a few functions with it:

```
(plot-function square)
(plot-function (lambda (x) (1+ (cube x))))
(plot-function (lambda (x) (if (even? x) 0 50)))
```

Even though our graphing program is reasonably thorough, there are still many improvements you might consider. For one thing, the graphs that we produce will usually have different scales on the *x*- and *y*-axes. That is, one axis will be "squished" relative to the other; the *x*-axis always ranges from -150 to 150, while the *y*-axis might represent a much smaller or larger range than that. This is a consequence of the last improvement that we made—and if you prefer, you can undo this change and use the function plotter as it was before (i.e., with our first version of make-plottable). Or you could change the program so that it labels the *x*- and *y*-axes on the screen.

Yet another possibility would be to make the range of *x*-values a parameter to the plot-function procedure: for instance, (plot-function test-function-1 -500 200) would graph test-function-1 between *x*-values of -500 and 200. Or you could plot graphs in various colors. Or you might try to enhance the efficiency of the procedures that we have written already; the strategy of the find-biggest-y-value-of procedure looks particularly improvable.

Procedures as Elements of Lists

Procedures are objects. And one thing that we can do with objects is make lists whose elements are those objects. So there is no reason that we can't make lists of procedure objects.

And thus, without further ado:

```
(define list-of-procedures (list square 1+ (lambda (no) (* 5 no))))
(car list-of-procedures)
```
#‹PROCEDURE SQUARE›
```
((car list-of-procedures) 4)
```
16
```
((cadr list-of-procedures) 3)
```
4
```
(map (lambda (function) (function 10)) list-of-procedures)
```
(100 11 50)

To the Reader   If you still don't feel entirely comfortable with the idea of procedures as objects, don't worry. It's a notion that needs playing with. Take your time, and try to make up some original examples of your own.

Exercises

1. Since symbols can be bound to procedures, it is possible to evaluate a procedure's name, as follows:
   ```
   car
   ```
   #‹PROCEDURE CAR›

   If we need another procedure that has exactly the same behavior as an already-existing one, we can simply provide another binding—a second name—for the already-existing procedure:
   ```
   (define first car)
   (first '(a b c))
   ```
   A

   There are a number of procedures in our sample project in Chapter 10 that may be rewritten (in a simpler way) along the lines of the definition of first above. Here's one of them:
   ```
   (define (first-element cue-list) (car cue-list))
   ```
   We could have just as easily written:

   ```
   (define first-element car)
   ```
   See if you can simplify some other procedure definitions in Chapter 10.

2. Write a procedure called sum-result-of-functions that takes three arguments: two functions (say, function1 and function2) and a number (say, no). The result should be the sum of applying the first function to the number and the second function to the number. Here are two examples (I'm assuming for these examples that the square and double procedures have already been defined):
   ```
   (sum-result-of-functions square double 3)
   15        ;that is, 9 + 6
   (sum-result-of-functions double 1+ 5)
   16        ;that is, 10 + 6
   ```

3. Write a procedure named apply-to-random-element that takes two arguments—a function and a list—and applies the function to one element of the list, chosen at random:
   ```
   (apply-to-random-element list '(this is a test))
   ```
   (is)
   ```
   (apply-to-random-element 1+ '(10 20 30))
   ```
   11

4. Often we are interested in how long it takes for some procedure call to be evaluated. Write a procedure named `time-this-call` for this purpose. `Time-this-call` should take two arguments—a procedure and a possible argument for that procedure—and should return the time taken to evaluate a call to the given procedure on the given argument, measured as accurately as possible. (You will need to use the PC Scheme primitive `runtime`; see Chapter 5, Exercise 11.) Here are two examples of `time-this-call` in use:

```
(time-this-call factorial 50)
6  ;The time taken to evaluate (factorial 50), in 0.01 second units

(time-this-call sort-high-to-low '(1 2 3 4 5 6 7 8 9 10 11 12 13 14 15))
11  ;The time taken to sort this list from highest to lowest.
    ;By the way, the sort-high-to-low procedure was shown in this chapter.
```

A procedure like `time-this-call` is particularly useful for choosing between different strategies for the same purpose. For instance, we might have three different list-sorting procedures; by using `time-this-call`, we could try each of the sorting procedures on some very long list, and compare the time required by each sorting strategy.

When you do this exercise, you will find that there is some variability in the time taken to evaluate a given expression. For instance, if we time the evaluation of (factorial 50) several times in a row, we may get different answers. Try writing another procedure, `find-average-time-of-n-calls`; this should take three arguments—a procedure, a possible argument for that procedure, and a number of calls to average—and should return the average time taken to evaluate the specified procedure call.

5. Write a procedure named `filter` that takes two arguments: a predicate procedure and a list. `Filter` should return a list of those elements in the original list for which the predicate returns #t. Here are several illustrative examples:

```
(filter even? '(3 4 5 7 8 9))
(4 8)
(filter negative? '(5 -9 55 -2))
(-9 -2)
(filter negative? '(2 3 4))
()
```

6. Consider the following two procedures:

```
(define (use-comparison-to-remove-elements comparison lis)
  (cond ((null? lis) '())
        ((comparison (car lis) (cdr lis))
         (use-comparison-to-remove-elements comparison (cdr lis)))
        (else (cons (car lis)
                    (use-comparison-to-remove-elements
                      comparison (cdr lis))))))

(define (proc-1 lis)
  (use-comparison-to-remove-elements memv lis))
```

Describe in words the operation of `use-comparison-to-remove-elements` and `proc-1`. (And of course, feel free to experiment with these procedures on your own!) What would be a more informative name for `proc-1`?

7. You may be wondering why I often use the name `lis` for a list argument, instead of the name `list`. For instance, you might ask, why didn't I write the `map` procedure as shown below?

```
(define (map proc list)
  (cond ((null? list) '())
        (else (cons (proc (car list)) (map proc (cdr list))))))
```

In point of fact, I could have written `map` this way, and there wouldn't have been any problem. But it's a good idea to get into the habit of avoiding the name `list` as an argument name, since you might want to use the primitive procedure `list` in the body of the same procedure. For instance, consider the following procedure:

```
(define (make-list-out-of-each-element lis)
  (cond ((null? lis) '())
        (else (cons (list (car lis))
                    (make-list-out-of-each-element (cdr lis))))))
```

If we call this procedure on argument `(1 2 3)`, the result will be `((1)(2)(3))`.

Now: what would happen if you rewrote this procedure with an argument name of `list`? Follow through the resulting procedure call using the Scheme evaluation rules and see if you can identify what will go wrong.

8. Look up the `procedure?` predicate in your Scheme manual. Using this predicate, write a procedure called `apply-to-1` that takes as its argument any Scheme object and—if the object is a procedure—applies it to 1. If the object is not a procedure, `apply-to-1` should respond with an error message. Here are two examples:

```
(apply-to-1 1+)
2

(apply-to-1 1)
```
You have to call APPLY-TO-1 with a procedure argument!
1

9. Use environment diagrams to work through the evaluation of the following expressions:

```
((lambda (number) (* number 5)) 3)
(map (lambda (element) (eqv? element 'up)) '(whats up doc))
((lambda (function) (function 3)) (lambda (number) (* number 5)))
```

10. Why is `lambda` a special form and not a procedure?

11. Use environment diagrams to trace the evaluation of the following expressions (you will have to transform each `let` expression into its equivalent `lambda` form):

```
(let ((x 1))
  (* x (+ x 1)))
(let ((x 2) (y 3))
  (+ x y))
(let ((x 2))
  (let ((y (+ x 1)))
    (+ x y)))
```

12. Suppose we type the following `define` expressions:

```
(define a 3)
(define b 4)
(define (test-procedure number)
  (let ((a (* b 3))
        (b (* a number)))
    (+ a b)))
```

Use environment diagrams to work through the evaluation of:

```
(test-procedure 5)
```

Try typing in these same expressions at the Scheme interpreter to see if your analysis was correct.

13. Write a procedure named nth-root-maker that takes as its argument a positive integer *n* and returns a procedure that takes the *n*th root of its numeric argument. Here are some examples:

```
(define cube-root (nth-root-maker 3))

(cube-root 27)
3.

(define tenth-root (nth-root-maker 10))

(tenth-root 544)
1.877
```

14. Suppose we create a giant list representing a deck of cards:

```
(define *cards*
   '((a spades) (k spades) ... 52 elements in all))
```

Write a procedure named make-card-dealer that takes a number *n* as argument and returns a "dealer" procedure. The "dealer" procedure, when called on no arguments, should return a list of *n* randomly chosen cards from the list above (all distinct). Here are two examples of make-card-dealer in use:

```
(define five-card-stud-dealer (make-card-dealer 5))

(five-card-stud-dealer)
((k spades) (j spades) (3 hearts) (10 clubs) (8 clubs))

(define bridge-dealer (make-card-dealer 13))

(bridge-dealer)
((k spades) (q spades) (8 spades) (a hearts) ... 9 more cards)
```

A more elaborate project would be to write a procedure called make-dealer-for-n-hands. This procedure should take two arguments—the number of hands to deal, and the number of cards in each hand—and should return a list of hands. Here is an example:

```
(define poker-game-dealer (make-dealer-for-n-hands 4 5))   ;4 players

(poker-game-dealer)
( ((a spades) (j spades) (4 spades) (q hearts) (10 clubs))
  ((2 spades) (9 hearts) (j diamonds) (10 diamonds) (7 clubs))
  two more hands of five cards each  )
```

15. Write a procedure named compose that takes two procedure arguments (say, f1 and f2). The value returned by compose should be a procedure that when given an argument first applies f1 to it, and then applies f2 to the result. Here are some examples:

```
(define square-then-double (compose square double))

(square-then-double 3)
18  ; that is, (double (square 3))

(define question?
  (compose (lambda (lis) (list-ref lis (-1+ (length lis))))
           (lambda (symbol) (eqv? symbol '?))))

(question? '(is this a question ?))
#t

(define all-positives?
  (compose (lambda (lis)(filter negative? lis)) null?))

(all-positives? '(2 4 7))
#t
```

For these examples, I am assuming that `square`, `double`, and `filter` have all been defined. `Filter` is shown in Exercise 5 above.

16. Imagine that we have two numeric functions, each of which is a function of time—for instance, we might have the functions

```
(lambda (time) (* 30 (cos time)))
(lambda (time) (* 30 (sin time)))
```

Now, suppose we use these two functions to determine the *x*- and *y*-coordinates of a point to plot at a given time. Thus, at time `0`, the first function returns a value of `30` and the second a value of `0`, so the point we want to plot is (30, 0). We could use the same two functions to plot another point at time `0.01`, and then another point at time `0.02`, and so on. The result of plotting these points, one after another, would be a sequence of points—in fact, the result will look like a curve if the points are very close together (which they often will be, if we choose a small time increment like 0.01).

Write a graphics procedure named `follow-path` that exploits this idea. `Follow-path` should take two numeric functions as arguments, and should use those functions to draw a curve on the screen: it will do this by plotting *x*- and *y*-coordinates (as obtained from the two functions) at time `0`, then at time `0.01`, then at time `0.02`, and so on.

Here's an example. Suppose we evaluate:

```
(follow-path (lambda (time) (* 30 (cos time)))
             (lambda (time) (* 30 (sin time))))
```

Evaluating the call to `follow-path` should plot the following points:

$$[(30 \times \cos 0), (30 \times \sin 0)] = (30, 0)$$
$$[(30 \times \cos 0.01), (30 \times \sin 0.01)] = (29.998, 0.300)$$
$$[(30 \times \cos 0.02), (30 \times \sin 0.02)] = (29.994, 0.600)$$

etc.

The points plotted should form a circle.

Now you can use the `follow-path` procedure to experiment with a family of curves known as *Lissajous figures*. Start with the following procedures:

```
(define (sin-maker number)
  (lambda (time) (* 30 (sin (* number time)))))

(define (cos-maker number)
  (lambda (time) (* 30 (cos (* number time)))))
```

And now try evaluating the following expressions:

```
(follow-path (cos-maker 5) (sin-maker 3))
(follow-path (cos-maker 7) (sin-maker 2))
(follow-path (cos-maker 2) (sin-maker 4))
```

The pictures that you get make your computer screen look like that of an oscilloscope.

Both the `sin-maker` and `cos-maker` procedures return procedures whose maximum returned value is `30`—that is, both the `sin-maker` and `cos-maker` procedures implicitly employ a "scaling-factor" of `30`. Rewrite these two procedures so that they take a second argument named `scale`; this should be a number providing the scaling factor for the returned procedure. Thus, to generate the same curve as in the first of our three examples above, we would evaluate:

```
(follow-path (cos-maker 5 30) (sin-maker 3 30))
```

Try some additional experiments with `follow-path`, juggling arguments to
`cos-maker` and `sin-maker`.

17. Generating cryptograms—coded messages—is a time-honored programming project. In this problem, your job will be to write a procedure named
`make-encoder`, which takes as argument a letter-substitution association list
and returns as its result a procedure—we'll call this new procedure an
"encoder." The encoder will take as *its* argument a list, and return an
encoded version of that list according to the appropriate letter substitution
rule.

This sounds a lot more complicated than it is. Here is a letter-
substitution list (we'll assume our alphabet has three letters):

```
(define *code-1* '((a b) (b c) (c a)))
```

The `*code-1*` list indicates that the letter a will be encoded as b, the letter b as
c, and the letter c as a. The `make-encoder` procedure that you will write should
take as its argument a list like `*code-1*` above, and return an encoder procedure as its result:

```
(define encoder-1 (make-encoder *code-1*))
```

Now we can call our `encoder-1` procedure on any given list, and `encoder-1` will
encode that list:

```
(encoder-1 '(a b a c a b))
(b c b a b c)
```

Why do things this way? Well, for one thing it is easy to write new encoders:

```
(define *code-2* '((a b) (b a) (c c)))
```

```
(define encoder-2 (make-encoder *code-2*))
```

```
(encoder-2 '(a b a c a b))
(b a b c b a)
```

We can even combine encoders:

```
(encoder-2 (encoder-1 '(a b a c a b)))
(a c a b a c)
```

Moreover, we can write "decoding" procedures as well. As a second problem, you should write a `make-decoder` procedure that takes a letter-substitution
list as argument and returns a decoder procedure. The newly-returned decoder
should take an encoded list as argument and return the unencoded list as its
result. Here are some examples:

```
(define decoder-1 (make-decoder *code-1*))
```

```
(decoder-1 '(c b a))
(b a c)
```

```
(decoder-1 (encoder-1 '(a a b b c c a)))
(a a b b c c a)
```

18. Write a procedure named `successful-predicates` that takes two arguments: a
list of predicates and some object. The `successful-predicates` procedure should
call each predicate on the object, one by one, and return a list of those
predicates that returned #t when called on the object. Here's an example:

```
(successful-predicates (list integer? negative? even?) 100)
(#<PROCEDURE INTEGER?> #<PROCEDURE EVEN?>)
```

19. Write a procedure named `check-all-predicates` which takes as its argument a
list of predicates and returns a procedure. This newly-returned procedure

takes one argument and returns #t if (and only if) all the predicates in the original list return #t when applied to that argument.

Here is an example:

```
(define big-negative-integer?
  (check-all-predicates
    (list (lambda (no) (> (abs no) 100))
          negative?
          integer?)))

(big-negative-integer? -200)
#t

(big-negative-integer? -20)
()
```

CHAPTER 13

Altering Bindings,
Altering Objects

The theme of this chapter is change: how to change existing bindings, and how to change certain types of Scheme objects. The techniques that we will acquire in this regard should be approached with some respect. Effecting change is a heady experience, tremendously powerful and deceptively simple in operation; but it has its pitfalls. In programming as in other realms, the acquisition of power can prove a mixed blessing. *Caveat hacker*.

Up until now, we have treated bindings as more-or-less immutable things, written in stone. For instance, suppose we create a new binding between a and 1 by evaluating the expression (define a 1). A diagram of our initial environment would now look like Figure 13.1.

Altering Bindings

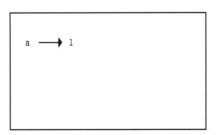

Figure 13.1. The variable a is bound to 1

Suppose we now want to change the binding for a—we want the name bound to 2 instead of 1. Our only method for effecting this change is to evaluate another define expression: (define a 2). This will work, but it's clumsy for several reasons. One problem is that the special form define really shouldn't do this kind of double duty—in Scheme culture, define is used to create new bindings, and it's considered awkward to use it to alter an existing binding.

A more serious problem is that we can't create a procedure to change the binding for a. Consider the following attempt:

```
(define (nice-try)
  (define a 2)
  a)
```

If we call nice-try on zero arguments, we will create a new frame with no bindings inside it; attach that frame to the initial environment; and then evaluate the body of the procedure inside the newly-created environment. (The final result returned will be 2, by the way.) After we evaluate the body of the procedure, our environment diagram would look like Figure 13.2.

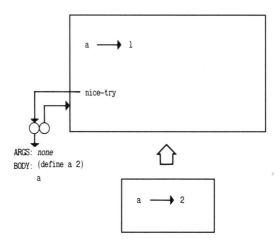

Figure 13.2. After evaluating the body of nice-try

The define expression inside nice-try created a new binding in the bottom frame, but it failed to alter the binding in the initial environment. Recall our discussion of define in Chapter 11: a define expression creates a binding (or alters an existing one) within the lowest possible frame of the environment in which the evaluation is taking place.

The Set! Special Form

There is a special form in Scheme—called set!—that is used to handle precisely the sort of task outlined above. The form of a set! expression is:

(set! *name expression*)

Here is the rule for evaluating a set! expression in some environment: first, evaluate the second subexpression following the set! (i.e., the thing labeled *expression* in the template above) within the given environment. Then, change the closest binding for *name* so that it is now bound to the result of evaluating *expression*.

To change the binding for a in the earlier example, then, we could type the expression (set! a 2). Or we could create a procedure to effect the change:

```
(define (better-try)
  (set! a 2)
  a)
```

Suppose we evaluate the procedure call (better-try). In this case (again following usual evaluation rules) we create a new frame with no bindings, attach that frame to the initial environment, and then evaluate the body of better-try in the environment just created. The relevant environment (before evaluating the body of better-try) is shown in Figure 13.3.

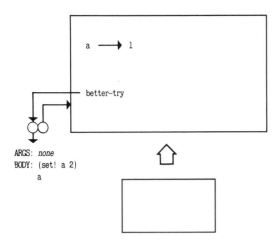

Figure 13.3. Before evaluating the body of better-try

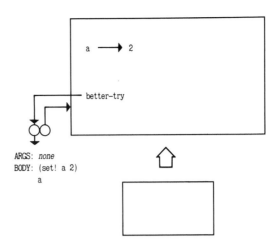

Figure 13.4. After evaluating the call to better-try

Evaluating the expression (set! a 2) in the environment of Figure 13.2 will now do exactly what we want—i.e., alter the binding of a in the initial environment. Figure 13.4 depicts the initial environment after the evaluation of the call to better-try.

There are two more general points you should be aware of. First, like all Scheme expressions, set! expressions do return some result when evaluated. However (as with define expressions, display expressions, and some others), we don't particularly care about the value returned. In other words, a set! is used "for effect"—because it alters some binding—and not because it returns an interesting value. In fact, the value returned by a set! expression is deliberately left unspecified in Scheme.

The second point is this: when you evaluate a set! expression, it is assumed that the variable name after the symbol set! is already bound. If it isn't—for instance, if you evaluate (set! b 3) before creating a binding for b—then you will receive an error message.

Global Variables

Often in writing a program, we find that many separate procedures refer to some particular object throughout the "running lifetime" of the program. As an illustration, let's say that we wish to create a program to generate form letters (we'll pretend that we're running an unscrupulous junk mail operation). One way to structure this program would be to have a number of procedures, each of which takes as argument the name of the current letter-recipient. In rough outline, the program might look as follows:

```
(define (print-form-letter name)
  (salutation name)
  (body name)
  (sign-off name))
(define (salutation name)
  (display "Dear ")
  (display name)
  (writeln ",")
  (newline))
(define (body name)
  (writeln "You may already have won the vacation")
  (display "of your dreams! Yes, ")
  (display name)
  (writeln ",")
  etc.)
```

To print out a form letter, we would call the `print-form-letter` procedure with the recipient's name (in string form) as argument. This string object is then used by several other procedures—`salutation`, `body`, and `sign-off`—each of which binds its own local argument name, `name`, to the object and incorporates it at various crucial spots in the printed text. But an alternative way to structure our program would be to define a variable `*current-patsy*` that is bound to the string object representing our recipient's name. Here is how this newer version of the program (again, in outline) might look:

```
(define *current-patsy* "Mr. Ingoldsby-Smythe")
(define (print-form-letter)
  (salutation)
  (body)
  (sign-off))
(define (salutation)
  (display "Dear ")
  (display *current-patsy*)
  (writeln ",")
  (newline))
(define (body)
  (writeln "You may already have won the vacation")
  (display "of your dreams! Yes, ")
  (display *current-patsy*)
  (writeln ",")
  etc.)
```

In our new program `*current-patsy*` is a *global variable*. Its value is a string object to which other procedures like `salutation` and `body` (and possibly many others not shown) may refer. We have used this programming strategy before; for instance, if you look back at Chapter 7, you will see that `screen-region-left-x` and `screen-region-bottom-y` served as global variables in the circle[2] project. Global variables are so called because they are bound in the initial environment and hence, in the language of Chapter 9, are globally bound. Of course, there isn't anything all that special about these variables: *any* name bound in the initial environment is globally bound. What distinguishes global variables is the way they are used: if many other procedures make use of some variable, then we tend to refer to that variable as global.

In the case of our letter-writing program, the advantage of this arrangement is that now we do not have to include a `name` argument to every relevant procedure. And because we have encountered the `set!` special form, we are able to write a `change-name!` procedure.

```
(define (change-name! name)
  (set! *current-patsy* name))
```

We could even throw in a `write-letter` procedure that takes the recipient's name as argument:

```
(define (write-letter name)
  (change-name! name)
  (print-form-letter))
```

The use of global variables is extremely common—in fact, you have most likely already incorporated this technique in your own programming projects. I have mentioned the subject here mainly to emphasize the fact that by using `set!` expressions within procedures it is possible to alter the bindings of global variables. In a similar vein, it is possible to improve the circle² program of Chapter 7 by incorporating three new global variables and as many judiciously placed set! expressions (see Exercise 6).

As long as we're on the subject of global variables and set! expressions, it's worth making explicit some of the naming conventions that we have already encountered. You may recall that whenever a new predicate procedure is created it is advisable (as a matter of etiquette) to give that procedure a name ending in a question mark; that way, other programmers will recognize it as a predicate by its name.

Similarly, procedures that use set! expressions to change the bindings of existing variables often have names ending in an exclamation point; the change-name! procedure above is an example. The purpose of this convention is that it makes it easier to read the program and find out which particular procedures are responsible for altering bindings. And since set! expressions are often responsible for hidden bugs (as we will see shortly), it is definitely worthwhile to be able to locate potentially risky procedures quickly within a program.

It should be noted, however, that the exclamation-point convention is a little looser than the question-mark convention for predicates. As an example, consider the write-letter procedure from the example above.

```
(define (write-letter name)
  (change-name! name)
  (print-form-letter))
```

Calling write-letter changes a binding (via the call to change-name!). Should the procedure then be named write-letter! instead? How about any other procedure that happens to call write-letter—should those others include exclamation points in their names? The answer, really, is that it is a matter of taste. The purpose of naming conventions is to communicate the structure of a program and aid in debugging. If the conventions are overused to the point of confusing the reader, then their utility is lost.

Another convention of sorts involves the naming of global variables. Programmers often name these variables with "markers" like the asterisks in *current-patsy*. This identifies the variable as global; and if there are several such variables, their definitions are typically grouped together within a program:

```
;; Here are the global variables
(define *some-global* '())
(define *some-other-global* 0)
etc.)
```

Again, this convention makes it easier to read the program and locate those variables whose values are used (and whose bindings may be altered) by many procedures.

Besides changing bindings with set!, it is also possible to change the contents of Scheme pairs by using two primitive procedures: set-car! and set-cdr!. Now, what do I mean, "change the contents of Scheme pairs"? Well, consider the following expression:

```
(define sample-pair (cons 1 2))
```

The name sample-pair is now bound to a pair object that we can represent graphically as in Figure 13.5. If we evaluate the name sample-pair at the Scheme interpreter, the printed result will be (1 . 2).

Figure 13.5. The pair to which sample–pair is bound

Suppose we now evaluate the expression

```
(set-car! sample-pair 6)
```

What this expression does is change the value associated with the first pointer of the pair in Figure 13.5. That pair now appears as in Figure 13.6. And if we evaluate the name sample–pair now, we will see (6 . 2) as the printed result.

Figure 13.6. The pair to which sample–pair is bound, after the call to set–car!

Thus, the set–car! expression changed the contents of the pair to which sample–pair is bound. The way that we think of this is that the pair object has changed; however, sample–pair is still bound to the same thing (albeit with new contents) that it was bound to before. Think of the pair object as a box, or container, with two pointers inside pointing to two Scheme objects; the name sample–pair is bound to that particular box, even if the particular pointers inside the box should change.

Before attempting any more examples, let's look at formal definitions of set–car! and set–cdr!. The primitive set–car! takes two arguments: the first should be a pair object, and the second may be an object of any type at all. The result of evaluating the set–car! expression is to change the car pointer in the pair so that it points to the object (the second argument value). As with set!, the result returned by evaluating the set–car! expression is left unspecified.

The set–cdr! primitive is similar except—as you might have predicted—the cdr pointer of the pair object is changed instead of the car pointer.

See if you can predict, given these definitions, the effects of evaluating the sequence of expressions below. Suppose that after each set–car! or set–cdr! operation you evaluated the names sample–pair–1 and/or sample–pair–2 (if relevant). What would the contents of these pairs be?

```
(define sample-pair-1 (cons 1 2))
(define sample-pair-2 (list 3 4))
(set-car! sample-pair-1 5)
(set-cdr! sample-pair-1 6)
(set-cdr! sample-pair-1 (list 7))
(set-car! sample-pair-2 8)
(set-car! (cdr sample-pair-2) 9)
(set-cdr! sample-pair-1 (cdr sample-pair-2))
(set-car! (cdr sample-pair-1) 10)
(set! sample-pair-1 (cons 11 12))
```

Here are the answers to the exercise above (they are also illustrated in Figure 13.7): after the first set–car! operation, the value of sample–pair–1 should print out as *(5 . 2)*. After the set–cdr! operation, the value of sample–pair–1 should print out

AFTER EVALUATING:

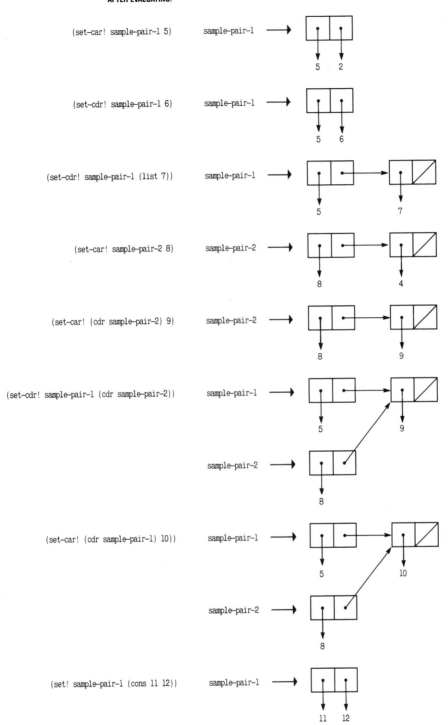

Figure 13.7. A summary of the sample session in the text

as *(5 . 6)*. The next `set-cdr!` operation changes the `cdr` pointer of this pair so that it points to a list; therefore evaluating `sample-pair-1` would cause the interpreter to print *(5 7)*. The following `set-car!` operation changes the contents of the pair to which `sample-pair-2` is bound, and evaluating this name would cause the interpreter to print *(8 4)*. The next `set-car!` operation affects the pair pointed to by the `cdr` of the pair to which `sample-pair-2` is bound (alternatively, we might say that we are changing the contents of the second pair in the list to which `sample-pair-2` is bound). The result of this operation is that the name `sample-pair-2` evaluates to a list that prints out as *(8 9)*.

The next set-cdr! operation changes the cdr pointer of the pair to which sample-pair-1 is bound; that cdr pointer is now directed at the same object as the cdr of sample-pair-2. Now the value of sample-pair-1 would print out as *(5 9)*. The set-car! operation that follows affects a pair that is part of the lists bound to both sample-pair-1 and sample-pair-2. Evaluating these names would cause the interpreter to print *(5 10)* and *(8 10)*, respectively. Finally, the set! operation actually binds the name sample-pair-1 to a different pair (which prints out as *(11 . 12)*, by the way). Unlike the earlier set-car! and set-cdr! expressions, the set! does not affect the *contents* of any object; rather, it changes the binding of the name sample-pair-1 so that it is now bound to a different object. The value of sample-pair-2 is unchanged.

Now that we've looked at some examples, it is worth pausing a moment to reflect on what it means to "change the contents of an object." By using set-car! and set-cdr! we are able to change the pointers within a given pair object; thus, pairs are objects capable of change. In technical terms, pairs are classified as *mutable* objects. With one exception, all the other types of objects that we have run across up until now have *not* been mutable. For instance, we cannot "change" the number object 4 so that it becomes some other number—say, 5; we think of the number objects 4 and 5 as two distinct objects, not one number object that has "changed" its contents. Similarly, we cannot change the symbol a so that it becomes b; nor can we change the square procedure object (in our standard example) so that it now performs, say, a square root operation. (The single exception—the other type of mutable object that we have run across, if only briefly—is the *string* type; in Chapter 16, we will encounter *vector* objects, which are also mutable.) The notion of mutability is explored further in Exercise 21 at the end of this chapter.

An Example: Circular Lists

Suppose we create a list as follows:

```
(define sample-list (list 1 2))
```

This list could be represented graphically as in Figure 13.8.

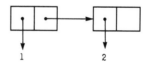

Figure 13.8. The list named sample-list

Now, suppose that we go on to evaluate the following expression:

```
(set-cdr! (cdr sample-list) sample-list)
```

The result of this operation is to create a *circular list*—a list with no "beginning" or "end." The new list is shown in Figure 13.9.

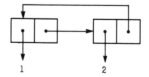

Figure 13.9. Sample-list is now bound to a circular list

The circular list to which the name sample-list is bound has some interesting properties. For one thing, we could keep applying cdr operations to it and never get to the end:

```
(null? (cddddr (cddddr (cddddr sample-list))))
()
```

Also, the way that circular lists are printed out on the screen is highly implementation-dependent. In PC Scheme, this list would print out endlessly as follows:

```
sample-list
(1 2 1 2 1 2 ... etc.)
```

Let's write a procedure called `circularize!` that takes as its input a standard list and returns the circularized list.[1] Here is one possible version:

```
(define (circularize! lis)
  (set-cdr! (last-pair lis) lis))
```

Our procedure is straightforward: we find the last pair in the list (the one whose cdr is ()) and change its cdr pointer to point to the first pair of the list. `Last-pair`, by the way, is a primitive that returns the last pair of its list argument (e.g., calling `(last-pair '(1 2 3))` would return `(3)` as its result).

Circular lists are useful data structures, since sometimes the data that we wish to model has a naturally "circular" structure. For instance, suppose we want to make a list representing the days of the week. We might go about it in the standard way:

```
(define *week*
  '(monday tuesday wednesday thursday
    friday saturday sunday))
```

In some respects, this list isn't really an optimal structure. We might, as one example, want to write a procedure that takes as argument the name of a day and returns the name of the following day. Here is one way of approaching the problem:

```
(define (day-after day)
  (let ((rest-of-week (cdr (memv day *week*))))
    (if (null? rest-of-week) (car *week*) (car rest-of-week))))
```

This will work: if we evaluate `(day-after 'monday)` the result will be the symbol `tuesday`. But we had to treat the last element in the list *week* as a special case, since to find the day after `sunday` we have to look back at the beginning of the list. A cleaner solution would be to make *week* a circular list:

```
(circularize! *week*)

(define (day-after day)
  (cadr (memv day *week*)))
```

The circular structure of the list *week* is now a better fit to our own mental picture of the days of the week.[2]

The Pitfalls of Changing Things

Changing bindings and pairs and so on is great fun, but—as noted at the beginning of this chapter—it has its dangerous side. One problem is that changing something in the middle of a program can often have effects that are widespread; an innocent-looking set! can potentially disturb the operation of hundreds of other procedures in our program (if those procedures directly or indirectly make use of the binding being changed). Moreover, we lose a certain amount of *predictability* in our code: it is possible, using set!, to write procedures that return different values every time we run them.

---

[1] Note that the "exclamation point naming convention" applies to procedures that alter pairs, as well as procedures that use set! to alter bindings.

[2] What happens if we call `day-after` with the name of a day that is not in our list, as in the expression `(day-after 'mardi)`?

This last point deserves a little elaboration. Consider the standard square procedure. Every time we evaluate (square 2), we get 4. Guaranteed. And because no set! expressions come into the picture, we only have to evaluate (square 2) once to know that the result of this expression will always and forever be 4. Now, in contrast, consider the following tiny program:

```
(define *counter* 0)
(define (add-to-counter number)
  (set! *counter* (+ *counter* number))
  *counter*)
```

We might now try a few successive calls to add-to-counter:

```
(add-to-counter 1)
1
(add-to-counter 1)
2
(add-to-counter 1)
3
```

Every time we evaluate (add-to-counter 1), we get a different result. Contrast this situation to that of square: the square procedure, unlike add-to-counter, can be viewed as a mathematical function—when provided with an input value, it always returns the same result. However we might wish to think about add-to-counter, we *cannot* think of it as a function.

This quality of "nonfunctionality" often makes programs that use set! problematic, as their behavior is hard to predict. Also, their bugs are hard to catch because every time we test the program we might get a different result, and testing a program is crucial to debugging it.[3]

Sharing

The set-car! and set-cdr! primitives pose additional problems as well. Suppose we are working with two lists, list-1 and list-2. We evaluate these names at the Scheme interpreter:

```
list-1
(a b c)
list-2
(a b c)
```

They look the same. But as it turns out, they are not eq? to one another:

```
(eq? list-1 list-2)
()
```

We might think, then, that it is safe to change one list without affecting the other. So we evaluate the expression:

```
(set-car! (cdr list-1) 'd)
```

And now our lists look as follows:

```
list-1
(a d c)
list-2
(a d c)
```

---

[3]We have already encountered a few cases of "nonfunctionality," albeit without paying much attention to the fact. The random primitive, for instance, also returns a (deliberately) unpredictable value every time it is called.

It seems that we have changed list-2 as well as list-1! How did this happen? Well, suppose we originally created list-2 by typing:

```
(define list-2 (cons 'a (cdr list-1)))
```

In this case, list-2 and list-1 exhibit a property known as *sharing* (or, sometimes, *aliasing*): they both provide access to the same pair object. Although the pairs named by list-1 and list-2 are not the same, their respective cdr pointers access the same list. The situation (before the set-car! operation) is shown in Figure 13.10.

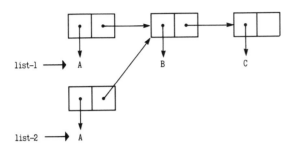

Figure 13.10. Sharing between list-1 and list-2

Now, you might say that we *could* have uncovered the sharing between these two lists by typing:

```
(eq? (cdr list-1) (cdr list-2))
#t
```

That's true. But the point is not that the sharing was undiscoverable; we discovered it, after all, with the set-car! operation. The point is rather that the sharing is not easily apparent: we can't tell list-1 and list-2 apart just by looking at their printed representations. Before we started playing with set-car! and set-cdr!, the issue was academic, but now that we can actually change the contents of pairs, the burden is upon us as programmers to keep straight all the occurrences of sharing in our code.

You might respond in turn that this is not a difficult problem. In fact, the example above is deliberately scaled down. But keeping track of sharing in a large program is an exercise demanding a great deal of care. *Someday*—mark my words—one of your programs will crash on account of unintended or neglected sharing. And then you'll think back to that weird book, years ago, that tried to warn you.

Object-Oriented Programming

Enough of the disadvantages of change—let's look at the bright side. Now that we have encountered set!, we are able to explore one of the most interesting themes in the history of programming: "object-oriented programming."

In the object-oriented programming style, the programmer's computational "world" is structured as a bunch of identifiable objects, each with its own local state. For instance, suppose we are programming a simulation of the solar system: we might want to create objects to represent the sun, the various planets, satellites, a few asteroids, and so on. For each object, the "state" might consist of its mass, its position (relative to the sun) and its velocity (relative to the frame in which the sun is stationary). Running the simulation would cause each object to periodically update its own state based on the current states of the other objects.

Or, to take another instance: suppose we are programming a simulation of international economic trade. In this case, the objects that we create might represent nations; their "states" might include population, agricultural resources, mineral resources, and so on. Again, as we run the simulation, the states of the objects would change in observable ways.

Among computer languages, there have been several notable champions of object-oriented programming: Smalltalk and Simula[4] are two of the better-known examples. Exploring the history of object-oriented programming is of course beyond the scope of this book; but we will see how this style of programming may be accommodated in Scheme.

An Extended Example: A Logo Turtle

As a sample project, we will create a "turtle object" similar to the kind made popular by the Logo language. Besides being fun, our program will illustrate some of the typical issues encountered in object-oriented programming.

A *turtle*—just to explain the nature of our project—is a little cursor that moves about on the display screen. (In Logo, the turtle is drawn as a tiny triangle, but our turtle will be invisible.) The turtle has a position—i.e., x- and y-coordinates—and a heading, or direction. Additionally, our turtle understands certain commands, like forward. When we tell the turtle to go (forward 50), it moves 50 "turtle steps" in the direction that it is pointing. Figure 13.11 shows the effect of telling the turtle (forward 50); note that the turtle draws a line when it moves, so that this command causes it to make a straight line on the screen.

Figure 13.11. Telling the turtle to go (forward 50)

Another important command is right. When we tell the turtle to turn (right 90), it changes its heading by turning 90 degrees to the right. Thus, if the turtle is pointing due north and we command it to turn (right 90), it will be pointed east after obeying the command. Figure 13.12 shows the effect of giving the turtle three commands in succession: (forward 50), (right 90), and then (forward 50).

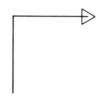

Figure 13.12. Telling the turtle to go (forward 50), (right 90), and (forward 50)

Finally, it is worth mentioning a standard Logo construct called repeat. By telling the turtle to repeat a sequence of commands some number of times, we can produce a variety of patterns. For example, telling the turtle to repeat the sequence (forward 50), (right 90) four times—i.e., to execute this sequence four times—produces a square. (See Figure 13.13.)

The few paragraphs above only hint at the fascinating programming projects you can undertake with turtles. Once you have played with these computational objects for a while, you might want to check out some other works on the subject.[5]

---

[4]Descriptions of these languages may be found in *Smalltalk-80: The Language and its Implementation* by A. Goldberg and D. Robson and *SIMULA: BEGIN* by G. M. Birtwistle et al. See also the References section at the end of this book.

[5]Some worthwhile readings are mentioned in the References section at the end of this book.

Figure 13.13. Telling the turtle to repeat the sequence (forward 50), (right 90) four times

A Proto-Turtle

Our first turtle implementation will be so simple that it will be unable to move. But this "proto-turtle" will at least get us started. Here is the central procedure in our implementation—a make-turtle procedure that can be used to create a new turtle object.

```
(define (make-turtle)
  (let ((heading 0)
        (x-position 0)
        (y-position 0))
    (lambda (message)
      (cond ((eq? message 'hdg) heading)
            ((eq? message 'x-pos) x-position)
            ((eq? message 'y-pos) y-position)
            (else (error "Message not accepted" message))))))
```

If you study the procedure above, you will find that calling make-turtle on no arguments returns a procedure object—a procedure object associated with a three-frame environment in which heading, x-position, and y-position are bound in the lowest frame. Let's take an example: suppose we evaluate the following expression at the Scheme interpreter.

```
(define joe (make-turtle))
```

Then we could represent joe graphically as in Figure 13.14. The middle frame in that diagram—the one with no bindings—is created when we apply the make-turtle procedure to zero arguments; the bottom frame results from calling the procedure of three arguments that is implicit in the let expression (recall the discussion of let in the previous chapter).

Note that joe is now the name of a procedure—that is to say, our "turtle object" is realized as a procedure. Moreover, the name joe is bound in the initial environment, but it is bound to a procedure associated with a different environment. The "state variables" of this turtle object (heading and so on) are bound in the procedure object's environment.

Let's take a closer look at the procedure to which joe is bound. The body of this procedure is just a big cond expression; each clause of the cond is intended to pick out a particular *message* to this turtle. For instance, if we type the following expression:

```
(joe 'hdg)
```

the returned result will be 0. (Unless this result is obvious to you, it is *strongly* recommended that you work through the evaluation of (joe 'hdg) using environment diagrams.) Something interesting is going on here: by sending the hdg message to joe, we are able to find the value to which heading is bound in the environment of Figure 13.14. Thus, although the value of heading is not *directly* accessible in the initial environment, we can find it by sending the appropriate message to joe.

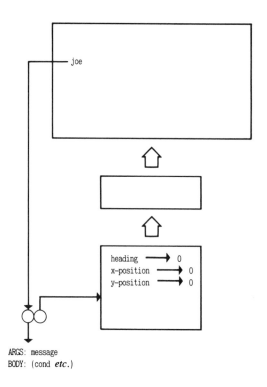

ARGS: message
BODY: (cond *etc.*)

Figure 13.14. The procedure object (in this case, "turtle object") named joe

The realization of objects as procedures is specific to Scheme; but the concepts of "hidden state variables" and "messages" crop up in some guise in virtually every realization of objects.

A Moving Turtle

The only messages that our first turtle understands are hdg, x-pos, and y-pos. That's all very well, but these messages only serve to *access* the state of a turtle. We would like to create a turtle whose state can change in response to certain messages. For instance, telling a turtle to turn right ought to change the value of its heading variable; telling it to move forward ought to change its x-position and/or its y-position.

Here is a new version of make-turtle that creates smarter turtles—objects that understand forward and right commands. The code looks difficult, but don't get intimidated.

```
(define (make-turtle)
  (let ((heading 0)
        (x-position 0)
        (y-position 0))
    (define (in-radians angle)
      (* (/ (* 2 3.14159) 360) (- 90 angle)))
    (define (forward steps)
      (let ((new-x (+ x-position
                      (* steps (cos (in-radians heading)))))
            (new-y (+ y-position
                      (* steps (sin (in-radians heading))))))
        (position-pen (round x-position) (round y-position))
        (set! x-position new-x)
        (set! y-position new-y)
        (draw-line-to (round new-x) (round new-y))))
    (define (right angle)
      (set! heading (modulo (+ heading angle) 360)))
```

```
(define (clear)
  (set! heading 0)
  (set! x-position 0)
  (set! y-position 0)
  (clear-graphics))
(lambda (message)
  (cond ((eq? message 'hdg) heading)
        ((eq? message 'x-pos) x-position)
        ((eq? message 'y-pos) y-position)
        ((eq? message 'fd) forward)
        ((eq? message 'rt) right)
        ((eq? message 'clr) (clear))
        (else (error "Message not accepted" message))))))))
```

The make-turtle procedure, when called on zero arguments, still returns a procedure object; but this new procedure has as its body a cond expression that chooses among six messages, instead of three as before. Before explaining the new fd, rt, and clr messages (short for "forward," "right," and "clear"), let's graphically depict the result of evaluating:

```
(define joe (make-turtle))
```

The resulting portrait of joe is shown in Figure 13.15.

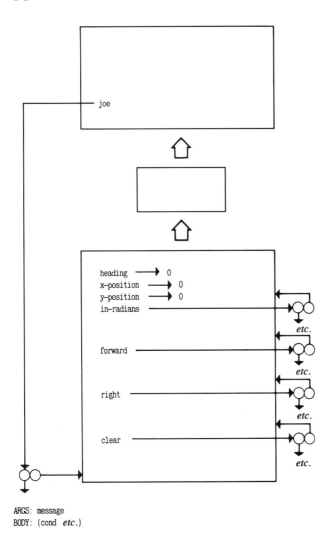

Figure 13.15. The new turtle object named joe

The bottom frame of the environment in Figure 13.15 now contains some names for procedures—right, forward, clear, and in-radians—as well as the state variables of the turtle.

Now, suppose we evaluate the expression:

((joe 'rt) 90)

The first subexpression, (joe 'rt), evaluates to the procedure object named right in the bottom frame of Figure 13.15. This procedure, then, is applied to 90. The result of this application (follow it through: create a new frame, bind angle to 90, attach that frame to the bottom frame in Figure 13.15, and so on) is simply to change the binding for heading so that this name is now bound to 90. If we evaluate

((joe 'rt) 90)

yet again, the result will be to change the binding for heading to 180. (See also Exercise 16 for an improvement to the rt message.)

The same sort of analysis applies to the fd message. If we evaluate

((joe 'fd) 50)

the first subexpression, (joe 'fd), evaluates to the procedure to which forward is bound in the bottom frame of Figure 13.15. This procedure is then applied to 50; the new values of x-position and y-position are calculated in accordance with the turtle's heading, and a line is drawn from the old to the new position. Let's examine that process in a little more detail.

The in-radians procedure, used in the body of forward, simply converts the turtle's heading into radians; in Logo, a heading of 0 corresponds to due north and 90 to due east (as opposed to the usual system in which 0 is due east and 90 is due north). I have kept the Logo system, so in-radians is a bit complicated; but if you check the code, you will see that it does correctly convert from "turtle heading in degrees" to "standard heading in radians." This conversion is necessary because the sin and cos primitives take radian-valued arguments.

Once we know the sine and cosine of the turtle's heading, the new x-position may be calculated as the present x-position plus the net change in the x-coordinate caused by moving forward; this change is the number of "turtle-steps" times the cosine of the heading. (See Figure 13.16.) The new y-position is calculated similarly, using the sine of the heading.

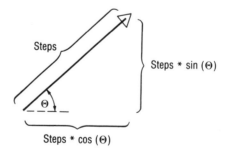

Figure 13.16. Finding the new position after an fd move

The clr message, finally, tells a turtle object to clear the screen and position itself back at coordinates (0, 0). I leave the examination of this message to you, as an exercise.

Using the Turtle

There are many extensions and modifications to make to our turtle program; some of these are suggested in problems at the end of this chapter. But we can get some mileage out of our present version. First, as a test, we can type:

```
(joe 'clr)
((joe 'fd) 50)
((joe 'rt) 90)
((joe 'fd) 50)
```

This should cause the turtle to draw a sort of "upside-down-L" shape.[6] We can go further, of course, and write procedures in the editor:

```
(define (square side)
  ((joe 'fd) side)
  ((joe 'rt) 90)
  ((joe 'fd) side)
  ((joe 'rt) 90)
  ((joe 'fd) side)
  ((joe 'rt) 90)
  ((joe 'fd) side)
  ((joe 'rt) 90))
```

If we now type (square 30) at the interpreter, our turtle should make a square of side-length 30.

A better idea is to make a repeat procedure that takes as argument a positive integer and a procedure of zero arguments:

```
(define (repeat number procedure)
  (cond ((= number 1) (procedure))
        (else (procedure) (repeat (-1+ number) procedure))))
```

The purpose of repeat is to run its procedure argument number times. Using this tool we can write turtle procedures more easily:

```
(define (square side)
  (repeat 4 (lambda () ((joe 'fd) side) ((joe 'rt) 90))))
(define (octagon side)
  (repeat 8 (lambda () ((joe 'fd) side) ((joe 'rt) 45))))
(define (pattern side)
  (repeat 8 (lambda () (octagon side) ((joe 'rt) 45))))
```

The result of evaluating (pattern 15) is shown in Figure 13.17.

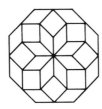

Figure 13.17. The result of evaluating (pattern 15)

Multiple Turtles

Every call to make-turtle results in a brand new procedure object, each with its own independent state variables. Thus, suppose we make a playmate for joe by typing:

```
(define sally (make-turtle))
```

An environment diagram depicting joe and sally is shown in Figure 13.18. We can thus write programs involving multiple turtles. For instance, we could create a program in which one turtle chases the other about the display screen; or perhaps the two turtles can be made to move about as "mirror images" of each other, one

---

[6]You will need to use the mode-switching procedures of Chapter 7 in order to use this program; you should enter "graphics mode" before giving fd commands to the turtle.

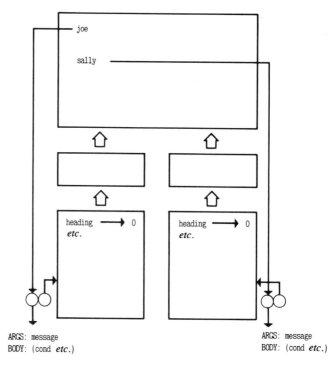

Figure 13.18. Two turtles

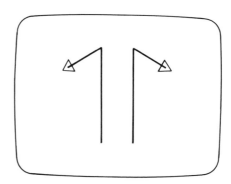

Figure 13.19. "Mirror-image" turtles

turtle moving on the left half of the screen, and the other—the "reflection"—moving on the right half. (See Figure 13.19.)

The notion of multiple objects interacting with each other is common in object-oriented programming. Another often-encountered notion is that of making a variety of different object types. For instance, we might create a system in which turtles interact not only with each other, but with other sorts of entities. We might have a "wall" object that can be placed on the screen and will not move, but will block the turtle's path. (To implement this idea, we would presumably have to write a make-wall procedure.) And then we could invent a "mole" object that can move like a turtle but can also burrow underneath walls. The possibilities are, literally, endless.

Exercises

1. Suppose we have a list of vegetable names, as follows:

```
(define *salad*
  '(lettuce tomato onion))
```

Write a procedure named `add-vegetable!` that takes a symbol as its argument (a new vegetable, presumably) and changes the list bound to `*salad*` so that it now contains that vegetable. The `add-vegetable!` procedure should return the new value of `*salad*` as its result.

Here are two examples:

```
(add-vegetable! 'cucumber)
```
(cucumber lettuce tomato onion)

```
(add-vegetable! 'radish)
```
(radish cucumber lettuce tomato onion)

2. Suppose we evaluate the following expressions:

```
(define a 1)

(define b 2)

(define (test! c)
  (define a 3)
  (set! a 10)
  (set! b 20)
  (set! c 30)
  (+ a b c))
```

Use environment diagrams to follow through the evaluation of the expression `(test! 0)`. If we evaluate the names a and b afterward, will either of their values have changed?

3. Suppose that we have left the "Who's on First?" program (from Chapter 10) running all day on our computer, and we want to know how many people played with the program while we were away. What we will do is maintain a "counter" variable, `*whos-on-first-count*`, which will be incremented every time someone calls the `whos-on-first` procedure; thus, it will provide a running count of people who have played with our program. Here's the counter:

```
(define *whos-on-first-count* 0)
```

Your job is to alter the original `whos-on-first` procedure:

```
(define (whos-on-first)
  (whos-on-first-loop '()))
```

Change this procedure so that every time it is called, it increments the value of `*whos-on-first-count*`.

4. Suppose we have the following global variables, indicating the current date:

```
(define *day-of-week* 'monday)
(define *month* 'march)
(define *day-of-month* 15)
(define *year* 1989)
```

Write a procedure named `ask-user-for-todays-date!` This procedure might work as follows:

```
(ask-user-for-todays-date!)
```
Day of week? tuesday

Month? march

Day of month? 16

Year? 1989

The example above depicts the user typing in various new values for the day of the week, month, and so on. Your procedure should use the values typed in to change the values of the global variables. In other words, if we were now to evaluate the name `*day-of-month*`, the result would be 16. (You will probably need to use the `read` primitive for this problem.)

As a second and more difficult problem, try writing a next-day! procedure that changes all the global variables to reflect the passage of one day. (You will probably find the leap-year? predicate from Chapter 4 helpful.)

⊛   5. Suppose we have a global variable named *current-base* that can have as its value any integer between 2 and 10 inclusive:

```
(define *current-base* 8)
```

Write procedures named add-in-current-base and subtract-in-current-base. Both of these should take two arguments—lists of single-digit numbers—and treat these lists as multidigit numbers to be added (or subtracted) in the current base. Here's an example (recall the current base is 8):

```
(add-in-current-base '(1 5) '(2 3))
(4 0)  ; that is, 15 + 23 = 40 in base 8
```

Your procedures should check that the arguments are valid numbers in the current base (e.g., an argument of '(9) is impossible in base 8), and should print an error message if they are not.

Finally, write a change-base! procedure that changes the value of the current base.

Suppose there were no global variable named *current-base*. How would you now go about writing add-in-base and subtract-in-base procedures that add or subtract numbers in a given base? What conceivable advantages are there to maintaining a global *current-base* value, as we did above?

6. Here is the top-level circle-squared procedure from Chapter 7.

```
(define (circle-squared sq-left-x sq-bottom-y sq-side-length)
  (clear-graphics)
  (region-loop
    screen-region-bottom-y sq-left-x sq-bottom-y sq-side-length))
```

The values of sq-left-x, sq-bottom-y, and sq-side-length, as you may remember, correspond to the bottom left coordinates and side length of the "hypothetical square" that we are using to create our graphic design on the screen. But one problem with our Chapter 7 program is that these values must then be passed, unchanged, as arguments to a variety of other procedures—for example, take a look at the call to the region-loop procedure that concludes the body of circle-squared.

It would be easier to create three global variables as follows:

```
(define *square-left-x* 0)
```

```
(define *square-bottom-y* 0)
```

```
(define *square-side-length* 0)
```

Now we can rewrite our program in a cleaner fashion. The circle-squared procedure should still take three arguments, but it should use these to set the values of the three global variables shown above. Any other procedure that formerly required these three values as arguments can now obtain those values by evaluating the names of the global variables. See if you can rewrite the program along these lines.

⊛⊛   7. Write a program that plays the game of hangman with the user. The program might maintain a list of words from which to make the choice of "unknown word" for a particular game:

```
(define *possible-unknown-words*
  '((v a r i o u s)
    (w o r d s)
    (f r o m)
    (w h i c h)
    (t o)
    (c h o o s e)))
```

Note that words will be represented as lists of letters (to be precise, one-character-long symbols); if you prefer, you might employ strings instead.

You will probably also find it helpful to use two global variables—lists—representing the mistaken letters guessed so far and the letters of the word that have been guessed so far:

```
(define *mistaken-letter-list* '())
```

```
(define *word-guessed-so-far* '())
```

Beyond this start, I will leave the rest of the project to you, except to present a hypothetical session with the game:

(hangman)

Word so far: (* * * *)*

Mistaken letters: ()

Guess a letter: e
Sorry!

Word so far: (* * * *)*
Mistaken letters: (E)

Guess a letter: o

Word so far: (O * * *)*
Mistaken letters: (E)

etc.

The game might end after the user completes the entire word or makes, say, ten mistaken guesses (whichever comes first). You might also consider different strategies for handling repeated guesses—for instance, what if the user foolishly guessed e again on the next try in the game above?

And by the way, if you *really* want to get fancy, you might combine this program with appropriate graphics procedures and depict the little "hanged man" taking shape over the course of the game.

8. Use box-and-pointer notation to work through the evaluation of the following expressions:

```
(define pair-1 (list 1 2 3))

(define pair-2 (cons 4 5))

(set-car! pair-2 6)

(set-car! (cdr pair-1) 7)

(set-car! pair-2 (cons 8 9))

(set-cdr! pair-2 (list 10 11))

(set-cdr! (cdr pair-1) (list 12 13))

(set-cdr! (car pair-2) (cdr pair-2))

(set-cdr! (cdr pair-1) (cdr pair-1))
```

9. Investigate the behavior of the PC Scheme primitives `delete!` and `delq!`. Compare the behavior of `delq!` with that of the following procedure:

```
(define (delq obj lis)
  (cond ((null? lis) '())
        ((eq? obj (car lis)) (delq obj (cdr lis)))
        (else (cons (car lis) (delq obj (cdr lis))))))
```

Here is a hint for comparing the two procedures `delq!` and `delq`. Suppose we define a sample list:

```
(define sample-list '(a b c))
```

Now we might try both our procedures using `sample-list` as the second argument:

```
(delq 'b sample-list)
(A C)
```

```
(delq! 'b sample-list)
(A C)
```

The two results look the same; what, then, is the difference between using `delq!` and using `delq`?

10. Write a procedure named `add-into!` that takes three arguments: a Scheme object, a list, and a position (a nonnegative integer). The result of calling `add-into!` should be to alter the list by adding in the given Scheme object immediately after the specified position (adding something after the zeroth position makes it the second element in the list). Here are some examples:

```
(define sample-list '(1 2 3))
```

```
(add-into! 4 sample-list 0)
(1 4 2 3)
```

```
(add-into! 'b sample-list 1)
(1 4 b 2 3)
```

```
(add-into! 'c (cdr sample-list) 0)
(4 c b 2 3)
```

11. Suppose we have an alphabetized list of strings:

```
(define *string-list*
  (list "banana" "orange" "pear"))
```

Write a procedure named `add-new-string!` that takes a string as argument and changes `*string-list*` so that it includes the new string in the correct (alphabetical) position. Here are some examples:

```
(add-new-string! "melon")
```

```
*string-list*
("banana" "melon" "orange" "pear")
```

```
(add-new-string! "apple")
```

```
*string-list*
("apple" "banana" "melon" "orange" "pear")
```

As a slightly more elaborate project, write a procedure named `ask-for-string-to-add` that repeatedly asks the user to type in a string and inserts the typed-in string into `*string-list*`. There are many ways to implement this procedure; for some, you will find PC Scheme's `read-line` primitive helpful, and you should investigate this primitive on your own.

12. Exercise 12 in Chapter 5 involved an investigation of random walks—we described a situation in which a bug on a number line flips a coin that tells him whether to move one integer unit left or right. (You might review that

problem now, to refresh your memory.) Suppose we wish to create a global variable—a list named *places-visited* that will keep track of the number of times the bug has visited any particular integer on the number line. The *places-visited* list will consist of a set of two-element sublists, each of which contains a "position" value (an integer that was visited at least once), and a "number-of-visits" value (the number of times that the particular integer was visited). Thus, if the list *places-visited* looks as follows:

```
*places-visited*
((-1 2) (0 3) (1 1) (2 1))
```

then we can conclude that the bug has arrived at −1 twice, at 0 three times, at 1 once, and at 2 once.

Write a random-walk procedure analogous to the one you created in Exercise 12, Chapter 5. Your new procedure should alter the *places-visited* list every time the bug moves to a new spot; thus, when the walk is complete, the *places-visited* list will provide a record of the number of times any individual site was visited. Note that if the bug starts at position 0 on the number line, the initial value of *places-visited* may be either the empty list or ((0 1)) depending on whether you want to count the bug's initial state as a visit at position 0. The sample value of *places-visited* above would result from a random walk in which the bug's itinerary was as follows: 0, −1, 0, −1, 0, 1, 2. (Here, I decided to count the initial position as a visit to 0.)

13. Keeping in mind the discussion of the concept of sharing in this chapter, investigate and compare the behaviors of the PC Scheme primitives append and append! Use box-and-pointer notation to depict the results of some sample calls to append and append!, and devise some experiments at the keyboard to justify your theories of how these primitives behave.

14. Suppose that we have two lists named list-1 and list-2. We don't know what expressions were originally used to create these lists (this was done by the programmer next door), but we can see how the two lists appear when printed out:

```
list-1
((1 2) (1 2))
list-2
(1 2)
```

Now, suppose we evaluate the expression:

```
(set-car! list-2 3)
```

What are the possible changes that could have occurred in the list to which list-1 is bound? For each possible change that you propose, show how it is compatible with some way in which the two lists might have been originally created. For instance, if the two lists were created as follows:

```
(define list-1 (list (list 1 2) (list 1 2)))
(define list-2 (list 1 2))
```

then evaluating the set-car! expression above would have no effect on list-1.

15. The following procedure, make-counter, may be used to create "counter objects." Before discussing just what a counter object might be, let's first look at our procedure:

```
(define (make-counter)
  (let ((count 0))
    (lambda ()
      (set! count (1+ count))
      count)))
```

Here is an example of how the make-counter procedure might be employed:

```
(define counter-1 (make-counter))
(define counter-2 (make-counter))
(counter-1)
1
(counter-1)
2
(counter-1)
3
(counter-2)
1
```

The sample session above illustrates the basic features of counter objects. The idea is that make-counter, when called on no arguments, returns a procedure which itself may be called on no arguments to return an increasing sequence of positive integers. (This returned procedure is what we are referring to as a "counter object.") Note that each call to make-counter returns an entirely *independent* counter object: thus, the names counter-1 and counter-2 in the example above refer to independent objects, each of which maintains its own "counting state." As an example of this notion of independence, observe that the very first time we call the counter-2 procedure the returned value will be *1* no matter how many times we have previously called the counter-1 procedure.

Now for the problem portion of this problem:

(a) Define the make-counter procedure as specified, and spend some time playing with counter objects to get a feeling for how they work.

(b) Use environment diagrams to analyze the sample session above. You should show the environments associated with the procedure objects named counter-1 and counter-2: by doing this you can explain, in particular, why these two counter objects are independent of each other.

(c) Rewrite make-counter so that it creates more elaborate counter objects; the new objects should accept "messages" like increment, reset, and current-count. Here is an example of how the new make-counter might work:

```
(define counter-1 (make-counter))
(counter-1 'current-count)
0
(counter-1 'increment)
1
(counter-1 'increment)
2
(counter-1 'reset)
0
(counter-1 'current-count)
0
```

The current-count message tells the counter to return its current count value (but does not increment that value); the increment message tells the counter to increment and return its count value; and the reset message tells the counter to set its count value back to 0.

16. There are many improvements that we can make to the turtle object that we created in this chapter. As a start, we might note that our turtle can only turn

right by integer-valued angles. In other words, we can tell the turtle named
joe to turn right by 90 degrees:

```
((joe 'rt) 90)
```

But we cannot tell joe to turn right by 22.5 degrees:

```
((joe 'rt) 22.5)
```

The reason the second expression signals an error is that the modulo procedure
(which we used to implement the internal right procedure inside make-turtle)
accepts only integer-valued arguments. Thus, evaluating (modulo 380 360)
returns a value of 20, but evaluating (modulo 380.5 360) results in an error
message.

Write a new procedure named float-modulo that accepts a noninteger
value as its first argument. Here are some sample calls to float-modulo:

```
(float-modulo 20 360)
20

(float-modulo 380.5 360)
20.5

(float-modulo 23.2 11)
1.2
```

Using the new float-modulo procedure, rewrite the internal right procedure
inside make-turtle so that turtle objects can turn right by noninteger-valued
angles.

17. This problem suggests some additional extensions to turtle objects. Each of
these extensions may be implemented by changing the make-turtle procedure
so that the turtles we create accept some new message (or messages).

(a) Add pen-up and pen-down messages to our turtle objects. When a turtle is
sent a pen-up message, it "picks up its pen" and no longer draws lines
when it moves. By sending the turtle a pen-down message, we tell the
turtle to "put its pen back down" and henceforth draw lines when it
moves. (The rationale for the names of these new messages is that we
imagine the turtle as having a little pen in its stomach: if the pen is up,
then the turtle doesn't draw lines when it moves, while if the pen is
down the turtle does draw lines when it moves.) As an example, here is
how we can tell the turtle joe to draw two vertical lines with a space
between them:

```
(joe 'clr)
((joe 'fd) 20)
(joe 'pen-up)
((joe 'fd) 10)
(joe 'pen-down)
((joe 'fd) 20)
```

(b) Add a set-heading message to our turtle objects. By telling a turtle to set
its heading to 0, we cause the turtle to face due north; by telling it to set
its heading to 90, we cause the turtle to face east; similarly, due south
represents a heading of 180 and due west a heading of 270. (See Figure
13.20.)

You can see by looking at this scale that if we tell the turtle to set
its heading to 45, the turtle will face northeast. Note that the turtle's
heading is determined modulo 360; thus, a heading of 360 is equivalent
to a heading of 0. Similarly, a heading of 370 is equivalent to a heading
of 10; so, for that matter, is a heading of 730 or -350.

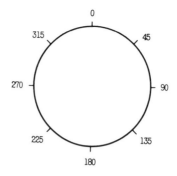

Figure 13.20. Scale of headings

As an example of how to use the set–heading message, consider the following sample session:

```
((joe 'set-heading) 45)
((joe 'fd) 20)
((joe 'set-heading) -90)
((joe 'fd) 10)
```

These commands will cause joe to draw a pattern rather like the number 7. Since the turtle should be able to set its heading to noninteger values, you will probably need the float–modulo procedure of Exercise 16 above.

(c) Add a set–position message for turtle objects. The set–position command should move the turtle directly to some position (specified by *x*- and *y*-coordinates) on the screen. Here is an example:

```
(joe 'clr)
((joe 'set-position) 0 50)
((joe 'set-position) 50 50)
((joe 'set-position) 50 0)
((joe 'set-position) 0 0)
```

Evaluating these expressions will cause the turtle joe to draw a square on the screen. Note that when the turtle sets its position to some new value, it draws a line between its present position and the new one—unless, of course, the turtle's pen is up (see part *a* of this exercise). Note also that since the coordinates of the PC screen have integer values, your set–position message should tell the turtle to move to the nearest appropriate pixel on the screen. For instance, if we evaluate the following expression:

```
((joe 'set-position) 10.3 -7.9)
```

then the turtle should move to the screen location with *x*- and *y*-coordinates of 10 and -8, respectively.

(d) Add a set–color message to our turtle objects. If we tell the turtle to set its color to 1, the turtle will henceforth draw lines in cyan; setting the turtle's color to 2 draws lines in magenta; setting the color to 3 draws lines in white; and setting the color to 0 draws lines in black. (Note that these four colors are derived from the "standard IBM PC configuration" that was described in Chapter 7; your system might provide more colors.)

Here is an example of the set-color message in action:

```
(joe 'clr)
((joe 'set-color) 1)
((joe 'fd) 20)
((joe 'set-color) 2)
((joe 'fd) 20)
```

Evaluating these commands causes the turtle named joe to draw a vertical line in two colors—half in cyan, half in magenta.

18. In this book, we have made extensive use of the concept of recursion. The patterns drawn by our turtle object may also be recursive—that is to say, we may create recursive "turtle-walk" procedures. Here is an example of such a procedure:

```
(define (c-curve level)
  (cond ((= level 0) ((joe 'fd) 4))
        (else (c-curve (-1+ level))
              ((joe 'rt) 90)
              (c-curve (-1+ level))
              ((joe 'rt) 270))))
```

This procedure can be used to draw a family of patterns known as *c-curves*. Try calling the c-curve procedure with arguments of 0, 1, 2, and so on (clearing the screen before each call). You will see a series of increasingly elaborate patterns, each composed of two copies of the previous pattern in the series. (Naturally, in order to run this particular version of the procedure, you will need to create a turtle object named joe.)

Dragon curves are another pretty family of recursive turtle walks. Here are two procedures that can be used to draw this series:

```
(define (left-dragon-curve level)
  (cond ((= level 0) ((joe 'fd) 4))
        (else (left-dragon-curve (-1+ level))
              ((joe 'rt) 270)
              (right-dragon-curve (-1+ level)))))

(define (right-dragon-curve level)
  (cond ((= level 0) ((joe 'fd) 4))
        (else (left-dragon-curve (-1+ level))
              ((joe 'rt) 90)
              (right-dragon-curve (-1+ level)))))
```

Try calling right-dragon-curve with increasing argument values, starting from 0. How does this series of patterns differ from the c-curve series?

19. Create a procedure named make-slot-machine that (as the name suggests) makes "slot machine objects." The state of a slot machine should consist of three tumbler values and a store of money. Tumbler values are strings: some possible values might be "orange", "cherry", "bar", and so on. Slot machine objects should accept at least three messages: money, add-money, and spin. The first returns the amount of money left in the slot machine; the second may be used to refill the money inside the machine; and the third effects a spin of the three tumblers, changing the amount of money in the machine according to whether the spin is a winning or losing one.

I am deliberately leaving many decisions up to you—among them, how to determine the odds of various spins. But to provide a rough example of how your program might work, here is a possible session with the finished program:

```
(define machine-1 (make-slot-machine))

(machine-1 'money)
100

(machine-1 'spin)
Tumbler 1: ORANGE
Tumbler 2: CHERRY
Tumbler 3: BAR

(machine-1 'money)
101

(machine-1 'spin)
Tumbler 1: BAR
Tumbler 2: BAR
Tumbler 3: BAR

You win: $100

(machine-1 'money)
1

((machine-1 'add-money) 200)
DONE

(machine-1 'money)
201
```

20. Write a procedure named make-hotel that takes a positive integer argument n and creates a "hotel object" representing a hotel of n rooms. Among the messages accepted by hotel objects should be the following:

all-full?

Returns #t if every room is booked.

next-empty-room

Returns the lowest-numbered currently empty room. If there are no empty rooms, this message might return (), or perhaps should result in an error message.

add-customer-to-room

Returns a procedure that takes a (currently unoccupied) room number and a customer's name as arguments, and books the room for the customer.

delete-customer-from-room

Returns a procedure that takes a room number as argument and frees up the room. (In other words, this procedure is used when a customer checks out of a room.)

whos-in-room

Returns a procedure that takes a room number as argument and returns the name of the customer in the room (or (), if the room is unoccupied).

21. In this chapter we have seen that pairs are mutable objects in Scheme—that is, they can have their contents changed by the set-car! and set-cdr! primitives. Not every type of Scheme object is mutable: for instance, there is no Scheme primitive that will change the number object 4 into the object 5. But we *have* encountered another mutable Scheme object type—namely, strings. In this problem, we will explore the concept of mutability as it applies to strings. (A brief introduction to strings was provided in Chapter 8, Exercise

24, and you may want to look at that problem now or do some poking around on your own before attempting this exercise.)

The most important Scheme primitive for mutating strings is named string-set! String-set! takes three arguments: a string, a nonnegative integer *n*, and a character object (I'll explain that last very shortly), and it changes the string so that its *n*th character becomes the one specified by the third argument. Before proceeding any further, let's look at a few examples:

```
(define *some-string* "abc")

(string-set! *some-string* 0 #\d)

*some-string*
"dbc"

(string-set! *some-string* 1 #\o)

*some-string*
"doc"
```

The third argument to string-set! is a character object; in Scheme, character objects are preceded by the characters #\; this prefix identifies the following letter as a character, much as surrounding double quotes identify a piece of text as a Scheme string. Thus, the first string-set! expression above is intended to change the starting character of the string named *some-string* to the character #\d. (Note, by the way, that the zeroth character refers to the starting character of the string.) Just as with set!, set-car!, and set-cdr!, evaluating a string-set! expression returns an unspecified value.

Here is a more elaborate example. The purpose of this procedure, named change-question-to-a, is to change a given string so that all instances of the question-mark character #\? will be changed to the character #\a. The procedure uses the primitives char=?, which tests for equality between characters; string-ref, which returns a single character from a string; and string-length, which returns the number of characters in a string. I leave it to you to read about these primitives in your Scheme manual.

```
(define (change-question-to-a string)
  (define (go-through-string char-no limit)
    (cond ((= char-no limit) 'done)
          ((char=? (string-ref string char-no) #\?)
           (string-set! string char-no #\a)
           (go-through-string (1+ char-no) limit))
          (else (go-through-string (1+ char-no) limit))))
  (go-through-string 0 (string-length string)))
```

Here is an example of our new procedure in use:

```
(define *sample-string* "b?n?n?")

(change-question-to-a *sample-string*)
done

*sample-string*
"banana"
```

Your job is to write a procedure named change-c1-to-c2. This procedure should take three arguments, a string and two characters, and mutate its string argument so that all instances of the first character are changed to the second character. Here's an example:

```
*sample-string*
"banana"
```

```
(change-c1-to-c2 *sample-string* #\n #\l)
done

(change-c1-to-c2 *sample-string* #\b #\f)
done

*sample-string*
"falala"
```

Finally, you might continue the exploration begun here and in Exercise 24, Chapter 8, by playing with the following PC Scheme string-mutating primitives:

```
string-fill!
substring-fill!
substring-move-left!
substring-move-right!
```

And the following are some helpful character-manipulating primitives:

```
char<?
char>?
char-ci=?
char-ci<?
char-ci>?
char?
```

CHAPTER 14

Debugging II

If you have been diligently working your way through this book, trying out programming examples and so forth, you have no doubt encountered your share of bugs. And you have probably become a near expert at CTRL-Qing your way out of the PC Scheme Inspector (or similarly exiting whatever debugger your system may include). In this chapter, armed with an understanding of environments, we will take a closer look at the Inspector and the process of debugging.

I should tell you that our coverage will be brief and somewhat narrow. In particular, we will only discuss the notion of breakpoints and some half dozen or so Inspector commands. There are two reasons for this brevity. First, a thorough examination of the Inspector, while interesting, would take us into a number of complex topics beyond the scope of this book. Second, many features of the Inspector are implementation-dependent and unique to PC Scheme; hence, this chapter will focus on those features that are likely to occur across Scheme implementations and that illustrate general debugging techniques.

Breakpoints

In Chapter 6, we encountered the error special form, which enables us to create our own customized error messages. We also encountered the trace primitive, which provides a signal every time a procedure is used.

Both of these are good to know, but there is an even more valuable technique for debugging programs—the use of *breakpoints*. Breakpoints are like "stop signs" inside a program; they cause the program to halt execution temporarily so that we can examine the state of our running process. Thus, rather than confine ourselves to typing expressions at the Scheme interpreter and waiting until results are returned, we have the option of studying the working program at some intermediate point.

To introduce a breakpoint within a procedure, we use a new special form: bkpt. The syntax of bkpt is reminiscent of that of error:

(bkpt *message expression*)

The *message* following the symbol bkpt is usually a string; this string will be printed out on the screen every time the bkpt expression is evaluated. The second

204

subexpression, labeled *expression* above, is evaluated and the result is likewise printed out. But the most important step in evaluating the bkpt expression is yet to come—namely, the program halts and an Inspector prompt is provided (alternatively we might say that we have "entered the Inspector"). This Inspector prompt enables us to evaluate expressions *in the environment that exists at the time the breakpoint expression is evaluated*. This is a first for us: up until now, we have typed expressions at the Scheme interpreter, and they have all been evaluated in the initial environment. But now we will have the opportunity to type in expressions that will be evaluated in some *other* environment. An ambitious prospect.

Let's start with an artificially simple example. Suppose we introduce a bkpt expression in the body of our standard square procedure:

```
(define (square no)
  (bkpt "The value of NO is: " no)
  (* no no))
```

Now when we evaluate (square 3) at the Scheme interpreter, we will see the following on the display screen:

```
[BKPT encountered!] The value of NO is:
3

[Inspect]
```

Both the string and the result of evaluating no have thus been printed out, as promised; and we now have an Inspector prompt to work with. The Inspector responds to a variety of special-purpose keys—like (CTRL)-C, which tells the Inspector to print out the bindings in the lowest frame of the current working environment. Before trying this first experiment, let's see if we can predict the result. In our evaluation model, a diagram of the current environment would look like Figure 14.1.

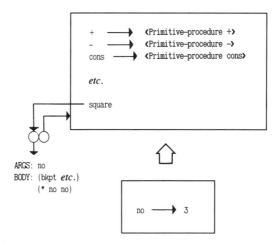

Figure 14.1. The environment that we expect

Figure 14.1 shows the environment in which the bkpt expression was evaluated and with which our Inspector prompt is now associated. Thus, if we type (CTRL)-C at the prompt, we would expect to see a binding between the name no and the number object 3. This is in fact what we do see—the Inspector's response to the (CTRL)-C key looks as follows:

```
[Inspect] Current environment frame
Environment frame bindings at level 0
  NO              3
[Inspect]
```

So far, so good: we are now able to look at bindings in some frame other than that of the initial environment. But further experiments reveal that our evaluation model, as realized by Figure 14.1, is not quite the whole story.

First, we need two more Inspector commands: the (CTRL)-P key and the (CTRL)-S key. The first of these enables us to move to the parent (next higher) frame of the current environment; the second moves us back to the son (next lower) frame.

When we use the (CTRL)-P key to move to the parent frame, we would expect—from Figure 14.1—that this would place us in the initial environment. But instead we see:

```
[Inspect] 'Parent' environment frame
Environment frame bindings at level 1
   SQUARE          #<PROCEDURE SQUARE>
[Inspect]
```

What's going on? Why don't we see the initial environment bindings—car and * and so on? Before answering that question, let's continue exploring. If we use (CTRL)-P yet again, we will see the following (henceforth the final Inspector prompt will be omitted):

```
[Inspect] 'Parent' environment frame
Environment frame bindings at level 2 <USER-INITIAL-ENVIRONMENT>
   SQUARE        #<PROCEDURE SQUARE>
```

The "label" in the second line says USER-INITIAL-ENVIRONMENT, but the only binding that we see is for the name square. Where are the bindings for primitive names that we expect to see in the initial environment? And anyway, why do we see yet another frame in which the name square is bound? Answers are on their way—but first let's go up one more frame. Before doing this, however, I should tell you that this next frame *will* contain the bindings for Scheme primitives, and these can take a while to print out. To stop the printing-out process—in case you're following along at the keyboard—you can type any key at all.

Now, if we venture up one more frame with the (CTRL)-P key, this is what we see:

```
[Inspect] 'Parent' environment frame
Environment frame bindings at level 3 <USER-GLOBAL-ENVIRONMENT>
   BREAKPOINT-PROCEDURE  #<PROCEDURE BREAKPOINT-PROCEDURE>
   %COMPILE-REGION       #<PROCEDURE COMPILE-REGION>
    OPEN-INPUT-STRING     #<PROCEDURE OPEN-INPUT-STRING>
     .
     .
     .
```

... and all your favorite primitives.

So, overall, it looks as though the environment diagram deduced by our trip through the Inspector looks like Figure 14.2.

Why the discrepancy with Figure 14.1? Well, to begin with, the PC Scheme initial environment actually consists of two frames—the top two in Figure 14.2. Thus, what we have been viewing as a one-frame initial environment actually is split into two. In the terminology of PC Scheme, the "initial environment" is the two-frame structure of Figure 14.2, and the "global environment" is the single upper frame; hence the labels that we saw printed out in viewing the two uppermost frames.

There is good sense to this two-frame initial environment structure; and indeed we might have noticed that good sense during our journey with the Inspector, upon reaching the second frame from the top. The point is this: in order to look at the new bindings that we ourselves have created using define expressions, we can look at the bindings in the lower frame of the initial environment. Thus,

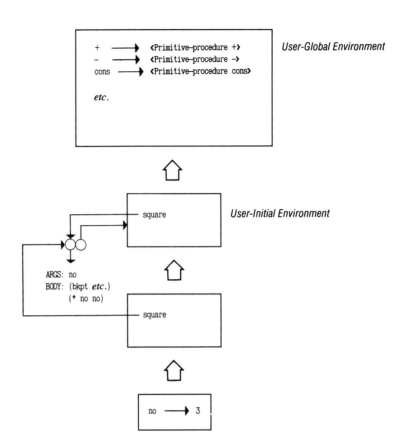

User-Global Environment

User-Initial Environment

Figure 14.2. The environment that we actually find

we don't have to hunt through all the bindings of primitive procedure names to find the few bindings of particular interest to us—which is what we'd have to do if Figure 14.1 were accurate. The two-frame structure of the initial environment is common to many Scheme systems, by the way, and was mentioned earlier in Chapter 11, Exercise 7.

What about the third frame from the top in Figure 14.2? This is a thornier issue, relating to the current version (3.0) of PC Scheme, and I will devote only this one hand-waving paragraph to it. The central point is that when PC Scheme procedures are applied, they actually create an intermediate frame in which the procedure name is bound, before creating the frame in which the argument names are bound. This arrangement is not common across Scheme systems, and it relates to the distinction between `lambda` and `named-lambda` that was alluded to in a footnote in Chapter 12. The discussion of `named-lambda` in the PC Scheme reference manual is essential reading if you want to explore this issue further on your own.[1]

In any case, I should mention that the discrepancies between Figure 14.1 and Figure 14.2 do not materially affect the accuracy of the evaluation model presented earlier, except in a few unusual cases. So the explanations in the previous several chapters ought to stand you in very good stead for a long time (in case you were worried).

To continue with our Inspector experiments: we can now wend our way back down the chain of frames using the (CTRL)-S command (here, S stands for "son"). If you are following along at the keyboard, you should (CTRL)-S your way back to the bottom frame of Figure 14.2 before proceeding to the next section.

---

[1] As mentioned, this paragraph applies to the version 3.0 of PC Scheme. The most recent official definition of the Scheme language does not include the `named-lambda` special form employed by PC Scheme, and future versions of PC Scheme may change accordingly.

Now that we are back in the bottom frame of Figure 14.2—i.e., the lowest frame of the environment in which the original bkpt expression was evaluated—we can try our hand at evaluating an expression or two. Here's how we do it: we simply type a space at the Inspector prompt (if you prefer, you can type (CTRL)-V). We now see a prompt that reads *Value of:*, indicating that we are supposed to type a Scheme expression to be evaluated.

As a test, we can type the expression no, followed (as usual) by the ↲ key. The result of evaluating this expression, printed out by the Inspector, is *3*. Clearly, had we evaluated no in the initial environment we would have received an error message; so this should give us confidence that we are in fact dealing with the environment of Figure 14.2.

We can now try a more interesting test. Let's type a space once more and evaluate the expression (set! no 4). This should change the binding of no in the lowest frame of Figure 14.2 to 4. After this has been done, we can again evaluate the name no just to check that its value has indeed been altered.

Once we're all done with the Inspector, we *could* go back to the Scheme interpreter by typing (CTRL)-Q, as we usually do. But in this case, it's more interesting to continue on with the temporarily halted evaluation process; we can do this by typing (CTRL)-G (for "go"). This command tells the interpreter to resume evaluation as always. The result, as printed out by the interpreter, is 16; this of course is consistent with the fact that we changed the binding for no midway in the evaluation of the body of square, before the call to the * primitive.

Now that we have become acquainted with breakpoints and the Inspector, let's try a slightly more interesting example. We will place a bkpt expression inside the factorial procedure:

```
(define (factorial no)
  (cond ((= no 0) 1)
        (else (bkpt "The value of NO is: " no)
              (* no (factorial (-1+ no)))))))
```

If we now evaluate (factorial 3) at the Scheme interpreter, we will again see the expected output on the display screen: the breakpoint message, the result of evaluating no (here, the result is 3), and the Inspector prompt. Suppose we now immediately type (CTRL)-G to continue the evaluation process. Because the continuing process results in a recursive call to factorial, we will again encounter a bkpt expression. And as before, the breakpoint message will print out along with the value of no—that is, 2, this time—and the Inspector prompt. If we continue one more time, we will see the result of the *next* breakpoint encounter, with no bound to 1.

Yet another (CTRL)-G here would finish off the evaluation process; but before doing that, let's try another two Inspector commands. The (CTRL)-U command allows us to look at the environment that was in effect when the current procedure (the one with the breakpoint) was invoked; in effect, (CTRL)-U moves up the "chain of actors" according to our model from Chapter 5. The inverse operation—moving down the chain—is performed by typing (CTRL)-D. (Think of U and D in this context as standing for "up" and "down.")

If we type (CTRL)-U at the Inspector prompt, we will see the following:

```
[Inspect] Up to caller
Stack frame for #<PROCEDURE FACTORIAL>
   NO          2
```

What we are seeing, then, is the lowest frame of the environment that was in effect when the current (halted) invocation of factorial was performed.[2] The call to factorial with an argument of 1 was done while evaluating the body of factorial in an *earlier* invocation, during which the argument no was bound to 2. By moving up the calling chain, we have arrived at the lowest frame of the environment associated with the previous call to factorial.

We can continue our trip up the calling chain by typing another (CTRL)-U at the Inspector prompt. This time, we will see the following:

```
[Inspect] Up to caller
Stack frame for #<PROCEDURE FACTORIAL>
    NO          3
```

The invocation of factorial with an argument of 2 was performed by yet another, earlier invocation of factorial, this one with an argument of 3. If we now type (CTRL)-U again, we will see:

```
[Inspect] Up to caller
Stack frame for ()
```

Without worrying about what in the world this response might mean, we can take it as an indication that we have reached the origin of the calling chain.[3]

We can now move back down the calling chain by typing (CTRL)-D. At every point along the calling chain, we find ourselves in the bottom frame of some environment; and, if we like, we can examine the bindings of parent frames in that environment by typing (CTRL)-P as we did before. Thus, by typing the appropriate commands at the Inspector, we can find our way into any frame we are interested in—the parent frame of the current invocation's lowest frame, the parent frame of the previous invocation's lowest frame, and so on. Wandering around like this can be extremely helpful for debugging programs: often, the bug that eventually "crashes" a program lies not in the procedure that is being invoked at the time of the crash, but rather in some earlier calling procedure. (We'll see an example of this shortly.) It should be mentioned, though, that it is easy to lose your bearings in a labyrinth of frames; you might find it helpful to make a map as you poke around with the Inspector (rather like playing an adventure game).

Listing Procedures

As a final experiment with the factorial procedure, let's first return to the original frame in which the latest bkpt was encountered (you can use (CTRL)-D to go back to this frame if you were following along in the previous section). Then read on. . . .

It's often desirable, once a breakpoint is encountered, to look at the code of the procedure whose invocation caused the breakpoint. In our current example, we might want to see the code for the factorial procedure. Of course, we might have a listing for our program sitting around; but there is also a way of examining the factorial code directly from the Inspector. To do this, we can type (CTRL)-L at the Inspector prompt.

If you try this command right now, however, you will find that it doesn't quite work—all you will see is the following:

```
[Inspect] List Procedure
#<PROCEDURE FACTORIAL>
```

---

[2] Don't worry about the phrase "stack frame" in the printed-out message. What we have informally called the "chain of actors" or "calling chain" is referred to as a *call stack* by PC Scheme. Explaining the term "stack" would take us far afield into language implementation issues; if you want to pursue the matter, start with the PC Scheme User's Guide and see also the References section at the end of this book.

[3] The exact message that you see in your PC Scheme system at this point may vary with the particular version you are running. Our attitude of unconcern for that message, however, remains unchanged.

Not very valuable: we wanted to see the code for factorial, not just its name. The problem is that in PC Scheme, the code for any given procedure is not stored in printable form. We can change this situation, however, by exiting the Inspector and typing the following at the Scheme interpreter:

```
(set! pcs-debug-mode #t)
```

You may recall the pcs-debug-mode variable from Chapter 6; we changed its value to #t so that we could use the trace primitive more informatively. In this case, by setting pcs-debug-mode to #t, we ensure that any procedure that we create in the future will have its code (in printable form) stored along with it. So what you should do, if you are following along at the keyboard, is:

1. Exit the Inspector (with (CTRL)-Q) and evaluate the set! expression above at the Scheme interpreter.

2. Go back to the editor and evaluate the definition of factorial once more, without changing any code; the idea is that now, when factorial is defined, its code will be retained with it.

3. Return to the Scheme interpreter and try evaluating (factorial 3).

4. When you encounter the first breakpoint, try using the (CTRL)-L Inspector command. What you should see at this point is the following:

```
[Inspector] List Procedure
#<PROCEDURE FACTORIAL> =
(LAMBDA (NO)
  (COND ((= NO 0) 1)
        (ELSE (BKPT "The value of NO is: " NO)
              (* NO (FACTORIAL (-1+ NO)))))))
```

A Brief Note on Pcs-Debug-Mode

The variable pcs-debug-mode is specific to PC Scheme. It is used to control certain features of the Scheme system relevant to debugging: as we have seen, by changing its value to #t, we enrich the trace primitive and the procedure-listing facility of the Inspector.[4] Generally, pcs-debug-mode is bound to #f, since our Scheme system will work more efficiently under these conditions; storing procedure code, for instance, is usually a waste of our computer's memory space unless we are really likely to examine that code.

Thus, the idea of pcs-debug-mode is that it is a "switch" that we can turn on when creating procedures that we wish to examine carefully (e.g., by using trace or printing out code). Under normal circumstances, as an efficiency measure, we leave the switch off—that is, we leave pcs-debug-mode with its original value of #f. Note that pcs-debug-mode may thus be used *selectively*. We can set it to #t for a while, and define some procedures that we want to treat carefully; then, later, we can set it back to #f and define less problematic procedures.

And one final word on the subject. According to the PC Scheme User's Guide, the bindings that are visible from within a breakpoint—that is, the bindings that we can look at with the Inspector—may differ depending on the value of pcs-debug-mode. In particular, when pcs-debug-mode is set to #f, some bindings may not be printable in the Inspector (again, as an efficiency measure). Thus, to get a full listing of all bindings in the frame created by invoking some procedure, you will probably want to create that procedure with pcs-debug-mode set to #t. This is yet another instance of using pcs-debug-mode to select those procedure definitions that we wish to perform "carefully." In our earlier examples, we defined both square and factorial with pcs-debug-mode set to #f; as an experiment, you should see

---

[4] See also Exercise 7.

for yourself if there is any additional information to be obtained when these procedures are defined while pcs–debug–mode is set to #t.

A Breakpoint Sampler

The examples of breakpoint usage shown above were deliberately simple. In small programs with only several procedures, it probably isn't necessary to debug with breakpoints—it's easier to use other methods, from putting a trace on a procedure to staring hard at the code and "playing computer" in one's mind. However, once your programs start to get larger and larger, it's important to have a broad arsenal of debugging techniques at hand. What follows is a brief smorgasbord of ways to use breakpoints. These are not, of course, the only "good" or "allowable" ways—just possibilities.

Finding the Caller of a Procedure

Suppose we have a large program that seems to crash every few hours by running out of space. We suspect that the problem may involve a recursive sum–squares–to–0 procedure:

```
(define (sum-squares-to-0 number)
  (cond ((= number 0) 0)
        (else (+ (square number)
                 (sum-squares-to-0 (-1+ number))))))
```

Our hypothesis is that this procedure is somehow being called with a negative argument and thus never reaches the appropriate base case (in which number is bound to 0).

Well, what to do? We know that the problem isn't really in sum–squares–to–0, but in whoever is calling this procedure with a negative argument. How do we find the caller?

Here is one possible strategy:

```
(define (sum-squares-to-0 number)
  (cond ((or (not (integer? number)) (< number 0))
         (bkpt "What joker called me with argument: " number))
        ((= number 0) 0)
        (else (+ (square number)
                 (sum-squares-to-0 (-1+ number))))))
```

Now, if sum–squares–to–0 is called with a negative (or noninteger) argument, the bkpt expression will be evaluated and the Inspector will be entered. We can then use the (CTRL)-U command to locate the offending caller.

Looking at State Variables Within an Object

Suppose we are programming with "objects" as described in the previous chapter. Often, we will design some sort of object that has many more internal state variables than we usually want to look at. For instance, we might create a "circuit" object that has, as its state variables, some "input wire values," some "output wire values," and some "internal wire values." Our object only accepts messages to set the values of the input wires, and to observe the values of both input and output wires; but because there are many internal wire values, we haven't included messages to look at them.

Under certain conditions, however, we may want to observe the bindings of the usually invisible state variables corresponding to internal wires. One approach is to include an emergency message to our object; sending this message causes a breakpoint and allows us to evaluate expressions in the environment of the object. Here, in outline, is what this idea might look like:

```
(define (make-circuit)
  (let ((input-1 0)
        (input-2 0)
        (internal-1 0)
        .
        .
        .
        (internal-n 0)
        (output-1 0)
        (output-2 0))
```

   presumably some internal definitions here
       .

```
    (lambda (message)
      (cond ((eq? message 'set-input-1!) etc.)
```

          .
          .

      A bunch of messages for setting and observing
      input and output wire values

          .

```
            ((eq? message 'emergency)
             (bkpt "You are now inside a circuit object." message))
            (else (error "Message not accepted" message))))))
```

The point of the `emergency` message is that it now allows us to enter the environment of any circuit object and examine the states of various bindings—we might even use `set!` to alter those bindings. This gives our computational objects a quality of user-accessibility that they didn't have before.

In the course of developing a large program, we sometimes run across a situation where some pieces of the program work but others don't. For instance, suppose we are writing a program to play chess: the program is intended to try some 300 rules in every playing situation, and to see if any of these rules are applicable. There might be a `king-in-check?` rule, a `queen-in-jeopardy?` rule, etc., etc.—and the next move will be determined by acceding to the suggestion of the highest-priority rule. Thus, if the `king-in-check?` rule is applicable, it will determine the next move (since this would be the highest priority situation).

Great idea for a program. The problem is, we've only implemented four rules so far this year. So we might decide that somewhere in our program, if we find that none of the current rules is applicable, we ourselves—the implementors—will decide the next move on behalf of the program. This, of course, is only a temporary "patch"; eventually, the program ought to play chess on its own. But for now, for the sake of not aborting every sample game, we will include a special facility for choosing the next move on behalf of the program.

Here, in very rough and fanciful outline, is how such a situation might look:

Providing Makeshift Interactivity

```
(define (find-next-move current-position)
  (let ((emergency-move '()))
    (cond ((king-in-check? current-position) ... )
          ((queen-in-jeopardy? current-position) ... )
          .
          .
          .
          (else (bkpt "Uh-oh! Set emergency-move!" '())
                emergency-move))))
```

In this case, if none of the current rules proves useful, we will enter a breakpoint. Should this happen, we can examine the binding of `current-position` and suggest a move by evaluating a `set!` expression for the variable `emergency-move`. After setting this variable, we allow the program to continue running; since the last `cond` clause ends by returning the value of `emergency-move`, our suggested move will be the value returned by the call to `find-next-move`. Okay, it isn't exactly pretty, but for now all we might want is a *running* program so that we can work our way toward a *finished* program.

Exercises

1. Suppose that, instead of writing `factorial` in our usual way, we write a tail recursive version; and suppose further that we include a breakpoint in our program, as follows:

```
(define (factorial n)
  (fact-helper 1 n))

(define (fact-helper result count)
  (cond ((= count 0) result)
        (else (bkpt "The values of result and count are: "
                    (list result count))
              (fact-helper (* result count) (-1+ count)))))
```

Try working with the sample program above and compare your results with the `factorial` example in this chapter. For instance, suppose you call the new `factorial` with an argument of 3 and then continue on from the first two breakpoints that you encounter; eventually, you will reach a breakpoint where the values of `result` and `count` are 6 and 1, respectively. Now, what happens when you type (CTRL)-U at the Inspector prompt to find the caller of the current invocation of `fact-helper`? Can you see why this is consistent with the actor model and with what you know about tail recursive procedures?

2. Consider the following two-procedure program:

```
(define (blah x)
  (bar x))

(define (bar y)
  (bkpt "The value of y is: " y)
  (* y 5))
```

Define these procedures and evaluate the expression `(blah 3)`; you can see that you will encounter a breakpoint when the call to `bar` is evaluated. Try typing (CTRL)-U at the Inspector prompt to find the caller of `bar`. Can you explain the result that you get? (The issues involved in this example are similar to those in Exercise 1 above.)

What do your results imply about the `sum-squares-to-0` example in this chapter: in particular, can we always find the caller of a procedure?

3. What happens when you evaluate a `bkpt` expression in the initial environment (by typing it at the interpreter)?

4. Try redoing one of the examples in this chapter (e.g., the `square` example), but with one alteration: namely, replace any `bkpt` expression in the program with a similar `error` expression. When you test your rewritten program, you will again encounter an Inspector prompt; what environment is the prompt associated with now?

5. PC Scheme contains a number of additional useful debugging procedures. Find the descriptions of the following in your manual: break, break-entry, break-exit, and break-both. Compare these procedures with their "tracing cousins" trace, trace-entry, trace-exit, and trace-both. Try defining some simple procedure—say, double—and use break to enter a breakpoint every time the procedure is called.

   Once you've got your example working, you can use the PC Scheme procedure unbreak to "undo" the effect of the call to break; see the manual for a description of this procedure (as well as unbreak-entry and unbreak-exit).

6. Suppose you have been using the various commands (CTRL)-U, (CTRL)-D, (CTRL)-P, and (CTRL)-S to explore some complicated environment structure; and by now, you have trekked through so many frames that you are totally lost. You can "reinitialize" the PC Scheme Inspector by typing the exclamation point character "!" at the Inspector prompt (note that you do *not* use the (CTRL) key in this instance). By typing "!," you can return to the original frame in which you started—that is, the frame associated with the last bkpt expression that you evaluated.

   Try experimenting on your own with the "!" Inspector command.

7. By now, you have probably encountered some situations in which you felt it would be helpful to look at the code of a procedure without entering the editor. For instance, suppose we want to check the double procedure to ensure that we wrote it correctly. The standard way of doing this would be to go back to the editor and find the definition of double; or perhaps, if we printed out a listing of our program on paper some time earlier, we could look at that.

   A quick and easy way to look at the code for double is to use PC Scheme's pp procedure (short for "pretty-print"). By evaluating the expression (pp double) at the interpreter, it is possible to examine the code for the double procedure:

```
(pp double)

#<PROCEDURE DOUBLE> =
(lambda (no)
  (* 2 no))
```

Before you try this, however, there is one important point to note: when you use pp to examine the code of a procedure, that procedure should have been defined with pcs-debug-mode set to #t. Otherwise, calling pp on a procedure will simply return the name of the procedure.

   In sum, then, you might try the following experiment:

   1. Define some new procedure with pcs-debug-mode set to #f.

   2. Try calling pp on this procedure and note the result that you get.

   3. Set pcs-debug-mode to #t; then reevaluate the definition of your procedure.

   4. Now call pp on the procedure and note the result.

CHAPTER 15

Sample
Projects IV

In this chapter, we will bring together some of the techniques we have explored throughout this book to create a prototype of a "rule-based expert system." Our example will be on a very small scale, and some issues involved in the construction of real-world systems will unavoidably be slighted; but our system will provide an introduction to many of the principles involved in creating those larger programs.

We will proceed with our project in two major phases. The first phase will be to create a pattern-matching program that enables the user to create a database of "assertions" (i.e., known facts) and to explore that database in a flexible and interesting way. This program is itself useful, but the second phase of our project will augment our pattern matcher with a set of rules that enables the system to draw simple "inferences."[1]

Pattern Matching

As the first step in our project, we will create a database program that employs *pattern matching* to retrieve facts. Loosely, pattern matching is the activity of deciding whether certain test objects match up with (or, as is sometimes said, *instantiate*) a particular pattern (or *template*). For instance, we might say that the sentence "Springfield is the capital of Illinois" matches the pattern *"wild-card-1 is the capital of wild-card-2,"* where each *wild-card* is allowed to match up with any word at all; other matching objects for this pattern would be "Sofia is the capital of Bulgaria," and "What is the capital of Brazil?"

The notion of what, exactly, constitutes a pattern is not written in stone; rather, it varies from one program to another depending on our purpose. Under some interpretations, we might say that the sentences in the previous paragraph match the pattern "Sentences about Capitals." Or, to take a different example, we might say that the problem of deciding that the cartoon character Daffy Duck is

---

[1]Our program incorporates many of the ideas found in the "query system" described in *Structure and Interpretation of Computer Programs*, and the forward chaining rule-based system depicted in Winston and Horn's book *Lisp*.

intended to represent a bird requires a kind of pattern matching—namely, matching salient visual features of the character against some general "bird template."

In our program, we will work with a database of assertions about rock groups, and these will act as the objects against which we match our patterns. The purpose of our pattern-matching program is that it can be used to answer questions about the entries in our database—for instance, we can use the program to discover the names of all musicians in a particular group, the albums put out by that group, or the instruments played by some musician in the group. As we proceed in this chapter, we will extend our program so that it can handle more elaborate types of questions.

Before describing our method for pattern matching in greater detail, let's look at the assertions that constitute our database.

The Assertions

Assertions will be represented as lists of three (or occasionally, two) elements. Here are some examples:

```
(group (becker walter) steely-dan)
(plays (becker walter) guitar)
(album steely-dan aja)
```

We can think of these assertions as indicating that Walter Becker is[2] a member of the group Steely Dan, and that he plays guitar; and that *Aja* is an album by Steely Dan. In our system, the first element of each assertion represents some relationship that holds between the remaining two elements. There are, of course, many alternative conventions we could have used for writing assertions; we *could* have structured our assertions as follows:

```
((walter becker) plays guitar)
((walter becker) group steely-dan)
```

As long as we are consistent, the differences between these assertion formats are irrelevant for our purposes.[3] "Consistency" in this context simply means that we don't want to employ different formats for similar assertions, as in the following example:

```
((walter becker) group steely-dan)
(group (collins philip) genesis)
```

Anyhow, without further ado, here is the list of assertions that we will use in our sample system:

```
(define *the-assertions*
  '(
    (group (becker walter) steely-dan)
    (group (fagen donald) steely-dan)
    (plays (becker walter) guitar)
    (plays (becker walter) bass)
    (plays (fagen donald) keyboards)
    (plays (fagen donald) vocals)
    (album steely-dan aja)
    (album steely-dan pretzel-logic)
    (album (fagen donald) the-nightfly)
```

---

[2]Okay, "was."

[3]Under other circumstances, the formatting of assertions might make an important difference to our program. Some assertion formats might lead to much more efficient pattern-matching strategies than others. But exploring these ideas would lead us too far afield.

```
(group (hoffs susanna) bangles)
(group (peterson debbi) bangles)
(group (peterson vicki) bangles)
(group (steele michael) bangles)
(plays (hoffs susanna) guitar)
(plays (hoffs susanna) vocals)
(plays (peterson debbi) drums)
(plays (peterson debbi) vocals)
(plays (peterson vicki) guitar)
(plays (peterson vicki) vocals)
(plays (steele michael) bass)
(plays (steele michael) vocals)
(album bangles all-over-the-place)
(album bangles different-light)
(group (banks tony) genesis)
(group (collins philip) genesis)
(group (rutherford mike) genesis)
(plays (banks tony) keyboards)
(plays (collins philip) drums)
(plays (collins philip) vocals)
(plays (rutherford mike) guitar)
(plays (rutherford mike) bass)
(album genesis abacab)
(album genesis and-then-there-were-three)
(album (collins philip) no-jacket-required)
))
```

We're going to start out with a very simple pattern matcher; but before we can write that program we have to do some ground clearing. Our goal is to employ a pattern with "variable" entries, and to compare that pattern with every assertion in our database to find all the assertions that match. Here's an example of a pattern:

Comparing Patterns with Assertions

```
(plays (?v who) drums)
```

In our system, "variable elements" (written as lists beginning with the special symbol ?v) can be matched by any object (usually a symbol or list). In the example above, the list (?v who) is a variable element; thus, our pattern will match any three-element assertion whose first element is the symbol plays and whose last element is the symbol drums. The matching assertions in our database are:

```
(plays (peterson debbi) drums)
(plays (collins philip) drums)
```

Note that by saying that the pattern:

```
(plays (?v who) drums)
```

matches the assertion:

```
(plays (peterson debbi) drums)
```

we are implicitly matching the variable (?v who) with the list (peterson debbi). Thus, the question of which assertions match a given pattern is equivalent to the question of which assertion elements match the variable elements in our pattern. In other words, we could have completely specified the match between the pattern and assertion above by stating that we can match the variable (?v who) with the list (peterson debbi).

Let's pursue this idea by constructing a data structure called a *dictionary*. A dictionary is a list, each of whose elements is itself a list containing a variable name and its matching element in some assertion. In the example of the previous paragraph, the relevant dictionary would look as follows:

```
((who (peterson debbi)))
```

This list contains one variable-name-and-element sublist, specifying that the variable (?v who) is being matched with the list (peterson debbi). The other assertion in our database that matches our original pattern is:

```
(plays (collins philip) drums)
```

We could specify this matching assertion with the following dictionary:

```
((who (collins philip)))
```

And going one step further, we could say that whenever we wish to find all the possible matches for any given pattern, we will specify those matches by a list of dictionaries. Thus, comparing the pattern:

```
(plays (?v who) drums)
```

with our entire set of assertions yields a list of two dictionaries representing the two possible matches:

```
( ((who (collins philip)))
  ((who (peterson debbi))))
```

Similarly, comparing the pattern:

```
(plays (peterson (?v first-name)) (?v instrument))
```

against all the assertions in our database will yield the following list of dictionaries:

```
( ((first-name debbi) (instrument drums))
  ((first-name debbi) (instrument vocals))
  ((first-name vicki) (instrument guitar))
  ((first-name vicki) (instrument vocals)))
```

In this case, each dictionary in our list contains two entries—one for the variable (?v first-name) and one for the variable (?v instrument).

As a final quick example, you should verify for yourself that comparing the pattern:

```
((?v relation) (fagen donald) (?v something))
```

against all our assertions yields the following list of dictionaries:

```
( ((relation group) (something steely-dan))
  ((relation plays) (something keyboards))
  ((relation plays) (something vocals))
  ((relation album) (something the-nightfly)))
```

Our First Pattern Matcher

Now we're ready to write our first pattern matcher. Our program will allow us to find all assertions that match a given pattern, and to return a list of dictionaries representing the matching assertions.

The heart of our program is the procedure match. This procedure takes as its arguments a pattern, an expression (to which the pattern is being compared), and a dictionary (representing the current proposed assignments of pattern variables). Here is the procedure: take a look at it, and then we will discuss it more carefully below.

```
(define (match pattern expression dictionary)
  (cond ((eq? dictionary 'failed) 'failed)
        ((atom? pattern)
         (if (eqv? expression pattern)
             dictionary
             'failed))
        ((null? expression) 'failed)
        ((variable? pattern)
         (extend-dictionary pattern expression dictionary))
        ((atom? expression) 'failed)
        (else
          (match (cdr pattern) (cdr expression)
                 (match (car pattern)(car expression) dictionary)))))
```

Our `match` procedure uses several other procedures. The `atom?` predicate is a Scheme primitive that returns #t if its argument is not a pair. The `variable?` predicate is one that we have to write; it returns #t if its argument is a variable. This one is easy, so let's digress a moment to write it:

```
(define (variable? pattern)
  (eq? (car pattern) '?v))
```

Finally, the `extend-dictionary` procedure takes as its arguments a variable, an expression (i.e., a list or symbol), and a dictionary, and returns a new dictionary containing all the variable-and-element lists of the original plus (if not redundant) a new variable-and-element list consisting of the given variable and expression. We'll get to this procedure very shortly, but first let's examine the overall strategy of `match`.

The point of `match` is to compare a pattern and expression and return a dictionary that represents a match between the two. If the pattern and expression do not match, our procedure returns the symbol `failed`. Here are some examples of `match` in action:

```
(match '(a b (?v letter)) '(a b c) '())
((letter c))
(match '(a b (?v letter)) '(a d c) '())
failed
(match '(a (?v letter1) (?v letter2)) '(a b c) '())
((letter2 c) (letter1 b))
(match '(a b c) '(a b c) '())
()
(match '(a (?v letter1) (?v letter1)) '(a b c) '())
failed
(match '((a (?v letter)) c) '((a b) c) '())
((letter b))
```

Let's start our exploration of `match` with the fourth example above. None of the first five `cond` clauses applies here: the value of `dictionary` is not the symbol `failed`, the value of `pattern` is a pair, the expression isn't (), the pattern is not a variable, and the expression is a pair. So we will call `match` on three new arguments: namely, the list (b c), the list (b c), and the result of calling `match` on the symbol a, the symbol a and (). The result of this latter "internal" call to `match` is () (since here, the first argument, a, is not a pair, and the first two arguments are `eqv?` to each other). Thus, the recursive call to `match` is performed with arguments (b c), (b c), and (). I will leave it to you to follow through the rest of this example; the only point you may need to remember (for the final recursive call to `match`) is that the empty list () is not a pair and hence calling the atom? predicate on this object returns #t.

Now let's try the second example above. Here, we will eventually arrive at a recursive call to match with arguments (b (?v letter)), (d c), and (). (I will leave to you the exercise of following through the recursive calls to match until this point is reached.) Again, none of the first five cond clauses applies, so we call match on three new arguments: ((?v letter)), (c), and the result of calling match on b, d, and (). But this latter internal call to match returns the symbol failed; thus, the recursive call to match with arguments ((?v letter)), (c), and failed will itself return failed, and this will be the result of our entire original call to match.

Finally, let's look at the first example. Here, we will eventually arrive (again, this is your exercise) at a call to match with arguments ((?v letter)), (c), and (). The first five cond clauses don't apply, so we will call match on (), (), and the result of calling match on (?v letter), c, and (). For this internal call, the first argument is a variable, so the result returned by extend–dictionary (we'll show this in a moment) will be the dictionary:

```
((letter c))
```

The call to match with arguments (), () and ((letter c)) will simply return the last of these, since the first two arguments are nonpairs that are eqv? to each other.

We will continue our examination of match in a moment, but first let's clear up the question of the extend–dictionary procedure. Here it is:

```
(define (extend-dictionary variable expression dictionary)
  (let ((vname (variable-name variable)))
    (let ((v (assq vname dictionary)))
      (cond ((null? v) (cons (list vname expression) dictionary))
            ((equal? (cadr v) expression) dictionary)
            (else 'failed)))))

(define variable-name cadr)
```

A couple of sample calls to extend–dictionary:

```
(extend-dictionary '(?v letter) 'a '())
((letter a))
(extend-dictionary '(?v letter) 'a '((letter a)))
((letter a))
(extend-dictionary '(?v letter) 'a '((letter b)))
failed
```

Here is the strategy of extend–dictionary in prose: First, find the variable name—the name after the ?v marker—of the variable argument. Then see if there is already an entry for this variable name in the given dictionary. (This is the point of the call to the primitive assq, whose behavior is left to you to investigate. See also Exercise 3.) If there is not (the point of the first cond clause), return an augmented dictionary. If there is, and if the current dictionary entry for this variable is the same as the expression argument, return the original dictionary (there's no point augmenting the dictionary with a redundant variable-name-and-element list). Finally, if the current dictionary entry is inconsistent with the expression argument (as in the third sample call to extend–dictionary above), then the procedure returns the symbol failed.

Now, with all this experience behind us, let's take a top-level look at match once more. The first five cond clauses test for "simple" calls to match. If the dictionary argument is the symbol failed, then there is no possible match, and we return the symbol failed. If the pattern is not a pair, then see if it is eqv? to the expression; if so, return an unchanged dictionary, and if not, return the symbol `failed`. The point here is simply that if the pattern isn't a pair, it must be a symbol,[4] and the only way it can match the expression is if the expression is also a symbol and the two are `eqv?`. The third cond clause returns `failed` if the expression is (); the only way we could get past the second clause is if the pattern is not (), since () is not a pair, and therefore the pattern and expression can't match. The fourth clause applies if the pattern is a variable, in which case we use `extend-dictionary` to return (if possible) an augmented dictionary as explained above. The fifth clause checks for the situation in which the pattern argument to `match` is a nonvariable pair and the expression argument is not a pair; in this case, no match is possible, so the clause returns `failed`.

Finally, the `else` clause is reached in the event that both the pattern and expression are pairs (and the pattern is not a variable). In this case, we find the dictionary that results from calling `match` on the `car` of our pattern and `car` of our expression (and the current dictionary), and use *that* result as the new dictionary for calling `match` on the `cdr` of our pattern and the `cdr` of our expression.

You should test your understanding of the `match` procedure now by going back to the earlier set of six examples of `match` in action, and working through the third, fifth, and sixth of these (i.e., the ones we haven't discussed).

Now that `match` is understood, the rest of our program is relatively straightforward. We want a procedure that will take a given pattern and compare it with every assertion in our database, returning a list of all dictionaries that are not the symbol `failed`. Here is such a procedure, named `try-all-assertions`.

```
(define (try-all-assertions pattern assertion-list)
  (throw-away (lambda (dictionary)
                (eq? dictionary 'failed))
              (map
                (lambda (assertion) (match pattern assertion '()))
                assertion-list)))
(define (throw-away predicate lis)
  (cond ((null? lis) '())
        ((predicate (car lis)) (throw-away predicate (cdr lis)))
        (else (cons (car lis) (throw-away predicate (cdr lis))))))
```

The `try-all-assertions` procedure takes a pattern and a list of assertions as arguments. The call to `map` in the body of `try-all-assertions` will return a huge list of dictionaries: the result of calling `match` with the given pattern and each assertion in the assertion-list. The call to `throw-away` will effectively remove all instances of the symbol `failed` from that list. The `throw-away` procedure, which is also shown above, is analogous to `map` in that it takes a procedure and a list as arguments, and returns a list as its result; however, in `throw-away`'s case the procedure is a predicate, and `throw-away` returns only those elements of its list argument that are not "tossed out" by that predicate (i.e., only those elements such that the predicate returns #f when applied to them).

Finally, we need a top-level procedure for our pattern matcher. Here it is:

```
(define (try pattern)
  (try-all-assertions pattern *the-assertions*))
```

We are now able to use the `try` procedure to retrieve facts from our database. Here are some examples, along with the English versions of the questions to which they correspond:

What instrument(s) does Tony Banks play?

```
(try '(plays (banks tony) (?v inst)))
( ((inst keyboards)) )
```

What are the names of the players in Steely Dan?

```
(try '(group (?v player) steely-dan))
( ((player (becker walter))) ((player (fagen donald))) )
```

What are the names of the albums by Genesis?

```
(try '(album genesis (?v alb)))
( ((alb abacab)) ((alb and-then-there-were-three)) )
```

What are the first names of the players named Peterson in the Bangles?

```
(try '(group (peterson (?v first-name)) bangles))
( ((first-name debbi)) ((first-name vicki)) )
```

Is Fats Domino a member of Steely Dan?

```
(try '(group (domino fats) steely-dan))
()
```

Adding And **and** Or

Our next step will be to expand the kinds of questions that we can pose of our system: specifically, we would like to combine questions using notions like "and" and "or." For instance, suppose we want to find out all those people in our database who play both guitar and bass. An appropriate expression to type would look as follows:

```
(try '(and (plays (?v person) guitar)
           (plays (?v person) bass)))
```

Similarly, we might be interested in finding all those people who can either play drums or sing (or both). An appropriate expression would look like this:

```
(try '(or (plays (?v person) drums)
          (plays (?v person) vocals)))
```

Let's think out the sort of strategy we need to include and-type questions in our pattern matcher. Suppose we have the pattern:

```
(and (plays (?v person) guitar) (plays (?v person) bass))
```

We know how to retrieve the appropriate assertions for either one of these patterns individually. Suppose we get the list of dictionaries corresponding to the first pattern:

```
( ((person (becker walter)))
  ((person (hoffs susanna)))
  ((person (peterson vicki)))
  ((person (rutherford mike))))
```

Now, we would like to proceed as follows:

1. Choose a dictionary from the list above.

2. Check the second pattern—i.e., the second and clause—against all assertions, using the chosen dictionary as the starting dictionary in the match procedure for each new assertion we check.

3. Any calls to match that return a non-failed dictionary will return a dictionary whose assignments are compatible with both and clauses. We now have a dictionary that corresponds to a match for the entire and question.

4. Do steps 1–3 for each dictionary in the list and return all the resulting dictionaries.

Let's illustrate these steps with our example, just to make things more concrete. We take the first dictionary in our list of guitar players:

```
((person (becker walter)))
```

Now, we check the pattern:

```
(plays (?v person) bass)
```

against every assertion in our database by repeatedly calling the match procedure with this pattern and the dictionary that we chose. The only matching assertion in our database compatible with the chosen dictionary is:

```
(plays (becker walter) bass)
```

Thus, the dictionary returned by checking the second pattern against all assertions is just:

```
((person (becker walter)))
```

Figure 15.1 illustrates our example thus far.

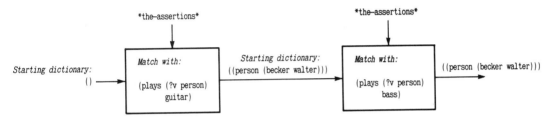

Figure 15.1. Part way in matching an and pattern

Now we choose the next dictionary in our list:

```
((person (hoffs susanna)))
```

and again check the pattern:

```
(plays (?v person) bass)
```

against all assertions using this new dictionary as a starting dictionary. This time there are no matching assertions, so there are no new dictionaries to add to our net result. Figure 15.2 depicts this next stage of our matching process.

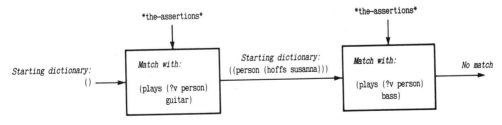

Figure 15.2. Matching an and pattern, continued

We repeat the same process for the remaining two dictionaries in our list, and the net result—the set of all dictionaries compatible with both clauses—is

```
( ((person (becker walter)))
  ((person (rutherford mike))))
```

Thus, we now know that, of the musicians in our database, only Walter Becker and Mike Rutherford play both bass and guitar.

Let's express the strategy outlined above in the form of code. We are going to rewrite the try-all-assertions procedure as follows:

```
(define (try-all-assertions pattern assertion-list starting-dictionary)
  (throw-away (lambda (dictionary)
                (eq? dictionary 'failed))
              (map (lambda (assertion)
                     (match pattern assertion starting-dictionary))
                   assertion-list)))
```

The difference between this version and our older one is that now try-all-assertions uses a particular starting dictionary for all the calls to match.

Now we need a procedure that realizes the four steps above. Our procedure must take a list of dictionaries and a (second) pattern as arguments, and then must try each of the dictionaries, one by one, as the starting dictionary for try-all-assertions:

```
(define (check-assertions-for-each-dictionary
           pattern dictionary-list assertions)
  (map-append
    (lambda (dictionary)
      (try-all-assertions pattern assertions dictionary))
    dictionary-list))
(define (map-append procedure lis)
  (cond ((null? lis) '())
        (else (append (procedure (car lis))
                      (map-append procedure (cdr lis))))))
```

The check-assertions-for-each-dictionary procedure meets our requirements. The point of the map-append procedure is that we want to append together the lists of dictionaries returned by all the calls to try-all-assertions.

Now all we need are some top-level procedures. The two procedures try-depending-on-type and do-and-clauses, shown below, together incorporate the ability to handle and patterns into our program. Finally, the try procedure is rewritten so that it calls try-depending-on-type.

```
(define (try-depending-on-type pattern dictionary-list assertions)
  (cond ((eq? (car pattern) 'and)
         (do-and-clauses (cdr pattern) dictionary-list assertions))
        (else (check-assertions-for-each-dictionary
               pattern dictionary-list assertions))))
(define (do-and-clauses clauses dictionary-list assertions)
  (cond ((null? clauses) dictionary-list)
        (else (do-and-clauses (cdr clauses)
                              (try-depending-on-type
                               (car clauses)
                               dictionary-list assertions)
                              assertions))))
(define (try pattern)
  (try-depending-on-type pattern (list '() ) *the-assertions*))
```

The try-depending-on-type procedure works with patterns of two types: either the pattern begins with and, or it is a "simple" pattern of the kind we used in the previous version of our program. Let's look at the simple case first. Suppose we call try-depending-on-type with a simple pattern, the list (()) as the list of dictionaries, and *the-assertions* as our list of assertions. In this case, try-depending-on-type will call check-assertions-for-each-dictionary and will simply return the list of dictionaries compatible with our simple pattern, just as the earlier version of the program did.

Now suppose instead we call try-depending-on-type with a pattern beginning with and. In this case, we call do-and-clauses, which itself calls try-depending-on-type on each and clause, each time using the list of dictionaries compatible with all previous and clauses. The final result is the list of all dictionaries compatible with every and clause.

The try procedure is, as before, our top-level procedure: it simply starts off try-depending-on-type with an initial dictionary list of (()) and *the-assertions* as the list of assertions.

Finally, let's add to our program the capability of working with or-type patterns as well. We will add one more cond clause to try-according-to-type, and add a new procedure, try-or-clauses. Examining this new addition—and seeing where it differs from our strategy for handling and patterns—is left to you. The only point that I will mention here is that the overall strategy for or patterns is similar to that for and, except that our final list of dictionaries should be those compatible with *any* of the or clauses (rather than *all* of the clauses, as is the case with and patterns).

Here are the changes needed to handle or patterns:

```
(define (try-depending-on-type pattern dictionary-list assertions)
  (cond ((eq? (car pattern) 'and)
         (do-and-clauses (cdr pattern) dictionary-list assertions))
        ((eq? (car pattern) 'or)
         (do-or-clauses (cdr pattern) dictionary-list assertions))
        (else (check-assertions-for-each-dictionary
               pattern dictionary-list assertions))))

(define (do-or-clauses clauses dictionary-list assertions)
  (cond ((null? clauses) '())
        (else (append (do-or-clauses
                       (cdr clauses) dictionary-list assertions)
                      (try-depending-on-type
                       (car clauses) dictionary-list assertions)))))
```

Here are some examples of our program in use:

What are the names of the people who play on the album 'Aja'?

```
(try '(and (group (?v person) (?v group))
           (album (?v group) aja)))
( ((group steely-dan) (person (becker walter)))
  ((group steely-dan) (person (fagen donald))))
```

Who are the people who play keyboards or drums?

```
(try '(or (plays (?v person) keyboards)
          (plays (?v person) drums)))
( ((person (peterson debbi)))
  ((person (collins philip)))
  ((person (fagen donald)))
  ((person (banks tony))) )
```

Which members of the Bangles play either bass or drums?

```
(try '(and (group (?v person) bangles)
           (or (plays (?v person) bass)
               (plays (?v person) drums))))
( ((person (peterson debbi))) ((person (steele michael))) )
```

As it stands now, we have a reasonably useful program for retrieving information from databases. We will make another addition to our program in the next section, when we add the ability to handle "restrictions" in our patterns; but before getting to that, we can do a little cleaning-up work.

First, suppose we want to know which musicians play either bass or guitar:

```
(try '(or (plays (?v person) bass) (plays (?v person) guitar)))
( ((person (becker walter))) ((person (hoffs susanna)))
  ((person (peterson vicki))) ((person (rutherford mike)))
  ((person (becker walter))) ((person (steele michael)))
  ((person (rutherford mike))) )
```

There is some redundancy in our result—for instance, Walter Becker is included twice because the dictionary:

```
((person (becker walter)))
```

specifies matching assertions for both or clauses.

One improvement, then, is to remove all duplicate dictionaries from the list that we return. There are a number of approaches we could try, but one simple approach is to augment our try procedure with a call to a new procedure named remove–duplicates:

```
(define (try pattern)
  (remove-duplicates
    (try-depending-on-type pattern (list '() ) *the-assertions*)))
(define (remove-duplicates lis)
  (cond ((null? lis) '())
        ((member (car lis) (cdr lis))
         (remove-duplicates (cdr lis)))
        (else (cons (car lis) (remove-duplicates (cdr lis))))))
```

Examining the remove–duplicates procedure is left to the reader.

A second major improvement is to have our program print out not just a list of dictionaries, but rather a series of patterns in which the variables have been replaced by the appropriate dictionary elements. Here is an example of how we want our program to behave:

```
(try '(and (plays (?v person) guitar)
           (plays (?v person) bass)))
(and (plays (becker walter) guitar) (plays (becker walter) bass))
(and (plays (rutherford mike) guitar) (plays (rutherford mike) bass))
```

Later on, when we add "if-then" rules to our program, we will actually implement a procedure that can help realize this improvement. For now, it may be worthwhile for you to try making this change on your own. (See also Exercise 5.)

A third improvement is to use subprocedures to make some of the structure of our program a bit more visible. For pedagogical reasons, I presented each procedure separately, but it is possible to go back now and "subproceduralize" our program. One example of this approach would be to make do–or–clauses and do–and–clauses subprocedures of the try–according–to–type procedure. (See also Exercise 6.)

Finally, it is interesting to note that by using different lists of assertions, we can employ our procedures as the basis for a variety of independent database systems. Suppose, for example, we have a bunch of assertions regarding Greek mythology:

```
(define *greek-myth-assertions*
  '((father zeus athena)
    (father zeus heracles)
    (husband zeus hera)
    (wife hera zeus)
    ...))
```

And suppose we have another set of assertions about a hypothetical soap opera:

```
(define *soap-opera-assertions*
  '((loves joe jane)
    (loves jane bill)
    (husband bill sue)
    (loves sue joe)
    ...))
```

We could write a procedure, make-database-matcher, that takes as its argument a database (i.e., a list of assertions) and returns a pattern matcher that employs the given database:

```
(define (make-database-matcher assertion-list)
  (lambda (pattern)
    (remove-duplicates
      (try-depending-on-type pattern (list '() ) assertion-list))))
```

Using the make-database-matcher procedure, we can create pattern matchers for each of our various lists of assertions:

```
(define try-rock-database
  (make-database-matcher *the-assertions*))

(define try-greek-myth-database
  (make-database-matcher *greek-myth-assertions*))

(define try-soap-opera-database
  (make-database-matcher *soap-opera-assertions*))

(try-soap-opera-database '(loves (?v who) jane))
(((who joe)))
```

One more major addition to go, and the first phase of our project will be complete. Along with and and or patterns, we would like to include a dont-keep pattern that enables us to place restrictions on the dictionaries returned by our pattern matcher.

Suppose, for instance, that we want to know the names of all guitarists who are *not* members of Genesis. The sort of pattern that we would like to use is as follows:

```
(try `(and (plays (?v person) guitar)
           (group (?v person) (?v group))
           (dont-keep ,(lambda (g)(eq? g 'genesis)) (?v group))))
```

There are some unfamiliar aspects to this example. First, you may have noticed that the entire pattern begins with a *backquote* symbol ` instead of the usual quote. Second, the list beginning with lambda is preceded by a comma. I will explain these new symbols in a moment, but first it's worth expressing the meaning of the above expression in prose. The idea is that we want all dictionaries that meet the requirements of the first two and clauses, but we want to throw out all those dictionaries for which the variable (?v group) is associated with genesis.

The dont-keep clause is followed by a predicate procedure and a variable name, and it tests each dictionary by applying the procedure to the value associated with that variable name. If the predicate procedure returns #t, the dictionary will not be included in the list of dictionaries ultimately returned by the matcher.

We'll continue our discussion of dont-keep clauses in a moment, but first a brief word about that backquote.

Digression: The Quasiquote Special Form

In Chapter 8, we encountered the quote special form (typically abbreviated with the single quote mark '), which acts as a "don't evaluate" signal to the Scheme interpreter. There are times, however, when we would like to precede a list by another sort of marker which means "selectively evaluate certain portions of this list." This is the point of the quasiquote special form (typically abbreviated with the single backquote mark `).

When the Scheme interpreter evaluates a list preceded by a backquote marker, it behaves as though the list were quoted in the usual way . . . *except* for those expressions within the list preceded by a comma. Any expression following a comma is evaluated, and the result is inserted into the list. Here are some examples:

```
`(a b c)
(a b c)
`(a b ,(* 3 5) d)
(a b 15 d)
(define c 3)
`(a b ,c)
(a b 3)
`(a b ,(car '(1 2)))
(a b 1)
`(a ,* b)
(a #<PROCEDURE *> b)
```

The quasiquote special form is a convenience. We *could* have constructed the second sample list above by typing:

```
(list 'a 'b (* 3 5) 'd)
```

This would work, but the backquoted version of the expression is easier to read.

More explorations of the quasiquote special form are provided in Exercises 7 and 8; and we will meet up with this topic again in the final chapter when we discuss the macro special form.

Adding Restrictions, Continued

Okay, back to our example. If you look once more at our sample pattern:

```
(try `(and (plays (?v person) guitar)
           (group (?v person) (?v group))
           (dont-keep ,(lambda (g)(eq? g 'genesis)) (?v group))))
```

you will see why the backquote symbol comes in handy. We want the first expression following the symbol dont-keep to be a procedure, so we precede that expression by a comma. Note that we *could* have typed the following:

```
(try (list 'and
            '(plays (?v person) guitar)
            '(group (?v person) (?v group))
            (list 'dont-keep
                  (lambda (g) (eq? g 'genesis))
                  '(?v group))))
```

Again, this expression would work as well as our backquoted version—but you can see that the backquoted version is much easier to read.

Now that we know how we want our typed-in expressions to look, we need to incorporate dont-keep patterns into our matching program. First, we'll add a new clause to the try-depending-on-type procedure:

```
(define (try-depending-on-type pattern dictionary-list assertions)
  (cond ((eq? (car pattern) 'and)
         (do-and-clauses (cdr pattern) dictionary-list assertions))
        ((eq? (car pattern) 'or)
         (do-or-clauses (cdr pattern) dictionary-list assertions))
        ((eq? (car pattern) 'dont-keep)
         (use-dont-keep-proc (cdr pattern) dictionary-list))
        (else (check-assertions-for-each-dictionary
               pattern dictionary-list assertions))))
```

Our rewritten procedure employs a new procedure named use-dont-keep-proc. This procedure takes as its arguments the portion of a dont-keep pattern following the symbol dont-keep, and a list of dictionaries. It should return a "filtered" list of dictionaries—namely, all those dictionaries that do not meet the condition implied by the dont-keep pattern.

Here is a possible version of use-dont-keep-proc, along with some other subsidiary procedures:

```
(define (use-dont-keep-proc clause dictionary-list)
  (let ((dont-keep-proc (car clause))
        (clause-variables (cdr clause)))
    (throw-away (lambda (dictionary)
                  (apply dont-keep-proc
                         (get-list-of-values clause-variables dictionary)))
                dictionary-list)))
(define (get-list-of-values list-of-variables dictionary)
  (map (lambda (var)(get-value var dictionary))
       list-of-variables))
(define (get-value variable dictionary)
  (let ((vname (variable-name variable)))
    (cadr (assq vname dictionary))))
```

The only unusual aspect of this code is the procedure apply, which appears in the body of use-dont-keep-proc. Apply is a Scheme primitive that takes as its arguments a procedure and a list of values, and returns the result of applying the procedure to those values as arguments. Here are some examples of apply in action:

```
(apply 1+ '(2))
3
(apply (lambda (number lis)(+ number (car lis))) '(3 (5 6)))
8
```

```
(apply * (list 2 3 (+ 1 4)))
```
30

The other possibly noteworthy aspect of this code is that it uses the throw-away procedure that we wrote earlier.

Phase One Completed

Well, we're done with the first phase of our program: we now have a reasonably useful pattern matcher. Here are three more examples of our program in use:

Find the guitarists in our database who are not members of Genesis.

```
(try '(and (plays (?v person) guitar)
           (group (?v person) (?v group))
           (dont-keep ,(lambda (g) (eq? g 'genesis)) (?v group))))
( ((group steely-dan) (person (becker walter)))
  ((group bangles) (person (hoffs susanna)))
  ((group bangles) (person (peterson vicki))) )
```

Who are the members of the Bangles not named Peterson?

```
(try '(and (group ((?v last-name) (?v first-name)) bangles)
           (dont-keep
             ,(lambda (lname) (eq? lname 'peterson)) (?v last-name))))
( ((first-name susanna) (last-name hoffs))
  ((first-name michael) (last-name steele)) )
```

Which musicians play two different instruments (not counting vocals)?[5]

```
(try '(and (plays (?v person) (?v inst1))
           (plays (?v person) (?v inst2))
           (dont-keep
             ,(lambda (i1 i2) (or (eq? i1 'vocals)
                                  (eq? i2 'vocals)
                                  (eq? i1 i2)))
             (?v inst1) (?v inst2))))
( ((inst2 bass) (inst1 guitar) (person (becker walter)))
  ((inst2 guitar) (inst1 bass) (person (becker walter)))
  ((inst2 bass) (inst1 guitar) (person (rutherford mike)))
  ((inst2 guitar) (inst1 bass) (person (rutherford mike))) )
```

Phase Two: Incorporating Rules

Now it's time to embark on the second phase of our project—namely, adding "if-then" rules to our program.

We can begin by outlining what we mean by a "rule." Suppose we want to express the following notion: a *versatile* musician is one who plays two or more instruments (not including vocals). We could phrase this idea as a rule: *if* a musician plays two or more (nonvocal) instruments, *then* she is versatile.

Now, one method for finding versatile musicians would be to type the following:

```
(try '(and (plays (?v person) (?v inst1))
           (plays (?v person) (?v inst2))
           (dont-keep
             ,(lambda (i1 i2)
                (or (eq? i1 'vocals)(eq? i2 'vocals)(eq? i1 i2)))
             (?v inst1) (?v inst2))))
```

---

[5] You will no doubt notice a special kind of redundancy in the program's response to this question. It may be a worthwhile project to attempt a fix for this problem.

Another approach, however, would be to add a new kind of entity to our program
—a representation of the rule that we stated above:

```
( (and (plays (?v person) (?v instl))
       (plays (?v person) (?v inst2))
       (dont-keep
         ,(lambda (il i2)
            (or (eq? il 'vocals) (eq? i2 'vocals) (eq? il i2)))
         (?v instl) (?v inst2)))
  (versatile (?v person)) )
```

The list above contains two sublists: the first of these represents the "if-part"
of the rule, and the second the "then-part." The idea is that if a dictionary can be
found to specify a match for the if-part of the rule, we can propose a new assertion
specified by the then-part. This rule, accordingly, is an assertion generator: it can
be used to create new assertions to add to our database.

In the example above, only Walter Becker and Mike Rutherford meet the
conditions of the if-part of the rule; therefore, the new assertions that our rule
should propose are:

```
(versatile (becker walter))

(versatile (rutherford mike))
```

To sum up: in our system, a rule will be written as a list of two patterns. The
first pattern, the "if-part," is matched against the assertions in our database; the
second pattern, the "then-part," specifies a new assertion that can be added to our
database for every successful match of the if-part.

Now that we have a rough idea of what rules are, we still have to decide how to
incorporate them into our program. The strategy that we will use is as follows: we
will maintain, along with our list of assertions, a list of rules. As always, we can
retrieve information from our assertion database by specifying patterns to match
against the database. In addition, however, we can *add* new assertions to the
database. Whenever a new assertion is added, we use our list of rules to see if any
more assertions are suggested. In other words, rules are things that hang around
until a new assertion is proposed; should that happen, all proposed rules are tried
to see if there are any more assertions—that is, besides the original one that was
proposed—to add to our database.

To continue with the example above: suppose we found out that Susanna
Hoffs plays bass as well as guitar. We would like to add the assertion:

```
(plays (hoffs susanna) bass)
```

to our database. But, according to our sample rule, this new assertion also implies
that Susanna Hoffs should now be classified as a versatile musician; therefore, we
would like our program to add yet another assertion in addition to the one proposed:

```
(versatile (hoffs susanna))
```

Now, if we were to look for all versatile musicians as follows:

```
(try '(versatile (?v person)))
```

we would expect to see three matching dictionaries:

```
( ((person (becker walter)))
  ((person (rutherford mike)))
  ((person (hoffs susanna))) )
```

**Forward Chaining:
A Strategy for
Proposing New
Assertions**

In the example above, we assume that the two assertions:

```
(versatile (becker walter))
(versatile (rutherford mike))
```

were already in our database before the new assertion regarding Susanna Hoffs was proposed. Thus, there are now three matches to our pattern, where there were only two before.

Now, how do we go about implementing our strategy? Here's the plan: every time a new assertion is added to the database, we will try all the rules (in a manner to be specified shortly) to see if there are any new assertions to propose. It is entirely possible that the new assertions suggested by our rules will *themselves* cause some rule to become applicable; that is, we have to try all our rules whenever *any* new assertion is proposed, whether it is the original assertion that we wanted to add or the newer assertions deduced from our rules. This means that we have to try all our rules repeatedly until we are sure that no new assertions can be proposed.

Let's pick up our example again, just to demonstrate the point of the last paragraph. Suppose our program contained another rule in addition to the "versatility" rule:

```
( (and (versatile (?v person))
        (plays (?v person) vocals))
  (versatile-singer (?v person)) )
```

This rule indicates that a versatile musician who also sings may be classified as a "versatile singer."

Now, when we added the assertion:

```
(plays (hoffs susanna) bass)
```

to our database, the only new assertion suggested by either of our two rules is the one that we mentioned above:

```
(versatile (hoffs susanna))
```

But now that *this* assertion is proposed, our database has a match for the if-part of our second rule. Thus, yet another assertion may now be added:

```
(versatile-singer (hoffs susanna))
```

The point of this last example, again, is to show that we have to try rules *repeatedly*. Our second rule did not suggest any new assertions when we added our original assertion; however, it did suggest a new assertion based on the assertion proposed by the first rule.

The overall strategy, then, is that when a new assertion is added, all rules are tried to see if there are still other assertions to propose; after that, if the rules have indeed proposed new assertions, we try all the rules again; and if this second "pass" results in still more assertions, we try all the rules yet again, and so on until our rules no longer suggest any new assertions. This strategy of finding all possible deductions from a particular set of rules is known as *forward chaining*.

Using a Single Rule to Propose New Assertions

The programming task outlined above may sound formidable; but in fact, it requires fewer than a dozen procedures to implement. Let's start with one chunk of our plan: we want a procedure that will test one rule against all existing assertions to see whether the if-part of the rule can find any matches in the database. Our procedure should return a (possibly empty) list of new assertions to propose.

Here is the procedure we will use. Note that its body contains references to as-yet-undefined procedures; we'll get to those in a moment.

```
(define (do-one-rule rule assertions)
  (let ((matching-dictionaries
           (find-dictionaries (if-part rule) assertions)))
     (let ((possible-new-assertions
              (map (lambda (dictionary)
                      (plug-dictionary-values-into dictionary (then-part rule)))
                   matching-dictionaries)))
        (remove-duplicates
          (throw-away (lambda (new-assertion) (member new-assertion assertions))
                      possible-new-assertions)))))
```

In prose, the strategy of do-one-rule is as follows: first, use the if-part of the rule to obtain a list of dictionaries representing possible matches in our database. Once that list is obtained, create a new list of assertions by plugging the values obtained from each matching dictionary into the then-part pattern of the rule. This list may contain needless assertions: there may be duplicates within the list, or assertions already contained in our database. Therefore, we return only those proposed assertions that are not redundant (this is the point of the throw-away and remove-duplicates expressions above).

The find-dictionaries procedure, which is used in the body of do-one-rule above, is very similar to the try procedure that we wrote in developing the first phase of our program. The only difference is that this new procedure takes a second argument—namely, a list of assertions—along with the first (pattern) argument.

```
(define (find-dictionaries pattern assertions)
  (remove-duplicates
    (try-depending-on-type pattern (list '() ) assertions)))
```

The plug-dictionary-values-into procedure takes as its arguments a dictionary and a pattern, and returns a new assertion in which the pattern variables have been replaced by their values in the dictionary. Here are two sample calls to plug-dictionary-values-into:

```
(plug-dictionary-values-into '((word test)) '(this is a (?v word)))
(this is a test)
(plug-dictionary-values-into '((word stickup)) '(this is a (?v word)))
(this is a stickup)
```

Here is the procedure itself:

```
(define (plug-dictionary-values-into dictionary pattern)
  (cond ((null? pattern) '())
        ((atom? (car pattern))
         (cons (car pattern)
               (plug-dictionary-values-into dictionary (cdr pattern))))
        ((variable? (car pattern))
         (cons (get-value (car pattern) dictionary)
               (plug-dictionary-values-into dictionary (cdr pattern))))
        (else (cons (plug-dictionary-values-into dictionary (car pattern))
                    (plug-dictionary-values-into dictionary (cdr pattern))))))
```

This is a standard garden-variety tree-recursive procedure, and nothing more needs to be said about it . . . except that this procedure can be used to realize one of the aforementioned improvements to our "phase one" pattern-matching program. (See also Exercise 5.)

Finally, we need two selector procedures to retrieve the if-part and then-part of some given rule:

```
(define if-part car)

(define then-part cadr)
```

We can test the portion of the program that we have written so far by trying an example:

```
(define test-rule '( (or (plays (?v person) guitar)
                         (plays (?v person) bass))
                     (string-player (?v person)) ) )

(do-one-rule test-rule *the-assertions*)
((string-player (steele michael))
(string-player (becker walter))
(string-player (hoffs susanna))
(string-player (peterson vicki))
(string-player (rutherford mike)))
```

Using All the Rules to Propose New Assertions

Our next step is to use all the rules in a large rule-list to find the possible new assertions that we can propose. The procedure that we will employ—like many others we have seen in this chapter—uses a mapping strategy:

```
(define (do-all-rules rules assertions)
  (remove-duplicates
    (map-append
      (lambda (rule) (do-one-rule rule assertions))
      rules)))
```

The call to map-append returns a list of newly-proposed assertions—the appended results of each call to do-one-rule for each individual rule. Since this list may contain duplicates, we call remove-duplicates on it and return the result.

Note that do-all-rules represents only one "pass" of the rules over a list of assertions; as per our discussion above, we will have to call do-all-rules repeatedly until there are no new assertions to propose. Let's move on to that issue now.

Using All Rules Repeatedly

The next procedure that we have to write will call do-all-rules over and over again, each time with a set of assertions augmented by the previous pass, until there are no new assertions to propose. The result returned by this procedure will be a list of all the new assertions that were suggested—i.e., all those assertions above and beyond the original ones in the database.

Here is our procedure:

```
(define (do-all-rules-repeatedly rules new-assertions old-assertions)
  (let ((newly-inferred-assertions
          (do-all-rules rules (append new-assertions old-assertions))))
    (cond ((null? newly-inferred-assertions) new-assertions)
          (else
            (do-all-rules-repeatedly
              rules
              (append newly-inferred-assertions new-assertions)
              old-assertions)))))
```

In words: for each pass, we will find the newly inferred assertions that result from trying every rule on all the assertions we have accumulated. If we find that no new assertions are proposed, we return the current set of new assertions—that is, the current set of all assertions proposed in addition to the original set. Otherwise, we call do-all-rules-repeatedly again, this time augmenting the set of new assertions by all those that we found in the previous pass.

Adding New Assertions

The naive way to add a new assertion to our database would simply be the following:

```
(define (add-new-assertion! assertion)
  (set! *the-assertions* (cons assertion *the-assertions*)))
```

This is probably the way we would have written add-new-assertion! had we wanted a procedure to add assertions within our "phase one" program; and indeed, it would be a useful addition to that program. But now, when we add a new assertion, we want all the other assertions deduced by our rules to be added as well.

Here, then, is a better version of the add-new-assertion! procedure:

```
(define (add-new-assertion! assertion)
  (cond ((member assertion *the-assertions*) '())
        (else
          (set! *the-assertions*
                (append (do-all-rules-repeatedly
                          *the-rules* (list assertion) *the-assertions*)
                        *the-assertions*))
          'done)))
```

Cleaning Up

We're just about done—only a little more effort is needed. First, let's construct a list of rules analogous to our list of assertions:

```
(define *the-rules*
  '( ( (and (plays (?v person) (?v inst1))
            (plays (?v person) (?v inst2))
            (dont-keep
              ,(lambda (il i2)
                 (or (eq? il 'vocals) (eq? i2 'vocals) (eq? il i2)))
              (?v inst1) (?v inst2)))
       (versatile (?v person)))
     ( (and (group (?v person) (?v group))
            (album (?v person) (?v album)))
       (made-solo-album (?v person)))
     ))
```

Now, we need a procedure that will take our original lists of both assertions and rules and "initialize" the list of assertions so that it contains all the assertions we can possibly deduce:

```
(define (initialize-assertion-list)
  (set! *the-assertions*
        (append (do-all-rules-repeatedly
                  *the-rules* '() *the-assertions*)
                *the-assertions*))
  'done)
```

The point of this procedure is simply to try all the rules repeatedly on our original list of assertions, and to reset that list so that it contains all the assertions deducible from our set of rules.

Finally, as a little added frill, we can once more rewrite our top-level try procedure so that it uses the find-dictionaries procedure we created earlier:

```
(define (try pattern)
  (find-dictionaries pattern *the-assertions*))
```

Phase Two Completed

We now have a program that employs pattern matching to retrieve information from a database of assertions *and* uses forward chaining to deduce additional information whenever new assertions are added to the database. Here are some examples of our system at work:

```
(initialize-assertion-list)
done
```

Who are the versatile musicians in our database?

```
(try '(versatile (?v person)))
( ((person (becker walter))) ((person (rutherford mike))) )
```

Which groups in our database include musicians who have made solo albums?

```
(try '(and (group (?v person) (?v group))
           (made-solo-album (?v person))))
( ((group steely-dan) (person (fagen donald)))
  ((group genesis) (person (collins philip))) )
```

Here is a new musician to add to our database.

```
(add-new-assertion! '(plays (jackson joe) vocals))
done

(add-new-assertion! '(plays (jackson joe) keyboards))
done

(add-new-assertion! '(plays (jackson joe) clarinet))
done
```

Now who are the versatile musicians in our database?

```
(try '(versatile (?v person)))
( ((person (jackson joe)))
  ((person (becker walter)))
  ((person (rutherford mike))) )
```

Possible Extensions and Things We've Swept Under the Rug

Because this chapter has to occupy a finite number of pages, it is not possible to go any further in constructing our sample program. But responsibility demands that some of the weaknesses of our project—as well as feasible improvements—be mentioned.

First the improvements. In the program we have constructed, it is only possible to add new *assertions*. Naturally, we might like to add new *rules* as well. This is a straightforward task, and it is given as Exercise 9 at the end of this chapter. Another improvement—also straightforward—is to allow the user to *hypothesize* new assertions and see what other assertions would be deduced if the hypothesized assertion were true. For example, we might want to see all the new assertions that would be proposed if Tony Banks were to learn to play the sousaphone:

```
(hypothesize '(plays (banks tony) sousaphone))
( (versatile (banks tony)) (plays (banks tony) sousaphone) )
```

This extension is also given as an exercise, in Exercise 10.

A third improvement, substantially more complicated to implement, would be to develop a more advantageous data structure than a simple list as our "assertion structure." One of the difficulties of our present implementation is that the list *the-assertions* has to be checked in its entirety whenever we try to match a simple pattern. But it should be possible to construct a more efficient arrangement of assertions. To take one idea, we might employ a list of twenty-six sublists, each of which contains assertions whose first element starts with a given letter. Thus, the assertions:

```
(album bottomless-pits horrible-metallic-noise)

(group (doe john) bottomless-pits)

(plays (doe john) guitar)
```

would be placed in the first (for "a"), seventh (for "g"), and sixteenth (for "p") sublist, respectively. The advantage of this arrangement is that when we wish to match a pattern whose first element is not a variable (this happens in the great majority of cases), we know exactly which sublist in our list of assertions to search. For example, the pattern:

```
(plays (?v person) guitar)
```

would now be matched only against those assertions in the sixteenth sublist of our giant assertion list, instead of being matched against every assertion as before. For our sample system, this arrangement may not save a great deal of searching time, but its advantages would become noticeable for larger collections of assertions.

Considering what happens when our set of assertions (and rules) gets large leads us to the weaknesses of our sample program. One well-known difficulty associated with the strategy of forward chaining is that it may be possible to deduce huge numbers of new assertions just by adding a new assertion or two; and as a result, we may find that the number of assertions in our database grows astronomically as we add assertions.[6] There are a number of possible strategies for constraining the deduction process, but considering these would take us too far afield.[7]

Finally, you may have noticed that although our system allows us to *add* assertions to our database, we are not able to *delete* assertions. Deleting assertions is a trickier problem than it may appear. For instance, suppose we find out that Walter Becker does not play guitar after all, and we want to delete this assertion from our database. It may seem that we only have to alter the assertion list (using set-car! and set-cdr!) to remove this assertion; but recall that we *also* have an assertion in our list stating that Walter Becker is a versatile musician. This second assertion will have to be removed as well, since it was deduced by a rule whose premises are no longer valid.

One approach to the problem of deleting assertions is the following: we maintain, along with each assertion A, a list indicating the additional assertions derived from A. (That is to say, a list of all assertions that were added by rules whose premises used A as a matching assertion.) Then, if we want to delete A from our database, we can use the "derived-assertion" list associated with A to find all the other assertions that we have to delete; and naturally, deleting each of these assertions may necessitate deleting still *other* assertions, and so on.

---

[6]Under certain circumstances, it is even possible for an infinite number of new assertions to be derived via forward chaining from finite initial sets of assertions and rules.

[7]See also the References section at the end of this book.

< n/a>

Strategies of this kind are part of the technique of creating so-called *truth maintenance systems*—systems that attempt to work with highly changeable sets of "known assertions."[8]

Exercises

1. Use the pattern matcher to answer the following questions:

   What are the names of the albums by Steely Dan?

   What are the names of the albums by Philip Collins (solo)?

   What is the first name of the guitarist named Hoffs?

   What instruments are played by musicians whose last name is Peterson?"

2. Compare the results of evaluating the following two expressions:

   ```
   (try '(group (steele michael) bangles))
   ```

   ```
   (try '(group (welk lawrence) bangles))
   ```

   Explain the source of the difference between the two results.

3. The Scheme primitive assq, which appears in the extend-dictionary procedure, takes two arguments: the first can be any object at all (often a symbol), and the second is a list of lists (i.e., a list each of whose elements is itself a list). The result of the call to assq will be the first element of the large list whose car is eq? to the object. Here are some examples:

   ```
   (assq 'a '((a 1) (b 2) (c 3)))
   (a 1)
   (assq 'dog '((cat chat) (dog chien) (cow vache)))
   (dog chien)
   (assq 'horse '((cat chat) (dog chien) (cow vache)))
   ()
   (assq 'a '((a 1) (a 2) (a 3)))
   (a 1)
   ```

   The third example illustrates the fact that the call to assq returns #f if the object argument is not eq? to the car of any element in the list. The fourth example shows that the element returned will be the *first* matching element, even if other matches exist.

   Here is the problem part of this problem: first, suppose we have a list representing the menu of a Chinese restaurant. (We'll use the same menu as the one in Chapter 8, Exercise 12.)

   ```
   (define menu
     '((egg-drop-soup 1.75)
       (won-ton-soup 2.00)
       (beef-with-snow-peas 7.00)
       (chicken-with-almonds 6.75)
       (shrimp-lo-mein 6.50)
       (mixed-vegetables 5.00)))
   ```

   Use the assq primitive to rewrite the price-of procedure in Chapter 8, Exercise 12. This procedure should take as its argument the name of a dish (a symbol) and should return the price of the dish.

---

[8]The strategy for deleting assertions outlined in this paragraph is itself problematic. For instance, if we delete A we need not delete another assertion B derived from A if B can be derived from yet other (still-existing) assertions. All of this merely goes to show that maintaining flexible sets of assertions can be a difficult task. Again, see the References section for suggestions for future reading.

Note that assq is particularly useful in conjunction with *association lists*, as described in Chapter 8, Exercise 12. Our "dictionaries" are, in fact, simply association lists.

You should also examine the assoc and assv primitives in your language manual, and compare these procedures with assq.

4. Use the pattern matcher (employing and and or patterns where necessary) to answer the following questions:

    What are the names of people who sing and play guitar?

    What are the names of the (solo) albums by keyboard players?

    What are the names of instruments played by Debbi Peterson or Donald Fagen?

5. Change the pattern matcher program so that it returns, rather than a list of dictionaries, a list of patterns in which the variables have been replaced by matching dictionary elements. (This can be done before the addition of rules to the program; see the section entitled "Extensions to Our Program.") Here is an example of the desired behavior:

    ```
    (try '(plays (hoffs susanna) (?v instrument)))
    ((plays (hoffs susanna) guitar) (plays (hoffs susanna) vocals))
    ```

    If you need a head start, you might find the plug–dictionary–values–into procedure helpful.

6. Try "cleaning up" the program by introducing subprocedures where you think appropriate. (This can be done at various times; you might try cleaning up once and and or patterns have been introduced, and again after the entire program as described in this chapter has been completed.)

7. To familiarize yourself with the quasiquote special form, try predicting the results of evaluating the following expressions. Then type the expressions at the Scheme interpreter to see if your predictions were correct.

    ```
    `((+ 2 3) ,(+ 2 3))
    (define a 1)
    `(a ,a ,(+ a 3) (+ ,a 3) ,(list 'a a))
    (car `(,(* 8 5) ,(* 4 5)))
    (cons '(a `(b ,a)) `(a ,a))
    ```

8. Sometimes, inside a backquoted expression, we see a comma followed by an at-sign (@), as in this expression:

    ```
    `(1 ,@(list (+ 3 4) 8))
    ```

    The meaning of the comma-at-sign combination is that the following expression (i.e., the one right after the comma-at-sign) should be evaluated, and the result should be a list; this list should then have its parentheses "stripped away" (or "dissolved," if you prefer that metaphor) and its elements should be placed in the next-higher-level list. The example above should thus evaluate to:

    ```
    (1 7 8)
    ```

    Note that if the at-sign had *not* been included, the example above would have evaluated to:

    ```
    (1 (7 8))
    ```

    Here are some other examples:

    ```
    `(1 ,(list (* 8 5)) ,@(list (* 8 5)))
    (1 (40) 40)
    ```

```
'(list 1 ,@(map 1+ '(1 2 3)))
(list 1 2 3 4)
'((1 ,@(list 2 3)) 4)
((1 2 3) 4)
```

Try to predict the results of evaluating the following expressions. Then type them at the Scheme interpreter to see if your predictions were correct.

```
(list 1 '(2 3) '(4 ,(* 5 6) ,@(cons 7 '(8 9))))
(define b '(1 2))
'(b ,b ,(cdr b) ,@(cdr b))
'(list ,@b (list b) ,(list b) ,(list 'b) ,@(list 'b) ,@(list b))
'(,@(append b '(3 4)))
```

9. The add-new-assertion! procedure only allows us to add one new assertion to our database at any one time. Write a procedure named add-list-of-assertions! that takes as its argument a list of new assertions, and adds all of them (as well as all new assertions that can be derived from rules) into the database.

10. Write a procedure named hypothesize-new-assertion that takes as its argument an assertion and returns all the assertions that *would* be added to the database if the new assertion were true. Note that our procedure should *not* change the existing database, as add-new-assertion! does; it should treat its argument, rather, as a hypothetical assertion.

☑ ✳ 11. Write a procedure named add-new-rule! (analogous to the add-new-assertion! procedure) that allows us to add a new rule into our database. Note that when we add a new rule, we should also find all the new assertions that can be deduced by virtue of adding the rule, and we should include these new assertions in our database.

CHAPTER 16

A Sampler of Advanced Topics

This chapter is going to introduce—all too briefly, I'm afraid—a number of advanced topics in Scheme programming. Any one of these topics could easily be the subject of a chapter in its own right, but limitations of time and space preclude delving into these subjects in the depth that they ultimately deserve. So you might think of this chapter as a three-day economy tour of Scheme—you're going to see a lot of wonderful things and then get hustled away from them before you even have time to appreciate them. But of course you will be able to return to the places you like and explore them on your own afterward.

What to Do When You Meet a New Type of Object

Most of the topics that we will cover here focus on the introduction of some new Scheme object type. Up until now, we have encountered six object types—numbers, booleans, pairs, procedures, symbols, and strings—but there are still quite a few that we haven't met. Each Scheme object type, familiar or unfamiliar, has its own particular specialty: numbers are used for mathematical programming, booleans are integral to the notion of testing, pairs are helpful in building compound data structures, and so on. And each object type is associated with its own set of Scheme primitives and special forms—a set that specifies the elementary operations we can perform with objects of that type. For instance, the pair type is associated with primitives like cons, car, cdr, set-car!, list, etc.

When you encounter a new object type, then, you should be thinking along the following lines: why is this object type useful? What is its "domain of expertise"? What are the primitives and special forms associated with this object type? Most of all, see if you can incorporate this new, strange beast into your own projects—for just as the best way to learn a word is to use it in conversation, the best way to learn a new programming concept is to program with it.

Vectors

The first new object type that we will explore is the *vector* type. Scheme vectors are analogous to *arrays* in languages like Basic and Pascal. If you have used arrays in some other language, then—just by virtue of the previous sentence—you probably already have a good idea of what vectors are; but if Scheme is your first programming language (lucky you!), then the comparison with arrays isn't likely to be too helpful.

Here is the idea. A vector is a compound data structure composed of a set of other objects—rather like a list. Each object (or *element*) in the vector is accessed by position: thus, if a vector is composed of the four elements 3, (1 2), (), and 5, then the zeroth element is 3, the first element is the list (1 2), and so on. (The zeroth element, by convention, is the starting element in the vector.)

The important difference between vectors and lists is that a vector is stored in one large "chunk" of memory space within the computer. What this means is that the nth element of a vector may be located very quickly; in a list, the nth element would have to be found by doing a series of n repeated cdr operations. (In fact, this is how the list-ref primitive works.) For a very long list, then, finding the nth element can be slow work for large values of n. By contrast, the nth element of a vector can be found directly no matter how large n might be.[1]

Before getting to the uses of vectors, and some other contrasts between vectors and lists, let's look at a few relevant Scheme primitives. Vectors may be constructed by the make-vector procedure, which is called as follows:

(make-vector *number-exp exp*)

The first argument expression should evaluate to a number object; this indicates the size (in elements) of the vector to be created. The second argument may evaluate to any type of object at all; this object will be the initial value of every element of the resulting vector.[2] Here are two examples, showing how make-vector may be used to create two vector objects named test-vector-1 and test-vector-2.

(define test-vector-1 (make-vector 10 0))

(define test-vector-2 (make-vector 20 '(5)))

Test-vector-1 is now the name of a vector of ten elements, each with value 0; while test-vector-2 is the name of a vector of twenty elements, each with the list value (5).

In order to do anything interesting with these vectors, we need two more primitives—vector-ref and vector-set!. Vector-ref takes a vector object and a number n as argument, and returns the value of the nth element of the vector. Thus, to find the final element of test-vector-1, we could type:

(vector-ref test-vector-1 9)

0

This tells us that the ninth element of test-vector-1 is 0. (Recall that the starting element has index 0, so the index number that we used in this example was 9.)

We can change the vector so that it has a new nth element value by using the vector-set! primitive. Vector-set! takes three arguments: a vector, a number n, and an object. The result of a call to vector-set! is to change the vector so that its nth element is the specified object. Thus, to change the initial value of test-vector-1 to 75, we could type the following at the Scheme interpreter:

(vector-set! test-vector-1 0 75)

---

[1]Just to elaborate on the discussion above: suppose a vector is implemented in the computer as a series of pointers with each pointer taking up one memory location. (This is an idealized picture of how vectors are implemented, but it's close enough to the truth to get the important ideas across.) Then a vector of 1,000 elements would be a set of 1,000 pointers in contiguous memory locations; let's say, for the sake of example, that these pointers occupy locations 500 to 1499 in the computer. To find the zeroth element of the vector, we find the object pointed to by the pointer in location 500; to find the 700th element of the vector, we find the object pointed to by the pointer in location 1200. Thus, we know how to find the desired object simply by knowing its location within the vector (e.g., the 700th element), and the starting location of the vector in memory (e.g., location 500). In contrast, lists may use a large number of noncontiguous memory locations: one pair may be at location 2000, the next at location 2040, the next at location 1766, and so on; thus, to find a particular pair—and the object pointed to by the car of that pair—might require chasing down a lot of cdr pointers.

[2]Actually, the second argument is optional—you can leave it out if you like. In that case, the vector created by make-vector will have unspecified initial values for every element.

Finally, a useful primitive to know is `vector-length`, which takes a vector as argument and returns the number of elements in that vector:

```
(vector-length test-vector-1)
10
```

Let's put some of these ideas together in a brief example. Suppose we want to write a vote-counting program for an election in which there are six candidates (for convenience, we will label the candidates by number—Candidate 0, Candidate 1, and so on). First, we might create a vector of six elements: each element will represent the number of votes thus far for the given candidate.

```
(define *vote-vector* (make-vector 6 0))
```

Now we will write a useful procedure called `increment-nth!` that takes a vector (of numbers) and an index *n* as arguments and increments the *n*th element of the vector:

```
(define (increment-nth! vector n)
  (vector-set! vector n (1+ (vector-ref vector n))))
```

And now, using `increment-nth!`, we can write a voting procedure:

```
(define (vote)
  (display "Which candidate do you want to vote for? ")
  (let ((candidate-no (read)))
    (cond ((> candidate-no (-1+ (vector-length *vote-vector*)))
           (writeln "No candidate with that number exists!")
           (vote))
          (else (increment-nth! *vote-vector* candidate-no)
                (writeln "Thank you!")))))
```

Obviously, this program leaves all kinds of room for improvements and elaborations. As a start, you might want to write a `find-leader` procedure that returns the number of (and number of votes for) the currently leading candidate.

It may have occurred to you that we *could* have written the program above using a list as our basic data structure instead of a vector. That's true, and it reflects a more general truth—namely, that you can do with lists just about anything that you can do with vectors. Lists are in fact a more flexible data structure; for instance, you can extend the length of a list (by using `set-cdr!` on the last pair), whereas once a vector is created it cannot change in size.

So why use vectors? Well, as mentioned earlier, finding the *n*th element of a large vector is a very quick process—much quicker than finding the *n*th element of a list. So if you have very large data structures that will be accessed according to position, vectors are a more efficient choice than lists. Beyond this, there are certain questions of taste that enter into the choice of one data structure or other. Specifically, making extensive use of `set-car!` and `set-cdr!` is considered clumsy by most Scheme programmers; if you have a data structure that you intend to change often, you should at least consider using vectors. (In other words, vectors are considered a "naturally alterable" kind of data structure in a way that lists are not.)

Environments

In Chapter 11, we encountered the concept of environments—a concept that has proved tremendously useful to us ever since. With the environment model as our foundation, we have been able to explore a variety of subjects: procedures as first-class objects (in Chapter 12), the `set!` special form (in Chapter 13), and breakpoints (in Chapter 14). Environments, however, are more than just a helpful diagrammatic fiction; it may surprise you to know that in many implementations of Scheme—PC Scheme included—environments are themselves first-class Scheme objects.

Recall the essential nature of environments: they are places in which to evaluate expressions. That's their whole point. And that's how our new "environment objects" are used; specifically, environments are most often employed in conjunction with a primitive procedure named eval. A call to eval has the form:

(eval *exp env*)

Here, *exp* is some expression, and *env* is an environment object. The result of a call to eval is the result of evaluating the expression *exp* within the environment *env*.

Before we can look at some examples of eval in action, we will need a little more apparatus. We want to call eval on two arguments—an expression and an environment. The expression might be a symbol object, like + or a, or a list like (* 2 b), or even a number like 555. So our call to eval might look as follows:

(eval '+ *env*)

Here, we want to evaluate the symbol + in some environment. But what should the second argument to eval be? Well, one possibility is to use the initial environment. In PC Scheme, the variable user-initial-environment is bound to the initial environment. So we could type the following expression:

```
(eval '+ user-initial-environment)
#<Procedure +>
```

The result of evaluating the symbol + in the initial environment is, of course, just the primitive addition procedure.[3]

This is all very well: we have just used the eval procedure to evaluate the symbol + in the initial environment. But we could have done the same thing by typing the symbol + at the Scheme interpreter. So what's so interesting about eval?

The real interest begins when we use other environments besides the initial environment as the second argument to eval. One way to do this is to use another PC Scheme primitive named the-environment. When this primitive is applied to no arguments, it simply returns the current environment. Thus, consider the following procedure:

```
(define (sample-env-maker)
  (let ((a 2)
        (b 7))
    (the-environment)))
```

If the procedure sample-env-maker is called on zero arguments, it will return an environment in which the name a is bound to 2 and b is bound to 7. Thus, we might create a new environment named env-1:

```
(define env-1 (sample-env-maker))
```

And now we can evaluate expressions in this new environment:

```
(eval 'a env-1)
2

eval '(* a b) env-1)
14
```

Another relevant PC Scheme primitive is procedure-environment. This primitive takes a procedure object as its argument and returns the environment associated with that procedure object. (Remember that a procedure object is composed of two parts: the procedure code, and the environment with which the procedure is

---

[3]Note that we used the quoted symbol + as the first argument to eval. This is because eval is a procedure, and thus its arguments are evaluated before the procedure is applied (just as with every other procedure). We wanted the first argument expression to evaluate to a symbol, and the expression '+ fills the bill. Had we left out the quote mark, the first expression + would have evaluated to a primitive procedure instead of a symbol.

associated.) Now, in many standard cases, the environment associated with a procedure is just the initial environment; square and double and all of our "classics" are examples. So evaluating an expression in one of these procedures' environments isn't very interesting:

```
(eval 'car (procedure-environment square))
#<Procedure CAR>
```

It is much more intriguing to evaluate an expression in the environment of a procedure like sample-procedure below:

```
(define sample-procedure
   (let ((a 5)) (lambda (number)(* a number))))
```

In this case the name sample-procedure is bound to a procedure object whose associated environment contains a binding for the name a. (Draw an environment diagram if you don't believe me!) So now we can eval an expression in the environment associated with sample-procedure:

```
(eval 'a (procedure-environment sample-procedure))
5
```

Let's try a more interesting example. At the end of Chapter 13, we wrote a program to create "turtle objects." Our implementation, if you recall, involved the use of procedures to represent turtles: that is, a "turtle" was really a procedure with an environment that contained bindings for a bunch of local "turtle state variables." Figure 16.1 below (which is actually identical to Figure 13.15) is an environment diagram for a typical turtle:

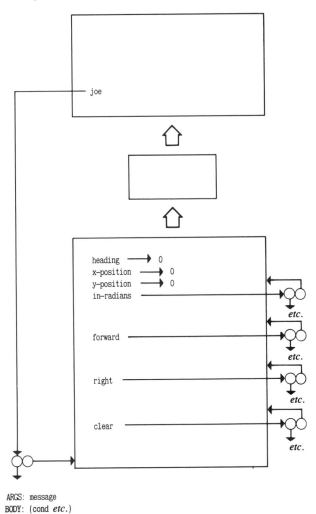

Figure 16.1. Portrait of a Turtle

What we're going to do is write a procedure that allows us to type expressions and have them evaluated in the environment of some turtle object—just as we now type expressions at the Scheme interpreter and have them evaluated in the initial environment. To take a concrete example, if we were to type the symbol heading at the Scheme interpreter we would receive an error message, because that symbol is not bound; however, if we type heading at some "turtle environment" we should see the appropriate turtle's heading.

Here are two procedures that together implement this idea. The type-at-environment procedure takes as argument a string (to use as a prompt) and an environment in which to evaluate typed-in expressions. The talk-to-turtle procedure takes a turtle (procedure) as argument and allows us to type expressions "inside" that turtle's environment.

```
(define (type-at-environment prompt-string env)
  (newline)
  (display prompt-string)
  (let ((exp (read)))
    (writeln (eval exp env))
    (type-at-environment prompt-string env)))
(define (talk-to-turtle turtle)
  (type-at-environment "TURTLE> " (procedure-environment turtle)))
```

Let's look at type-at-environment for a moment. You can see that it is a tail recursive procedure; each call to type-at-environment terminates with a recursive call. So type-at-environment will generate an infinite loop. Each time the procedure is invoked it will print out the given prompt; read in some expression to evaluate; print out the result of evaluating that expression in the given environment; and finally call itself recursively.

So the type-at-environment procedure, when called, generates a simple example of a "read-eval-print loop." In a sense, this procedure sets up a little "miniature interpreter." As a matter of fact, the Scheme interpreter itself works along similar principles: print out a prompt, read in an expression, print out the evaluated result, go back and do it all over again.

Here is an example of our new talk-to-turtle procedure in use:

```
(define joe (make-turtle))
(talk-to-turtle joe)
TURTLE > heading
0
TURTLE > (set! heading 90)
90
    .
    .
    .
etc., etc.
```

What we have done here should recall to you one of the uses of breakpoints that we saw in Chapter 14: namely, we have created a way of "talking" to some environment other than the initial environment. You might compare the styles of the program above and the Chapter 14 example in which we inserted a breakpoint message into a "circuit" object.

Procedures as Lists: Or Eval's Real Value Reevaluated

In the very first chapter, while discussing the interesting features of Lisp, I mentioned that the choice of lists as basic data structures was an extremely fruitful one. What I said at that time was that since programs are themselves represented as lists, it is possible to write Lisp programs that accept other Lisp programs (in list form) as data.

Here's an example of what I was referring to. This is a procedure that takes a list as argument and uses that list to create a procedure which will then be applied to the number 1.

```
(define (run-list-on-1 lis)
  (eval (list (cons 'lambda lis) 1) user-initial-environment))
```

We could now use this procedure as follows:

```
(run-list-on-1 '((no)(+ 7 no)))
8
(run-list-on-1 (cons '(number) (list '* 'number 5)))
5
```

Although this is a tiny example, there are interesting ideas to pursue here. One could write procedures that put together lists beginning with the symbol lambda and then eval those lists to create new procedures, and so on. The essential point is that Scheme procedures are all written as large lists, and those lists may be treated as "merely" lists in some contexts and evaluated to yield procedures in other contexts.

As I say, these are neat ideas. And I would hardly discourage you from exploring them. But, truth to tell, no Scheme programmer that I know of has made extensive use of the "lists-that-look-like-procedures" technique of programming. The idea appears to have had historical importance, in that it helped people to reconsider the distinction between procedures and data; but in most cases that I can think of, it is easier to use other techniques[4] than it is to use eval to change lists into procedures. In short, then, the list representation of programs does embody extremely important concepts, as stated in Chapter 1—but it itself is no longer widely used in Scheme. Those same concepts have been incorporated into other, more popular language features.

Windows

So far in this chapter, we have encountered two new types of objects: vectors and environments. Not every Scheme system will contain environments as an object type, although many do—including PC Scheme. The next type of object that we will discuss, however, really is specific to PC Scheme. I'm referring to "window objects"; and if your Scheme system is not PC Scheme, you may want to skip this section altogether (although if your version of Scheme includes some similar type of object, you may still get some value from this section).

A *window object* in PC Scheme is a rectangular region of the screen. The sorts of things that we can do with windows include:

- Creating them
- Placing them in a specified position on the screen
- Specifying a size (length and width) for them
- Displaying text inside them
- Clearing them of all text
- Erasing them from the screen

There are a number of other games that one can play with windows, but we will discuss only the operations listed above. Some other possible topics are mentioned in the problems at the end of the chapter; and, to be honest, I haven't experimented with windows much beyond these basic operations myself, so I'd

---

[4]Such as first-class procedures, as covered in Chapter 12.

feel pretty insecure writing about the more baroque side of window programming.

First things first. The typical display screen has 24 rows (numbered 0 to 23) and a line length of 80 columns (numbered 0 to 79, assuming that we are in the standard "text mode"). When we place a window on the display, we will specify its size (in rows and columns) and its upper left-hand corner position. Thus, a window of 5 rows and 20 columns positioned at row 10, column 5 would appear as in Figure 16.2.

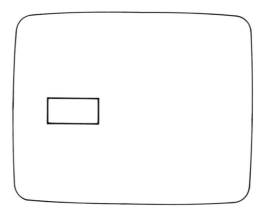

Figure 16.2. A window at row 10, column 5

In almost every situation where we are working with windows, we do not want their borders on the screen to overlap. (Overlapping windows interact in ways that are usually unintended and too messy to go into here.) Thus, if we want to use two windows of, say, 15 rows and 40 columns each, we will almost certainly want to place the upper left-hand corners of the two windows in columns 0 and 40, as in Figure 16.3 below.

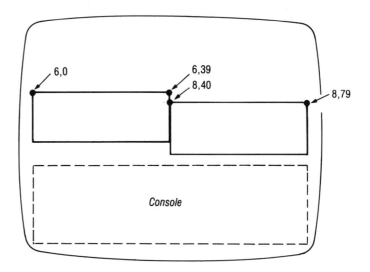

Figure 16.3. A window arrangement

The window that we typically interact with on the screen is called the *console*, and when we place additional windows on the screen, we do not want them to overlap the console. Thus, in Figure 16.3, you will note that the console window has been "squished" to make room for the other two windows.

Enough theory. Here are the PC Scheme primitives for working with windows.

◆ Make–window

The `make-window` primitive takes two arguments: a string to be used as a label (this value can be `#f` if you don't want a label), and a boolean to indicate whether the window should have a visible border (if this argument is `#t` a border line will be displayed; if `#f`, no border will be displayed). If you decide to give the window a label, it will appear toward the upper left-hand portion of the window's edge.

The value returned by a call to `make-window` is a window object large enough to take up the entire screen. Usually, this will be larger than we want, and we will employ the `window-set-size` primitive (to be described below) before actually placing our new window up on the screen.

Here are two examples of `make-window` in use:

```
(define invisible-window (make-window #f #f))
```

```
(define *north-window* (make-window "North" #t))
```

The first expression binds `invisible-window` to a window without a label or border; the second binds `*north-window*` to a window that will have a label of `"North"` and a visible border. Note that neither of these windows will appear on the screen; we will need to call the `window-clear` primitive (to be described below) for that purpose.

◆ Window–set–position!

The `window-set-position!` primitive takes three arguments: a window object, a row number, and a column number. Calling this primitive will position the given window at the appropriate row and column. If the window is already visible on the screen, it will change position the next time we clear it or display text in it; but if we haven't yet displayed the window, it will remain undisplayed until we use the `window-clear` primitive.

Here's an example:

```
(window-set-position! *north-window* 1 20)
```

◆ Window–set–size!

The `window-set-size!` primitive takes three arguments: a window object, a number (of rows), and another number (of columns). Calling this primitive changes the size of the specified window. As with `window-set-position!` above, the change isn't visible until the next time we clear the window or (for an already-visible window) display text inside it. By the way, if the window has borders, these will cause the window to occupy a larger screen region than prescribed by the `window-set-size!` command: in particular, the window will occupy two more rows (due to the presence of the upper and lower border lines) and two more columns (due to the left and right border lines) than specified by the call to `window-set-size!`.

To take an example, suppose we continue working with the window *north-window* from the previous paragraphs:

```
(window-set-size! *north-window* 4 32)
```

If *north-window* had no borders, then it would take up 4 rows and 32 columns of screen space, with its upper left corner at row 1, column 20 (as specified by the earlier call to `window-set-position!`). However, since *north-window* is in fact a window with a visible border, it will take up 6 rows and 34 columns of screen space, and the upper left corner of its border will be at row 0, column 19.

♦ Window-clear

This primitive takes a single argument—a window object. Calling window-clear will cause an undisplayed window to appear on the screen, or will clear out whatever text exists inside an already-visible window.

An example:

```
(window-clear *north-window*)
```

♦ Window-delete

This primitive also takes a window object and erases it from the screen. Note that the window object itself isn't destroyed—just gone from the screen. We may, if we want, display the object on the screen at some later time by using window-clear.

An example:

```
(window-delete *north-window*)
```

♦ Display

You're probably wondering why display is in this section at all. Don't we already know what display does? . . . Well, not entirely. The display primitive, besides taking an argument of something (often a string) to display, may also take an optional second argument—a window object.[5] When this second argument is included, the printed output appears inside the specified window. A similarly useful fact is that the newline primitive, like display, may take an optional window argument to which the "start a new line" command will apply.

Here is an example:

```
(display "hello" *north-window*)
```

Evaluating this expression would cause the word *hello* to appear inside the *north-window* window on the screen (assuming that *north-window* is visible on the screen).

Let's use our window primitives in a sample project. We are going to create a small piece of a program that plays bridge. Specifically, we're going to write the portion of the program that displays bridge hands. (By the way, you don't have to know how bridge is played to follow along—just take a look at some bridge column in the newspaper. Our goal is to create a screen display like the one shown in the column.)

We'll start by creating four windows to display the four hands:

```
(define *north-window* (make-window "North" #t))
(define *south-window* (make-window "South" #t))
(define *east-window* (make-window "East" #t))
(define *west-window* (make-window "West" #t))
```

Next, we'll write a procedure that takes some window as argument—along with a screen position—and displays a short, fat window in the appropriate position. This procedure will be used to render visible the four windows above.

```
(define (initialize-window window upper-row left-col)
  (window-set-size! window 4 32)
  (window-set-position! window upper-row left-col)
  (window-clear window))
```

Our next procedure initializes the display screen for the entire game. It positions the console window toward the bottom of the screen, and then displays

---

[5]Actually, a *port* object, but we'll get to that in a while.

the four bridge windows. Note that all five windows are positioned to avoid any overlap.

```
(define (initialize-game-windows)
  (window-clear 'console)     ; start out by clearing the screen
  (window-set-position! 'console 20 0)
  (window-set-size! 'console 4 80)
  (window-clear 'console)      ; new position and size take effect
  (initialize-window *north-window* 1 20)
  (initialize-window *south-window* 13 20)
  (initialize-window *east-window* 7 47)
  (initialize-window *west-window* 7 1))
```

The only odd thing about this procedure is that it uses the symbol console as the argument to various window operations. The symbol console is treated specially by these window primitives; all we are doing, as you might expect, is operating on the console window.

If you have gotten this far, you might want to try typing (initialize-game-windows) at the Scheme interpreter; this should start up the bridge display.

We'll write two more procedures just to show how our new windows can be used. The display-bridge-hand procedure takes as its argument a bridge hand (structured as a list of four sublists—one for each suit) and a window, and displays the hand inside the given window.

```
(define (display-bridge-hand hand window)
  (let ((spades (car hand))
        (hearts (cadr hand))
        (diamonds (caddr hand))
        (clubs (cadddr hand)))
    (window-clear window)
    (display-suit "Spades: " spades window)
    (display-suit "Hearts: " hearts window)
    (display-suit "Diamonds: " diamonds window)
    (display-suit "Clubs: " clubs window)))
(define (display-suit string lis window)
  (newline window)
  (display string window)
  (display lis window))
```

If we now type the following expression at the interpreter, we should see a bridge hand displayed in the "North" window.

```
(display-bridge-hand '((A K 5) (J 10 8 3) (K Q) (7 6 5 2))
                      *north-window*)
```

Finally, here's a procedure to erase the four bridge windows and restore the screen to its original configuration:

```
(define (restore-screen)
  (window-delete *north-window*)
  (window-delete *south-window*)
  (window-delete *east-window*)
  (window-delete *west-window*)
  (window-set-position! 'console 0 0)
  (window-set-size! 'console 24 80)
  (window-clear 'console))
```

Obviously, there is much, much more of our program to be written—even the user interface portion has been barely begun—but this should give you some indication of how windows might be used.

Before moving on, I do have a promise to keep. I promised to explain the graphics-mode and text-mode procedures from Chapter 7. Here they are—they shouldn't look all that strange to you now:

```
(define (graphics-mode)
  (window-set-position! 'console 18 0)
  (window-set-size! 'console 6 80)
  (set-video-mode! 4)
  (set-line-length! 40)
  (clear-graphics)
  *the-non-printing-object*)
(define (text-mode)
  (window-set-position! 'console 0 0)
  (window-set-size! 'console 24 80)
  (window-clear 'console)
  (set-video-mode! 3)
  *the-non-printing-object*)
```

You can see that graphics-mode simply "squishes" the console window and changes the video mode to the IBM PC's four-color graphics mode; since the text-character size in this mode is larger than usual, the call to set-line-length! is needed to make sure that only 40 characters are included in a line, rather than the usual 80. As for text-mode, you can see that it is analogous to the bridge-program procedure that we wrote to restore the screen to normal. The only additional feature is that we have to set the video mode back to its normal "text-only" setting (which, on the IBM PC, is video mode 3). Once more—if you haven't discovered the fact by now—the set-video-mode! primitive works differently on TI machines. If you have PC Scheme but are not using an IBM PC with a Color Graphics Adapter, you should consult the PC Scheme User's Guide.

Continuations

Continuations are probably the most puzzling object type in Scheme—at least, most students seem to think so. The usual description of a continuation is that it represents the "future of a computation." But the notion of a computation's "future" is not at all obvious. By way of explication (I hope), consider the following simple expression:

```
(+ 4 (* 8 5))
```

By now, evaluating an expression like this in our heads is old hat. First, we evaluate subexpressions: for the sake of this discussion, let's evaluate them from left to right. The first subexpression, +, evaluates to a primitive procedure. The second, 4, evaluates to itself. The third is itself a procedure call, and again we evaluate subexpressions from left to right. The first, *, evaluates to a primitive procedure. The second, 8, evaluates to itself. The third . . .

But let's hold it right here. Obviously, we could continue our hypothetical evaluation right through to the end; but let's imagine that we can take a "snapshot" of the evaluation process right at this point. The crucial idea is that as soon as we "unfreeze" our snapshot and evaluate the upcoming subexpression, there is a *computation waiting to proceed.* That is, there is a sequence of operations prepared to happen: first multiply by 8, then add the result to 4, then print that result and return to the top-level Scheme prompt. You can think of this waiting computation as a *procedure* that takes as its argument the result of evaluating the next subexpression and uses it to complete the evaluation of the entire top-level expression. This procedure is the *current continuation* at the point where we took our snapshot of the running process.

Perhaps another metaphor for continuations will prove helpful. You may recall the "actor model" that we used in Chapter 5 for understanding recursive processes. That model treated each invocation of a given recursive procedure as the "hiring" of a new actor to enact the "script" (code) of the procedure. Now, suppose we view each invocation of *any* procedure—including primitive procedures—as requiring some new actor to be hired. And additionally, each time an expression beginning with a special form is evaluated, a new actor is hired to enact the particular special form. Thus, consider the following sample expression:

```
(and (= 0 0) (> 4 5) (= 3 3))
```

In evaluating this expression, we hire an actor to enact the and "script"; this actor (let's call him Humphrey) hires a new actor, Meryl, to evaluate the call to =; Meryl returns a result of #t, and now Humphrey hires a new actor, Dustin, to evaluate the call to >; Dustin returns a value of #f to Humphrey and this is the result of evaluating the entire expression.

All we have done here is expand our Chapter 5 model to include an actor-hiring step for every procedure call and every special form expression. The point of introducing this model is just this: a continuation may be viewed as the current chain of actors waiting to finish the reading of their script. For instance, at the point of the evaluation at which we evaluated the 5 in the expression above, there were two actors still reading their scripts: Dustin and Humphrey. Dustin is now waiting for a value to compare to 4, and Humphrey is waiting for Dustin's result which will tell him (if #t) whether to hire another actor or (if #f) to return a result of #f and go back to the top-level Scheme prompt.

We can view this two-actor chain—Dustin followed by Humphrey—as a procedure which takes some value as its argument and proceeds on with the computation. That is, we have a procedure that takes its argument, finishes Dustin's script (compare the argument to 4), then finishes Humphrey's script (either go on to evaluate (= 3 3), return that result, and go back to the top-level prompt; or else simply return #f and go back to the top-level prompt). This procedure is the current continuation at the time that we evaluate the subexpression 5 in the expression above. So, to reiterate the main point, you can view a continuation as a chain of actors all waiting in line to finish reading their scripts.

Now that we've been introduced to continuations, we can proceed to the next level of confusion.

In Scheme, continuations are first-class objects. The most relevant primitive to learn in working with continuations is call-with-current-continuation, or call/cc for short. This procedure takes as argument a procedure *proc* and calls *proc* on one argument—the current continuation. Let's take an example based on the one we used above:

```
(define *stored-continuation* '())

(and (= 0 0)
     (> 4 (call/cc (lambda (current-c)
                      (set! *stored-continuation* current-c)
                      5)))
     (= 3 3)))
```

If we evaluate the two expressions above, the result of the second will be #f. But in addition to returning #f, the evaluation of the second expression has had another effect: the continuation that exists just at the point where the second argument to > is being evaluated is now the value of *stored-continuation*. Let's look at this notion more closely. In evaluating the second expression after the and, we evaluated a call to call/cc. When the call/cc expression is evaluated, we take the current continuation (which is waiting for a value to compare with 4) and call the given procedure:

```
(lambda (current-c) (set! *stored-continuation* current-c) 5)
```

with the current continuation as argument. The result of calling this procedure is to save the current continuation as the value of *stored-continuation* and return the value 5. Now we proceed with the evaluation of the and expression, and the result is #f; but we have a continuation object (namely, the value of *stored-continuation*) to play with.

Let's see how we can use our continuation object. If we view this object as the two-actor chain described above, then by calling this object on an argument of, say, 10, we should see the result of our two actors' combined operations—namely, a printed result of *()* and a return to the top-level Scheme prompt:

```
(*stored-continuation* 10)
()
```

On the other hand, if we call our continuation procedure on a value of, say, 3, then we should see a printed result of *#t* (since the final subexpression of the original and expression evaluates to #t), and a return to the top-level Scheme prompt:

```
(*stored-continuation* 3)
#t
```

Note that *stored-continuation* may be used as often as we like; it is a permanent "snapshot" of the computation that we created via the original call to call/cc. We could write a procedure that includes a call to *stored-continuation* in its body:

```
(define (try-this no)
  (* 9999 (+ 37 (/ 764 (*stored-continuation* no)))))
```

If you try calling the try-this procedure on a numeric argument, the result may surprise you—until, that is, you stop and think. The call to *stored-continuation* results, as we know, in a comparison with 4, a conclusion of the evaluation of the and expression, and then *a return to the top-level prompt*. The return to top level is an integral part of our continuation procedure. Thus, as soon as we call *stored-continuation*, we will immediately return to the top-level prompt; and that concludes the evaluation of the body of try-this. No number will ever be divided into 764 or added to 37 or multiplied by 9999:

```
(try-this 5)
()
(try-this 3)
#t
```

What we have done, then, is created a procedure with a *nonlocal exit* (to use the technical phrase). When we call try-this on some numeric argument, the evaluation process "jumps" out of its normal path; that is, it sidesteps the normally-expected control path of evaluation, in which every invoked procedure returns—barring error—some result. (Here, the try-this procedure was invoked, but never returned a result.)

Time and space do not permit a thorough exploration of the kinds of tricks one can do with continuation objects. But the technique exemplified above—that of using a continuation to provide a nonlocal exit—is one of the most widespread uses of continuations. To provide one quasi-realistic example, suppose we want to write a procedure that finds the maximum of a list of positive numbers but returns `failed` if the list contains a negative number. Here is one way that we could write the procedure:

```
(define (max-of-positives lis)
  (cond ((negative? (car lis)) 'failed)
        ((null? (cdr lis)) (car lis))
        (else (let ((max-of-rest (max-of-positives (cdr lis))))
                (if (eq? max-of-rest 'failed)
                    'failed
                    (max (car lis) max-of-rest))))))
```

This would work. . . . But there is some inefficiency here. If we call `max-of-positives` on a very long list whose last element happens to be the only negative number in the list—e.g., a list like:

$$(1\ 2\ 3\ 4\ \dots\ etc.\ \dots\ -1000)$$

we will arrive at a situation in which our waiting chain of "actors" is huge; and each will end up passing a value of `failed` back up the chain until a net result of `failed` is printed out. (If you don't believe me, use the actor model to work through a call to `max-with-positives` with an argument of (1 2 -3).)

An alternative plan is to create a ready-made "failure continuation" at the outset of our recursive process; then, if any element of the list proves to be negative, we call this failure continuation directly and sidestep the waiting chain of actors (just as we did with *stored-continuation* a little earlier).

```
(define (max-of-positives lis)
  (call/cc
    (lambda (failure-exit)
      (define (max-helper lis)
        (cond ((negative? (car lis)) (failure-exit 'failed))
              ((null? (cdr lis)) (car lis))
              (else (let ((max-of-rest (max-helper (cdr lis))))
                      (max (car lis) max-of-rest)))))
      (max-helper lis))))
```

Now suppose we call `(max-of-positives '(1 2 -3))`. The continuation to which `failure-exit` is bound within the body of the procedural argument to `call/cc` is the continuation that exists just at the time that the `call/cc` procedure is invoked; since there are no other expressions in the body of `max-with-positives`, then calling this continuation on some argument value will cause that value to be returned as the net result of the call to `max-with-positives`. In particular, calling this continuation with an argument of `failed` will cause the symbol `failed` to be returned as the result of the call to `max-with-positives`. So when we eventually make our final recursive call to `max-helper`, with an argument of (-3), the call to the `failure-exit` procedure will cause a net result of `failed` to be returned directly; there is no need to pass the value `failed` back up the chain of actors that was created by earlier recursive calls to `max-helper`.

Some additional examples of programming-with-continuations are provided in the problems at the end of this chapter.

Ports

In the section before last we were introduced to PC Scheme's "window objects." As it happens, windows are special instances of a more general object type—

namely, the *port* object type. Ports, in Scheme, are things that one can "read from" or "write to"; that is, they are things that can provide input or accept output. When we worked with windows we used the display command to send output to particular window objects; so in that case we might have said that we were treating the windows as "output ports" for the characters written by display.

Window objects are ports associated with a given region of the display screen; but another way to use ports is to associate them with *files*. We have been working with files, of course, right along; in Chapter 2 we saw how Scheme program files could be saved on a floppy disk from the Edwin editor, and how they could likewise be retrieved from a disk into the editor. You have no doubt become proficient by now in saving and restoring your own personal Scheme files.

Since files may be associated with port objects, however, we can actually incorporate file operations into the programs that we write. That is to say, we can write Scheme programs that create new disk files, save data objects of various kinds in those files, and read back the data objects at some later time. The best way to become familiar with these notions is to look at some relevant Scheme procedures:

♦ Open-output-file, Close-output-port

The open-output-file primitive takes a string—the name of a new file—as its argument, and returns an output port associated with the given file. By using the write primitive procedure with the new output port as its second argument, we can send output to the file. Finally, when we are done writing to the file, we call the close-output-port procedure, which takes a port as argument and closes the appropriate file. Here is an example:

```
(define new-file (open-output-file "a:test.scm"))

(write 'testing new-file)

(newline new-file)

(close-output-port new-file)
```

If we type these expressions at the Scheme interpreter, we will create a new file called "TEST.SCM" on the floppy disk in drive A:. The first expression opens this file for output and binds the name new-file to an output port corresponding to the newly-opened file. The second expression writes the symbol testing into the new file; the third expression starts a new line in the file (we'll see the rationale behind that very soon). Finally, the call to close-output-port closes the file.

♦ Open-input-file, Close-input-port

Open-input-file takes a string—the name of an already-existing file—as its argument, and returns an input port as its result. By using the read primitive, we can obtain input values from this port. Once we are done reading input from the port, we can use close-input-port, which takes a port as its argument and closes the given input file. Here's an example, continuing the one we began above.

```
(define disk-file-for-input (open-input-file "a:test.scm"))

(read disk-file-for-input)
```
TESTING
```
(close-input-port disk-file-for-input)
```

The first expression opens the file that we created earlier and binds the name disk-file-for-input to an input port corresponding to this file. The second expression reads one Scheme expression—in this case, the symbol testing—from the input port. The last expression closes the file.

♦ Write

You may have noticed that in the example above, we sent output to our file by using a new procedure—the write procedure. Up until now, whenever we wanted to print out some value or other on the screen, we used display (or occasionally, writeln). These primitives are especially well suited to printing out objects on the display screen—they employ certain formatting conventions that make the printed-out object easier to read. For instance, if we type (display "Hi"), what we see on the screen is simply the word *Hi*, without the surrounding quotation marks. (Presumably, we don't really want to see the quotation marks in the printed message.)

However, the write procedure is often better suited to sending output to files, since in this case the file is intended to be read (eventually) by the Scheme interpreter, using the read procedure. That is to say, the formatting conventions used by write are appropriate when the printed values are going to be read by calls to read. Some experiments comparing write and display are suggested in Exercise 15 at the end of this chapter; but for now suffice it to say that write is likely to be the more useful procedure in working with files. Note, too, that when we use the read procedure to read input from a port, what we expect to read is one Scheme object—e.g., a symbol, or number, or list—followed by a "line return" character. In other words, the read primitive is intended to be used with files that contain one Scheme object per line. That is why we used the newline command in our example, after we had sent output to our file with write; as a default, it is good policy when using output ports to follow write operations with newline operations.

Having come this far, we can use our newfound knowledge to create half of a useful program (the other half is left to you in Exercise 17). As you know if you worked through the sample project in Chapter 7, our circle-squared graphics designs take a long time to draw. Worse yet, we have no way of saving the designs that we like—if a particular design strikes our fancy, the only way to recover it is to redraw it from scratch.

Well, now our troubles are over. Let's augment our circle-squared program so that it saves all the relevant information that we need to recreate our designs at will. Here are the values that we intend to save:

• The coordinates of the bottom left corner of our design.

• 10,000 numbers corresponding to the chosen pixel values that make up our 100-by-100-pixel region on the screen. (In our four-color version, each pixel has a value of 0, 1, 2, or 3.)

Our first addition to the circle-squared program will be used to create an output port object:[6]

```
(define *picture-output-port* '())

(define (set-output-port! filename)
  (set! *picture-output-port* (open-output-file filename)))
```

Our next procedure will be used to save the bottom left coordinates of our screen region:

```
(define (save-coordinates)
  (write screen-region-left-x *picture-output-port*)
  (newline *picture-output-port*)
  (write screen-region-bottom-y *picture-output-port*)
  (newline *picture-output-port*))
```

---

[6]See Chapter 7 for the original program. The changes we are making here can be directly incorporated into that code.

We'll write yet another procedure that saves the current pen color:

```
(define (save-pen-color color)
  (write color *picture-output-port*)
  (newline *picture-output-port*))
```

Finally, we have to change two procedures in our earlier program: the single-row-loop procedure and the circle-squared procedure:

```
(define (single-row-loop row-y column-x sq-left-x sq-bottom-y sq-side-length)
  (cond ((= (- column-x screen-region-left-x) 100) row-y)
        (else (let ((new-color
                      (choose-pen-color
                        column-x row-y sq-left-x sq-bottom-y sq-side-length)))
                (set-pen-color! new-color)
                (save-pen-color new-color)
                (draw-point column-x row-y)
                (single-row-loop
                  row-y (1+ column-x)
                  sq-left-x sq-bottom-y sq-side-length)))))
(define (circle-squared sq-left-x sq-bottom-y sq-side-length filename)
  (clear-graphics)
  (set-output-port! filename)
  (save-coordinates)
  (region-loop
    screen-region-bottom-y sq-left-x sq-bottom-y sq-side-length)
  (close-output-port *picture-output-port*))
```

Our new program will save the created design in a file whose name (a string) is passed as an argument to circle-squared. This file will consist of 10,002 numbers: the first two of these are the *x*- and *y*-coordinates of the bottom-left corner of our screen region, and the remaining 10,000 are the pixel colors of our region. Thus, we might use the circle-squared procedure as follows:

```
(circle-squared -83 -83 166 "A:design1.scm")
```

Evaluating this expression would store our design in numeric form as a file named "DESIGN1.SCM" on the floppy disk in drive A:.

Of course, we are not done with our new version of circle-squared. We will need some new procedures to retrieve a stored design and display it on the screen. That job is left to you, with some suggestions provided by Exercise 17.

Creating New Special Forms with Macro

The earlier sections in this chapter were devoted to introducing new types of Scheme objects: vectors, environments, windows, continuations, and ports. This last section is a change of pace: we won't meet any new objects, but we *will* acquire an interesting new technique—namely, a method for creating special forms.

Over the course of this book, we have worked our way through a large variety of programs. And the bedrock of our programming technique has been the use of the define special form to create our own procedures. Perhaps, at some point or other, you found yourself wondering whether there is any similar way in Scheme to create our own special forms.

The answer is "yes and no." There is no standard way in Scheme to create new special forms; that is to say, there is no one method that is guaranteed to work in every implementation of the language. However, most implementations do include *some* features for this purpose. In PC Scheme, the macro special form is one such feature.

Before delving into the formal details of using macro expressions, let's look at an example. Suppose we would like to create a new special form called name! that has the same purpose as set! but that takes its "arguments" in the opposite order. That is, we want

    (name! 3 baz)

to have the same meaning as

    (set! baz 3)

Here is a macro expression that will accomplish this purpose:

    (macro name! (lambda (exp) (list 'set! (caddr exp) (cadr exp))))

The expression above illustrates the general format of macro expressions—namely, the special form macro; then the name of the new special form that we are creating; and finally, a procedure of one argument. We'll analyze these elements more closely in a moment, but let's take the broad picture first. The point of our sample expression might best be expressed as a letter to the Scheme interpreter:

"To the Scheme interpreter:

Any time an expression of the form (name! x y) occurs within any expression that you read, you should behave as though what you *actually* read was:

    (set! y x)

To take an example, if we define a new procedure as follows:

    (define (change-some-global-to value)
      (name! value *global-variable*))

you should behave as though the procedure was actually defined as:

    (define (change-some-global-to value)
      (set! *global-variable* value))

Thank you."

Our macro expression thus provides a kind of rewriting rule for the Scheme interpreter: any time an expression beginning with name! is included in an expression read by the Scheme interpreter, it is automatically (and invisibly) rewritten as a set! expression during the reading-in step. Note that this means that a name! expression will be rewritten even when it occurs within the body of some procedure (as in fact happened in the example using change-some-global-to above); even though we haven't used the procedure yet, the name! expression that occurred in the code of that procedure was rewritten as it was read.[7]

Now, how is some particular rewriting rule specified? Let's look again at the method we used to create the name! special form:

    (macro name! (lambda (exp) (list 'set! (caddr exp) (cadr exp))))

The argument exp in the lambda expression above refers to the entire list beginning with name!. In other words, when the following expression is read by the Scheme interpreter:

    (name! 3 baz)

then the appropriate rewriting rule is specified by the lambda expression above, with exp bound to the list (name! 3 baz). The cadr of this list is 3, and the caddr is baz, so evaluating the body of the rewriting rule:

    (list 'set! (caddr exp) (cadr exp))

---

[7]There are some subtleties here, and in fact I am not telling the whole truth. But this explanation is sufficiently close to the truth so that you shouldn't get into trouble. See also Exercise 18 for additional obscure details.

will return the list (set! baz 3). The Scheme interpreter will behave as though it had actually read this rewritten expression.

Let's try out our new special form. Here is a sample session illustrating name! in action:

```
(define *test-variable* 0)

(name! 2 *test-variable*)

*test-variable*
2
(define (increment-test-variable)
  (name! (1+ *test-variable*) *test-variable*)
  *test-variable*)

(increment-test-variable)
3
```

As an aside, it is usually easier to create macro rewriting rules by using the backquote notation that we encountered in Chapter 15. Thus, a simpler way of specifying the name! special form would be the following:

```
(macro name!
  (lambda (exp) '(set! ,(caddr exp) ,(cadr exp))))
```

This is easier to read than our earlier macro expression, and would work just as well.

Let's sum up this discussion. A macro expression is of the form:

(macro *new-special-form rewriting-rule*)

Evaluating a macro expression in the initial environment creates a special form with the name *new-special-form*.[8] Any time an expression beginning with the name *new-special-form* is read by the Scheme interpreter, the *rewriting-rule* procedure is first called on that expression. The result will be a new, rewritten expression; and the Scheme interpreter will now behave as though it were actually reading the rewritten expression.[9]

It is important to state once more that this is the rule for PC Scheme's macro special form—at least in its present implementation—but that other Scheme systems may work differently. The overall message that you should take away from this discussion is simply that most Scheme systems have features like macro that allow new special forms to be created via the use of "rewriting rules." Check your own system manual for details.

Let's conclude with two examples—one brief, one a little more extended. First, we'll create a new special form, unless. The unless special form is followed by two expressions: only if the first evaluates to #f will the second be evaluated. Otherwise, we simply return #f. Here are two examples illustrating the desired behavior of unless:

```
(unless (= 0 0) 'hello)
()
(unless (= 0 1) 'hello)
hello
```

Here's a macro expression to create the unless special form:

```
(macro unless
  (lambda (exp)
    '(if (not ,(cadr exp)) ,(caddr exp) #f)))
```

---

[8]Throughout this discussion, we will assume that all macro expressions are evaluated in the initial environment; one cannot create "locally defined" special forms.

[9]By the way, a terminology note: special forms created in this way are called *macros*.

If you try typing in this expression, you can play with the `unless` special form and verify for yourself that it works. I will leave this to you as an exercise.

Finally, let's try one more example. In Chapter 13, when we created a "turtle object," we also defined a procedure called `repeat`. This procedure took two arguments—a number `number` and a procedure of no arguments—and invoked the procedure the appropriate number of times:

```
(define (repeat number procedure)
  (cond ((= number 1) (procedure))
        (else (procedure) (repeat (-1+ number) procedure))))
```

The problem with this solution is that calls to `repeat` look a little clumsy:

```
(repeat 4 (lambda ()((turtle 'fd) 50) ((turtle 'rt) 90)))
```

It would be preferable to employ a form for `repeat` that enables us to dispense with the `lambda` expression:

```
(repeat 4 ((turtle 'fd) 50) ((turtle 'rt) 90))
```

Here, then, is a new incarnation of `repeat` as a special form:[10]

```
(macro repeat
  (lambda (exp)
    '(repeat-helper ,(cadr exp) (lambda () ,@(cddr exp)))))

(define (repeat-helper number procedure)
  (cond ((= number 1) (procedure))
        (else (procedure) (repeat-helper (-1+ number) procedure))))
```

Here, the body of the `macro` expression for `repeat` rewrites an expression like:

```
(repeat 4 ((turtle 'fd) 10))
```

so that it becomes:

```
(repeat-helper 4 (lambda ()((turtle 'fd) 10)))
```

Any procedure with a `repeat` expression in its body will behave as though it were actually written with a `repeat-helper` expression. And the `repeat-helper` procedure looks, as you might expect, exactly like our old version of `repeat`.

Some additional problems involving `macro` are included among the following exercises.

Exercises

Vectors

1. Find descriptions of the following Scheme primitives in your language manual, and try to use these primitives in some sample expressions:

   ```
   vector
   vector-fill!
   vector->list
   list->vector
   ```

2. This problem concerns a well-known (but simple) solitaire peg game. The game board is just a row of seven holes with three black pegs in the three

---

[10]This `macro` expression uses the at-sign notation @ within a backquoted expression. The idea is that we want the following evaluated list to have its parentheses "stripped away" and to have its elements inserted in the surrounding list. Thus, the expression `'(1 2 ,@(cdr '(5 3)))` evaluates to the list `(1 2 3)`. The at-sign notation was discussed in Chapter 15, Exercise 8, so you may want to go back and examine that exercise now if you didn't before.

leftmost holes and three white pegs in the rightmost holes, as represented below:

$$B \quad B \quad B \ldots W \quad W \quad W$$

A move can be one of the following: a white peg may be moved one space to the left, or a black peg one space to the right, as long as the peg ends up in the empty hole. Also, a white peg may jump a single black peg to its left, or a black peg may jump a single white peg to its right, if by doing so it ends up in the empty hole. The object is to get the three white pegs in the leftmost holes, and the three black pegs in the rightmost holes. Here is the beginning of a sample game:

$$B \quad B \quad B \ldots W \quad W \quad W$$
$$B \quad B \ldots B \quad W \quad W \quad W$$
$$B \quad B \quad W \quad B \ldots W \quad W$$
$$B \quad B \quad W \ldots B \quad W \quad W$$
$$B \ldots W \quad B \quad B \quad W \quad W$$

Create a program that allows you to play the peg game. Your program should represent the game board by a vector of seven elements: each element is one of the three symbols b, w, or empty. Thus, the initial game board would be represented as[11]

```
#(b b b empty w w w)
```

Your peg game program should allow the user to input moves and should display (ideally using graphics) the game board as the game progresses. Compare your program to the one you might have written had the game board been represented as a list instead of a vector.

By the way, once you have this version of the peg game working, you can try extending the game: you might, for instance, invent more elaborate game boards (e.g., two-dimensional boards) and more complex rules.

3. We have made extensive use of the map procedure in working with lists. Write an analogous procedure named map-over-vector! that takes two arguments—a procedure and a vector—and replaces each element in the vector by the result of applying the procedure to that element. Here's an example:

```
(define sample-vector (make-vector 3 0))

(map-over-vector! 1+ sample-vector)
#(1 1 1)

sample-vector
#(1 1 1)
```

Note that the map-over-vector! procedure does not return a new vector—rather, it alters the vector that it gets as its second argument.

4. Just as lists can contain lists among their elements, so vectors can include other vectors as elements. As one example, suppose we want to create a program that will keep track of "reminders" for a calendar year. A reasonable data structure to use would be a twelve-element vector; each element (representing a month) will itself be a vector—the initial "month vector,"

---

[11]As an aside: the pound sign # in this representation is Scheme's "vector marker"; it indicates that the following parenthesized expression is intended to represent a vector. Whenever the Scheme interpreter prints out a vector value, it does so using the pound-sign-plus-parentheses marker; and if you type a parenthesized expression preceded by a pound sign at the Scheme interpreter, that expression will evaluate to a vector object. Thus, if you type (make-vector 3 0) at the interpreter, you will see a printed result of #(0 0 0), and if you type the expression (vector-ref #(1 2 3) 0), you will see a printed result of 1.

representing January, will have thirty-one elements, the next will have twenty-eight (or maybe twenty-nine) days, and so on. Each element of the month vectors will be a list of reminders (which might be strings). Thus, to get a list of reminders for, say, Valentine's Day, we would find the thirteenth element of the first element in our calendar structure:

```
(vector-ref (vector-ref *year* 1) 13)
("Send cards" "Tickets to basketball game at 8 PM")
```

Here, *year* is assumed to be a global variable bound to our twelve-element "calendar" vector. (Remember that the starting element in a vector is the zeroth element: hence the numbers 1 and 13 in our sample expression.)

Using the description above as a starting point, write a program that will maintain reminders for a calendar year. Your program should include procedures like add-reminder!, which takes a string (reminder) and date as arguments and adds the string to the list of reminders for the appropriate date; and get-reminders, which takes a date as argument and returns the list of reminders for that date. Note that when your initial calendar structure is created—before any reminders have been inserted into it—all twelve month vectors should have their elements initialized to ().

Environments

5. Just to see the printed representation of an environment object, evaluate the name user-initial-environment at the Scheme interpreter; in PC Scheme, this name is bound to the initial environment. Another way of seeing the printed representation of an environment is to call the sample-env-maker procedure (which we created in this chapter) on no arguments.

6. Two useful PC Scheme special forms are unbound? and make-environment. The unbound? special form is used to find whether a symbol has a binding in a given environment; the make-environment special form is used to create new, "custom-made" environments. Find these special forms in the PC Scheme language manual and concoct some sample expressions to see how they work.

7. Try to predict the results of typing the following sequence of expressions at the Scheme interpreter. Then run the experiment to see if your predictions were correct.

```
(define a 1)
(define b 'a)
(eval 'a user-initial-environment)
(eval a user-initial-environment)
(eval 'b user-initial-environment)
(eval b user-initial-environment)
```

8. We have seen procedures that take an environment as argument (eval is an example), and we have seen procedures that, when invoked, return environments (sample-env-maker is an example). This, of course, is consistent with the fact that environments are first-class objects in PC Scheme. And since they are first-class objects, it is also possible to create lists (also vectors) of environments.

Write a procedure named symbol-values that takes two arguments—a symbol, and a list of environments—and returns a list of the values to which the symbol is bound in each of the various environments. Here's an example of the procedure at work:

```
(define (sample-env-maker-1)
  (let ((a 1))
    (the-environment)))
(define (sample-env-maker-2)
  (let ((a 2))
    (the-environment)))
(symbol-values 'a (list (sample-env-maker-1) (sample-env-maker-2)))
(1 2)
```

Windows

⊡ 9. One common rationale for using windows in a program is to allow separate areas on the screen for reading input and displaying output—that is, we want the things typed by the user to appear in one region of the screen, and the responses of the program to appear in another.

As an example of this technique, write a trivia question-and-answer program in which the questions are presented in a "question window" and the user types in his answers in an "answer window." After the answer is typed in, the correct answer should be displayed in the question window.

By way of a hint: the only difficult part of this program is creating the "answer window" in which the user's input is typed. There are several approaches you could take. The simplest is to make the console the answer window; another approach is to note that the read primitive in PC Scheme takes an optional window argument (more accurately, an optional port argument—see the section in this chapter on ports), and if the following expression is evaluated:

```
(read *answer-window*)
```

the next expression typed by the user will appear in the window bound to the name *answer-window*.

⊡ 10. Extend the hangman game project of Chapter, 13 Exercise 7, so that it incorporates windows. The current word (blank letters and correctly-guessed letters) should appear in one window; the current set of incorrectly-guessed letters should be displayed in a second window; and the player's input should be read from a third window. If your program includes graphics, the pictures should be displayed in a region of the screen that does not interfere with the various windows.

⊡ 11. Besides using window-clear to display a window, it is also possible to use another PC Scheme primitive: window-popup. The point of this procedure is that we can display a window on top of some other window (i.e., overlapping that other window), but the contents of the window underneath will be restored after the top (popup) window is deleted from the screen. Window-popup, then, is useful for displaying temporary windows: things that appear, present some quick message (like an error message), and disappear afterward.

Investigate the PC Scheme primitives window-popup and window-popup-delete. As an example of how these procedures might be used, consider a further extension to the hangman game described in Exercise 10. Suppose that if the user guesses the character "?" instead of a letter, a temporary "help window" will appear in which the rules of the game will be printed out; this window is deleted from the screen when the user types any key at all. Thus, the help window is something that can be displayed momentarily (overlapping some other region of the screen) and then erased without disturbing the text underneath.

12. Consider the following Scheme code:

```
(define *stored-continuation* '())

(define (continuation-test)
  (let ((message (call/cc
                   (lambda (continuation)
                     (set! *stored-continuation* continuation)
                     "This is a test."))))
    (newline)
    message))
```

If we now call continuation-test on zero arguments by typing (continuation-test) at the Scheme interpreter, the value of *stored-continuation* will be set to a continuation that, when invoked with a string as argument, will print out that string and return to the top-level prompt:

```
(continuation-test)
```
This is a test.
```
(*stored-continuation* "This is another test.")
```
This is another test.
```
(*stored-continuation* "And another.")
```
And another.

Try defining the continuation-test procedure and performing your own experiments; you will probably find it helpful to use the actor model of evaluation in order to understand the code.

Now, why would a procedure like continuation-test ever be useful? Well, consider what this procedure is doing. It is setting the value of *stored-continuation* to a continuation: when this continuation is called with a string argument, that string is printed out on the screen and we return to top level. In a sense, then, calling *stored-continuation* is like using the error special form: when an error expression is evaluated, a message is printed out and we return to the Inspector prompt. The difference between calling *stored-continuation* and evaluating an error expression is that in one case the user is returned to the Scheme interpreter, while in the other the user is returned to the Inspector. To make this distinction a bit more visible, consider the following two procedures, both of which are intended to sum up the numbers in a list:

```
(define (sum-list-A lis)
  (cond ((null? lis) 0)
        ((number? (car lis)) (+ (car lis) (sum-list-A (cdr lis))))
        (else (error "This isn't a number: " (car lis)))))

(define (sum-list-B lis)
  (cond ((null? lis) 0)
        ((number? (car lis)) (+ (car lis) (sum-list-B (cdr lis))))
        (else
          (*stored-continuation* "The list contains a non-number."))))
```

If we call both these procedures on the list (1 2 3 a), the first will return us to an Inspector prompt, and the second to the interpreter prompt.

There are sometimes good reasons for avoiding the use of the error special form: if we were writing a program to be used by people unfamiliar with Scheme, we might want to employ the second strategy (i.e., something rather like *stored-continuation*) to ensure that even when errors are encountered, our users will not have to deal with the (potentially intimidating) Inspector prompt.

13. Suppose we are writing a recursive procedure that takes as its argument a list of numbers and returns the product of all the numbers in the list. Here are two possible versions of this procedure:

```
(define (product-A lis)
  (cond ((null? (cdr lis)) (car lis))
        (else (* (car lis) (product-A (cdr lis))))))

(define (product-B lis)
  (call/cc
    (lambda (continuation)
      (define (product-loop lis)
        (cond ((= (car lis) 0) (continuation 0))
              ((null? (cdr lis)) (car lis))
              (else (* (car lis) (product-loop (cdr lis))))))
      (product-loop lis))))
```

As it turns out, both procedures work:

```
(product-A '(2 4 5))
40

(product-B '(4 5 6))
120
```

Compare the behavior of the two procedures. In particular, suppose that the argument list is:

```
(1 2 3 4 5 0 1 2 3 4 5)
```

Clearly the product of the numbers in this list is just 0. How do the procedures product-A and product-B differ in their operation when given this list as argument? Are there reasons to prefer one procedure over another in certain situations?

14. Here is the match procedure from Chapter 15.

```
(define (match pattern expression dictionary)
  (cond ((eq? dictionary 'failed) 'failed)
        ((atom? pattern)
         (if (eqv? expression pattern)
             dictionary
             'failed))
        ((null? expression) 'failed)
        ((variable? pattern)
         (extend-dictionary pattern expression dictionary))
        ((atom? expression) 'failed)
        (else
          (match (cdr pattern) (cdr expression)
                 (match (car pattern)(car expression) dictionary)))))
```

Now, consider what happens when we evaluate the following expression:

```
(match '(((((a))))) '(((((b))))) '())
```

If you work through this example using the actor model, you will see that the evaluation process involves the creation of a long chain of actors, each of which must eventually pass the value failed back to the previous one.

Using what you know of continuations, rewrite the match procedure so that it avoids this sort of inefficiency. Your procedure should call a special "failure continuation" when an impossible match situation is encountered (e.g., when the first two arguments to match are two distinct symbols). If you need an additional hint: the new version of match should be written along the same general lines as the max-of-positives example in this chapter.

Ports

15. There are a number of differences between display and write; but for our purposes, the most commonly encountered difference between these primitives is in the way that they print strings. Display prints strings without surrounding double quotes, while write prints the double quotes. Thus, when a string is printed by write the result "looks like" a string, but when a string is printed by display it might "look like" a symbol:

```
(display 'hello)
HELLO

(display "HELLO")
HELLO

(write 'hello)
HELLO

(write "HELLO")
"HELLO"
```

The key point here is that write and read are intended to be compatible: when a string is printed out by a call to write, it is in the same form that we would use if we were typing a string to be returned by a call to read. Thus, if we write a string to a file (more accurately, if we write a string to a port object assigned to a file), and then read the string back later, the result of the call to read will be a string.

To elaborate on this point, consider the following example:

```
(define *output-port* '() )

(define (do-test)
  (set! *output-port* (open-output-file "A:test.scm"))
  (display "hello" *output-port*)
  (newline *output-port*)
  (display 'hello *output-port*)
  (newline *output-port*)
  (write "hello" *output-port*)
  (newline *output-port*)
  (write 'hello *output-port*)
  (newline *output-port*)
  (close-output-port *output-port*))
```

Calling do-test on zero arguments will output four expressions to the file TEST.SCM.

Your job is to create a program that will read back the expressions in the file TEST.SCM. In particular, we are interested in whether the objects read in from this file are symbols or strings; so your program should use the predicates symbol? (which returns #t if its argument is a symbol) and string? (which returns #t if its argument is a string) to see exactly what kinds of objects are read in from TEST.SCM.

16. Sometimes when we are obtaining input from a file, we don't know how many lines the file contains: perhaps the file contains, say, ten numbers—or perhaps a thousand. In this situation, the PC Scheme primitive eof-object? comes in handy. This predicate returns #t if its argument is the special "end-of-file object" that concludes every PC Scheme file. Here is an example of eof-object? in action: the following procedure, read-until-done, takes a

port (one that is assigned to a file) as its argument, and prints on the screen the value of every object in the file. Note that read–until–done works no matter how large the file might be.

```
(define (read-until-done port)
  (let ((object (read port)))
    (cond ((eof-object? object) (close-input-port port) (writeln "Done."))
          (else (writeln object)
                (read-until-done port)))))
```

Your job is to write a procedure named size-of-file that takes a port (again, one assigned to a file) as its argument and returns the number of objects in the file. For simplicity's sake (although it really isn't important), you can assume that the file contains only numbers.

17. Earlier in this chapter, we wrote a program to save the information for "circle-squared" designs in disk files. This problem will provide some suggestions for a program to read those design files and display the saved picture on the screen. I want to stress that that this is only one possible programming strategy among many; it won't hurt my feelings if you ignore my suggestions entirely and write the program on your own.

Anyway, if you're still with me, you might start out by defining a global variable named *picture–input–port*:

```
(define *picture-input-port* '())
```

Now the procedures in the program might be structured more or less as follows:

```
(define (set-input-port! filename)
  Sets *picture-input-port* to a port
  object assigned to the specified file.
)

(define (read-coordinates)
  Sets *screen-region-left-x* and
  *screen-region-bottom-y* to the
  values specified by the file
)

(define (draw-one-row row-no)
  Reads in 100 values from the
  file and uses them to set the
  pixels of one row on the screen.
  You will probably need a subprocedure here.
)

(define (draw-rows)
  Calls draw-one-row 100 times, once
  for each row on the screen.
  You will probably need a subprocedure.
)
```

Here is the top-level procedure for the program, given the structure that we have employed thus far:

```
(define (retrieve-and-draw-file filename)
  (set-input-port! filename)
  (read-coordinates)
  (draw-rows)
  (close-input-port *picture-input-port*))
```

18. One of the potentially confusing aspects of macro expressions is that the rewrite-rule they specify is applied even before the new special form is actually "used." To see what I mean, look at the special form unless that we created earlier in this chapter:

```
(macro unless
  (lambda (exp)
   '(if (not ,(cadr exp)) ,(caddr exp) #f)))
```

Having evaluated the macro expression above, we can now use unless just like any other special form. Here are a couple of sample expressions typed at the Scheme interpreter:

```
(unless (= 1 1) 'hello)
()
(unless (= 1 2) 'hello)
HELLO
```

Now, suppose we define a procedure whose body includes an unless expression:

```
(define (print-if-not-0 no)
  (unless (= no 0) (display no)))
```

This ought to work—and in fact, it does. But suppose, before we even invoke our new procedure, we try to recreate the unless special form so that it returns #t instead of #f when the condition isn't met:

```
(macro unless
  (lambda (exp)
    '(if (not ,(cadr exp)) ,(caddr exp) #t)))
```

Here is the key question: if we *now* call print-if-not-0 on an argument of 0, will it return #t or #f? In other words, is the unless expression in the body of our procedure an "old" or "new" unless expression?

In point of fact, the unless expression in the body of our procedure is the "old" version. This is because the rewrite-rule for unless is applied at the time the procedure using unless is defined. Thus, the print-if-not-0 procedure will continue to use the original meaning of unless; if we want it to use the new definition, we will have to redefine the procedure.

Try working through this example at the keyboard. First create the old version of unless, and then define print-if-not-0. Then evaluate a new macro expression to change the meaning of unless. You can prove to yourself that print-if-not-0 uses the older meaning of the unless special form. Finally, redefine print-if-not-0 without changing its code; you will see that now it uses the new meaning of unless.

The upshot of all this is that changing a special form's meaning is more "dangerous" than redefining a procedure. If you redefine a procedure, any call to that procedure will of course use the new definition; you don't have to redefine all the other procedures that happen to use the one that you changed. However, if you rewrite a macro expression, you must take care to redefine all those procedures that include the newly-changed special form; otherwise, all existing expressions employing the special form will continue to use the original (and presumably faulty) version.

19. Suppose that, in the course of writing a large program, we find ourselves creating a lot of similar "yes-or-no" procedures:

```
(define (print-random-number?)
  (display "Want to see a random number? (Type Y if yes) ")
  (if (eq? (read) 'y) (writeln (random 100)) '()))

(define (want-to-play-again?)
  (display "Want to play again? (Type Y if yes) ")
  (if (eq? (read) 'y) (run-some-game-procedure) (writeln "Goodbye!")))
```

Create a new special form named make-yes-or-no-procedure that is followed by four expressions: the name of the procedure to create, the "question string" to use, the expression to evaluate if the user types "y," and the expression to evaluate if the user types anything besides "y." For instance, here is how we would use our new special form to create the first procedure shown above:

```
(make-yes-or-no-procedure
  print-random-number? "Want to see a random number? (Type Y if yes) "
  (writeln (random 100)) '())
```

⟨✳⟩ 20. It is possible to create special forms that in turn create other special forms. Consider the following (admittedly somewhat convoluted) example:

```
(macro alternative-name-for
  (lambda (expression)
    '(macro ,(caddr expression)
       (lambda (exp) (cons ',(cadr expression) (cdr exp))))))
```

The new special form alternative-name-for allows us to give alternative names to any procedure or special form:

```
(alternative-name-for car first)

(alternative-name-for cadr second)

(first (second '((1 2) (3 4))))
3
```

Try experimenting with the alternative-name-for special form. Use it to create a new name just-in-case for the if special form.

Miscellaneous

⟨✳✳⟩ 21. This chapter has been largely concerned with introducing a variety of new object types, but there are a few species that we haven't examined for lack of space. As a project of your own, you might explore one or more of the following PC Scheme object types:

    • Structures   • Engines   • Delayed Objects

It should also be mentioned that although we have used strings from time to time throughout this book, we never really made a systematic investigation of this object type. Look up the following PC Scheme procedures in your language manual and devise some string-manipulating experiments of your own:

make-string	string-ref	string-null?
string-append	string-set!	list->string
string-copy	substring	string->list

22. For every type of object in PC Scheme, there is an associated "type-checking predicate"—a predicate that returns #t if its argument is an object of the given type. For instance, here are the appropriate "type predicates" for numbers, booleans, and pairs:

number?	boolean?	pair?

Look through your PC Scheme language manual and see if you can find some other "type predicates."

An Edwin Mini-Manual

This appendix is intended to provide a brief overview of PC Scheme's Edwin editor. By reading this section, you will gain some initial familiarity with Edwin; you should follow your reading of this section by looking at the extensive material on Edwin in the PC Scheme User's Guide and by doing some leisurely exploration on your own.

Edwin is a text editor not unlike those that you might find in many word-processing systems. It is in fact a version of EMACS, a text editor developed (largely by Richard Stallman) at MIT.

General Information

The basic idea in using Edwin is that you type text at the keyboard, and the text appears on the screen just about as fast as you type it. The new text is inserted just before the *cursor* (the white mark, sometimes flashing, that you see on the screen). Occasionally in using Edwin, you will type key combinations that do not insert text but that instead have some special function (for instance, moving the cursor on the screen, or saving the text that you have typed in some file on a disk). Most of these special key combinations employ the *control* or *meta* keys, which will be described in the next section.

When we work with PC Scheme, the Edwin editor is a handy tool for writing programs. As mentioned in Chapter 2, the typical Scheme programming scenario is one in which programs are first written in the Edwin subsystem and subsequently tried out by typing expressions at the Scheme interpreter. There are special commands in Edwin that allow us to "go back to" the Scheme interpreter, and that allow us to treat our text (as typed in the editor) as a series of expressions to be evaluated by the Scheme interpreter; we'll get to all these matters a little later in this appendix.

By far the easiest way to familiarize yourself with Edwin is to play with it. You will find that you can get by very comfortably using only a small number of special commands. By perusing the Edwin manual from time to time, you will gradually expand your Edwin repertoire.

Control and Meta Commands

Most of the special Edwin commands are so-called *control* or *meta* commands. A control command is one in which the (CTRL) (CONTROL) key is held down at the same time as some other key; for instance, the (CTRL)-F command is given by holding down the (CTRL) key and then pressing the F key (while still holding down (CTRL)). A meta command is one in which the (ESC) (ESCAPE) key is pressed first (and then released), and then some other key is pressed. Thus, for example, the (ESC)-F command is given by pressing the (ESC) key, releasing it, and then pressing the F key.[1] If your keyboard does not have an (ESC) key, you can use the (CTRL)-Z command as a substitute; the (ESC)-F command would then be given by first holding down the (CTRL) key and pressing the Z key; then, after releasing both the Z and (CTRL) keys, pressing the F key.

Moving the Cursor Around: Simple Editing

The first skill to acquire in using Edwin is moving the cursor around on the screen. You will see that when you type ordinary text at the screen, the cursor moves one character to the right for every character you type. By pressing the ↵ (or RETURN) key, you can start a new line.

Suppose you find that you have typed the following text in the editor:

```
(defile (square no)
  (* no no))
```

Your cursor is at the end of the expression—that is, after the second close parenthesis character on the second line—and you notice that you have typed defile instead of define (an interesting Freudian slip, but we won't pursue that). How can you fix the misspelling?

The first step in fixing the problem is to move the cursor until it is just after the letter l in defile (in other words, until the cursor is over the final e in defile). If your keyboard has arrow keys, you can move the cursor with these. For instance, the up-arrow key will move the cursor upward, a line at a time: one press will move the cursor to the top line of the expression. Pressing the left-arrow key will move the cursor back, one character at a time, until it is over the target e.

Another way of moving the cursor is to use the following control commands:

- (CTRL)-N moves the cursor to the Next line (like the down-arrow)
- (CTRL)-P moves the cursor to the Previous line (like the up-arrow)
- (CTRL)-F moves the cursor Forward one character (like the right-arrow)
- (CTRL)-B moves the cursor Back one character (like the left-arrow)

There are other cursor-movement commands—and we'll see a few more in a moment—but the four listed above are a good set to learn first. In our example, you could move the cursor from the second line of the defile expression to the first by using the (CTRL)-P command, then the (CTRL)-B command until the cursor is over the target e.

Once you have moved the cursor to the desired position, you can delete the offending l by pressing the ← (BACKSPACE) key; pressing this key erases the character immediately before the cursor. Now, by typing n, you can complete your repair of the original misspelled expression.

Merely by using the information given so far—i.e., how to type in new text, how to move the cursor around and how to delete characters—you are now able to do a surprising amount of editing. Before moving on to other matters, however, it is worth mentioning some other cursor-movement commands. The problem

[1]The term "meta command" derives from the fact that the original EMACS was developed on a machine whose keyboard included a META key. For our purposes, you can think of (ESC) as the META key, if you like.

with the four above is that they can only move the cursor a short distance at a time; but if you have written a large amount of text, it is possible that you will want to move the cursor over a longer distance.

By way of explanation, suppose you are writing a sizable Scheme program, with many procedures. As you type new text, the cursor approaches the end of the Edwin screen; and if you continue to type text past the final visible line, the screen will scroll upward to accommodate the new characters. You will eventually find that your program takes up well over a "screen's-worth" of space. Now, if you wanted to move the cursor from the end of your text to the beginning, you could use CTRL-P to shift the cursor a line at a time; but for situations like this, the following commands are likely to come in handy.

- CTRL-V scrolls the text displayed down by one screen
- ESC-V scrolls the text displayed up by one screen
- ESC-< moves the cursor to the top of the buffer
- ESC-> moves the cursor to the end of the buffer

In our current example, to move the cursor back to the very beginning of our text, we would use the ESC-< command. To return the cursor to its original position at the end of our text, we could use the ESC-> command; or we could scroll the screen by one screen's-worth of text at a time by using the CTRL-V command. (You are encouraged to experiment with these commands on your own.)

By the way, the term *buffer* in the description of the ESC-> and ESC-< commands refers to the working text area (from the beginning of our text to the end). Thus, when people are working with Edwin they may say that they are "typing text into the buffer" or "moving the cursor around in the buffer."

Killing and Unkilling Text

In the previous section, we saw how to use the ← key to delete one character. We often want to delete larger portions of text. In this case, the CTRL-K key is useful—by typing CTRL-K, you can delete all characters after the current cursor position on the current line. For instance, if you position your cursor over the e in the line

        this is a test

and type CTRL-K, the result is

        this is a t

If you type CTRL-K at the end of a line (i.e., in a position in which there are no more characters in this line to delete), then the effect will be to bring the following line up to the current one. (You can think of this as deleting the "line return" at the end of the current line.) Here's an example: suppose you position your cursor over the t in time in the following lines:

        Now is the time for all good men to come to the aid of their
        party.

By typing CTRL-K once, you will see the following:

        Now is the
        party.

And by typing CTRL-K yet again from the cursor's current position (at the end of the top line), you will see the following:

        Now is the party.

If you wish to delete a series of lines, you can position your cursor at the beginning of the series and type CTRL-K repeatedly. There are other, more elaborate ways of deleting large portions of text, but the only one that will be explored here is (CTRL)-K.

Now, suppose you delete a line (or series of lines) using (CTRL)-K and decide that you want to put them back? The way to do this is to use the (CTRL)-Y (for "Yank back") command. To see how this might be used, we can place the cursor in the previous example over the p in party, and then type (CTRL)-Y. The previously killed text is retrieved, and the line once more looks like:

```
Now is the time for all good men to come to the aid of their
party.
```

In other words, the entire killed line (and the line return at its end) are retrieved by typing (CTRL)-Y. The cursor, you will find, is positioned at the end of the retrieved text (in this example, over the p in party).

There are two very common uses for the commands (CTRL)-K and (CTRL)-Y. One is to move large chunks of text around. For instance, if you want to move some lines from the beginning of your program to the end, you can: (a) position your cursor before the lines to be moved, (b) kill those lines using (CTRL)-K, (c) move your cursor to the end of the program, and (d) retrieve the killed lines using (CTRL)-Y. As you get used to working with Edwin, you will no doubt find yourself making liberal use of (CTRL)-K and (CTRL)-Y to do what other editors call "cut and paste" operations.

A second use of the (CTRL)-K and (CTRL)-Y commands is to make multiple copies of some piece of text. This technique exploits the fact that if you type (CTRL)-Y a second (third, etc.) time, you get a second (third, etc.) copy of the previously killed text.

For example, suppose that we have written the following Scheme procedure:

```
(define (display-many-lines)
  (display "This")
  (display "should")
  (display "take")
  (display "five")
  (display "lines")
  )
```

We want to place the expression (newline) before each of the five display expressions. Here is how we could go about it: we write the first of our five desired lines:

```
(define (display-many-lines)
  (newline)
  (display "This")
  (display "should")
  (display "take")
  (display "five")
  (display "lines")
  )
```

Then we kill the entire line with the newline expression (and the line return following) by positioning our cursor at the very beginning of that line and typing (CTRL)-K twice. (At this point the text looks exactly as it did before we added the first newline expression.) Now we retrieve the killed text by typing (CTRL)-Y; then move the cursor down one line (to the beginning of the line with (display "should")) and type (CTRL)-Y again. Our text now looks like this:

```
(define (display-many-lines)
  (newline)
  (display "This")
```

```
(newline)
(display "should")
(display "take")
(display "five")
(display "lines")
)
```

By continuing to move the cursor down and using the (CTRL)-Y command, we can
eventually add all the desired newline calls:

```
(define (display-many-lines)
 (newline)
 (display "This")
 (newline)
 (display "should")
 (newline)
 (display "take")
 (newline)
 (display "five")
 (newline)
 (display "lines")
 )
```

There are still other tricks you can do by way of retrieving killed text; again,
you should consult the PC Scheme User's Guide for details.

Edwin includes a handy feature that allows you to search for specific portions of
text in the editor buffer. This feature is called *incremental search*, and as time
goes on you will find yourself using it more and more.

Searching for Text

The incremental search facility is best introduced by an example. Suppose
your cursor is at the beginning of a (very large) buffer, and you wish to locate
a particular define expression somewhere in the buffer—say, the following
expression:

```
(define (square x)
 (* x x))
```

One way to do this would be to use the (CTRL)-V command to repeatedly scroll the
screen, keeping a careful watch for the square definition as you do so. But this is
risky—if you lose concentration, you might miss the square procedure and thus
have to look through the entire buffer again and again.

A surer way to locate the square definition is to use the (CTRL)-S command,
which searches the buffer for the next occurrence of some particular piece of text.
Here's how you could use (CTRL)-S in the present example. First, type the (CTRL)-S
command; you will see a prompt at the bottom of the screen labeled *I-Search*. Now
if you type the character s you will see that character appear after the prompt, and
the cursor will "jump" to the next occurrence of the letter s in the buffer. If you
continue by typing the letter q at the search prompt, the cursor will move from its
current position (where it has found the letter s) to the nearest position further on
where it finds the letter pair sq. (If the cursor's original s-position was *already*
followed by the letter q, then the cursor will only move over one character—i.e.,
to the nearest sq-position.) By continuing to type characters at the search prompt,
you can cause the cursor to move until it finds the first occurrence of the entire
sequence that you have typed. Thus, if you continue with our example by typing
the letters u, a, r, and e, the cursor will move to the spot where the letter sequence
square first occurs.

We are not yet done with our example; so far, we have only seen how to use (CTRL)-S to locate the first occurrence of the letter sequence square in our buffer. Let's suppose for now that we have gotten lucky, and that the first occurrence of the letter sequence square is in fact within the define expression we are looking for (that is, there were no *other* occurrences of the letters square earlier in the buffer). In this case, our search has been successful; we now want to terminate the search operation. The easiest way to do this is with some cursor-movement command like (CTRL)-F or (CTRL)-B; typing either of these commands will cause the search prompt to disappear from the bottom of the screen, and will leave the cursor near the sought-for letter sequence.

Suppose, however, that the first occurrence of the letter sequence square occurs before the define expression that we were looking for. Now, our search operation has positioned the cursor over the first occurrence of square—but this is not the occurrence we are interested in and we wish to keep searching. In this case, all we have to do is type the (CTRL)-S command once more and the cursor will jump to the *next* occurrence of the letters square in the buffer. If this is still not the one we seek, we can keep typing (CTRL)-S and eventually locate all the occurrences of the letter sequence square in the buffer.

Thus, we have used (CTRL)-S to move the cursor to each occurrence of square until we found the particular expression we want. You can see that this is a good deal more effective than scrolling through a large program and trying to find the expression we want by "eyeballing" the text.

There are still some observations to be made about our example. First, we might ask what happens if in fact there are no (or no more) occurrences of the sequence square in our buffer; that is, what happens if the search operation fails to find some specified sequence further on in the buffer? In this case, we will see a message reading *Failing I-Search* at the bottom of the screen, and the cursor will not move from its latest position. Second, it is worth stressing the fact that each time we type a character at the search prompt, the cursor jumps to the next appropriate position; thus, when we type letters sq at the prompt, the cursor locates the first occurrence of this sequence. If the first occurrence of the letters sq is in fact within the define expression we are seeking, then we don't have to type the entire word square at the prompt—merely typing the letters sq is sufficient to find the sought-for expression in the buffer.

It is possible to search backward in the buffer, as well as forward, for some letter sequence. If you type (CTRL)-R instead of (CTRL)-S, you will see a prompt labeled Reverse I-Search, and by typing characters you can now locate occurrences of some letter sequence *before* the original cursor position.

There are still more interesting properties to the search facility in Edwin, but the discussion here should be enough to get you started. One topic worth noting before we leave the subject—and it's a topic rarely documented—is that there is a certain craft to using the search facility. Recall our previous example, and suppose that instead of searching for the word square we decided instead to search for the word define (which is, after all, also a letter sequence within the expression that we are looking for). In this case, we could cause the cursor to find, one by one, each occurrence of the letter sequence define in our buffer. But because the letter sequence define is likely to occur many times in the buffer, we will probably have to search through a lot of unwanted defines until we locate the one we want. The point of this is simply that when we are searching for some piece of text, it is shrewd to choose a letter sequence within that text that is unlikely to occur anywhere else. In the example above, we might have done even better by using the letter sequence e (square—that is, starting our sequence with the letter e, a space, and an open parenthesis character—since this would almost certainly lead us immediately to the square definition (rather than some other occurrence of the word square). You should note (and will no doubt eventually take advantage of) the fact that spaces, line returns, parentheses, and so on are all permitted as part of a sought-for character sequence.

Any time you are working with Edwin, you can save the current contents of the buffer in a file on disk.[2] One way to do this is by using the (CTRL)-X (CTRL)-W command (where the "W" stands for "Write Buffer"; note also that this command requires two separate keystrokes). If you type the (CTRL)-X (CTRL)-W command, you will see a prompt at the bottom of the screen asking for a file name under which to save the contents of the buffer. You can then type the name that you wish to give your new file (say, A:MYCODE.SCM) and press ↵; the contents of the buffer will be saved in a file of that name.

Saving and Retrieving Files

The (CTRL)-X (CTRL)-W command is typically used when you are creating a new file with a given name. Suppose, however, that after saving your code as in the example above, you continue to work with Edwin and add a few more procedures to your program; and you wish to save the new buffer contents in a file with the same name as before (in effect, you wish to erase the previous file with that name and create a new file with the same name and the updated buffer contents). In this case the simplest command to use is (CTRL)-X (CTRL)-S (where the "S" stands for "Save Buffer"). When you type this command, Edwin will attempt to save the buffer contents under the name that you used for the previous (CTRL)-X (CTRL)-W operation (in our current example, Edwin will attempt to save the buffer contents under the name A:MYCODE.SCM). You will see a message at the bottom of the screen telling you that a file with this name already exists, and asking whether you really intend to replace the earlier version; if you reply by pressing Y, Edwin will save the new buffer contents in a file with the original name.

Now, suppose you wish to retrieve a stored file from your disk and load its contents into the Edwin buffer. The (CTRL)-X (CTRL)-V command (for "Visit File") will serve your purpose. When you type this command, you will see a prompt asking you for the name of the file to retrieve; and when you type a file name (and press ↵), the contents of the desired file will be loaded into the Edwin buffer, and the previous contents of the buffer will disappear.[3]

One key concept to understand in all this is that the Edwin buffer is *not* a file, but rather the text that we are currently working with in the editor. Thus, altering the contents of the buffer does not affect the contents of any stored file. The only way to change the contents of a file is to save the buffer contents (e.g., by using (CTRL)-X (CTRL)-S) into a new file of the same name. Moreover, retrieving the contents of a file into the Edwin buffer does not alter that file in any way; the file is still stored on the disk after the retrieval operation. Similarly, saving the buffer contents into a file does not alter the buffer contents.

Let's sum up this section on file manipulation by describing two typical scenarios that illustrate how we might use the commands introduced above:

Scenario 1: Creating a New Program

1. Enter the Edwin editor and begin writing the program.
2. After writing a bit of the program, save it under a new file name using (CTRL)-X (CTRL)-S.

---

[2]For the purposes of this discussion, I will assume that your system has a floppy disk drive that uses "A:" as a device name; but you can save files on other storage media, such as hard disk, as well.

[3]If those previous buffer contents have been altered since the last time they were saved in a file, Edwin will ask whether you want to save the current buffer contents before they disappear; and if you reply with a Y, Edwin will prompt you for a file name under which to store the current buffer contents. If, on the other hand, you reply with an N, Edwin will simply load the visted file's contents into the buffer, and the original contents will be lost for good.

3. Add to and/or alter what you have written; and try out what you have written in the Scheme interpreter (this last step, going back to the Scheme interpreter from Edwin, will be discussed in the next section).

4. Periodically resave the updated contents of the Edwin buffer by using (CTRL)-X (CTRL)-S.

Scenario 2: Working with a Previously-Written Program

1. Enter the Edwin editor and use (CTRL)-X (CTRL)-V to load the contents of the file into the buffer.

2. Try out (in the Scheme interpreter) and/or alter (in Edwin) the program.

3. If there are changes in the program that you wish to keep, use (CTRL)-X (CTRL)-S to resave the program under the original name (or use (CTRL)-X (CTRL)-W to save the changed program under a new file name without affecting the original file).

One final point, on the subject of appropriate file names: there are some general stylistic rules worth following. When typing a file name in response to an Edwin prompt, you should be sure to begin with a device name (like "A:"); you should conclude the names of Scheme program files with a ".SCM" extension; and you should use file names no longer than eight characters (not including the device name and the extension).[4]

Interaction with Scheme

There is not much use in writing a Scheme program in the editor if you cannot work with that program in the Scheme interpreter. Once you have a certain portion of your program written and wish to go back to the interpreter to try it out, you can use the (ESC)-O command (that's the letter O, not zero). This command causes the Scheme interpreter to evaluate, in order, every one of the expressions in the current Edwin buffer, and returns you to the Scheme interpreter. Note that typing (ESC)-O does not change the contents of the buffer; the next time you enter the editor by evaluating the expression (edwin) at the interpreter, the Edwin buffer will reappear unchanged from the last time you left the editor.

It is worth driving home the point that the (ESC)-O command tells the Scheme interpreter to evaluate expressions *in order*—just as if you typed those expressions, one by one, at the interpreter. Thus, suppose the following two expressions appear in the buffer:

```
(define b a)
(define a 1)
```

If we type (ESC)-O, the Scheme interpreter will print out an error message when it tries to evaluate the first of these expressions because the name a has not been bound to any value.[5] However, if the order of the two expressions is reversed, as follows:

```
(define a 1)
(define b a)
```

the (ESC)-O command can be used without any problems.

Let's say you have changed or added only one expression in the Edwin buffer, and wish to go back to the Scheme interpreter without evaluating *every* expression in the buffer. In this case, rather than using (ESC)-O, you can move the cursor to the beginning of the single new expression to be evaluated, and type

---

[4]The eight-character limit on file names (as well as a three-character limit on extension names) derives from the rules of the MS-DOS operating system. You should consult your operating system manual if you want to investigate the subject of file names and the conventions surrounding them.

[5]The Scheme concepts needed to understand this example are introduced in Chapter 3.

(ESC) (CTRL)-X. (The technique for doing this is to first press (ESC); release it; then press (CTRL) and, while (CTRL) is still being held down, press X.) This command will cause the Scheme interpreter to evaluate the one indicated expression and will return you to the Scheme interpreter.

There is yet another, more flexible method of sending Scheme expressions back to the Scheme intepreter, but the two commands described above ((ESC)-0 and (ESC) (CTRL)-X) should serve you pretty well for a while. For further exploration, consult the section on "Marks and Regions" and the description of the (ESC) (CTRL)-Z command in the PC Scheme User's Guide.

Finally, one other method of returning from Edwin to the Scheme interpreter is by typing the (CTRL)-X (CTRL)-Z command. This is the command to use if you merely wish to return to the interpreter without evaluating any expressions in the buffer. If the buffer has been altered since the last time you saved its contents, then when you type (CTRL)-X (CTRL)-Z, Edwin will ask you with a prompt whether you want to save the buffer contents (though in any case those contents will not be lost—if you should return to the editor the buffer will reappear just as it was when you left).

Several Useful Tips for the Beginner

This section discusses some miscellaneous commands and topics not covered in the earlier sections.

The (CTRL)-G Command

The (CTRL)-G command is an all-purpose "abort" command in Edwin. (I don't know what the "G" stands for, but personally I always think of it as meaning "Get me out of here!") Discussing the fine points of the command would almost be counterproductive; suffice it to say that if you find yourself in a situation that you want to undo (for instance, you have accidentally typed (CTRL)-X (CTRL)-W and are now staring at an unwanted file name prompt), the (CTRL)-G command will often do the trick. In certain situations, typing (CTRL)-G twice is called for; for example, if you wish to abort a failed incremental search operation and bring the cursor back to its starting position (i.e., its position before the search operation began), you should type (CTRL)-G (CTRL)-G. Consult your manual for more details.

The (CTRL)-L Command

Typing the (CTRL)-L command will scroll the screen so that the text at the current cursor position will be repositioned at the center of the screen. This is a useful command if you are looking at some text way toward the top or bottom of the screen and wish to scroll that text so it is at screen center.

Using Edwin as a Programming Aid

There are several features of the Edwin editor that are especially useful for Scheme programmers. The first is the (TAB) key (also explored in Chapter 2, Exercise 7). If you press (TAB), the line on which the cursor is currently positioned will automatically be indented in accordance with standard Scheme indenting conventions. These indenting conventions are not worth describing explicitly; over time, you will come to recognize them almost unconsciously.[6]

There is good reason to maintain properly-indented Scheme code: if you press the (TAB) key and find that the current line of text is indented to some unexpected position, you have good reason to expect that there is some error (possibly, mismatched parentheses) somewhere in your code. In other words, the indentation rules—merely by dictating a "standard look" to Scheme code—can provide hints as to the location of mistakes. If a portion of Scheme code "looks wrong" to you, it probably *is* wrong.

While we're on the topic of indentation, the (ESC) (CTRL)-Q command can be used to indent an entire Scheme expression according to the standard conventions.

---

[6]As an example of an indenting convention, in case you need to see one written out: whenever all arguments in a procedure call expression are written on separate lines, they should all begin in the same column on the screen.

If you wish to indent a Scheme expression, you should first move the cursor to the beginning of the expression and then type the command (first press and release the (ESC) key, then type (CTRL)-Q). Here is an example of the command in use; suppose the following expression appears somewhere in our buffer:

```
(define (win-or-lose? number)
(if (= number 0)
(display "You won!")
                        (display "You lost!")
            ))
```

This code is formatted hideously, and we are not even positive at first glance that it includes no parenthesis-matching errors. Moving the cursor to the parenthesis before the word define and typing (ESC) (CTRL)-Q will cause each line in the expression to be indented correctly:

```
(define (win-or-lose? number)
  (if (= number 0)
      (display "You won!")
      (display "You lost!")
      ))
```

Yet another way in which Edwin helps to avoid programming errors is by parenthesis matching. You will find that when you type a close parenthesis character in Edwin, the matching open parenthesis character is highlighted momentarily. (If you type a close parenthesis for which Edwin can find *no* matching open parenthesis, the editor will sound a little beep.) It is a good habit to take note of which open parentheses are matched by the close parentheses that you type; by comparing your expectations with the visible evidence provided by the editor, you can often spot (and fix) parenthesis mismatches.

Backup Copies of Files

It is *always* a good idea to create at least one extra copy of any program file that you wish to keep. Moreover, if you are working with your Scheme system and editing some program text in Edwin, you should resave your program (using (CTRL)-X (CTRL)-S) often; if you do not, some horrible occurrence (e.g., your pet capuchin swats the computer plug out of its socket) may result in the loss of much editing work. *Ignore this paragraph at your own risk.*

Inserting Files into the Buffer

The (CTRL)-X (CTRL)-I command in Edwin is a file-manipulating command that allows you to insert the contents of some file into the buffer at the current cursor position. If you type (CTRL)-X (CTRL)-I, Edwin will prompt you for a file name; after you type in the name, the contents of the specified file will be inserted into the Edwin buffer (and the cursor will be positioned at the beginning of the inserted text).

One way in which this command is useful is that it allows us to create "tool files" that can be inserted into the programs that we write. These files might contain procedures (or portions of procedures) that we wish to include in many different programs.

Here is an example. In Chapter 7, three "graphics procedures" named graphics-mode, text-mode, and g-edwin are introduced. These procedures are handy for any program that involves graphics; so we might like to include them in our various graphics programs. One possible approach in this situation would be to save the three graphics procedures in their own little file named GPROCS.SCM; then, whenever we compose a new graphics program, we can insert the GPROCS.SCM file into our buffer.[7]

Cursor Movement

(CTRL)-N	Move cursor to Next line
(CTRL)-P	Move cursor to Previous line
(CTRL)-F	Move cursor Forward one character
(CTRL)-B	Move cursor Backward one character
(CTRL)-V	Scroll to next screen
(ESC)-V	Scroll to previous screen
(ESC)-‹	Move cursor to the start of the buffer
(ESC)-›	Move cursor to the end of the buffer
(CTRL)-L	Center the cursor position on the screen

Killing and Unkilling Text

← (BACKSPACE)	Delete character just before cursor
(CTRL)-K	Kill line
(CTRL)-Y	Yank back previously killed text

Incremental Search

(CTRL)-S	Search forward for some letter sequence
(CTRL)-R	Search backward for some letter sequence

File Manipulation

(CTRL)-X (CTRL)-V	Read a file's contents into buffer
(CTRL)-X (CTRL)-W	Write buffer contents to a file
(CTRL)-X (CTRL)-I	Insert file contents into buffer

Interaction with Scheme

(ESC)-0	Evaluate all expressions; go to Scheme
(ESC) (CTRL)-X	Evaluate next expression; go to Scheme
(CTRL)-X (CTRL)-Z	Go to Scheme

Miscellaneous

(CTRL)-G	Abort the current Edwin command
(TAB)	Indent the current line
(ESC) (CTRL)-Q	Indent the next expression

---

[7]Other, and possibly better, approaches exist; for instance, we might include the expression (load "A:GPROCS.SCM") in an "initialization procedure" within all our graphics programs; thus, when those programs run they will automatically load and evaluate the procedure definitions in GPROCS.SCM. If we go this route, the three graphics procedures need only exist in one file, rather than having many copies of the same procedures in many files. However, the file-insertion approach described in the text is also reasonable. See the description of the load command in your Scheme language manual for more information about the alternative described in this note.

Answers to
Selected Exercises

3. The first procedure returns the cube root of its argument, and so might be called cube-root. The second procedure returns the circumference of a circle whose radius is the argument number, and so might be called circumference—and we might change the name of the argument from number to radius while we're at it. The third procedure might be called average.

6.
```
(define (triangle-area-2 side-1 side-2 included-angle)
  (* side-1 side-2 (sin included-angle) (/ 1 2)))
```

This particular version makes use of the fact that the primitive procedure *, along with a few others like +, can actually take a variable number of arguments. In this case the * primitive takes four arguments.

8.
```
(define (sphere-volume radius)
  (* (/ 4 3) 3.14159 (expt radius 3)))

(define (shell-volume inner-radius outer-radius)
  (- (sphere-volume outer-radius) (sphere-volume inner-radius)))
```

9.
```
(define (batting-avg at-bats singles doubles triples home-runs)
  (/ (+ singles doubles triples home-runs)
     at-bats))

(define (slugging-pct at-bats singles doubles triples home-runs)
  (/ (+ singles (* 2 doubles) (* 3 triples) (* 4 home-runs))
     at-bats))

(define (on-base-pct
          at-bats singles doubles triples home-runs walks sac-flies)
  (/ (+ singles doubles triples home-runs walks)
     (+ at-bats walks sac-flies)))
```

3.  ```
    (define (triangle-area base height)
      (if (or (< base 0) (< height 0))
          (display "A triangle with a negative base or height?")
          (/ (* base height) 2)))
    ```

4.  ```
    (define (close? number-1 number-2 limit)
      (< (abs (- number-1 number-2)) limit))
    ```

8. The first variation continues to work. The second, with the cond clauses reversed, does not—consider calling the procedure with an argument of 1600.

Chapter 5

5. If you call familiar-number with large values of level, the result is very close to the golden ratio. The familiar-number procedure is based on the following formula:

    $$\text{goldenratio} = \sqrt{1 + \sqrt{1 + \sqrt{1 + \cdots}}}$$

    If you stare at this formula, you will see that this implies:

    $$\text{goldenratio}^2 = 1 + \text{goldenratio}$$

    And if you solve this equation, you will see that the result is indeed the same number that we encountered earlier in the chapter.

8. Here is a program that prints out the prime factors of a number.

    ```
    (define (factor number)
      (print-factors number 2))

    (define (print-factors number current-factor)
      (cond ((= number current-factor)
             (writeln number))
            ((zero? (remainder number current-factor))
             (writeln current-factor)
             (print-factors (/ number current-factor) current-factor))
            (else (print-factors number (1+ current-factor)))))
    ```

    Here is a modification for counting the number of prime factors of a particular integer.

    ```
    (define (count-prime-factors number)
      (count-prime-factors-helper number 2 1))

    (define (count-prime-factors-helper number current-factor count)
      (cond ((= number current-factor) count)
            ((zero? (remainder number current-factor))
             (count-prime-factors-helper
              (/ number current-factor)
              current-factor (1+ count)))
            (else (count-prime-factors-helper number (1+ current-factor)
                                               count))))
    ```

    Now we can write a prime? predicate to see whether a number is prime, and another procedure called number-of-primes-up-to-limit that counts the number of primes less than or equal to some upper limit:

    ```
    (define (prime? number)
      (= (count-prime-factors number) 1))

    (define (number-of-primes-up-to limit)
      (cond ((= limit 2) 1)
            ((prime? limit) (1+ (number-of-primes-up-to (-1+ limit))))
            (else (number-of-primes-up-to (-1+ limit)))))
    ```

    The problem of finding whether a number is prime has important applications in subjects such as cryptography. Our prime? predicate, though usable, could be improved to run much faster for very large values of number. One immediate observation is that we shouldn't have to count the total number of factors in a given number; if there are at least two factors, the number is not prime, and we don't care if the number has three or four or a hundred additional factors. Thus, our prime? predicate needn't really use count-prime-factors. Here is an alternative and somewhat faster version of prime?:

```
(define (prime? number)
  (only-one-factor? number 2))

(define (only-one-factor? number current-factor)
  (cond ((= number current-factor) #t)
        ((zero? (remainder number current-factor)) #f)
        (else (only-one-factor? number (1+ current-factor)))))
```

Can you think of additional improvements?

11. As a first cut at a solution, let's not worry about waiting until after midnight; that is, we'll assume that we are waiting for short periods of time, and that our procedure is always used well before midnight.

```
(define (simple-wait hundredths)
  (let ((start (runtime)))
    (simple-wait-helper start hundredths)))

(define (simple-wait-helper start hundredths)
  (cond ((>= (- (runtime) start) hundredths) (display "done"))
        (else (simple-wait-helper start hundredths))))
```

The following is a fancier wait procedure that can wait for an arbitrary amount of time (even more than one day if necessary).

```
(define (wait hundredths)
  (let ((start (runtime)))
    (wait-loop start start hundredths 0)))

(define (wait-loop start previous-time time-to-wait midnite-crossings)
  (let ((now (runtime)))
    (let ((midnites-crossed
            (+ midnite-crossings (new-day-test now previous-time))))
      (cond ((>= (- (+ now (* 8640000 midnites-crossed)) start)
                 time-to-wait)
             (display "done"))
            (else (wait-loop start now time-to-wait midnites-crossed))))))

(define (new-day-test now previous-time)
  (if (< now previous-time) 1 0))
```

8.
```
(define (average list-of-numbers)
  (cond ((null? list-of-numbers)
         (error "Trying to average zero numbers" list-of-numbers))
        (else (/ (sum list-of-numbers) (length list-of-numbers)))))

(define (sum list-of-numbers)
  (cond ((null? list-of-numbers) 0)
        (else (+ (car list-of-numbers)
                 (sum (cdr list-of-numbers))))))
```

11.
```
(define (filter-out-symbol lis symbol)
  (cond ((null? lis) '())
        ((eq? symbol (car lis))
         (filter-out-symbol (cdr lis) symbol))
        (else (cons (car lis)
                    (filter-out-symbol (cdr lis) symbol)))))
```

```
14.     (define (reverse-list lis)
          (cond ((null? lis) '())
                (else (append (reverse-list (cdr lis)) (list (car lis))))))
```

As it turns out, there is a Scheme primitive named reverse that works like our reverse-list. (A note to users of PC Scheme: for reasons that will be given in the appendix to Chapter 11, it is not a good idea to appropriate the name reverse for our own procedure in this case.)

Chapter 10

2. The following is one possible way of implementing "time-dependent hedges."

```
(define (whos-on-first-loop old-context costello-count)
  (let ((costello (read)))
    (let ((new-context (get-context costello old-context)))
      (let ((strong (try-strong-cues costello))
            (weak (try-weak-cues costello new-context)))
        (cond ((not (null? strong))
               (writeln strong)
               (whos-on-first-loop (get-context strong new-context)
                                   (1+ costello-count)))
              ((not (null? weak))
               (writeln weak)
               (whos-on-first-loop (get-context weak new-context)
                                   (1+ costello-count)))
              ((wants-to-end? costello) (wrap-it-up))
              (else (writeln (hedge costello-count))
                    (whos-on-first-loop
                      new-context (1+ costello-count)))))))))

(define *irritated-hedges*
  '((i keep telling you and telling you)
    (how many times do i have to tell you)
    (why cant you get it straight)))

(define (hedge responses-thus-far)
  (if (> responses-thus-far 4)
      (select-any-from-list
        (append *irritated-hedges* *hedges*))
      (select-any-from-list *hedges*)))

(define (whos-on-first)        ;we need a new top-level procedure
  (whos-on-first-loop '() 0))
```

Chapter 11

3. The first expression, (greeting? 'hello), is evaluated as follows:

First, each subexpression is evaluated. The name greeting? evaluates to a procedure object (the one shown in the initial environment of Figure B.1); the second evaluates to the symbol hello. Next, a new frame is created in which the argument name symbol of the greeting? procedure is bound to the symbol hello. This frame is attached to the initial environment (i.e., the environment with which the greeting? procedure object is associated), and this attachment produces the environment shown in Figure B.1. Now, the body of the greeting? procedure is evaluated in the environment shown in Figure B.1. Again, the first step is to evaluate subexpressions. The name memv evaluates to a primitive procedure, the name symbol evaluates to the symbol hello, and the final (quoted) subexpression evaluates to the list (hello hi greetings). Since memv is a primitive procedure, it may be applied directly, and the result of this application (and our entire original expression) is (hello hi greetings).

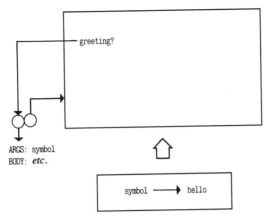

Figure B.1. Midway in evaluating (greeting? 'hello)

The second expression is evaluated as follows (I will not be quite as thorough as in the previous explanation):

First we evaluate the name conversation-boundary? and the quoted subexpression 'rosebud; we create a new frame in which the name symbol is bound to rosebud and attach that frame to the initial environment, as in Figure B.2.

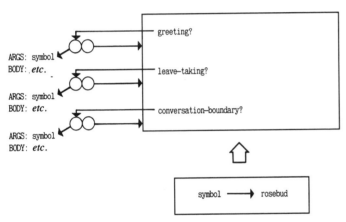

Figure B.2. Partway in evaluating (conversation-boundary? 'rosebud)

It is in this environment that we must evaluate the body of conversation-boundary?. This body is a single or expression; so we first have to evaluate the expression (greeting? symbol). In doing so, we evaluate the name greeting? and the name symbol; create a new frame in which symbol—the argument name for the greeting? procedure—is bound to the symbol rosebud; and attach that frame to the initial environment (since that is where the greeting? procedure object points). Now our diagram looks like Figure B.3 below.

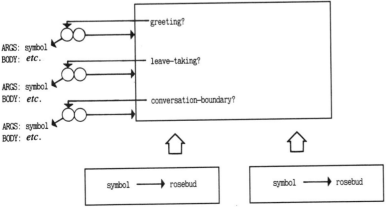

Figure B.3. Midway in evaluating (conversation-boundary? 'rosebud)

The result returned by evaluating the body of the greeting? procedure in the newly-created (rightmost) two-frame environment of Figure B.3 is () (you can show this), so we now go on to evaluate the second expression after the or in the body of conversation-boundary. This second expression is (leave-taking? symbol). We evaluate the names leave-taking? and symbol; create a new frame in which symbol—the argument name for the leave-taking? procedure—is bound to the symbol rosebud; and evaluate the body of the leave-taking? procedure in the newly-created (rightmost) two-frame environment of Figure B.4 below. This evaluation also returns () (you can show this), and so the value of the or expression (and the original call to conversation-boundary? is ().

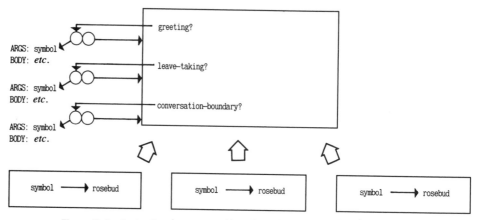

Figure B.4. Evaluating (conversation-boundary? 'rosebud), continued

I will not go through the evaluation of the final expression, except to say that at some point in the process you will find that you have drawn an environment diagram that looks like Figure B.5 below.

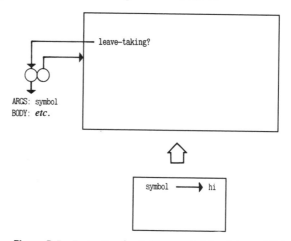

Figure B.5. Evaluating (not (leave-taking? (car '(hi there))))

Chapter 12
3.
```
(define (apply-to-random-element function lis)
  (let ((element (select-random-element lis)))
    (function element)))

(define (select-random-element lis)
  (list-ref lis (random (length lis))))
```

4. We won't worry about the problem of a procedure call running past midnight (see also Chapter 5, Exercise 11).
```
(define (time-this-call function number)
  (let ((start-time (runtime)))
    (function number)
    (- (runtime) start-time)))
```

```
5.    (define (filter predicate lis)
        (cond ((null? lis) '())
              ((predicate (car lis))
               (cons (car lis) (filter predicate (cdr lis))))
              (else (filter predicate (cdr lis)))))
```

12. First, we translate the `test-procedure` procedure into an equivalent one that does not use a `let` expression in its body:

```
(define (test-procedure number)
  ((lambda (a b) (+ a b))
   (* b 3)
   (* a number)))
```

Using this version of `test-procedure` we can work through the evaluation of `(test-procedure 5)`. We create a new frame in which the argument name `number` is bound to 5 and attach this to the initial environment. The body of `test-procedure` is a procedure call; the first subexpression is a `lambda` expression that evaluates to a procedure object (the one shown at the right of Figure B.6). The second subexpression evaluates to 12 (since the value of `b` is its value in the initial environment, or 4), and the third subexpression evaluates to 15 (the value of `a` is 3 and the value of `number` is 5). Now we make a frame in which the names `a` and `b`—the argument names of the procedure we created by evaluating the `lambda` expression—are bound to 12 and 15, respectively, and we bind this frame to the environment in which that unnamed procedure was created. Our environment diagram now looks like Figure B.6 below. We evaluate the body of the unnamed procedure, `(+ a b)`, in the newly-created three-frame environment, and the result is 27; this is likewise the result of the original call to `test-procedure`.

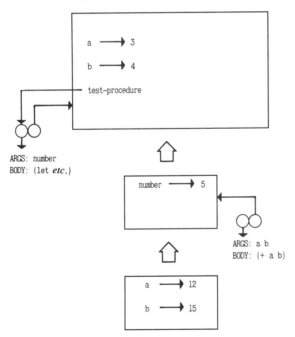

Figure B.6. Midway in evaluating (`test-procedure` 5)

```
15.    (define (compose f1 f2)
         (lambda (object) (f2 (f1 object))))
```

```
17.    (define (make-encoder code)
         (lambda (lis)
           (map (lambda (letter) (get-coded-letter letter code))
                lis)))
```

```
(define (get-coded-letter letter code)
  (cadr (assq letter code)))
(define (make-decoder code)
  (lambda (encoded-lis)
    (map (lambda (letter) (get-decoded-letter letter code))
         encoded-lis)))
(define (get-decoded-letter code-letter code)
  (define (code-loop code-list)
    (cond ((null? code-list)
           (error "This letter is not used by our code" code-letter))
          ((eq? (cadr (car code-list)) code-letter)
           (car (car code-list)))
          (else (code-loop (cdr code-list)))))
  (code-loop code))
```

18.
```
(define (successful-predicates pred-lis object)
  (cond ((null? pred-lis) '())
        (((car pred-lis) object)
         (cons (car pred-lis)
               (successful-predicates (cdr pred-lis) object)))
        (else (successful-predicates (cdr pred-lis) object))))
```

Chapter 13   4. Here is a very simple version of ask-user-for-todays-date!.

```
(define (ask-user-for-todays-date!)
  (newline)
  (display "Day of week? ")
  (set! *day-of-week* (read))
  (newline)
  (display "Month? ")
  (set! *month* (read))
  (newline)
  (display "Day of month? ")
  (set! *day-of-month* (read))
  (newline)
  (display "Year? ")
  (set! *year* (read))
  )
```

One improvement to this procedure would be to check the various typed-in expressions to make sure that they are valid. For instance, if the user indicates that the month is April and the day is the 31st, the procedure might point out the error and ask him to retype the date.

Here is a possible implementation of the next-day! project:

```
(define *weekdays*
  '(monday tuesday wednesday thursday friday saturday sunday))
(define *months*
  '(january february march april may june july
    august september october november december))
(define (next-item item lis)
  (let ((rest-items (memv item lis)))
    (if (null? (cdr rest-items))
        (car lis)
        (cadr rest-items))))
```

```scheme
(define (next-weekday day)
  (next-item day *weekdays*))

(define (next-month month)
  (next-item month *months*))

(define (end-of-year? month)
  (null? (cdr (memv month *months*))))

(define (leap-year? year)
  (define (divisible? number-1 by-number-2)
    (= (remainder number-1 by-number-2) 0))
  (or (divisible? year 400)
      (and (divisible? year 4)
           (not (divisible? year 100)))))

(define (final-day month year)
  (case month
    ((january march may july august october december) 31)
    ((april june september november) 30)
    ((february) (if (leap-year? year) 29 28))
    (else (error "This month is not in the year" month))))

(define (next-day!)
  (let ((possible-next-day (+ 1 *day-of-month*)))
    (cond ((> possible-next-day (final-day *month* *year*))
           (if (end-of-year? *month*)
               (set! *year* (1+ *year*)))
           (set! *month* (next-month *month*))
           (set! *day-of-month* 1))
          (else (set! *day-of-month* possible-next-day))))
  (set! *day-of-week* (next-weekday *day-of-week*)))
```

The final-day procedure above uses the case special form (see Exercise 17 in Chapter 8). We could easily have used a cond expression here as well.

10.
```scheme
(define (add-into! obj lis position)
  (splice-nth-cdr! obj lis position)
  lis)

(define (splice-nth-cdr! obj lis count)
  (cond ((null? lis)
         (error "Position must be less than the length of the list"
                position))
        ((= count 0) (set-cdr! lis (cons obj (cdr lis))))
        (else (splice-nth-cdr! obj (cdr lis) (-1+ count)))))
```

Chapter 14

2. The call to bar is the final expression in the body of the blah procedure. As a consequence, when blah calls bar, the frame created by the call to blah is no longer needed; the result of the call to bar will provide the result of the original call to blah. The Scheme system thus does not retain the information that the caller of bar is blah, and the memory space taken up by the blah frame is reclaimed. (This process of "frame reclamation" was described in Chapter 11 and explored further in Chapter 11, Exercise 9.)

The upshot of all this is that when we look for the caller of bar, we do not see the frame created by the call to blah, since our Scheme system is not retaining that frame.

4. The answer is "the initial environment." We are unable to look at bindings in the frame in which the error occurred; but we can use CTRL-G to continue

on from the error if we wish. We can also find the caller of the procedure in which the error was encountered by using $\boxed{\text{CTRL}}$-U.

Chapter 15　　4. Here are some calls to try that we could use:

```
(try '(and (plays (?v person) vocals) (plays (?v person) guitar)))

(try '(and (plays (?v person) keyboards) (album (?v person) (?v alb))))

(try '(or (plays (fagen donald) (?v inst))
          (plays (peterson debbi) (?v inst))))
```

5. This answer uses the plug-dictionary-values-into procedure, which is introduced toward the end of the chapter.

```
(define (try pattern)
  (map (lambda (dict) (plug-dictionary-values-into dict pattern))
       (find-dictionaries pattern *the-assertions*)))
```

11.
```
(define (add-new-rule! rule)
  (set! *the-rules* (cons rule *the-rules*))
  (initialize-assertion-list))
```

Chapter 16　　19.
```
(macro make-yes-or-no-procedure
  (lambda (exp)
    '(define (,(cadr exp))
       (if (yes-or-no ,(caddr exp))
           ,(cadddr exp)
           ,(car (cddddr exp))))))

(define (yes-or-no string)
  (display string)
  (let ((response (read)))
    (case response
      ((y yes) #t)
      ((n no) #f)
      (else (newline) (yes-or-no string)))))
```

In the example above, I used the case special form, just for kicks. Case is described in Chapter 8, Exercise 17.

References and Bibliography

The following list of references covers those works mentioned in the text as well as some additional pointers to related literature. This list is intentionally brief; the reader interested in pursuing some particular topic is referred to the more extensive bibliographies in the referenced works. All references listed by chapter are included in the bibliography.

References

Chapter 1

The text by Abelson and Sussman with Sussman [1985] uses Scheme as its "standard" language. It requires more formal background than this book; is faster paced; and covers a wider range of topics. (See also the accompanying teacher's manual by Sussman [1985].) The most current "official definition" of the Scheme language is the *Revised*[3] *Report on the Algorithmic Language Scheme* edited by Jonathan Rees and William Clinger [1986].

There are a large number of available books on Common Lisp. The standard reference is Steele [1984]. The books by Tatar [1987] and Winston and Horn [1984] both provide well-organized introductions to the language.

Brian Harvey's books on Logo—*Computer Science Logo Style, Volumes 1 and 2*—are marvelous reading. In this book I have made a conscious attempt to imitate Harvey's lucid style.

Chapter 5

The "multiple-model" technique for explaining recursion is based on that used by Brian Harvey in Volume 1 of *Computer Science Logo Style*. The golden ratio material is mostly taken from Ghyka [1977]. Beskin [1986] provides an introduction to the subject of continued fractions.

The procedure described in Chapter 5, Exercise 4, is taken from Beeler et al. [1972]. The quote in Chapter 5, Exercise 10, is from the delightful book by Levy [1984].

Chapter 7

The original account of the "circle-squared" program is in the Computer Recreations column of the September 1986 *Scientific American* (Dewdney [1986]).

Chapter 9

More technical discussions of scoping can be found in Horowitz [1984], Tennent [1981], and Abelson and Sussman with Sussman [1985].

Chapter 10

The quote from Paul Ceruzzi's essay is taken from the book edited by Corn [1986]. A brief nontechnical description of the ELIZA program can be found in Weizenbaum [1976].

My version of the "Who's on First?" routine was taken from memory. A transcript of (at least one variant of) the routine may be found in *The Fireside Book of Baseball* (Einstein [1956]).

Chapter 12

A formal definition of first-class objects is given in Stoy [1977].

Chapter 13

For those interested in pursuing the topics of Logo and/or turtle programming, there are many introductory Logo texts available. Again, Brian Harvey's books are recommended for those interested in the language—although they place much less emphasis on turtle programming than do most other Logo books. *Mindstorms* by Papert [1980] is an eloquent introduction to the spirit of Logo as an educational medium. As for turtle programming, *Turtle Geometry* by Abelson and diSessa [1980] includes a range of examples, from the elementary to the more advanced; the c-curve and dragon-curve examples in Chapter 13, Exercise 8, are adapted from that text.

Horowitz [1984] includes a chapter on object-oriented programming (written by Tim Rentsch). The books by Goldberg and Robson [1983] and Birtwistle et al. [1973] are popular references for Smalltalk and Simula, respectively.

Chapter 14

The final chapter of Abelson and Sussman with Sussman [1985] provides a good introduction to the subject of Scheme implementation.

Chapter 15

There are a large number of expert systems texts on the market; none of those which I am familiar with stand out enough to be mentioned here. For those interested in general concepts of artificial intelligence programming, the volumes by Barr, Cohen, and Feigenbaum [1981, 1982] are recommended, as is the text by Winston [1984]. The book on Lisp by Winston and Horn [1984] has a more elaborate treatment of forward chaining, and the book by Tatar [1987] includes a readable expert system example. Those familiar with the "query system" example in Abelson and Sussman with Sussman [1985] will no doubt see that the code in Chapter 15 owes a great deal to that program. Doyle's [1979] article, reprinted in Webber and Nilsson [1981], illuminates many of the issues in creating truth maintenance systems.

Bibliography

Abelson, Harold, and Andrea diSessa.
Turtle Geometry
MIT Press, Cambridge, Mass. 1980.

Abelson, Harold, and Gerald Jay Sussman with Julie Sussman.
Structure and Intepretation of Computer Programs
McGraw-Hill, New York; MIT Press, Cambridge, Mass. 1985.

Barr, Avron, Paul R. Cohen, and Edward A. Feigenbaum.
The Handbook of Artificial Intelligence (Volumes 1-3)
Heuristech Press, Stanford, California; William Kaufmann, Los Altos, California. 1981, 1982.

Beeler, M., R. W. Gosper, R. Schroeppel, et al.
Hakmem
AI Memo No. 239
MIT Artificial Intelligence Laboratory, Cambridge, Mass. 1972.

Beskin, N.M.
Fascinating Fractions
Mir Publishers, Moscow. 1986.

Birtwistle, G.M., O.-J. Dahl, B. Myrhaug, and K. Nygaard.
Simula Begin
Studentlitteratur, Lund, Sweden; Auerbach Publishers, Philadelphia, Pa. 1973.

Corn, Joseph J. (ed.)
Imagining Tomorrow: History, Technology and the American Future
MIT Press, Cambridge, Mass. 1986.

Dewdney, A. K.
Computer Recreations
Scientific American, September 1986.

Einstein, Charles (ed.)
The Fireside Book of Baseball
Simon and Schuster, New York. 1956.

Ghyka, Matila
The Geometry of Art and Life
Dover Publications, Inc., New York. 1977.

Goldberg, Adele and David Robson.
Smalltalk-80: The Language and its Implementation
Addison-Wesley, Reading, Mass. 1983.

Harvey, Brian
Computer Science, Logo Style
Volume 1: Intermediate Programming
Volume 2: Projects, Styles and Techniques
MIT Press, Cambridge, Mass. 1985, 1986.

Hofstadter, Douglas R.
Gödel, Escher, Bach: An Eternal Golden Braid
Basic Books, New York. 1979.

Horowitz, Eliis.
Fundamentals of Programming Languages
Computer Science Press, Rockville, Maryland. 1984.

Levy, Steven.
Hackers: Heroes of the Computer Revolution
Anchor Press/Doubleday, Garden City, N.Y. 1984.

296

Papert, Seymour.
Mindstorms
Basic Books, New York. 1980.

Rees, Jonathan and William Clinger. (eds.)
"Revised[3] Report on the Algorithmic Language Scheme"
ACM Sigplan Notices, 21(12), December 1986.

Steele, Guy L., Jr.
Common Lisp: The Language
Digital Press, Burlington, Mass. 1984.

Steele, Guy L., Jr., Donald R. Woods, Raphael A. Finkel, Mark R. Crispin,
Richard M. Stallman, and Geoffrey S. Goodfellow.
The Hacker's Dictionary
Harper & Row, New York. 1983.

Stoy, Joseph E.
*Denotational Semantics: The Scott-Strachey Approach to
Programming Theory*
MIT Press, Cambridge, Mass. 1977.

Sussman, Julie, with Harold Abelson and Gerald Jay Sussman.
*Instructor's Manual to Accompany Structure and Interpretation of
Computer Programs*
MIT Press, Cambridge, Mass. 1985.

Tatar, Deborah G.
A Programmer's Guide to Common Lisp
Digital Press, Bedford, Mass. 1987.

Tennent, R. D.
Principles of Programming Languages
Prentice-Hall International, Englewood Cliffs, New Jersey. 1981.

Webber, Bonnie Lynn and Nils J. Nilsson. (eds.)
Readings in Artificial Intelligence
Morgan Kaufmann, Los Altos, California. 1981.

Weizenbaum, Joseph.
Computer Power and Human Reason
W. H. Freeman, San Francisco, California. 1976.

Winston, Patrick Henry.
Artificial Intelligence
Addison-Wesley, Reading, Mass. 1984.

Winston, Patrick Henry and Berthold Klaus Paul Horn.
Lisp
Addison-Wesley, Reading, Mass. 1984.

Scheme Names

This index contains the names of all Scheme primitives and special forms encountered in this book; it also contains the names of Scheme procedures defined in the various examples throughout the text. Page numbers marked with "E" indicate that the entry appears in an exercise; the two numbers following the "E" refer to the chapter and exercise number in which the entry occurs.

INDEX 2

Subject